T0333426

Mexico, Central, and South America:
New Perspectives

Volume 3
Social Movements

Series Content

Mexico, Central, and South America:
New Perspectives

Volume 3
Social Movements

Edited with introductions by

Jorge I. Domínguez
Harvard University

ROUTLEDGE
New York/London

Published in 2001 by

Routledge
29 West 35th Street
New York, NY 10001

Published in Great Britain by
Routledge
11 New Fetter Lane
London EC4P 4EE

Routledge is an Imprint of Taylor & Francis Books, Inc.
Copyright © 2001 by Routledge

Printed in the United States of America on acid-free paper.

All rights reserved. No part of this book may be reprinted or reproduced or utilized in any form or by any electronic, mechanical, or other means, now known or hereafter invented, including any photocopying and recording, or in any information storage or retrieval system, without permission in writing from the publishers.

10 9 8 7 6 5 4 3 2 1

Library of Congress Cataloging-in-Publication Data

Democracy in Latin America in the 1990s / edited with introductions by Jorge I. Domínguez.
      p. cm. -- (Mexico, Central and South America : the scholarly literature of the 1990s ;
   v. 2)
   Includes bibliographical references.
   ISBN 0-8153-3692-6 (set : alk. paper) -- ISBN 0-8153-3694-2 (v. 2 : alk. paper)
   1. Latin America--Politics and government--1980- 2. Democracy--Latin
America--History--20th century. I. Domínguez, Jorge I., 1945- II. Mexico, Central and
South America ; v. 2.

F1414.2 .D4317 2001
320.98--dc21

                                                                      2001524240

ISBN 0-8153-3692-6 (set)
ISBN 0-8153-3693-4 (v.1)
ISBN 0-8153-3694-2 (v.2)
ISBN 0-8153-3695-0 (v.3)
ISBN 0-8153-3696-9 (v.4)
ISBN 0-8153-3697-7 (v.5)

Contents

Introduction

Social movements, nongovernmental organizations, and communities of faith are among the building blocks of civil society. They connect citizens to one another and to a vision of their collective selves and hopes for their societies. At times they undertake activities to shape neighborhoods, regions, or aspects of national public life. At other times they principally aim to assist their members in realizing shared goals; even in the latter cases, the linkages among citizens in one endeavor may facilitate and foster linkages in other endeavors.

Among the oldest and most enduring social movements are labor unions. They have organized workers, and at times peasants, to improve conditions at their workplaces, and they typically shape the wider political arena. The first three articles in this volume look at dimensions of the role of labor unions.

Ruth Berins Collier and James Mahoney examine the role of labor unions in the democratization of South American and southern European countries in the 1970s and 1980s. They argue against the dominant explanation for processes of democratization during those years— namely, that elite strategic choice accounts sufficiently for the process of democratic transition. Instead, they claim that the labor movement was one of the major actors in the political opposition, explicitly demanding a democratic regime. In some cases, union-led protest for democracy contributed to a climate of ungovernability and delegitimation that led directly to a general destabilization of authoritarian regimes. Continual protest kept the transition moving. Moreover, labor-union protest also expanded the scope of contestation in the successor regime, secured the legalization of labor-affiliated parties, and contributed to deepening the process of democratization. Within that framework, the authors identify two principal patterns. In some countries (such as Spain and Peru in the late 1970s and Argentina in the early 1980s), authoritarian incumbents had adopted projects to bring about a democratic transition. Labor protest destabilized the authoritarian regime, triggered the transition, and forced authoritarian elites to retreat. In other countries (such as Uruguay and Brazil in the early 1980s), authoritarian incumbents had adopted a project to enhance their legitimacy, but labor protest helped to derail that project and reshaped and advanced the transition.

Victoria Murillo focuses on the role of labor unions in a different transition, that from statist to market-oriented economies, especially in Argentina, Mexico, and Venezuela. In each of these countries, populist labor-based parties advanced protectionist and state interventionist economic policies from the 1940s to the 1980s. Presidents elected from these parties between December 1988 and July 1989, however, reduced state intervention and opened the economies of their countries. This policy change, the most important in these three countries during the second half of the twentieth century, challenged the historic relationship between these parties and their long-term labor-union allies. Murillo argues that the terms of the new relationship between labor unions and labor-party-based governments hinged on two key variables: the extent of competition among labor unions and the extent of competition among parties for leadership of labor unions. First, cooperation between government and labor unions is most likely when there is only one union confederation and only the party that controls the government fills all key leadership posts in that confederation. Party loyalty reduces union militancy, while union monopoly boosts its bargaining power. Second, labor unions are likely to subordinate their goals to the party that controls the government if there is extensive labor-union competition but all key leaders of the relevant union federations are affiliated with the same party. Party loyalty again constrains union militancy, while government officials play off one union against another, rewarding the compliant. This pattern was most common in Mexico. Third, labor unions are likely to succeed in their militant opposition to the policies of the party that controls the government if there is a single union confederation but many parties effectively compete to fill its leadership posts. Union leaders affiliated with one party fear being outflanked by union leaders affiliated with another party, resulting in generalized militancy from a single powerful union confederation. This pattern was most common in Venezuela. Fourth, when there is both competition among unions and competition among parties, coordination is difficult; the unions resist but are weak and ineffective.

Charles Davis, Edwin Aguilar, and John Speer focus on urban informal-sector workers in Costa Rica and Nicaragua. They seek to understand the relative impact of civil society and partisan organizations on the political behavior of workers. They find that the level of associational involvement is low in both countries; the economic vulnerability of the urban informal sector impedes collective organization. Among workers who do belong to organizations, however, the greater their organizational involvement, the greater their cognitive engagement with politics and the more intense their forms of participation. Costa Rica and Nicaragua differ, nonetheless, in terms of the impact of parties on political participation. In Costa Rica, parties are associated with voting and campaign activism; other, more demanding forms of participation are independent of parties and associated with civil society organizations. In Nicaragua, in contrast, affiliation with the Frente Sandinista de Liberación Nacional (FSLN) is strongly associated with all forms of political activism. The FSLN's impact narrowed the participatory gap that might have been expected between Nicaragua and Costa Rica simply on the bases of Costa Rica's much greater social and economic resources.

Social movements often flourish in rural settings because, although the presence of the state and political parties may be weak, rural folk remain vulnerable to encroachment from landlords or business enterprises. Social movements may thus be the principal organizational instruments available to peasants and agricultural workers. The next four articles in the volume explore these themes.

Margaret Keck examines the case of rubber tappers from rural Acre state in Brazil who began to organize in the mid-1970s against the encroachment of cattle ranchers and land speculators. The rubber tappers had to create their means for resistance. Keck's argument employs three levels of analysis. The first level, a "resource mobilization" approach, helps to provide an account of the growth of the movement and its relative success in meeting some of its goals. It highlights the importance of funds, communication networks, leadership, the use of information, and the gathering of members. A second level emphasizes that organizational and political strategies were inseparable from the deliberate way the struggle was portrayed and, in particular, its connection to the international environmentalist movement. The social construction of this new environmentalist identity (on top of its domestic identity as a labor and partisan struggle) helped to frame the case and the attention and resources it received. The third level calls attention to the reframing of the story, that is, the reinterpretation of the experiences of an "old" labor movement among rubber tappers into a new frame that joined environmental and other social movements and issues. This reframing was easier during the transition from a military to a democratic regime because the new unionism in the labor movement and its political ally the Workers Party also emphasized participatory grassroots values and unconventional styles as part of a shared identity opposing the decaying dictatorship.

The presence of the state in rural areas, however, is best conceptualized as a variable. This is the key insight proposed by Peter Houtzager and Marcus Kurtz. They argue that a strong state can foster associational activity and help create the bases for a dense civil society that in turn would increase the efficacy of state action. They study rural popular mobilization in Brazil and Chile before, during, and after their military dictatorships. Before the dictatorships, the Chilean countryside was one of Latin America's most highly organized and politicized, whereas few rural regions of Brazil had experienced significant popular mobilizations. After the dictatorships, the Chilean countryside was quiescent, whereas new rural movements in Brazil mobilized support and forced agrarian issues to the forefront of the national political debate. The different paths to economic modernization pursued by the military governments— developmental in Brazil, neoliberal in Chile— created, the authors argue, different possibilities for agrarian mobilization in the post-authoritarian years. Brazil's developmental model established an interventionist state in rural areas, a corporatist system of labor relations, a broad-based program of social provision, and increased state regulation of land. This institutional configuration facilitated the expression of collective identities around new issues and provided rural social groups with material and organizational resources. In contrast, neoliberalism in Chile produced a minimalist state in the rural areas, heavily reliant on market forces, a decentralized system of labor relations, a privatized pension system, and an efficient land market. The state's retreat from economic and social spheres eroded material and organizational resources in rural communities and undermined collective identification; rural social movements in Chile became weak or rare.

Yianna Lambrou offers a focused case study of changes experienced by a nongovernmental organization (NGO) in rural southern Chile in order to understand the level of activity in a countryside under severe pressures to depoliticize. During the dictatorship, she argues, NGOs maintained a critical distance from the government and became agents for resistance and oppositional expertise. They created a niche for opposition researchers and activists and a possibility of economic survival for professionals working on proposals to address the needs of the poor. International funding provided the resources but also created a cliental relationship to donors. After the restoration of democracy, many of the same professionals joined the government. NGOs became more pragmatic and efficient. But they lost their altruism and their position as independent sources of criticism of the government; they may also have lost their role as builders of democratic community.

Henry Veltmeyer studies the Zapatista insurrection in rural Chiapas, Mexico, in order to assess the utility of social-class analysis. He takes note of postmodernist critiques of previous class analyses. Class essentialism, these critics suggest, assumed that the poor acted as members of a social class; instead, the critics argue, new social movements constructed a social identity in each new case of collective action. Members of women's movements constructed a social identity as women that enabled them to act collectively; indigenous peoples likewise constructed their identity to recover and express cultural goals. Veltmeyer argues that the Chiapas rebellion stemmed from structural and objective causes; its members responded with a clear awareness of their social identity as an exploited class. However variable the methods of these peasant social movements, the indigenous peasants in Chiapas were constituted as a class under the objective conditions of the relationship to the means of production and to the state, but they also constituted themselves as a class in subjective terms through their actions. In this way, Veltmeyer seeks to reconnect the study of new social movements with the study of older social movements, in particular labor movements and their partisan allies.

Social movements may be rooted not just in social-class considerations, the relationship to the state, or other material sources of collective identity creation but also in communities of faith. Two articles consider these issues.

Patricia Pessar analyzes millenarian movements in northeast Brazil to explore the intertwining of their religious, ideational, and political-economic underpinnings. She criticizes scholars of millenarianism who dismiss the religious meanings and motives in the ideologies and actions of messianic leaders and their followers and emphasize exclusively such factors as social change, modernization, or class struggle. She also criticizes those who examine these movements purely as religious phenomena. Instead, she argues, folk Roman Catholicism provided the meanings and motives— such as a moral economy encompassing patrons and clients as well as resentment— that assisted rural Brazilians in interpreting the changes that threatened their way of life. Divine vengeance would punish economic and political elites for their acts of suppression against the poor. Millenarian messiahs would be the Lord's avenging angels on this earth to bring retribution and justice. Thus folk Catholicism also provided for remedial action against injustice. The key organizing principle of Brazilian millenarianism was the dynamic relationship between religion and politics.

Jean-Pierre Bastian examines the metamorphosis of Latin American Protestant groups. The Protestant movements of nineteenth-century Latin America, he argues, were culturally liberal and promoted individual free will; they emphasized rationalism and the written word. The Protestant movements that grew rapidly in Latin America during the second half of the twentieth century derived from popular Roman Catholic religious culture; these are oral, unlettered religions. They are often vehicles for caudillo-style models of religious and social control. They are predominantly syncretic and represent a redeployment of popular Latin American religiosity. Some Protestant movements have served in various countries as means of resistance to oppression. More such movements, however, have displayed strong authoritarian political features and strategies for dealing with the state. Not surprisingly, clientelist-oriented right-wing politicians, such as Presidents Efraín Ríos-Montt and Jorge Serrano in Guatemala and President Alberto Fujimori in Peru, developed close alliances with some of these new religious movements.

During the last third of the twentieth century, social movements in Latin America were particularly common among women activists. They also at times served to improve the quality of civic life and the efficacy of local governments. Many social movements that evolved into NGOs often established valuable international connections that were essential to fulfilling their goals. The following three articles in the volume exemplify each of these.

Karen Kampwirth examines the role of gendered issues and strategies during the elections held in Nicaragua in 1990 and in El Salvador in 1994 and the role of the organized feminist movement in these elections. The 1990 Nicaraguan election opened the way to ending the civil and international wars swirling in and around Nicaragua; the 1994 El Salvadoran election was the first one held after the government and the revolutionaries reached a peace accord to end similar wars affecting their country. In Nicaragua, the victorious candidate, Violeta Chamorro, ran as a long-suffering mother who preferred familial reconciliation to war and who made antifeminist claims during the election campaign. Daniel Ortega, in turn, ran as both a good father and a male sex symbol. During the campaign, the organized feminists, directly connected to the FSLN, did little to counter antifeminist themes and simply supported their party. The feminist movement's lack of political autonomy crippled its capacity to shape the gendered content of the new political regime. In El Salvador, in contrast, neither campaign emphasized gendered issues; each was met with an active response from feminist groups. Neither the government party nor the revolutionaries had established their supremacy over feminist groups, freeing the latter to contest them and seek concessions from all political parties and making it important for the parties not to take their support for granted.

Rebecca Abers explores the transformation of civic life in the city of Pôrto Alegre, Brazil, and the causative role of politics in that change. In 1988 the Workers Party won the mayoral election and proceeded to create a decentralized participatory budget process. Neighborhood associations would discuss the part of the budget pertinent to their section of the city. The effect was to even out opportunities to participate because the Workers Party successfully mobilized the poorer neighborhoods. Associationalism blossomed as citizens began to join other civic groups. People participated because there were new windows of opportunity, the issues were comprehensible and pertinent, and the results were palpable. Led by a left-wing political party, municipal government invested in a new relationship between the state and the citizenry.

Finally, Mara Loveman analyzes the conditions under which individuals risk their lives to resist repressive states. She focuses on the emergence of human-rights organizations under military dictatorships in Chile, Uruguay, and Argentina. At their installation, military dictatorships successfully increased state repression to bring about political demobilization. However, some individuals respond to such repression by increasing their participation in acts of resistance. Face-to-face dense interpersonal networks insulate, protect, and motivate activists. These were reactive social movements. How they frame their process of resistance in turn helps them link their struggle to wider national and international issue networks that generate publicity and funds. These movements developed strongly and early in the experience of dictatorship in Chile thanks in part to preexisting partisan networks that connected to networks developed through the Roman Catholic Church. Uruguay, on the other hand, stands out as the most successful case of state repression and demobilization. The Roman Catholic Church there was too weak to provide the necessary networks of its own or to connect to secular networks. Argentina is an intermediate case because the Roman Catholic Church there provided little support for human-rights networks but its secular (including partisan) networks operated more effectively than in Uruguay.

Social movements can give voice to the weak, empower the powerless, and challenge the state. Effective social movements, however, should be understood in the context of their intricate relationship with the state. That has long been the story of the labor movement. That explains reform in Pôrto Alegre, the prospects for rural mobilization, and the willingness of citizens in moments of suffering and anguish to risk their lives in order to redress moral wrongs.

High-Risk Collective Action: Defending Human Rights in Chile, Uruguay, and Argentina[1]

Mara Loveman
University of California, Los Angeles

Under what conditions will individuals risk their lives to resist repressive states? This question is addressed through comparative analysis of the emergence of human rights organizations under military dictatorships in Chile, Uruguay, and Argentina. While severe state repression is expected to lead to generalized demobilization, these cases reveal that repression may directly stimulate collective action. The potential for sustained collective action in high-risk contexts depends upon the relationship between strategies of repression and the particular configuration of embedded social networks; it is more likely where dense yet diverse interpersonal networks are embedded within broader national and transnational institutional and issue networks.

> First, we will kill all the subversives; then we will kill their collaborators; then their sympathizers; then the indifferent and finally, the timid. (attributed to Brig. General Ibérico Manuel Saint-Jean, former governor of Buenos Aires)

INTRODUCTION

From the mid-1960s into the late 1980s, military governments in Latin America systematically and ferociously violated human rights as defined by the international community with the adoption of the Universal Decla-

[1] I would like to thank the following individuals for their comments on earlier versions of this article: Rogers Brubaker, Rebecca Emigh, Elizabeth Lira, David Lopez, Brian Loveman, Michael Mann, Gerardo Munck, Jeffrey Prager, William Roy, Caleb Southworth, Jay Sundu, Ivan Szelenyi, and Maurice Zeitlin. I also wish to thank the participants in the UCLA Comparative Social Analysis Workshop, fall 1997, and the *AJS* reviewers. Revisions were supported in part by the Andrew A. Mellon Foundation. Direct Correspondence to Mara Loveman, Department of Sociology, University of California, 264 Haines Hall, Box 951551, Los Angeles, California 90095.

© 1998 by The University of Chicago. All rights reserved.
0002-9602/99/10402-0006$02.50

1

ration of Human Rights in 1948. Barbaric torture, murders, "disappearances,"[2] and disregard for civil liberties and rights became commonplace. In response, individuals and small groups of citizens protested against these policies, called for changes in government behavior, and sought to support and assist victims. Human rights organizations (HROs) formed, and a diffuse human rights movement arose in most of Latin America.

In some countries, HROs formed quickly and had significant social support. In others, HROs developed relatively later, were more fragile, and were less influential. In all cases, however, those participating in HROs faced potential retribution, even death, for opposing the incumbent dictatorships.

This article seeks to explain the emergence of sustained collective action in such "high-risk" contexts. Specifically, it attempts to account for the emergence of HROs in Chile, Uruguay, and Argentina in contexts where the potential consequences included arrest, torture, disappearance, or murder of participants, their friends, and their family members.[3] In short, why and how did individuals organize resistance in the face of extremely repressive governments? Further, what accounts for the significant differences in the timing of the emergence of HROs in these countries?

Asking these questions draws attention to the paucity of explicit attempts in the social movement literature to explain the emergence of sustained collective action in contexts of life-threatening risk. Most social movement theory stems from research into low-risk forms of mobilization. However, as McAdam (1986) suggests, the mobilization dynamics of high-risk movements are likely to be qualitatively different from those of low-risk movements. This article suggests that explanation of the emergence of HROs in Chile, Uruguay, and Argentina requires a synthetic theoretical approach that focuses attention on links between interpersonal and embedded social and political networks, resource mobilization capacity, identity construction prior to and in the process of participation, and the

---

[2] The word "disappearances" refers to kidnappings and murders not acknowledged by governments.

[3] The central empirical focus of this article is the human rights organizations (HROs) that emerged in each country. Recognizing that social movement organizations are only one possible form of the *organization of collective action* in a social movement (Tarrow 1994, p. 136), this account focuses on HROs for two reasons: first, available accounts of the early years of these movements by participants and scholars suggest that they consisted first and foremost of the networks of individuals working under the auspices of HROs. Second, these accounts also indicate that HROs provided the "mobilizing structures" (Tarrow 1994, p. 136) that linked diverse elements of the movement domestically and internationally.

modalities and extent of state repression that shape the political opportunity structure.[4]

THEORETICAL APPROACH

This investigation on human rights organizations in Latin America in the 1970s and 1980s asks two basic and interrelated theoretical questions: (1) When (under what conditions) do high-risk social movements and organizations emerge? (2) Why do people participate in such movements and organizations?

Different levels of abstraction and varying levels of theory yield distinct "explanations" for collective action, of which high-risk social movements and organizations are particular instances.[5] Theories operating at different levels of abstraction are generally presented in competition with other "schools" or "paradigms," although, often, "competing" theories present more of a contest between "most important variables" than between more profound paradigmatic differences. Rather than insist on the uniform predominance of micro, meso, macro, *or* "supra" macro variables or on variables emphasizing human agency *or* structural and conjunctural variables, the richness of social movement theories provides the possibility of improving explanations for social movements by reference to *composite causal contingencies* (Lofland 1996). In short, explanations for collective action involve multiple variables whose influence in particular instances of collective action is complexly and contingently interrelated.

SOCIAL MOVEMENT THEORIES AND HIGH-RISK
COLLECTIVE ACTION

Different social movement theories offer varying answers to the two basic questions posed above. The following overview considers how prevailing

---

[4] Recognizing that in comparative historical research there is always a tension between idiographic rigor and nomothetic explanation, a central aim of this article is to provide an initial consideration of how well a careful synthesis of selected theories can account both for the emergence of particular Latin American HROs and for differences among them.

[5] The social movements literature is replete with competing definitions of "social movement" (leading Marwell and Oliver [1984, p. 4] to conclude "the concept 'social movement' is a theoretical nightmare"). This article adopts a working definition based on Tarrow's (1994, p. 11) conceptualization: "collective challenges by people with common purposes and solidarity in sustained interaction with elites, opponents and authorities." Adopting this definition does not imply that I accept Tarrow's theoretical arguments regarding the sociological *bases* for collective challenges in their entirety.

approaches to these two questions account for the emergence of, and participation in, social movements and organizations *in high-risk contexts.*

Micro-Level Approaches

Approaches based on the premises of methodological individualism focus on the decisions and actions of discrete individuals to explain *why people engage in collective action.* These approaches can be divided into two (not necessarily mutually exclusive) general categories: those that adopt a rational choice framework and those that focus on individual characteristics or psychology to explain motivation.

Focusing attention on individual calculations of the costs and benefits of participation in collective action (Oberschall 1973, 1993; Klandermans 1984), rational choice approaches help explain why individuals participate in some movements but not others, and at some moments but not others, by assessing the changing incentives and disincentives for participation. While accepting Olson's (1965) basic framework, many rational choice theorists have qualified (or relaxed) his assumptions, expanded their analyses from individual to "collective" decision making, and introduced nonmaterial incentives into calculations of cost/benefit ratios (Oliver 1984; Fireman and Gamson 1979; Oberschall 1993). Despite such efforts, both formal and more "relaxed" rational choice models are particularly *un*helpful for explaining participation in collective action in situations involving high levels of risk or contexts of extreme instability and unpredictability.

Rational choice models work best when the "rules of the game"—the costs and benefits of choosing one action versus another—are clear and predictable (Geddes 1995, p. 87). But many "high-risk" contexts are high risk precisely because the consequences of actions are impossible to predict.[6] Additionally, it is difficult for rational choice models to avoid tautology when they attempt to incorporate noninstrumental incentives or to explain what Weber ([1992] 1968, p. 25) referred to as "value-rational behavior." In such cases, the "preferences" of actors are often deduced from the very actions they are meant to explain (e.g., Fireman and Gamson 1979, p. 24).

In part, this is because the language and grammar of rational choice tends to obstruct rather than facilitate understanding of human action in contexts where nonmaterial incentives, or "meanings," are *central* to individual decisions. It is analytically useful to distinguish "costs" ("expen-

---

[6] The military regimes in Southern Cone countries pursued (to varying degrees) deliberate strategies of seemingly arbitrary and disproportionately cruel forms of repression, creating fear, confusion, and terror with the intention of paralyzing any opposition.

4

ditures of time, money, and energy required of a person engaged in a particular form of activism") and "risks" ("anticipated dangers of engaging in a particular type of activity") (McAdam 1986, p. 67). However, in the rational choice framework, psychosocial processes such as *fear* are not formally theorized. Hence, risks simply weigh in as potential "costs" in individual calculations. And if risk or cost is calculated as a high probability of "death," while benefit is calculated at a minimal probability of "maintenance of honor" or "respect for human rights," how is this "ratio" to be assessed in the grammar of rational calculation in order to predict the outcome? If the likely result of action is death, rational choice models would predict inaction, unless they determine ex post facto, with reference to the individual's behavior, that the first order preference is a certain "value" that requires such a sacrifice. This, of course, is tautological.

Combinations of material and nonmaterial incentives are usually involved in individual decision making, and the reasons for individual participation in social movements may change over time. Different types of social movements, different moments in a movement's development, and different stages and levels of individual participation may be characterized by different combinations of material, solidary, and purposive motivations (Hirsch 1986; Snow et al. 1986). It is possible that at some moments of participation in high-risk social movements, material self-interest may become increasingly important for some participants (i.e., for individuals who become "movement entrepreneurs"); in such instances, a rational choice approach may have considerable explanatory potential. In general, however, it is likely that solidary and purposive motivations usually outweigh material incentives in decisions to participate in high-risk, and especially life-threatening, collective action.[7]

In addition to rational choice approaches, numerous other theories operating at the "micro" level of analysis also focus on individual motivations for participation but offer alternative motivational rationale. Some theorists emphasize how "prosocial" commitments motivate individuals to act collectively to achieve social goals (Martín-Baró 1983). Many "new social movement" (NSM) theorists argue that the expression of "new" or previously unarticulated "identities" forms the basis for collective action. Such approaches may be helpful for explaining participation in contexts of high risk if they avoid essentializing "identity" and instead are sensitive to social processes of identity construction leading up to and in the process of

---

[7] See, e.g., Calhoun (1991). Additionally, recent studies emphasizing the role of social networks and processes of collective identity construction suggest that material incentives may be less important determinants of participation than was once thought, even in less risky contexts (Gould 1995; McAdam 1986; Snow and Benford 1992; Snow et al. 1986). Of course, some high-risk collective action is motivated primarily by material incentives.

struggle and how socially constructed "identities" may be threatened by social change.

This contribution of NSM theorists may be linked to approaches that explore how "relative deprivation" or "status strain" may induce participation in social movements (Gurr 1970; Lipset and Raab 1970). The insights of these contributions can be applied to contexts of high risk by considering how sudden social change affects the self-understandings of particular individuals or groups in specific ways. Sudden threats to lifestyle or fundamental values may make life-risking behavior appear like the only viable option—as "self-saving" rather than "self-sacrificing" (Calhoun 1991, p. 69; Weber [1922] 1968, p. 25). Under such conditions, taking high risks may seem "the only choice."

Constructivist Approaches

A recurrent criticism of motivational accounts is that they fail to make problematic the social processes, or "micromechanisms," through which shared grievances or "latent" motivations are translated into collective action. One line of this criticism argues that explanations of participation in collective action need to consider how interactive processes of *interpretation* of grievances influence the propensity to participate (Snow et al. 1986, p. 465). Other theorists emphasize the importance of "identity" to social movements. However, theorists disagree over the extent to which identity *explains*, or is *explained by*, participation in a social movement.

Rather than accepting preexisting identities or feelings of solidarity as causal explanations for participation in social movements, some theorists have emphasized how individual and collective interests, identities, and solidarity are conceived, constructed, maintained, and reproduced in the process of struggle itself (Gould 1995; Melucci 1988; Calhoun 1991; Hirsch 1986; Snow et al. 1986). As Calhoun (1991, p. 52) explains: "The issue of identity is not adequately dealt with in terms of *legitimation, expression,* or other terms that imply that it exists prior to and is the basis of a struggle. Identity is, in many cases, forged in and out of struggle, including participation in social movements."

This insight is of particular importance for understanding participation in high-risk social movements, where the nature of the risks taken and sacrifices made are likely to heighten processes of self and collective (re)-definition in ways that have important consequences for continued and intensified participation. While, to the detached observer, the decision to risk life for a cause may appear stupid, pathological, or at best irrational, Calhoun (1991, p. 51) suggests instead that risks may be borne "because participation in a course of action has over time committed one to an identity that would be irretrievably violated by pulling back from risk."

Social Networks

Micromobilization processes are affected by the types of social networks within which potential participants are embedded. This is especially the case for recruitment to potentially risky forms of collective action (McAdam 1986; della Porta 1988; Morris 1984; Laitin 1995). Specifically, as Gould (1995, pp. 203–4) suggests and as McAdam (1986) demonstrates in the case of Freedom Summer volunteers, personal ties such as kinship or close friendship are particularly important for recruitment to high-risk activism. This is supported by Wickham-Crowley's (1989) finding that kinship or patron-client relationships were important bases of recruitment for guerrilla movements in Venezuela, Colombia, and Cuba. Personal ties are particularly important for sustaining contentious collective action in extremely repressive contexts because they provide a foundation for constructing the types of dense and insulated social networks required for effective resistance to state attempts at infiltration. The lack of anonymity also heightens individual accountability and can thus help to prevent defection (Laitin 1995). At the same time, it is within such insulated networks built on ties of kinship and friendship that collective and individual identities are constructed that make life-risking action appear as "self-saving" (Calhoun 1991, p. 69).

In addition to the importance of personal social networks, connections to certain types of organizations or institutions are also consequential for recruitment to high-risk collective action. Local social networks are generally embedded within broader regional, national, and sometimes international institutional networks. Theorists have shown that political parties can be an important basis for recruitment to guerrilla movements (Wickham-Crowley 1989) or terrorist groups (della Porta 1988), both forms of high-risk activism. In certain contexts, linkages to religious institutions, at the local, national, or international level, may also facilitate involvement in high-risk social movements (Wickham-Crowley 1989; Morris 1984; Orellana and Hutchison 1991; Lowden 1996; Osa 1989). The way in which face-to-face social networks are embedded within, and structured by, broader organizational networks influences the likelihood of participation in risky collective action.

Resource Mobilization

Connections to certain types of institutions may also help to explain *when (under what conditions) high-risk social movements and organizations emerge.* As numerous theorists in the "resource mobilization" tradition have convincingly argued, for grievances or beliefs in a cause to be translated into collective action requires availability and access to organizational and other resources (Zald and McCarthy 1979; Tilly 1978; Ob-

7

erschall 1973). Much like "low-risk" social activists, high-risk activists must have access to basic resources in order to begin and sustain mobilization and act collectively to achieve goals. Institutional and personal linkages to churches (Morris 1984), political parties, labor unions, universities, professional organizations, and national and international nongovernmental organizations (NGOs), among others, may provide potential activists in high-risk contexts with resources such as funding, information, and access to physical and symbolic space, which make sustained collective action possible. These sorts of connections frequently provide the "missing links" between feelings of deprivation and injustice, the "interpretation" of these feelings through social networks and processes of identity construction, and contentious collective action.

Frequently, critical resources are provided by "outsiders"—individuals or organizations other than the aggrieved population (Zald and Mayer 1979; Wickham-Crowley 1989). The case studies that follow suggest the acute importance of external financial or material support, information and expertise (services), and access to physical, sociopolitical, and symbolic space for HROs to emerge and be sustained under repressive military dictatorships.

Political Opportunity Structure

Access to resources, existing social networks, and availability of sociopolitical space are not sufficient to account for *when* social movements emerge. To explain the timing of social movement ebbs and flows, theorists have focused on how the political opportunity structure and long-term cycles of protest largely determine the possibility of contentious collective action (Tilly 1978; Tarrow 1994; Diani 1996). Social movements form in response to changes in society and in the political opportunity structure (Tarrow 1994, p. 18). In Tarrow's formulation, political opportunity structure is "external" to potential collective actors, so even resource-poor, "weak or disorganized challengers" can take advantage of changing opportunities. External changes may reduce the costs of collective action, reveal potential allies, and expose the vulnerabilities of authorities (Tarrow 1994, p. 18).

Changes in the political opportunity structure may go a long way toward explaining the timing and tactics of high-risk social movements.[8] However, it may not always be *improvements* in political opportunity that

[8] The inherent ambiguity of "changes in the political opportunity structure" may also introduce methodological difficulties. "Opportunity" is highly subjective, and "changes" in opportunity are necessarily relative. Looking back, it is possible to see "opportunities" where movement activists saw only "constraints" (and vice versa) (see Tilly 1978, p. 7).

induce social movement participation. In some cases, state policies and actions may themselves *create* new social movement "constituencies." In the cases examined here, political repression and human rights violations created new constituencies in a particularly dramatic and terrible fashion. Thus, while it may be the case that severe state repression tends to correspond with generalized demobilization (Tilly 1978), excessive abuses by the state may *directly stimulate* the emergence of *certain types* of contentious collective action. A basic assumption of opportunity structure and resource mobilization arguments, that "grievances" remain relatively constant, is violated in cases of sudden and severe state repression. The "early risers" in such contexts may mobilize in response to, *not despite,* severe repression; their actions may then create space for later waves of participants who may indeed be responding to *relative* improvements in the structure of opportunities.

In sum, the insights gained from an overview of theoretical literature on social movements suggest that explanations of participation in high-risk collective action should consider the influence of face-to-face, personal social networks, the way in which immediate social networks are embedded within broader institutional networks, and the forging of increasingly committed self and collective identities in the process of participation. Additionally, in contexts of high risk, social movements and organizations are more likely to emerge when individual and institutional networks facilitate access to critical resources such as information, financial assistance, and physical, sociopolitical, and symbolic space from which to launch contentious challenges. As is true for social movements in general, "external" support enhances the possibility for the emergence of social movements and organizations in high-risk circumstances. Finally, repression (a worsening of the political opportunity structure) may induce certain types of collective action.

EMERGENCE OF HROs IN CHILE, URUGUAY, AND ARGENTINA

Despite significant variations in their political histories and socioeconomic systems, the common experience of military dictatorship characterized by extensive human rights violations invites comparison of the HROs that developed in Chile, Uruguay, and Argentina in the 1970s and 1980s. Of course there were significant differences between the Southern Cone military regimes, as well as in the character of the military governments over time. The particular historical and institutional role of the military in politics differed in each country. The 1973 coups in Chile and Uruguay interrupted long traditions of civilian rule with only a few brief interludes of military involvement. In Argentina, military intervention in politics was a recurrent historical routine. Southern Cone military governments also varied in their internal structure, from relatively tight, top-down hierarchical control under General Pinochet in Chile, to interforce (army, navy, air force) divisions in Argentina, to hard-line/soft(er)-line factions in Uruguay. Despite such differences among and within these military governments, they shared a common commitment to national security doctrines that articulated the military's historical mission and duty, as ultimate protector of the "patria" from external and internal threats, to eradicate "subversive" elements from society. In all three cases, repression targeted organizations and individuals with linkages or associations with the left, especially labor unions, political parties, and students; however, in no case were government attacks limited to these sectors.[9] Evidence suggests communication and collaboration among the military intelligence services across nation-state frontiers, including the sharing of novel torture techniques (*Centro de Estudios Legales y Sociales* 1984).

However, the overall repressive strategy of each regime in accomplishing its "mission" varied, from the infamous "dirty war" in Argentina that left as many as 10,000–15,000 people dead or disappeared, to the relatively low number of fatalities but extraordinarily high incarceration and torture rates in Uruguay, where prisons were geared toward psychological torture and systematic destruction of the personality (Weschler 1990). Variations in repressive strategies across countries and over time subjected activists to different sets of risks and constraints in their efforts to create and sustain HROs. Differences existed both in the opportunity structure and the *perception* of risk for human rights activists. Such differences help to account for variations in the participation and timing of HROs in these countries, as the nature and extent of physical and psychological repression confronted by potential participants shaped their perceptions of the risks and opportunities. The timing and extent of legal restrictions on personal liberties and rights also varied across countries.[10] Together with the extent and intensity of repression (see fig. A3 in the appendix), such restrictions provide an indirect measure of the sociopolitical space provided by the "political opportunity structure" at different moments beneath the military regimes in each country.

To compare the political opportunity structure—"dimensions of the political environment that either encourage or discourage people from using collective action" (Tarrow 1994, p. 18)—across countries, this article fo-

[9] Part of the repression in each country was intended to dismantle labor movements in order to impose neoliberal economic models (see Drake 1996).

[10] Tables listing formal restrictions on political and sociocultural activity in Chile (1973–77), Uruguay (1967–77), and Argentina (1975–76) are available from the author upon request.

cuses on two features of the political environment of particular relevance to potential participants in HROs: (1) the extent and intensity of repression, and (2) formal (legal) restrictions on political and sociocultural space. These two "factors" do not fully operationalize what is meant by the concept "political opportunity," let alone *perceptions* of political opportunity, but together they provide a way to approximate the "space" available in each country and to compare in relative terms the degree of risk confronted by potential participants.

While repressive strategies varied, in all cases HROs emerged in response to sudden and dramatic increases in state abuses of civil and human rights. These were *reactive* social movements, in which human rights activists and constituencies were "created" by the abuses they then sought to end.[11] In each country, HROs emerged in contexts characterized by what Corradi, Fagen, and Garretón (1992) refer to as a "culture of fear," where the intentional propagation by a regime of a climate of uncertainty, insecurity, and terror aims to paralyze forms of collective action. Threats of persecution, arrest, torture, disappearance, or assassination of opponents of the regime are meant to create insurmountable obstacles to collective action; they exacerbate existing incentives to free ride.[12] Yet in spite of selective *dis*incentives to participate in HROs, such organizations emerged in each of the countries chosen for study.[13] In this context, how were HROs formed despite both generalized perceptions and actual situations of high risk in Chile, Uruguay, and Argentina? What accounts for cross-country variations?

[11] Prior to the 1960s, there was only one organization in the Southern Cone explicitly concerned with human rights: the Liga Argentina por los Derechos del Hombre was created in 1937 in response to political persecution that followed the military coup of Uriburu in 1930 (see Veiga 1985, pp. 15–26; Frühling et al. 1989).

[12] Olson's (1965) formulation of the "free rider" problem, with its emphasis on "proportional participation," does not adequately capture the dynamics of collective action in cases where small numbers may be more of an advantage than a liability (see Tarrow 1994, p. 15).

[13] The existence of "selective *dis*incentives" to participate means that the free rider problem was not overcome through olson's suggested solution of selective incentives for participants. In some ways, however, the creators and early participants in HROs can be conceptualized as analogous to Olson's "privileged group"—the other possible solution to the free rider problem. While referring to a group of individuals who lived with the constant fear of repression and potentially horrific mental and physical abuse as "privileged" is an obvious misnomer, this group played a role analogous to the "privileged group" in Olson's terminology. For reasons to be explored below, they were willing and able to assume the "costs" and risks of defying the military regime in the hope of providing the "public good" of basic respect for human rights.

11

CHILE

Rapid Formation of HROs during the Height of Repression

Chile is unique among the cases in the extent to which organized moral opposition (Lowden 1996) to the military regime by individuals not directly affected by human rights abuses began and was sustained during the height of repression.[14] How do the theoretical approaches to social movements reviewed above help account for the emergence of HROs during the worst years of repression (1973–76), and how do they help explain why individuals risked their lives to participate in the earliest HROs in Chile?

The literature on the human rights movement in Chile emphasizes that HROs formed in successive generations, with the first wave based in religious organizations, especially the Catholic Church, the second wave primarily composed of family members of victims, and later waves based in political parties or some combination of these three (Orellana and Hutchison 1991).[15] The creators and participants in the first HROs in Chile were predominantly religious leaders of various denominations and professionals, including academics, politicians, social workers, psychologists, and lawyers. The first organizations were formed in collaboration with international human rights and religious organizations under the protective umbrella of the Catholic Church. Immediately after the coup, the United Nations High Committee for Refugees (UNHCR), the World Council of Churches, through its representative to Chile, and representatives from evangelical churches petitioned the junta for permission to create an organization to evacuate the 10,000–15,000 non-Chilean political refugees residing in Chile and threatened by persecution. The National Committee for Aid to Refugees (CONAR) facilitated the safe exodus of approximately 4,000 refugees by 1974 (Lowden 1996, p. 32). An organization to assist Chileans was created in October of 1973. The Comité de Cooperación para la Paz en Chile (COPACHI), which included Catholic, Jewish, Orthodox, Lutheran, and various evangelical religious leaders, also emerged during the most intense period of repression. Programs under the auspices of COPACHI aimed at providing legal aid and general assistance to vic-

[14] The literature on HROs in the Southern Cone distinguishes between organizations made up primarily of *afectados* or *victimas*, people personally affected by repression through loss of family member, and organizations of *no-afectados*, people indirectly affected by human rights abuses (although there is some overlap in membership).

[15] Some sources refer to groups of family members of *desaparecidos* and victims of human rights abuses as "movements" and reserve the label "organization" for other types of HROs. Since this does not correspond with predominant usage in the social movement literature and would only add to terminological confusion, I have not adopted this usage.

12

tims of political persecution and their families, assisting refugees, and helping those hardest hit by the regime's austere economic policies through self-help employment projects, day care centers, and children's soup kitchens (Smith 1982, p. 334). In 1975, COPACHI was dissolved under pressure from the military junta and was replaced by the Vicaría de la Solidaridad, which together with La Fundación de Ayuda Social de las Iglesias (FASIC) continued to provide crucial support to those affected by repression.

Subsequent waves of HROs, such as organizations of family members of the disappeared, followed by more explicitly antiregime HROs, emerged in the space opened up by earlier organizations (Vidal 1986, pp. 26–33). The programs and strategies of later waves of HROs varied depending on the political context and particular goals but generally included some combination of public denunciation of human rights abuses, legal and material aid for victims and their family members, popular education, and eventually mass mobilization in opposition to the military regime.[16]

Several HROs emerged after 1977, as the dictatorship gradually loosened its control over social life, lending support to Tarrow's thesis that changes in the political opportunity structure that reduce the costs or potential risks of organization largely account for the timing of contentious collective action. Tarrow's formulation helps to account for the emergence of these third-generation Chilean HROs, because it recognizes that *relative* improvements in the opportunity structure may incite collective action. However, the earliest Chilean HROs do not fit neatly in Tarrow's model. What insights does the synthetic theoretical framework outlined above shed on why and how HROs emerged and were sustained during the height of repression in Chile?

The most salient feature of the early HROs in Chile, and the one that distinguishes the Chilean human rights movement from the other cases under consideration, is the prominence of the Catholic Church.[17] But the involvement of the Church per se is not itself an *explanation* for the quick and enduring formation of HROs in Chile compared with the more delayed or relatively weaker responses in other cases. A theoretically in-

---

[16] Tables listing HROs created in Chile, Uruguay, and Argentina prior to democratic transition in each country are available from the author upon request. Tables include name, date of origin, principal participants, and primary objectives and activities of each organization.

[17] For the purposes of this article, I consider the consequences of the Catholic Church's position vis-à-vis the military regime for HROs without attempting to explain *why* the Church as institution reacted differently to human rights abuses in each country. Though a fascinating question, it is beyond the scope of the present analysis. For Chile, see Smith (1982). For Argentina, see Mignone (1988).

formed assessment of the emergence of and participation in the earliest HROs in Chile suggests specific ways in which the Church and other religious organizations were influential.

First, accounts of the formation of COPACHI reveal the importance of *preexisting transnational and national social and political networks* linking religious leaders from diverse denominations in the creation of the earliest HROs. In the first months of the dictatorship, characterized by massive disappearances and political repression,[18] the church as an institution did not openly criticize the regime. To the contrary, it lent the military government at least tacit support and hence contributed to its legitimacy.[19] Brian Smith (1982) describes the position of the Church during this period of extreme repression as ambiguous at best, with Silva Cardinal Henriquez, the Permanent Committee of the Episcopal Conference, and several bishops expressing confidence in the regime and counting on the "good faith" of the military junta "as Christians" to bring a rapid end to the repression.[20]

In the days following the September 11, 1973, coup, a representative of UNHCR, a representative of the World Council of Churches (Charles Harper), and several Chilean ecumenical leaders created CONAR to secure the exit of the large refugee population. Following on the heels of CONAR, COPACHI was created to extend ecumenical support to Chilean nationals. Harper contacted Bishop Helmut Frenz, the head of the Lutheran Church in Chile, who spoke with the auxiliary bishop of Santiago, Fernando Ariztía, who enlisted the support of Raul Cardinal Silva Henriquez, the Archbishop of Santiago. Cardinal Silva Henriquez held a meeting for selected representatives of the Catholic, Orthodox, Lutheran, Methodist, Pentecostal, and Baptist churches and the Jewish community, and COPACHI, officially under the jurisdiction of the archdiocese of Santiago, was set in motion (Lowden 1996, p. 32). The *Comité para la Paz,* then, was not a product of the Catholic Church as institution; rather, it

[18] Estimated numbers of disappeared persons vary widely depending on the source. The Chilean Truth Commission, whose estimates are widely recognized as conservative due to its stringent criteria for accepting cases, reports 1,156 deaths and disappearances from September to December 1973. The CIA reported 11,000 dead between September and November 1973, while the U.S. State Department estimates ranged to 20,000 for the same period (cited in Smith 1982, p. 288). For a comparison and analysis of diverse estimates for Chile, Argentina, Uruguay, and Brazil, see King (1989).

[19] Isolated criticisms of "individual aberrances of power" emerged from 1974 onward; however, the Church did not officially criticize the systematic abuse of power by the regime until mid-1976 (see Smith 1982, chap. 9).

[20] The Church's official position of good faith toward the "Christian" military junta should be understood in contrast to its discomfort with the preceding Marxist regime that it perceived as a threat to traditional Catholic values (see Smith 1982, chap. 9).

developed through the personal and professional relations of religious leaders and others who, regardless of denomination, shared certain basic life commitments and values and recognized the threat of the regime to those values.

The preexisting social networks of progressive religious leaders also linked them to leftist politicians, university faculty, social workers, lawyers, and other professionals who participated in the first generation of HROs (Camus 1985; Lowden 1996; Orellana and Hutchison 1991). The Chilean case is unique in the extent to which institutional connections between the Church, Catholic left political parties, labor unions, community organizations, and Catholic universities had facilitated the prior development of personal networks linking individuals from these spheres of society. Personal ties were formed through institutional connections and shared values linking students and faculty at the prestigious Catholic University to progressive leaders within the Church, to political leaders, activists, and party members of the Catholic left. Institutional and personal connections between representatives of the Chilean Catholic Church and progressives in the universities and political parties were facilitated by the Church's official identification with the social reformist principles espoused at Vatican II in 1968 and reaffirmed a few years later at Medillín (Smith 1982).[21]

Many political leaders on the left had studied at Catholic universities, met each other through involvement in student politics, and maintained ties with faculty and priests. These networks, sometimes going back to the 1930s, proved crucial, as the individuals who became involved in human rights activities in the early years of the dictatorship through COPACHI, and later through the Vicaría and FASIC, were for the most part Catholics from outlawed or suspended political parties. According to Smith (1982, p. 334), the "backbone of the original core team" who initiated programs under the auspices of COPACHI "were Catholics formerly associated with leftist parties," such as Movimiento de Acción Popular Unitaria (MAPU) and the Christian Left Party (IC). Some non-Catholics who had been active in the communist or socialist parties also volunteered, along with several priests and nuns, totaling over 300 professional and staff personnel working as lawyers, social workers, physicians, and clerical help (Smith 1982, p. 334). Because of the high risks and the importance of trust and solidarity in the early 'wave' of resistance, participants

---

[21] The Church's discomfort with the Allende government was much more a reaction to that government's Marxist ideology than its plans for social reform (see interviews and survey results in Smith [1982]). Mainwaring (1986, p. 170) suggests that "since the late 1950s, the Chilean hierarchy has been one of the most progressive in Latin America."

were recruited exclusively through the personal networks of the core members. According to a psychologist active in FASIC, "The first generation of human rights activists was clearly made up of a network of persons who, if they didn't all know each other personally, had faith in the friends of those they did. Nobody came in off the street ('Nadie llegó desde la calle')" (Lira 1997).

Whether for primarily religious, ethical, or political reasons, some degree of personal commitment and "solidarity" (Fireman and Gamson 1979; Martín-Baró 1983) toward confronting the abuses of the regime characterized the early participants in HROs. Those who began to organize during the first wave, in the midst of unprecedented political repression and state terror, were motivated to do so in part because of moral, personal, and political commitments developed in their life experiences prior to the coup. Preexisting ties and solidarity among certain religious leaders, academics, politicians, and professionals (e.g., lawyers, social workers) facilitated the formation of COPACHI.

As outlined above, recent theories suggest that, to understand why individuals risked their lives by engaging in human rights work in the early to mid-1970s in Chile, it is helpful to consider both participants' self understanding and commitments prior to their involvement and how their "sense of self" is affected by involvement in high-risk collective action (Calhoun 1991, p. 69). Calhoun's (1991, p. 51) suggestion that risks may be borne "not because of the likelihood of success in manifest goals but because participation in a course of action has over time committed one to an identity that would be irretrievably violated by pulling back from risk" is supported by the account of a psychologist working with FASIC who became deeply involved in human rights activism: "In my view, motivations to participate were ethical, political, and very personal. For me, the suffering of the people I was helping was intolerable, the persecution of my students, their disappearance and death still cause me pain today. I believe that one commits oneself to things because of who one is. I believe that I would have lost my own dignity and self-respect if I hadn't done the work I did" (Lira 1997).

Once involved in the daily activity of assisting victims of human rights abuses and their families, saving lives by coordinating asylum for targets of persecution, and helping subjected communities to meet their basic needs, participants became increasingly committed to what Martín-Baró (1983) refers to as "prosocial" collective action and identity, in which commitment to the community or greater good of society outweighs concern for individual needs or satisfactions. As the FASIC psychologist notes: "For many people on the left who were unemployed, it was work. For others, it was a cause, a meaning of life. And if that's how it is, risks lose their importance" (Lira 1997).

The tight personal networks that made up the first generation of HROs were relatively effective and sustainable during the most intense period of repression (1973–76) because they were embedded within extended organizational networks that included the Catholic Church; as a nexus linking immediate social networks of committed individuals to those in need of assistance, the Church as institution played an invaluable role. The "politically neutral" Church organizations provided a degree of symbolic and physical space within which religious leaders, political activists from banned political parties, and concerned professionals could meet and coordinate assistance for victims of persecution or repression.

In addition to organizations explicitly focused on human rights, the Church also facilitated or sponsored a plethora of NGOs, including research institutes such as the Academia de Humanismo Cristiano, which housed professors purged from the universities by the government (Vidal 1986). Along with the Church's own information gathering and publications (Garretón 1983, p. 179; CEP 1974[22]) those of the Academia became an important source of information and "counterinformation" in combating government censorship. Because of the breadth of the Church's ties to Chilean society, expanded further under the dictatorship as it increasingly served as a "surrogate" for outlawed forms of organization, the Church's "organizational network offered a unique opportunity to work for human rights" (Smith 1982, p. 334). The particular way that personal networks reflecting the institutional linkages in Chilean society were embedded within the Church partly explains why and how certain individuals managed to organize HROs in the first months after the coup.

The embeddedness of personal networks of committed activists within the domestic and international institutional networks of the Church also accounts in part for Chilean HROs' ability to inspire and coordinate international resistance to the Pinochet regime. The embedded networks facilitated the development of an elaborate, clandestine web connecting grassroots activists in Chile to high-level international Church officials, to private and government foundations, to Chilean exiles living abroad. Through these channels, many individuals whose lives were threatened under Pinochet were smuggled out of Chile. These networks also helped to sustain political activity of the Chilean exile community trying to influence international opinion of the Pinochet regime. Although human rights activists from Argentina, and to a lesser extent Uruguay, also testified intermittently in international forums, the Chilean activists were exceptional

[22] For a fascinating collection exemplifying the type and extent of "counterinformation" being produced within the Church, see CEP (*Centro de Estudios y Publicaciones* 1974).

in their ability to sustain a veritable international political lobby over a considerable period of time.

The Church as institution was also influential in that even before it began to make official its opposition to the military junta, its historical and institutional role in Chilean society was crucial in providing a shield of legitimacy behind which the early HROs were able to coordinate assistance for victims of persecution. The Catholic Church in Chile had been deeply and directly involved in politics since colonial times and in numerous ways remained extremely influential in the moral, social, and political life of Chilean society after the separation of Church and state in 1925 and throughout the decades leading up to the coup in 1973 (Smith 1982).

In its first year in power, the military junta did not wish to risk an open attack on the "humanitarian work" of COPACHI, for fear of risking a confrontation with the Church hierarchy, which might undermine its legitimacy in the eyes of Chileans and in the international community. While not immune to persecution, the work carried out openly under the auspices of COPACHI escaped direct repression, at least for a while. However, toward the end of 1974, COPACHI volunteers and programs began to be targets of government harassment.[23] The implication of a group of priests and nuns linked to COPACHI in procuring asylum for four members of the Movimiento de Izquierda Revolucionaria (MIR) in foreign embassies led to the arrests of several religious members of COPACHI in November of 1975. Pinochet accused COPACHI of providing a front for Marxist-Leninist agitators and, in a letter to the cardinal, he requested that it be disbanded (Smith 1982, p. 318). Although the cardinal acquiesced, formally ending the interdenominational Comité para la Paz, the following month he created a new organization, the Vicariate of Solidarity (Vicaría de la Solidaridad), which essentially took up where COPACHI had left off. According to Smith (1982, p. 318):

> While there were some changes in personnel, the new organization continued the same services of COPACHI and was made an integral part of the juridical structures of the Archdiocese of Santiago. While the Church had lost a tactical skirmish with the government, the strategy of the cardinal was shrewd and foresighted. The new Vicariate of Solidarity was more closely tied to the official Church than its predecessor, making it both easier for the bishops to control and harder for the government to smash without directly attacking the core of the Church itself.

The Church as institution provided a "moral shield" for human rights work through its domestic influence as a source of legitimacy and its international symbolic, moral, and political weight. These characteristics of

---

[23] See Smith's (1982, p. 317) account of "paid spies" attending Church activities.

the Church also made it logistically possible for foreign religious and humanitarian foundations to send money in support of human rights activities without state interference. CONAR and COPACHI benefited from foreign funds from their first moments, as Bishop Frenz arranged for support from the World Council of Churches through his relationship with a member of the council, pastor Charles Harper. Other evangelical and Catholic organizations in Western Europe and the United States, as well as the Inter-American Foundation and the Ford Foundation, beginning in 1974, also made significant contributions (Frühling 1988, p. 149).

The significance of external financing of the Chilean HROs is difficult to overestimate. Smith (1982, p. 325) argues that "none of the new projects begun under the auspices of the Chilean Church since 1973 could have been inaugurated or sustained over time without very considerable outside support." Based on data provided by donating organizations, Smith calculated that between 1974 and 1979 over $67 million in financial and material assistance was sent to the Chilean Church from Catholic organizations in North America and Western Europe. The Inter-American Foundation contributed approximately $20 million in grants to Church-sponsored projects. And contributions from North American and Western European Protestant organizations, funneled through the World Council of Churches, totaled approximately $10 million (1982, p. 326). As Smith points out, these funds dwarfed the Chilean Church's $4 million in internal resources collected through "tithing campaigns" during this same period. Though the military government attempted on various occasions to obstruct the flow of external funds to the Chilean Catholic Church, it repeatedly backed down in response to international pressure from the Roman Catholic Church, the World Council of Churches, and in the case of Inter-American Development Bank (IDB) funds, members of the U.S. Congress, the U.S. ambassador, and representatives of the IDB (Smith 1982, pp. 327–29). Embedded within influential organizational networks at the international level, the Chilean Catholic Church was able to serve as a funnel for foreign funds for human rights programs, even when the Pinochet regime was willing to risk some domestic confrontation with the Church.

As suggested by resource mobilization approaches in the social movement literature, access to external funding or other resources is frequently crucial for explaining why social movements emerge precisely when they do and are able to sustain themselves over time. It is quite clear to observers and participants in the Chilean human rights movement that foreign funding facilitated both the implementation and the sustainability of human rights programs in Chile and that such funding was both forthcoming and technically possible due largely to Church sponsorship of HROs and their varied activities in Chile (Smith 1982; Lowden 1996).

19

The "framing" of human rights programs as such also facilitated the moral and technical support of international organizations tied into the international human rights issue network (Sikkink 1993). As indicated earlier, almost immediately after the coup, the UNHCR and the World Council of Churches intervened on behalf of the 10,000–15,000 political refugees residing in Chile. International organizations were thus involved in Chile from the first day after the coup and were not slow to spread the word of massive abuses of human rights. In the first six months after the coup, delegations from Amnesty International and the International Commission of Jurists made visits to Chile to examine the human rights situation. The international publicity and uproar over the abuses committed by the military government immediately following the coup were channeled into an effective political lobby by international HROs and the Chilean exile community, which pressured the U.S. government to pressure the Pinochet regime to halt abuses.[24]

The combination of foreign funds and international visibility helps to account in part for the sustainability of the first generation of HROs in Chile despite a political opportunity structure that was not conducive to sustained collective action. In the absence of "externally determined" advantageous fluctuations in the structure of political opportunities (Tarrow 1994), resourceful social actors sought out and *created* "opportunity"— through personal networks embedded in historically linked social, political, and institutional networks—where none seemed forthcoming. From there, the emergence of later waves of HROs and the eventual mass mobilization to oppose the continuation of Pinochet in power (1988), and later in the struggle for "truth" and "justice" in the transition to democracy, followed more closely Tarrow's conceptualization of increasing mobilization in response to improvements in the political opportunity structure.

Yet while the political opportunity structure, as captured by the intensity and extent of repression (see figs. A1 and A3 in the appendix) and restrictions on personal liberties and rights,[25] did not seem conducive to the emergence of collective action in defense of human rights between 1973 and 1976 in certain respects some Chileans enjoyed a somewhat greater degree of personal freedom in the first years after the coup than in Uruguay or Argentina. Repression peaked in Chile between 1973 and 1976. During and after 1976, arrests and disappearances were more selective than in either Uruguay or Argentina, and there were fewer "errors"

---

[24] A somewhat perverse indicator of the success of the publicity campaign to isolate the Pinochet regime in the international community is that several members of the Argentine armed forces have explained their decision to employ clandestine repressive measures as a means to avoid Pinochet's difficulties with international critics (see Sikkink 1993, p. 423).

[25] See n. 10 above.

or "unintended" detentions or murders (in part due to the international publicity mentioned above). For the most part, individuals recognized who the targets of persecution would be and why; this provided some minimal level of day-to-day security, if only for those who fell outside the ascriptive social categories persecuted by the state.

Significantly, in comparative perspective, some social spaces remained open, if constrained, in Chile, that were eliminated either before or upon the military coming to power in Argentina and Uruguay. Though political activity was proscribed, right and center political parties, including the Christian Democrats, were not outlawed until 1977. Some newspapers, including the generally conservative *El Mercúrio,* continued to operate without prior censorship, and most social organizations of a nonpolitical nature were allowed to continue to function. Although they were not viable sites for open *political* resistance to the regime, these social spaces allowed people to meet, talk, and develop shared understandings of the situation.

Of course, the relative selectivity of state persecution and the limited availability of certain social spaces would not qualify, by Tarrow's own definition, as aspects of the political opportunity structure that *encouraged* collective action; from Chileans' perspective, these features resulted from sudden changes in the political environment that drastically increased the costs and risks of contentious collective action, which in Tarrow's formulation should *discourage* the emergence of social movements. However, the potential "opportunities" of these features of the political environment may be seen as such when considered in comparative perspective, as will become evident below.

Conclusion

Analyzing the emergence of HROs in Chile within a synthetic theoretical framework suggests that such an approach can improve understanding of the interrelated social processes involved in the emergence of social movements and organizations in high-risk contexts. In lieu of considering either a single "most important variable," or what amounts to a check-off list of hypothetically independent variables operating discretely at distinct levels, this approach sheds light on how several processes discussed in the social movement literature are *interrelated* in particular ways in a historically specific case.

In Chile, certain individuals chose to participate in HROs despite the risks because of moral, personal, religious, social, or political commitments developed prior to the coup and because of preexisting personal connections linking them to others with similar commitments. Once involved, their personal and collective sense of commitment was increased through the experience of participation. These face-to-face networks, which reflected the institutional networks between the Catholic Church, Catholic University, Catholic left political parties, labor unions, and professional organizations, were embedded within the broader institutional networks of the Church and transnational NGO and religious networks. These networks permitted the rapid emergence and sustainability of HROs during the height of repression by facilitating almost immediate access to international funding and publicity and by providing the symbolic and moral legitimacy and the physical and sociopolitical space from which to coordinate programs in defense of human rights from the first moments after the coup.

URUGUAY

The Absence of HROs during the Height of Repression

Uruguay presents a striking contrast to Chile. Although the *autogolpe* in Uruguay occurred the same year as the Chilean coup,[26] the first and only HRO to operate as such under the dictatorship did not emerge until 1981 (Frühling, Alberti, and Portales 1989, p. 262; Weschler 1990, p. 154).[27] What requires explanation in the Uruguayan case, then, is the *absence* of HROs in the first seven years under the military regime.[28]

The Chilean case suggests the importance of access to resources such as funding, information, and sociopolitical or symbolic space, to account for the *timing* of emergence and sustainability of HROs in high-risk contexts. Additionally, it reveals that participation in collective action in high-risk contexts depends on particular types of face-to-face networks, the way in which immediate social networks are embedded within broader institutional networks, and the forging of increasingly committed self and collective identities in the process of participation. In the Chilean case, a particular configuration of these factors facilitated a rapid and sustained response by particular actors whose activities created additional space for subsequent waves of activists, whose mobilization corresponded to relative improvements in the political opportunity structure. The Uruguayan case provides the opportunity to assess how well this same combination

[26] The Uruguayan armed forces denied that a coup had taken place in Uruguay in 1973, when the National Congress was dissolved, because the elected president, Bordaberry, retained the office of chief executive. They place the date of the coup three years later, on June 12, 1976, when Bordaberry was forced to resign.

[27] See n. 16 above.

[28] To my knowledge, no one has explored why HROs formed so much later in Uruguay than in Chile during this period. Of course, the absence of collective action is the expected outcome for those who follow Mancur Olson (1965).

of factors accounts for the *absence* of the outcome they explain in the Chilean case.

Uruguayan and Chilean societies were similar in several important respects prior to the early 1970s. Each enjoyed a highly developed political party system, national labor unions, a large urban population, a prestigious education system, and a long electoral tradition with only a few brief interruptions.[29] In one important way, however, Chile and Uruguay could scarcely have been more different. The secular nature of Uruguayan society contrasted sharply with the permeation of religion and the Church in most all spheres of Chilean life, from education to politics. Uruguay is widely recognized as an extremely secular society, in which the Church has little influence outside a clearly demarcated and limited "religious" sphere. This contrasts with the Chilean Catholic Church's long history of strong political and social influence, which in recent decades had been exerted increasingly toward social reform. The Church in Uruguay has been "historically weak" and "has never assumed the defense of the persecuted or oppressed" (Gauding 1991, p. 86). The Church in Uruguay also lacked strong historical connections to the major political parties or labor organizations. The largest party in Uruguay, the Colorados, was ardently secular, even anticlerical, in contrast to Chile's most important political party, the Christian Democrats. When compared with the Chilean case, a theoretically informed consideration of this feature of Uruguayan society provides several insights that help to account for the absence of HROs in Uruguay until the political climate shifted following the plebiscite in 1980.

First, and perhaps reflecting the isolated and limited role of the Church in national political life, neither the Catholic Church nor other religious institutions were able to provide the kind of protective moral "shield" from direct persecution that COPACHI depended upon during the first months of the Pinochet regime. Whereas COPACHI's affiliation with the Church warded off (at least for a while) direct persecution by the military regime,[30] the Uruguayan armed forces openly confronted the Church *as institution* in their first years in power. In the years of armed struggle between the armed forces and *Tupamaro* guerrillas, which lead up to the *autogolpe*, several prominent members of the Uruguayan Bishop's Conference, including the archbishop of Montevideo, espoused increasingly progressive

---

[29] Due to its democratic legacy, large middle class, and commitment to a welfare state, Uruguay had earned the international reputation of the "Switzerland of Latin America." In specialists' rankings of "political development" in Latin America prior to the seventies, Uruguay is generally ranked first among Latin American countries, with Chile following close behind. See, e.g., Fitzgibbon (1954).

[30] Smith (1982, p. 312) suggests that regime's initial tolerance of COPACHI was a trade off for the acquiescence of the Church hierarchy during the first year after the coup.

23

views reflecting support of the principles of Vatican II and Medillín.[31] In 1969, and again in 1972, the Bishop's Conference issued letters that, despite their overall neutral tone and calls for "reconciliation," offered subtle critiques of the increasing use of torture and unjust imprisonment (Kaufman 1979, p. 45; Inter-Church Committee on Human Rights in Latin America 1978, p. 15). President Bordaberry's response to the 1972 letter essentially dismissed the bishops' concerns. In part, he replied: "In this struggle, conventional standards are not applicable. . . . Information is a decisive factor, it is the basis of success. . . . Information is obtained in some instances spontaneously . . . and in others after rigorous interrogations. I defend the rigor and the severity of interrogations, which avoid bloodshed and deaths in this war, and which make possible bloodless victories."[32]

Following the *autogolpe* in 1973, which sparked protests by unions and student organizations and resulted in massive arrests, the Church maintained a position of official silence (Rama 1987, p. 175). But as Uruguayans were soon to learn, neutrality was not an option in the generals' Uruguay. The Church's official silence was interpreted as a failure to cooperate with the military government, and the Church was considered infiltrated by communism "whose ruinous villainous and treasonous actions must be once and forever expurgated" (General Forteza in *La Opinión,* September 29, 1973; quoted in Kaufman 1976, p. 46). According to General Forteza, international communism "has reached the Church itself, violating in this institution the rights and obligations that the State has granted to the different religions" (Forteza in *La Opinión,* September 29, 1973; quoted in Kaufman 1976, p. 54).

In contrast to the church-state relationship under military rule in Chile, in Uruguay, not only were the Church and other religious institutions perceived as subordinate to the state, the Church was accused of violating the conditions of its existence as determined by the state. This is clear in the open verbal attacks on the Church as institution,[33] as well as in the

---

[31] Several prominent members of the Church hierarchy also defended the traditional, conservative role of the Church; overall, the Uruguayan Church was (by default) more progressive than in Argentina but much less so than in Chile. Mainwaring (1986, p. 115) suggests that Argentina and Uruguay are exceptional among Latin American Roman Catholic Churches in that they failed to become more progressive in the repressive situations of the 1970s.

[32] *Ahora,* June 16, 1972 (cited in Inter-Church Committee on Human Rights in Latin America 1978, p. 15).

[33] While the Pinochet government criticized particular members of the Church on numerous occasions, it avoided verbal attacks on the legitimacy of the Church as institution.

persecution and arrests of numerous religious functionaries. In addition to the arrest, torture, and, in some cases, death of individual Methodists and members of Catholic orders (such as Jesuits and Dominicans), the regime also created an official commission to investigate Catholic Church activities (Inter-Church Committee on Human Rights in Latin America 1978, p. 51). According to the former auxiliary bishop of Montevideo, Andrés Rubio: "The Uruguayan police tentatively watches the Catholic Church, controls and watches the content of sermons in the churches and investigates the text of the material circulated; several parishes and houses of clergymen have been subjected to searches and some priests have been arrested" (in the Mexican newspaper *Excelsior,* June 21, 1975; quoted in Kaufman 1979, p. 81).

Largely due to its relative isolation from the political process and historically marginal position in other spheres of Uruguayan society, the generals did not feel obligated even to feign respect for the Church. With members and leaders subject to arrest and imprisonment, the Church as institution could not provide "protected spaces" to the extent that it could in Chile, nor could it effectively perform the role played by the Chilean Church of collecting and disseminating "counterinformation." In Chile, the historical, political, and symbolic importance of the Church as institution forced the military junta to adopt a more cautious stance toward the Church, allowing it to become the single most important locus of resistance and moral opposition to the military regime. In Uruguay, the Church was much more easily controlled and repressed by the generals; it may well have been the "weakest of all political pressure groups in the country" (Kaufman 1979, p. 81).

While numerous sectors of "civil society" in precoup Uruguay were highly organized, the *particular type* of cross-sectoral personal networks that made such a difference in Chile were lacking. The contrast between the relationship of the church and the political left in Chile and Uruguay is particularly striking. Until quite recently, the left was historically insignificant as a political force in Uruguay, and the Christian left even more so. The two major political parties in Uruguay were both secular; the traditional Colorado and Blanco parties had monopolized political control through an elaborate electoral system and power-sharing arrangement that guaranteed the "loser" (for most of this century, the Blancos) one-third of the seats in legislative bodies. In the 1966 elections, the Christian Democratic Party won a mere 3% of the votes, and all leftist parties together accounted for only about 10% of the votes (Franco 1984, p. 95). With the formation of the Frente Amplio, a leftist coalition including the Socialist Party, the Frente Izquierda, the Christian Democratic Party, and the Union Popular, among other (even) smaller parties, the combined votes for the left in the 1971 elections rose to 18.28%, but the Christian Democratic Party still claimed only 3.86% of the electorate (Franco 1984, p. 95).

Whereas in Uruguay no significant Christian Democratic Party had developed prior to the *autogolpe*, in Chile before the coup, the Christian Democrats had governed from 1964 to 1970 and remained the country's single most powerful electoral force; the Christian left was an important if small part of the Allende coalition. In Chilean municipal and parliamentary elections since 1963, the Christian Democrats had received more votes than any other single party, and combined with the socialist and communist parties, claimed over 50% of votes in all elections through 1973 (Bravo Lira 1978, p. 203). In contrast to the 3% of votes won by the Christian Democrats in Uruguay in 1971, the Chilean Christian Democrats earned 25.72% of total votes in municipal elections the same year and 29.12% in the parliamentary elections two years later (Bravo Lira 1978).

The comparatively low support for the Christian Democratic Party in Uruguay, yet another indicator of the secular nature of Uruguayan society, reflects the historically low level of interconnectedness and ideological affinity between the Church, political parties, and labor organizations.[34] Institutional linkages between the Church and the most prestigious universities, where the political and professional elites were predominantly educated, were also lacking. In contrast to Chile, where Catholic and secular higher education are both esteemed, in Uruguay the production of future political leaders, lawyers, academics, psychologists, doctors, and social workers occurred almost exclusively in public, secular universities. Political leaders were not influenced by Catholic education, nor had they participated together along with other would-be professionals in Catholic youth groups, as was often the case in Chile since the 1920s. Hence, another crucial link in the type of face-to-face networks that were so consequential in Chile was missing in Uruguay. The lack of institutional linkages between Church, universities, and political parties in Uruguay suggests that even if the Church had been able and willing to provide a relatively secure space for coordinating efforts in defense of human rights following the *autogolpe*, it would have had few "secure" channels through

---

[34] Writing in 1964, Goran G. Lindahl commented: "The Catholic party, the Unión Cívica, has never gained much support, not only because Uruguay is probably the most atheistic country in Latin America, but possible also because Batlle [the country's most important political leader in the early 20th century] was strongly anti-Catholic: he said that the Catholic religion, like all other religions, was filthy. Today Batlle's son, who runs his old newspaper, *El Día*, goes on writing 'god' without a capital letter. The Unión Cívica has not even been able to gather many of the Catholic voters, most of whom seem to vote for the Nationalists" (Lindahl 1964, p. 450).

which to recruit participants from other sectors of society without the risk of infiltration from security forces.[35]

The Church's weak position in Uruguayan society helps to explain why the types of individuals who became involved through personal networks in the first generation of HROs in Chile—religious leaders and functionaries, party members from the Christian left, academics, lawyers, and social workers—did not create HROs in Uruguay in the face of military dictatorship. However, it only partly accounts for why no organizations emerged at all: Why did no other social actors, perhaps embedded in distinct types of social networks from those that linked the Chilean activists, act collectively to form HROs prior to the 1980s in Uruguay?

Though a reasonable question, the answer is rather obvious. In the Chilean case, *particular types* of social networks, embedded in the multidimensional organizational networks of the Church, were *key* for launching a quick and sustained collective effort in defense of human rights because other potential spaces, particularly political parties, the labor movement, the universities, and professional associations, were restricted following the coup in 1973. This was true to an even greater extent in Uruguay, where traditional spaces for both political and nonpolitical organization were rapidly and systematically eliminated or brought under military control. Uruguayans experienced "the systematic destruction of all the spaces (*ambitos*) that surrounded the State, or that developed autonomously and that could effectively, or eventually, contend for power, information, or cultural production, as well as [military] intervention or mediation in all intermediate forms of social organization that could possibly, regardless of intentions or objectives, become spaces of refuge for the persecuted or those excluded from power" (Rama 1987, pp. 169–70).

Consideration of the nature and extent of repression in Uruguay can largely account for why other social actors, embedded in diverse secular social networks, failed to coordinate and sustain HROs prior to 1981. To an even greater extent than the other countries under consideration, Uruguayan society was thoroughly and deeply penetrated by the monitoring and repressive apparatus of the military state.

Both geography and demography (over 50% of the population lives in the capital city of Montevideo) contributed to the armed forces' social control capabilities. According to the Lawyers Committee for International Human Rights, "Uruguay was the closest approximation in South America of the Orwellian totalitarian state. A small and demographically

---

[35] This was a danger even for the Chileans; however, in an interview with the author, a psychologist with FASIC commented that despite three separate attempts by security forces to infiltrate the Vicaría, they never succeeded because (in a situation where "nadie llegó desde la calle") they were always identified as outsiders.

homogeneous country, without internal geographical barriers, Uruguay became a laboratory for the national security state" (Lawyers Committee for International Human Rights 1985, p. 51).[36] An important difference from Chile is that the foundations and infrastructural skeleton of this "laboratory" were already in place prior to the disbanding of the Uruguayan congress in 1973. In Uruguay, as in Argentina, the armed forces had confronted real and violent "internal enemies" (the Tupamaros and Montoneros, respectively) before coming to power. As a consequence, the security forces were already organized and mobilized for waging a broadened "war against subversion,"[37] and important "wartime" legal restrictions on the population were already in effect when the military took control of the state.[38] In contrast to Argentina, the armed forces in Uruguay eschewed a clandestine "dirty war" strategy of massive "disappearance" and physical elimination of "subversives" (see table A1 in the appendix); instead, they enforced severe legal restrictions of individual freedoms and "legally" subjected thousands of Uruguayans to a prison system designed to systematically destroy individual personality through physical and psychological torture (Weschler 1990, pp. 131–47; Amnesty International 1983).[39]

In contrast to Chile, in Uruguay most potential spaces for organized resistance had already been restricted or eliminated before 1973. Although the repression in the first moments after the coup in Chile was severe, in comparative perspective, the Chilean security forces were not as prepared "logistically" (e.g., clandestine torture centers were not already established and fully functioning, the DINA [intelligence agency] had only just been created) to systematically persecute and paralyze all opposition from every sector of civil society as were their counterparts in Uruguay. When compared to Uruguay, it seems plausible that the confusion that followed the coup in Chile—both within civil society as well as within the armed

---

[36] The extent of social control is illustrated by the creation of a computerized classification system designating all public employees as "A" for politically "clean," "B" if involved in "some dissident political activity but capable of rehabilitation," or "C"— "banned." This system resulted in massive firings and facilitated identification of "inactive subversives."

[37] Evidence that security forces were organized and in operation prior to 1973 is provided by a report issued in 1969 by a senate named Special Investigative Commission of the Violation of Human Rights, Torture of Prisoners and Conditions of Detention Afflicting Human Dignity. The report includes testimonies of torture victims, coroners, public defenders, and lawyers. See *Acts of the Uruguayan Senate-11-7, Information documentaire d'Amerique Latine* (INDAL), Belgium: 247–82 (cited in Inter-Church Committee on Human Rights in Latin America 1978, p. 4).

[38] See n. 10 above.

[39] The main prison under the military was called, ironically, *Libertad*. Prisons were methodically designed, with the assistance of psychologists, to "demolish the mental, emotional and moral integrity of their inmate populations" (Weschler 1990, p. 131).

forces—regarding what had happened and what would happen in the months ahead left some spaces open and conducive to the coordination of collective resistance immediately following the coup. In short, the political opportunity structure in Uruguay was even less favorable for the creation of HROs than in Chile in 1973.

Observers of the repression in Uruguay emphasize that the breadth and depth of military involvement in all spheres of life, and the *extent* of state repression, was unmatched by other Southern Cone regimes. Though the statistical comparisons of deaths and disappearance under the Southern Cone dictatorships make the Uruguayan dictatorship seem relatively benign (see appendix table A1), these numbers are misleading as indicators of the extent of repression because the generals in Uruguay opted for a different repressive strategy: massive arrests, torture, prolonged imprisonment, and intervention in all spheres of life, public and private (*Servicio Paz y Justicia* 1989, chap. 3).[40] Under the military government, Uruguay had the highest concentration of political prisoners in the world. In 1976, Amnesty International estimated that "one in every 500 inhabitants of Uruguay was in prison for political reasons and that one in every fifty citizens had been through a period of imprisonment, which for many included interrogation and torture" (Amnesty International 1983, p. 1). The Lawyers Committee for International Human Rights (1985, p. 52) estimates that one in every 47 Uruguayans was "subjected to some form of repression during the dictatorship, whether in the form of house arrest, torture, beatings or a house raid." These numbers earned Uruguay the reputation of the "great lockup."[41] And though arrests generally targeted certain sectors of society (such as members of political parties, unions, and student organizations), due to the broad definition and interpretation of what constituted grounds for arrest in the interests of "national security," no one was immune.[42] The creation and persecution of "thought crimes" through laws that prescribed prison sentences for "the *intention* to commit a crime" or "to damage the honor of the armed forces" or otherwise threaten the nation, meant that anyone could be arrested without any

---

[40] The military intervened directly in all public administrations, universities, unions, and professional associations.

[41] The extraordinarily high numbers of exiles during this period is another indicator of the extent of repression. An estimated 300,000 people fled Uruguay in this period, including an estimated one-third of the population between the ages of 20 and 35 (Lawyers Committee for International Human Rights 1985, p. 4). For comparative estimates see Inter-Church Committee on Human Rights in Latin America 1978, p. 9; King 1989.

[42] Victims included priests, nuns, high school and university students, teachers, professors, journalists, lawyers, political party members, union leaders and members, and even medical workers (Servicio Paz y Justicia 1989, chap. 3).

legal recourse. Lawyers who defended those accused of such crimes were considered to be ideologically sympathetic to their clients and therefore also subject to arrest.[43] Hence, the Uruguayan generals' strategy effectively instilled a paralyzing culture of fear (Corradi et al. 1992) throughout society, and deep intervention by the military in all spheres of life closed off potential spaces for the emergence of HROs.

When the defeat of the generals' constitutional referendum in 1980 created temporary openings in the political opportunity structure, one HRO did emerge. Servicio Paz y Justica (SERPAJ)-Uruguay, created in 1981, "was the first organization devoted to work on behalf of the victims of repression and poverty to be established in Uruguay since the advent of the dictatorship" (Frühling et al. 1989, p. 262). In the same spirit as its sister organizations operating in Argentina since 1974 and Chile since 1977, SERPAJ-Uruguay sought to raise consciousness about human rights abuses (grassroots education programs), document human rights abuses committed by the military government, provide economic assistance for medical treatment for victims, and assist returned exiles. It also coordinated groups of family members of disappeared and political prisoners. However, the Christian-humanist organization, led by Perez Aguirre (who was arrested several times and released largely in response to international pressure; see Weschler 1990, p. 155) was severely limited in its efforts by a lack of external funding.

Here, another crucial role played by the Church in Chile again provides an important contrast; the Chilean Catholic Church made it logistically possible for international foundations to send financial support for humanitarian projects. In Uruguay, there was no institutional "funnel" through which funds could be "anonymously" received and diffused. According to a representative of a Swedish ecumenical NGO that funded several human rights programs in Latin America: "SERPAJ received a series of offers of economical support from foreign sources. However, it had to refuse in almost all cases because there was no way to introduce the resources into the country. Several people returning to Uruguay offered to take part and deliver money personally, but the founders [of SERPAJ] did not want to risk their safety" (Gauding 1991, p. 87). A member of SERPAJ-Uruguay commented, "I remember that when I was outside Uruguay people used to ask me, 'how can we send money to Uruguay?' There wasn't a single person who dared to receive a check, to give to a

---

[43] The fact that lawyers in Uruguay who defended those accused by the regime were themselves criminalized (which occurred to some extent in Argentina as well) undermined any possibility that the legal system might provide some recourse for the persecuted. On lawyers under the military in Uruguay, see Kaufman (1979, p. 77).

family member of a political prisoner, for fear of being sent to La Libertad prison" (as quoted in Gauding 1991, p. 87).

Conclusion

Unlike the other cases examined in this article, the Uruguayan case conforms quite neatly with sociological and commonsense expectations that severe state repression corresponds with generalized demobilization (Tarrow 1994; Tilly 1978). Comparative analysis suggests that this is due to the inability of the Church in Uruguay to play a role parallel to that played by the Church in Chile—as "moral umbrella" and as a funnel to capture a large and constant flow of resources—*combined with the regime's repressive strategy,* which effectively obstructed alternative sites of opposition. The combination of theoretical approaches applied to the Chilean case to explain the rapid emergence and sustainability of HROs under Pinochet can also account for the delayed emergence and nonsustainability of HROs in Uruguay. The Argentine case provides the opportunity to assess the utility of this approach to explain a more "intermediate" outcome.

ARGENTINA

An Intermediate Case

Attesting to the value of incorporating multiple cases in comparative research, the Argentine case suggests a challenge to the conclusions drawn from comparison of the Chilean and Uruguayan cases: without the support of the Catholic Church as institution, HROs still emerged under the harshest years of military rule in Argentina. In fact, not only did the Church—a powerful influence in Argentine politics and society—fail to support programs to defend human rights and assist victims of persecution, on numerous occasions it publicly voiced its support for the dictatorship.[44] Hence, while the Church in Uruguay seemed (at least somewhat)

---

[44] As previously mentioned, the reasons for the Argentine Catholic Church's complicity with the dictatorship are beyond the scope of this article. For a concise historical-institutional explanation, see Mignone (1986, pp. 72–92). Illustrative of the Church's complicity, Cardinal Aramburu publicly denied that the disappeared existed and maintained that position despite increasing evidence presented to the bishops by victims' families. According to Lowden (1996, p. 18): "The Episcopal Conference was even silent in the face of the persecution of clergy involved in human rights work, itself of unprecedented proportions: sixteen priests were murdered or 'disappeared' and two bishops died under highly suspicious circumstances" (see also Mignone 1988, chap. 2, chap. 8).

31

willing, but unable, to provide space and support for HROs and the Church in Chile proved both willing and able, the Church in Argentina was able but far from willing. This meant that neither the semiprotective "shield" of symbolic and moral legitimacy nor the multilevel organizational networks of the Catholic Church were available to human rights activists in Argentina. Despite the absence of conditions that were crucial for the emergence of Chilean HROs immediately following the coup, and that account for the absence of HROs in Uruguay until 1981, HROs arose in Argentina during the worst years of repression (1976–79). In the midst of massive and horrific repression in the mid- to late 1970s (see fig. A2 and table A1), and without the protective cover of the Church, why were certain individuals able to organize and act collectively in defiance of the military junta in Argentina? Did these organizations differ in significant ways from those that first emerged in Chile with Church support?

Much like in Chile, the Argentine Catholic Church is a powerful influence in Argentine society and is traditionally a major source of legitimacy for some political leaders.[45] In contrast, however, the two major political parties in Argentina, the Peronistas and the Radicals, were aggressively secular, if not anticlerical. As in Uruguay, there was no significant Christian Democratic Party and no generational or institutional connections of the Church to major labor, student, and professional associations. Thus, the embedded networks that connected activists to the Chilean Church were largely lacking in Argentina. The complicity of the church with the dictatorship in Argentina closed off what could have been a decisive source of opposition to the abuses of the military junta (Mignone [1986] 1988 p. 21). In stark contrast to the Chilean Church, the Argentine Church aligned itself with the military junta, granting its support and legitimacy to the imposed regime. As in Chile and Uruguay, divergent opinions and attitudes coexisted within the Church hierarchy; but in Argentina, radical and progressive members of the hierarchy were a marginalized minority.[46]

---

[45] In fact, in the 1970s, there was still no formal separation of Church and state in Argentina, and the constitution stipulated that the president must be Catholic.

[46] An organization of radical priests critical of the hierarchy emerged in 1968—the Movement of Priests for the Third World—but it was marginal and, as it earned a reputation of being a socialist organization, fell prey to repression under the 1976 junta (Mainwaring 1986, p. 168). Indicative of the minimal institutional penetration of progressive ideas in the Argentine Catholic Church, Mainwaring suggests that moderates and conservatives within the Argentine hierarchy were unwilling to defend progressive priests or bishops targeted by repression. This is supported in documents presented by Mignone (1988 chap. 8) revealing the collusion of the junta and the conservative hierarchy in the persecution of progressive sectors of the Church (the exact opposite occurred in Chile, where attacks on progressive religious functionaries caused the Church to finally take an official stand in opposition to the regime) (Smith 1982, chap. 9).

The historically conservative hierarchy—which had largely ignored, if not opposed, the social reformist tendencies stemming from Vatican II and Medillín—refused to denounce mounting evidence of human rights abuses, and the majority of churches closed their doors on family members of victims who came to plea for help (Mignone 1988, chap. 2). According to Mignone (1988, p. 19): "The Argentine episcopacy is made up of more than eighty active prelates, including heads of dioceses, auxiliary bishops, and military bishops. Only four of them took a stand of open denunciation of the human rights violations committed by the terrorist regime." The types of spaces, opportunities, and resources provided by the Church to activists in Chile were not forthcoming to their counterparts from the Church in Argentina.

With the Church doors closed and traditional spaces for organizing and coordinating collective action restricted or eliminated through legal and extralegal measures, HROs in Argentina emerged primarily through non-institutional channels. In addition to the Liga Argentina por los Derechos Humanos, a civil libertarian group dating to 1937 with unofficial links to the Communist Party, three other organizations came onto the scene *prior to* the 1976 coup that established the military dictatorship.[47] While these HROs emerged in response to repression, they did not initially confront the extent and intensity of repression imposed after 1976 by the military junta. Ecumenical leaders were active in forming all three of them, and two of them operated through personal relations of religious leaders to their parishes. This suggests an important contrast to Uruguay, where (for reasons discussed above) neither the Church—nor much less any other religious organizations—were fertile grounds for the emergence of HROs. Rising numbers of human rights abuses preceded the coup in Argentina because, as in Uruguay, sustained armed conflict between urban guerrillas and the armed forces had led to the erosion of legal protections of individual liberties and rights and to the escalation and institutionalization of extralegal forms of repression.[48] In response, in 1974, an Argentine section

---

[47] See n. 16 above.

[48] Like the Tupamaros in Uruguay, the Montoneros in Argentina provided justification for increasing military control over Argentine society. While neither the Tupamaros nor the Montoneros posed anywhere near the military threat claimed by the Uruguayan and Argentine armed forces to justify the tactics of their respective "wars against subversion," they were not "imaginary" enemies either. It is easy, and tempting, to overlook the provocative actions of these urban guerrilla movements in the face of evidence of the horrific abuses committed by the military regimes. But if their repressive actions remain unjustifiable, when the Montoneros were so bold as to wage armed attacks on military barracks, it was not totally unreasonable for the armed forces to speak of an "internal war." In contrast to Uruguay and Argentina, the Chilean armed forces did not face a significant armed threat before taking power, though smaller armed guerrilla movements later arose in response to the military regime.

33

of SERPAJ began providing assistance to grassroots sectors suffering effects of the heightened repression. The work of SERPAJ focused primarily on popular education and general assistance for marginalized communities, along with support for the creation of other HROs.

Some ecumenical leaders in Argentina who participated in SERPAJ grew frustrated by its "passive" stance in the face of the suffering they observed among their parishes and broke off to form the Movimiento Ecuménico por los Derechos Humanos (MEDH) in February 1976, on the eve of the coup. MEDH, which included dissident Catholic clergy and Protestant leaders among its founders, provided direct assistance to victims of human rights abuses and their families. As was the case for CO-PACHI in Chile, a combination of personal networks and external resources was crucial for the formation and activity of MEDH. In an interview, a member of MEDH recalled how "together with some friends, we considered forming a net of solidarity in different parishes to resolve concrete cases" (quoted in Gauding 1991, p. 103). Through mutual friends, members of MEDH were introduced to a representative of Diakonia, a Swedish NGO that offered financial assistance. Face-to-face relations were essential, as suggested by another member of MEDH: "In that period, it was impossible to work within any institutional structures. The Swedes ran the same risks as we did. We had to trust each other [Teniamos que confiar el uno en el otro]" (quoted in Gauding 1991, p. 103). Along with these two religious-based organizations, the Asamblea Permanente por los Derechos Humanos was formed by individual religious leaders, lawyers, academics, politicians, and other professionals as an alternative to the Liga with its reputed communist sympathies.[49] The primary activity of the APDH was the collection and systematic documentation of human rights abuses and disappearances. As in Chile, the prior religious, moral, and political commitments of certain individuals embedded in particular face-to-face networks facilitated the formation of HROs, despite severe repression in the mid-1970s in Argentina.

However, there are important differences in the early HROs that emerged in Chile and Argentina. If scholarly discussions of the human rights movement in Argentina rarely focus on the work of these organizations in the first years after the coup, it is only partly because the spotlight was diverted by the emergence of the Madres de Plaza de Mayo in 1977, followed by the Abuelas de Plaza de Mayo shortly thereafter. It is impressive that without the support of the Church—and at times with its explicit condemnation—HROs formed prior to the coup (before repression dra-

[49] Like MEDH, the APDH was created through personal networks, since, as Mignone explains (1991, p. 101), individuals formed APDH "without representing—and often against the wishes—of the collectivities to which they belonged."

matically increased) and managed to provide invaluable assistance to victims of human rights abuses and their family members. However, in comparative perspective, their development and activities "were severely limited due to the lack of support from the Catholic Church" (Frühling 1988, p. 161).

The absence of Church support affected these organizations in a number of overlapping ways. For example, in contrast to COPACHI, in their first moments, the activities of both MEDH and APDH were limited by lack of resources (Gauding 1991; Mignone 1991, p. 102). Eventually, both organizations benefited from connections to the World Council of Churches (Brysk 1994, p. 51; Mignone 1991, p. 102), which provided a degree of financial support and, particularly for MEDH, served as an alternative source of moral legitimacy. However, in predominantly (and officially) Catholic Argentina, the moral authority of the World Council of Churches could not offer the degree of protection from direct persecution that programs under the auspices of the Church in Chile enjoyed in the months after the 1973 coup.

During the mid- to late 1970s, the religious leaders involved in SERPAJ and MEDH and the heterogeneous members and leadership involved in APDH provided assistance to victims of repression at great risk to themselves. Brysk's (1994, p. 56) recounting of several cases of persecution of human rights activists is illustrative:

> Repression of the human rights movement touched every organization, affecting both the leadership and grass-roots membership. Many members of the original leadership of Las Madres "disappeared," while the Movimiento Ecuménico lost two nuns, several priests, and a Protestant minister. The co-founder of the Asamblea . . . was kidnapped, tortured, and imprisoned for several years. . . . Several Liga lawyers disappeared,[50] and a secretary of the Familiares was kidnapped, tortured, and forced to give false statements to the press denying her disappearance and alleging connections to guerrilla forces. Rank-and-file members of Las Madres were arrested repeatedly following demonstrations. . . . The offices of Asamblea, CELS, La Liga, and Movimiento Ecuménico were raided.

Mignone (1991, p. 104) recounts how the meeting places of APDH were bombed on numerous occasions. This repression prevented these organizations from providing nearly the extent of support or protection from state violence that programs under the auspices of the Church in Chile were able to provide in the first months under Pinochet. The absence of the Church umbrella also deprived Argentine HROs of the social and

---

[50] Again, this illustrates the less favorable political opportunity structure in Argentina than in Chile, where lawyers were exiled and jailed but none were killed or disappeared.

organizational networks that fostered the emergence, growth, and sustainability of the HROs in Chile. Overall, according to Frühling, in the first few years under the military junta "none of the Argentine human rights organizations reached the level of development or extent of human rights programs comparable to what was occurring in Chile at that time" (Frühling 1988, p. 162). Theoretically informed comparison of Chile, Uruguay, and Argentina, synthetically drawing on various strands of social movement theory, thus helps to explain both why these HROs emerged at all in Argentina and why they were relatively less effective than their counterparts in Chile in the early years after the coup.

Following the coup in March 1976, the Argentine military's chosen strategy in its "war against subversion" created a new category of social actor, as had occurred in Chile after 1973: relatives of the disappeared. This "ascribed identity" became the basis for the formation of three new HROs between 1976 and 1977, the Madres de Plaza de Mayo, the Abuelas de Plaza de Mayo, and the Familiares de Desaparecidos y Detenidos por Razones Políticas. Accounts of the emergence of these organizations invariably emphasize the extraordinary extent and cruel nature of repression under the military junta. Attempting to avoid the international criticism that plagued Pinochet, the armed forces in Argentina opted for a policy of clandestine state terror combined with official denial. Brysk (1994, pp. 36–37) describes the characteristic technique of disappearance: "'Disappearance' involved kidnapping of unarmed citizens (usually in the middle of the night, from their family homes) by a gang of armed men, followed by forced removal of the victims to clandestine detention centers, extensive torture, and mistreatment, and (almost always) murder. . . . Although the kidnappers usually sought a specific person, other family members or visitors often "disappeared" in lieu of or in addition to the intended victim."[51]

This strategy effectively instilled a culture of fear in Argentine society with all its paralyzing effects (Corradi et al. 1992); the majority of the population did their best to live day to day by trying to ignore or deny what was going on around them. The Argentine armed forces were determined to exterminate "subversive cancers" from the body of the nation, and to do so, they targeted vast numbers of Argentine citizens. In the words of Brigadier General Ibérico Manuel Saint-Jean, former governor of Buenos Aires: "First, we will kill all the subversives; then we will kill their collaborators; then their sympathizers; then the indifferent and, finally, the timid" (Comisión Argentina por los Derechos Humanos 1997,

---

[51] Eduardo Duhalde (1983, p. 146) discusses an internal military document from 1978 that places the margin of error of the disappearance campaign at "no more than 25 percent" (approximately 2,500 people).

p. 13).[52] The war against subversion in Argentina was not only a physical battle, it was also moral crusade. In response to a Mexican journalist seeking information on the fate of a woman confined to a wheelchair who had been detained, General Videla explained: "A terrorist is not only someone who kills with a gun or plants bombs, but anyone who encourages their use by others through ideas contrary to our Western, Christian civilization."[53] For this reason, the military government enacted sweeping censorship laws and even took the trouble to individually ban thousands of books, songs, and films, among them *"El Principito"* (The little prince), in its ninety-fifth edition in Argentina (Garcia 1995).

In these extremely repressive conditions, the founders of Madres de Plaza de Mayo met while searching for information about their disappeared children in government offices. Beginning in April 1977 a small group of these women decided to engage in symbolic protest against the regime by marching in the central public space of the nation, the Plaza de Mayo. Despite government attempts to crush the organization (nine of the original founders were "disappeared" after their meetings were infiltrated by an undercover military officer) and continuous persecution (members were frequently arrested following demonstrations), the Madres and Abuelas continued their weekly marches in the plaza, attracting international press coverage for their vigils. Under such an unfavorable political opportunity structure, why did these women risk their own security to protest the disappearance of their children and grandchildren?

Precisely because the decision by a small group of politically inexperienced women to stand up to the military junta seems so extraordinary and in many ways incomprehensible,[54] numerous authors have grappled with this question. Some accounts suggest that these women were able to confront the regime precisely because their claims—and the "identity" upon which they were based (motherhood)—were apolitical and were voiced in terms that challenged the regime's own discourse on "defense of the family." However, the disappearance of the founders seems to challenge the thesis that motherhood provided a protected space from which to launch symbolic protest. Other authors suggest that Las Madres protested the disappearance of their children because their sense of self, as

---

[52] Quoted in Comisión Argentina por los Derechos Humanos (1977, p. 13; Rock 1985, p. 444, n. 33; Camps 1983, p. 63). David Rock reports that Saint-Jean subsequently denied making the remark, citing an interview with General Ramón Camps in which Camps states he does not believe that Saint-Jean made the comment (Camps 1983). To my knowledge, there is no public record of Saint-Jean himself denying the comment.

[53] *Clarín*, Dec. 18, 1977 (cited in Frontalini and Caiati 1984, p. 24).

[54] Because of the likely consequences and improbability of success of the Las Madres' actions, within Argentina they earned the reputation of *"Las Locas de la Plaza de Mayo."*

mothers, compelled them to do so (Navarro 1989, p. 256).[55] However, this explanation fails to account for the vast majority of mothers of the disappeared who did nothing to make the personal political. Most attempts to account for the actions of Las Madres do so through a NSM framework that emphasizes how "new" (previously nonpolitical),[56] "powerless" actors employ "untraditional" forms of symbolic protest and emphasize the expression of particular "identities" to make claims on society. More insightful analyses combine this approach with "an appreciation of the strategic uses of maternal legitimacy" (Brysk 1994, 187 n. 31). Additionally, the nature of repression (which "created" a new category of social actor) and the institutional context were conditioning factors (most of the women had sought help from the Church but had been turned away). In Argentina, Las Madres' appeals to representatives of the state were directed to particular government offices, where relatives of the disappeared became aware of each other and came to recognize their shared plight and the futility of seeking help through traditional channels (Brysk 1994, p. 57). In contrast, in Chile, the Agrupación de Familiares de Detenidos y Desaparecidos (AFDD) was permitted to establish its office on Church property in the Vicaría.

Las Madres are often the focus of accounts of the Argentina human rights movement; this is likely because more than any other HRO to emerge in Latin America in this period, Las Madres captured the attention and support of the international community. Whatever limited political space they occupied was facilitated by international press coverage—skillfully manipulated by Las Madres leaders (MelliBovsky 1998). The image of defenseless mothers appealing to the military regime for information on the whereabouts of their children drew support from a number of international HROs and humanitarian foundations (Brysk 1994). "Framing processes" (Snow et al. 1986) were central in linking the plight of Las Madres to the international human rights issue network (Sikkink 1993). This allowed Las Madres to access international resources and support for their struggle without the benefit of the organizational networks of the Church. The publicity campaigns of Las Madres and their sponsors in a number of international forums contributed to growing international condemnation of the junta. And though their demands were ignored by

[55] In Navarro's (1989) account, the identity of "motherhood" is the primary causal factor. This interpretation is supported by interviews with founders and members who explain their participation in such terms. However, a politicized sense of "motherhood" may be more a result of their participation in Las Madres than the original cause (see Calhoun 1991).

[56] For a critique of the claims of novelty made by many NSM theorists, see Calhoun (1993).

the junta, together with Las Abuelas,[57] these women gained increasing international publicity, influencing the process of delegitimation of the military regime, which climaxed with the Malvinas crisis in the early 1980s.

While linkages to the international human rights issue network enabled Las Madres and the broader human rights movement to survive the dictatorship and exercise limited influence in the process of transition to democracy, (Brysk 1994) their effectiveness (in terms of their own stated goals) under the military government was quite limited. In comparison with Chile, where the Church's position vis-à-vis the dictatorship and its extensive linkages to other domestic institutions and to political parties facilitated the formation of dense and extensive embedded networks of human rights activists working in a variety of spheres and levels of society, in Argentina, the HROs essentially stood alone during the worst years of repression (though collaboration among HROs facilitated limited contacts between some of the same sorts of actors who were important in the Chilean case.) In Argentina, groups of *afectados* who engaged in symbolic protest largely isolated themselves from the rest of Argentine society during the worst years of repression. In contrast, in Chile, under the auspices of the Church, religious leaders, lawyers, social workers, academics, and political party members engaged in arranging safe exile for refugees, in providing monetary, legal, and medical assistance to victims and their families, in creating soup kitchens and work programs, and in working to expand the network of NGOs, which eventually became a type of "surrogate" political opposition to the regime (Loveman 1994).[58] It becomes clear in comparative perspective that the vitality of the early HROs in Argentina was limited both by the severely repressive context and by the fact that they were not linked to previously existing social and political networks.

Conclusion

Theoretically informed comparison with Uruguay and Chile reveals Argentina to be an "intermediate case." In contrast to Uruguay, HROs

---

[57] Las Abuelas (grandmothers) made claims on behalf of children born to pregnant prisoners or to the disappeared. Children of the disappeared were rarely returned to their blood relatives. Instead, they were given or sold to military families or their friends.

[58] This is not meant to downplay the overall significance of the human rights movement in Argentina, both nationally and internationally; as was apparent in the transition process with its famous trials and convictions (and later pardons) of the commanding officers of the junta, the claims of Argentine HROs had a powerful impact on political culture (even if their attempts to influence policy largely failed; see Brysk 1994).

emerged in Argentina both prior to and during the height of repression. However, the Argentine organizations lacked the foundation of extensive social networks, connected to domestic and international institutional networks of the Catholic Church, which characterized Chilean HROs. HROs in Argentina were thus much more vulnerable and hence less effective in terms of their own goals than their counterparts in Chile. Personal networks linking non-Catholic and dissident Catholic religious leaders to each other and to their parishes, and the previously developed prosocial religious and moral commitments of these leaders, enabled the development of SERPAJ and MEDH in response to the repression prior to the coup (1974–76). Individual politicians, lawyers, professionals, and religious leaders created the APDH as a (noncommunist) alternative civil-libertarian HRO (Mignone 1991, pp. 99–106). These groups, as well as Las Madres and Las Abuelas, emerged despite (or because of) a severely unfavorable political opportunity structure by operating within "noninstitutional" spaces that were not *formally* restricted. However, these spaces offered little or no protection from state persecution, restricting the development and activities of HROs under the dictatorship. Comparison with the extensive programs under COPACHI and later the Vicaría in Chile suggests the crucial significance of such a protected space for the effectiveness and sustainability of contentious collective action in high-risk contexts. The absence of Church support also limited the possibilities for the HROs to develop networks linking activists from different sectors of society; this further restricted the effectiveness of these organizations in terms of their own goals. This was particularly evident for Las Madres and Las Abuelas. Despite international fame, the domestic influence of these groups during the mid- to late 1970s was limited by their relative isolation from other sectors of society.[59]

CONCLUSION

By asking why and under what conditions individuals will risk their lives to confront state repression, I have identified an important area of research largely neglected in the existing social movement literature. Contrary to sociological and commonsense expectations, the cases examined

---

[59] The relative lack of domestic networks linking Argentine HROs to other social sectors, such as political parties, universities, and unions, may also partly account for their lesser influence during the transition to democracy, as compared to Chile. Comparative analysis of the role of HROs in the transitions in these countries, as well as their fate in newly democratic contexts, merits future research. For insights on Chile and Uruguay, see de Brito (1997); on Chile and Argentina, see Skaar (1994); on Chile in Comparative Perspective see Frühling and Orellana (1991).

here demonstrate that the onset of severe state repression, that increases dramatically both the potential risks and costs of collective action, may itself stimulate certain types of social movements. The generalized demobilization that is the expected outcome of dramatic increases in the scope and scale of state repression does not capture the entire picture; state repression may stimulate collective organization and opposition from certain sectors of society as a direct result of the severity and cruelty of its attempts to stifle it in others.

Comparative analysis suggests that participation in high-risk collective action depends largely on particular types of personal social network ties (McAdam 1986) and the particular way in which face-to-face networks are embedded within broader institutional networks (Morris 1984; della Porta 1988). Reliance on face-to-face networks permits a high degree of trust that helps to counteract the selective *dis*incentives to participate posed by threats of state persecution. Dense interpersonal networks tend to insulate activists, which contributes to their intensified commitment and willingness to act despite risks of horrific repercussions. The particular way in which certain types of face-to-face networks are embedded within previously existing domestic and international networks largely determines the ability of activists to organize and sustain collective action in high-risk contexts. To explain the actions of the "early risers" in high-risk contexts, it is also important to consider how forms of repression collide with personal, moral, or political commitments developed prior to and in the process of participation (Calhoun 1991; Martín-Baró 1983). The diversity and density of networks within which the personal networks of early risers are embedded influences whether, or to what extent, the efforts of the first core group of actors will develop into sustained and effective collective resistance and opposition, creating openings for later waves of activists by reducing the costs or risks associated with joining. But ultimately the emergence and sustainability of social movement organizations is constrained by the political opportunity structure, particularly the levels and types of repression—that is, the ability of the government to effectively curtail and control access to material and symbolic resources and physical and sociopolitical space.

When early risers are able to create or expand openings, whether they will be filled by new actors depends in part on the ability to frame the struggle in terms that resonate in the wider society. Framing processes are also important for linking local struggles into broader "international issue networks" that may generate international publicity and funds (Snow et al. 1986; Snow and Benford 1988; Sikkink 1993). Additionally, both timing and participation are intimately linked to how the structure of nested social networks creates or impedes access to crucial resources including physical, sociopolitical, and symbolic 'space,' information, and

41

material assistance, particularly from transnational and international sources.

Comparative historical analysis employing a synthetic theoretical framework facilitates identification of those social processes that influence the emergence of collective action in high-risk contexts that are generalizable across cases with the consequent potential to *generate theory*. This approach illuminates how *particular configurations* of 'variables' affect outcomes. In an example from this article, comparison of Argentina and Chile informed by a synthetic theoretical approach suggested that the emergence and effectiveness of HROs was related not merely to the presence or absence of particular types of personal ties, *plus* the presence or absence of institutional networks, but rather to the particular way in which personal networks were *embedded within* broader, multilevel institutional networks. This approach redirects attention of the theorist to *relationships among* social processes operating at different levels, resulting in improved understanding of the linkages between the how and the why of social movements.

This approach thus offers the potential to bridge some of the gaps between resource mobilization and NSM theoretical schools, a need that has been increasingly recognized and articulated by leading theorists in the field (Klandermans and Tarrow 1988; McAdam, Tarrow, and Tilly 1995). It also facilitates borrowing from, and integrating, the contributions of earlier pluralist, rational choice, structuralist, marxist, and social-psychological social movement theorists. If construction of social theory and social scientific knowledge is to be a cumulative enterprise, the contributions from diverse theories and comparative historical research must be incorporated and assimilated rather than discarded or forgotten in a battle of competing paradigms. The explanations generated through this comparative historical analysis of the emergence of HROs in Chile, Uruguay, and Argentina thus serve as a modest example of the utility of synthetic theory building and comparative research rather than pseudoparadigmatic intellectual warfare.

TABLE A1

ESTIMATED EXTENT OF REPRESSION IN THREE SOUTHERN CONE COUNTRIES

COUNTRY	TIME PERIOD	DEATHS		PRISONERS				EXILES		1976 POPULATION
				Long-Term		Cumulative				
		Total	Per 1,000 Population	Total	Per 1,000 Population	Total	Per 1,000 Population	Total	Per 1,000 Population	
Argentina	1976–83	10,000	.40	7,000	.03	30,000	1.1	500,000	18.9	26,480,000
Chile	1973–77	4,000	.40	6,500	.60	60,000	5.8	40,000	3.9	10,372,000
Uruguay	1973–84	36	.01	4,000	1.40	60,000	21.0	500,000	175.0	2,847,000

SOURCE: Repression statistics are from King (1989); population statistics are from United Nations (1987).
NOTE: King's estimates are derived from a comparative analysis of a wide range of estimates from government sources, international and domestic human rights organization sources, and academic sources.

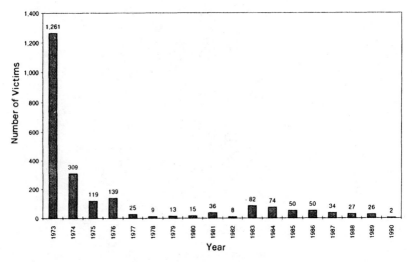

FIG. A1.—Victims of death and disappearance in Chile, 1973–90 (Chilean National Commission on Truth and Reconciliation 1993, p. 903).

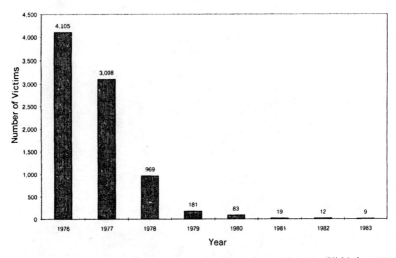

FIG. A2.—Victims of disappearance in Argentina, 1976–83 (Sikkink 1993, p. 427; Skaar 1994).

44

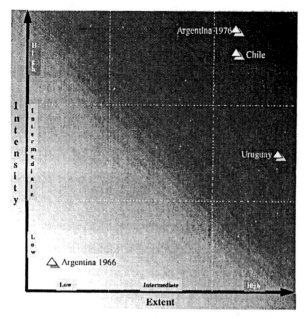

FIG. A3.—Comparative intensity and extent of repression (from King 1989); "extent" refers to the gross number of individuals affected by repression; "intensity" refers to the manner in which they were affected. Extent is the cumulative total of deaths, number of long-term political prisoners, total number of political prisoners, and number of political exiles. Intensity is determined by the number of deaths and long-term imprisoned, with greater weight given to deaths. Torture is not systematically incorporated into King's analysis (it is notoriously difficult to "measure"). However, he does mention that "qualitative aspects of the different cases are also evaluated in making the rankings."

REFERENCES

Amnesty International. 1983. "Mental Health Aspects of Political Imprisonment in Uruguay: An Amnesty International Special Briefing." New York: Amnesty International.

Bravo Lira, Bernardino. 1978. *Régimen de gobierno y partidos políticos en Chile, 1924–1973.* Santiago: Editorial Jurídica de Chile.

Brysk, Alison. 1994. *The Politics of Human Rights in Argentina: Protest, Change, and Democratization.* Stanford, Calif.: Stanford University Press.

Calhoun, Craig. 1991. "The Problem of Identity in Collective Action." Pp. 51–75 in *Macro-Micro Linkages in Sociology,* edited by Joan Huber. Newbury Park, Calif.: Sage.

———. 1993. "New Social Movements of the Early Nineteenth Century. "*Social Science History* 17:385–427.

Camps, Ramón J. 1983. "Los desaparecidos están muertos." *El Bimestre Político y Económico* 7 (January–February): 62–64.

Camus L., Carlos. 1985. "La experiencia de la Iglesia Chilena en la defensa de los derechos humanos." Pp. 51–58 in *Represión política y defensa de los derechos humanos*, edited by Hugo Frühling. Chile: Academia de Humanismo Cristiano.

Centro de Estudios Legales y Sociales. 1984. "Uruguay/Argentina: Coordinación represiva." Buenos Aires.

CEP (Centro de Estudios y Publicaciones). 1974. *Chile: Masacre de un pueblo.* Lima: Centro de Estudios y Publicaciones.

Chilean National Commission on Truth and Reconciliation. 1993. *Report of the Chilean National Commission on Truth and Reconciliation,* vol. 2. Translated by Phillip E. Berryman, with an introduction by Jose Zalaquett. Notre Dame, Ind.: Notre Dame University Press.

Comisión Argentina por los Derechos Humanos. 1977. *Argentina: Proceso al genocidio.* Madrid: Elías Querejeta Ediciones.

Corradi, Juan E., Patricia W. Fagen, and Manuel A. Garretón, eds. 1992. *Fear at the Edge: State Terror and Resistance in Latin America.* Berkeley and Los Angeles: University of California Press.

de Brito, Alexandra B. 1997. *Human Rights and Democratization in Latin America: Uruguay and Chile.* New York: Oxford University Press.

della Porta, Donatella. 1988. "Recruitment Processes in Clandestine Political Organizations: Italian Left-Wing Terrorism." Pp. 155–69 in *International Social Movement Research.* Vol. 1. Greenwich, Conn.: JAI Press.

Diani, Mario. 1996. "Linking Mobilization Frames and Political Opportunities: Insights from Regional Populism in Italy." *American Sociological Review* 61 (6): 1052–69.

Drake, Paul W. 1996. *Labor Movements and Dictatorships: The Southern Cone in Comparative Perspective.* Baltimore: Johns Hopkins University Press.

Duhalde, Eduardo Luis. 1983. *El estado terrorista argentino.* Spain: Talleres Gráficos.

Fireman, Bruce, and William Gamson. 1979. "Utilitarian Logic in the Resource Mobilization Perspective." Pp. 8–44 in *The Dynamics of Social Movements: Resource Mobilization, Social Control, and Tactics,* edited by Mayer N. Zald and John D. McCarthy. Cambridge, Mass.: Winthrop Publishers.

Fitzgibbon, Russell. 1954. *Uruguay: Portrait of a Democracy.* New Brunswick, N.J.: Rutgers University Press.

Franco, Rolando. 1984. *Democracia "a la Uruguaya": Análisis electoral, 1925–1985.* Montevideo: Editorial El Libro Libre.

Frontalini, Daniel, and Maria C. Caiati. 1984. *El mito de la "Guerra Sucia."* Buenos Aires, Argentina: Centro de Estudios Legales y Sociales.

Frühling, Hugo. 1988. "Organismos no gubernamentales de derechos humanos en el paso del autoritarismo a la democracia en Chile." Pp. 137–65 in *Una puerta que se abre,* Taller de Cooperación al Desarrollo. Chile: Imprenta la Union.

Frühling, Hugo, Gloria Alberti, and Felipe Portales. 1989. *Organizaciones de Derechos Humanos de America del sur.* San Jose, Costa Rica: Instituto Interamericano de Derechos Humanos.

Frühling, Hugo, and Patricio Orellana. 1991. "Organizaciones no gubernamentales de derechos humanos bajo regímenes autoritarios y en la transición democrática: El caso chileno desde una perspectiva comparada." Pp. 25–83 in *Derechos Humanos y Democracia,* edited by Hugo Frühling. Chile: Instituto Interamericano de Derechos Humanos.

Garcia, Prudencio. 1995. *El drama de la autonomia militar.* Madrid: Alianza Editorial.

Garretón, Manuel A. 1983. *El proceso politico Chileno.* Santiago: Talleres Gráficos.

Gauding, Anna-Karin. 1991. *Es mejor encender una luz que maldecir la oscuridad: Sobre el trabajo de Diakonia por los derechos humanos en America Latina.* Santiago: Diakonia.

Geddes, Barbara. 1995. "Uses and Limitations of Rational Choice." Pp. 81–108 in *Latin America in Comparative Perspective: New Approaches to Methods and Analysis,* edited by Peter Smith. Boulder, Colo.: Westview Press.

Gould, Roger V. 1995. *Insurgent Identities: Class, Community, and Protest in Paris from 1848 to the Commune.* Chicago: University of Chicago Press.

Gurr, Ted R. 1970. *Why Men Rebel.* Princeton, N.J.: Princeton University Press.

Hirsch, Eric L. 1986. "The Creation of Political Solidarity in Social Movement Organizations." *Sociological Quarterly* 27 (3): 373–87.

Inter-Church Committee on Human Rights in Latin America. 1978. *Violations of Human Rights in Uruguay (1972–1976).* Toronto: Inter-Church Committee on Human Rights in Latin America.

Kaufman, Edy. 1979. *Uruguay in Transition: From Civilian to Military Rule.* New Brunswick, N.J.: Transaction Books.

King, Peter J. 1989. "Comparative Analysis of Human Rights Violations under Military Rule in Argentina, Brazil, Chile, and Uruguay." Pp. 1043–65 in *Statistical Abstract of Latin America,* vol. 27. Edited by James W. Wilkie and Enrique Ochoa. Los Angeles: University of California, UCLA Latin American Center Publications.

Klandermans, Bert. 1984. "Mobilization and Participation: Social-Psychological Expansions of Resource Mobilization Theory." *American Sociological Review* 49 (5): 583–600.

Klandermans, Bert, and Sidney Tarrow 1988. "Mobilization into Social Movements: Synthesizing European and American Approaches." Pp. 1–38 in *International Social Movement Research,* vol. 1. Greenwich, Conn.: JAI Press.

Laitin, David D. 1995. "National Revivals and Violence." *Archives Europeenes de Sociologie* 36:3–43.

Lawyers Committee for International Human Rights. 1985. "The Generals Give Back Uruguay: A Report on Human Rights." New York: Lawyers Committee for International Human Rights.

Lindahl, Goran G. 1964. "Uruguay: Government by Institutions." Pp. 447–61 in *Political Systems of Latin America,* edited by Martin C. Needler. Princeton, N.J.: D. Van Nostrand.

Lipset, Seymour M., and Earl Raab. 1970. *The Politics of Unreason: Right Wing Extremism in America, 1790–1970.* New York: Harper & Row.

Lira, Elizabeth. 1997. E-mail interview with author. February 15.

Lofland, John. 1996. *Social Movement Organizations: Guide to Research on Insurgent Realities.* New York: Aldine de Gruyter.

Loveman, Brian. 1994. "Las ONG Chilenas: Su papel en la transición a la democracia." *Nuevas Políticas Urbanas,* edited by Charles A. Reilly. Arlington, Va.: Fundación Interamericana.

Lowden, Pamela. 1996. *Moral Opposition to Authoritarian Rule in Chile, 1973–90.* New York: Macmillan.

Mainwaring, Scott. 1986. *The Catholic Church and Politics in Brazil, 1916–1985.* Stanford, Calif.: Stanford University Press.

Martín-Baró, Ignacio. 1983. *Acción e ideologia psicología social desde Centroamérica.* San Salvador, El Salvador: Talleres Gráficos UCA.

Marwell, Gerald, and Pamela Oliver. 1984. "Collective Action Theory and Social Movements Research." *Research in Social Movements, Conflict and Change* 7:1–27.

McAdam, Doug. 1986. "Recruitment to High-Risk Activism: The Case of Freedom Summer." *American Journal of Sociology* 92 (1): 64–90.

McAdam, Doug, Sidney Tarrow, and Charles Tilly. 1995. "To Map Contentious Politics." Working Paper no. 222. New School for Social Research, Center for Studies of Social Change.

MelliBovsky, Matilde. 1998. Circle of Love over Death. Lecture given at the Latin American Studies Student Organization Conference on Human Rights in the Americas. April 14, at San Diego State University, San Diego, California.

47

Melucci, Alberto. 1988. "Getting Involved: Identity and Mobilization in Social Movements." Pp. 329–48 in *International Social Movement Research*, vol. 1. Greenwich, Conn.: JAI Press.

Mignone, Emilio F. (1986) 1988. *Witness to the Truth: The Complicity of Church and Dictatorship in Argentina, 1976–1983*, translated by Phillip Berryman. Maryknoll, N.Y.: Orbis Books.

———. 1991. *Derechos humanos y sociedad: El caso Argentino*. Buenos Aires: Centro de Estudios Legales y Sociales; Ediciones del Pensamiento Nacional.

Morris, Aldon. 1984. *The Origins of the Civil Rights Movement: Black Communities Organizing for Change*. New York: Free Press.

Navarro, Marysa. 1989. "The Personal Is Political: Las Madres de la Plaza de Mayo." Pp. 241–58 in *Power and Popular Protest: Latin American Social Movements*, edited by Susan Eckstein. Berkeley and Los Angeles: University of California Press.

Oberschall, Anthony. 1973. *Social Conflict and Social Movements*. Englewood Cliffs, N.J.: Prentice-Hall.

———. 1993. *Social Movements: Ideologies, Interests and Identities*. New Brunswick, N.J.: Transaction.

Oliver, Pamela. 1984. "'If You Don't Do It, Nobody Else Will': Active and Token Contributors to Local Collective Action." *American Sociological Review* 49 (5): 601–10.

Olson, Mancur. 1965. *The Logic of Collective Action: Public Goods and the Theory of Groups*. Cambridge, Mass.: Harvard University Press.

Orellana, Patricio, and Elizabeth Q. Hutchison. 1991. *El movimiento de derechos humanos en Chile, 1973–1990*. Santiago: Centro de Estudios Políticos Latinoamericanos Simón Bolívar.

Osa, Maryjane. 1989. "Resistance, Persistence, and Change: The Transformation of the Catholic Church in Poland." *Eastern European Politics and Societies* 3 (2): 268–99.

Rama, German W. 1987. *La democracia en Uruguay*. Buenos Aires: Grupo Editor Latinoamericano.

Rock, David. 1985. *Argentina, 1516–1987*. Berkeley and Los Angeles: University of California Press.

Servicio Paz y Justicia. 1989. *Uruguay nunca más: Human Rights Violations, 1972–1985*, translated by Elizabeth Hampsten. Philadelphia: Temple University Press.

Sikkink, Kathryn. 1993. "Human Rights, Principled Issue-Networks, and Sovereignty in Latin America." *International Organization* 47 (3): 411–41.

Skaar, Elin. 1994. "Human Rights Violations and the Paradox of Democratic Transition." Master's thesis. University of Bergen, Department of Comparative Politics.

Smith, Brian H. 1982. *The Church and Politics in Chile: Challenges to Modern Catholicism*. Princeton, N.J.: Princeton University Press.

Snow, David, and Robert Benford. 1988. "Ideology, Frame Resonance, and Participant Mobilization." Pp. 197–217 in *International Social Movement Research*. Vol. 1. Greenwich, Conn.: JAI Press.

———. 1992. "Master Frames and Cycles of Protest." Pp. 133–55 in *Frontiers in Social Movement Theory*, edited by Aldon Morris and Carol M. Mueller. New Haven, Conn.: Yale University Press.

Snow, David, E. Burke Rochford, Jr., Steven Worden, and Robert Benford. 1986. "Frame Alignment Processes, Micromobilization, and Movement Participation." *American Sociological Review* 51 (4): 464–81.

Tarrow, Sidney G. 1994. *Power in Movement: Social Movements, Collective Action, and Politics*. Cambridge: Cambridge University Press.

Tilly, Charles. 1978. *From Mobilization to Revolution*. Reading, Mass.: Addison-Wesley.

United Nations. 1987. *1985 Demographic Yearbook*, 37th issue. Department of International Economic and Social Affairs, Statistical Office. New York: United Nations.

Veiga, Raúl. 1985. *Las Organizaciones de derechos humanos*. Buenos Aires: Centro Editor de America Latina.

Vidal, Hernan. 1986. *El Movimiento contra la tortura "Sebastián Acevedo": Derechos humanos y la producción de símbolos nacionales bajo el fascismo Chileno.* Edina, Minn.: Institute for the Study of Ideologies and Literature, Society for the Study of Contemporary Hispanic and Lusophone Revolutionary Literatures.

Weber, Max. (1922) 1968. *Economy and Society*. Berkeley: University of California Press.

Weschler, Lawrence. 1990. *A Miracle, a Universe: Settling Accounts with Torturers.* New York: Pantheon Books.

Wickham-Crowley, Timothy P. 1989. "Winners, Losers, and Also-Rans: Toward a Comparative Sociology of Latin American Guerrilla Movements." Pp. 132–81 in *Power and Popular Protest: Latin American Social Movements*, edited by Susan Eckstein. Berkeley and Los Angeles: University of California Press.

Zald, Mayer N., and John D. McCarthy, eds. 1979. *The Dynamics of Social Movements: Resource Mobilization, Social Control, and Tactics.* Frontiers of Sociology Symposium. Cambridge, Mass.: Winthrop.

 Pergamon

Bull. Latin Am. Res., Vol. 16, No. 1, pp. 107–116, 1997
Copyright © 1997 Society for Latin American Studies
Published by Elsevier Science Ltd. Printed in Great Britain
0261-3050/97 $17.00 + 0.00

S0261-3050(96)00020-4

The Changing Role of NGOs in Rural Chile After Democracy

YIANNA LAMBROU

*International Development Research Centre (IDRC), Ottawa, Ontario,
Canada*

Abstract — The article examines how NGOs in rural Chile operated during the dictatorship and how their role changed after the return of democracy. An NGO (OPDECH) in Southern Chile is used as a case study. During the Pinochet regime, NGOs maintained a critical distance from the government by creating a niche for opposition researchers and activists. They provided a possibility of economic survival for professionals whilst working on alternative proposals to address the socio-economic needs of the poor majority. External funding from international agencies provided much needed resources but created as well a culture of reliance and a clientelistic middle class of professionals. The NGO in Southern Chile became a nucleus of resistance and expertise on regional development by safekeeping democratic tradition and providing a range of solutions to local development problems. After the restoration of democratic government many professionals joined the government. NGOs exchanged their altruism for a more pragmatic, opportunistic and, in some cases, more efficient role as executors of government programmes. The case study in Southern Chile illustrates this trajectory well. After municipal elections a collaborative role with local government was sought by OPDECH that aimed to implement local initiatives as well as advise local and regional governments on environmental and developmental issues. Given the NGOs historical commitment to grassroots development, it remains to be seen what role they can play in supporting local government while forging a new role for themselves in a democratic context. Copyright © 1997 Society for Latin American Studies

Key words — Chile, NGOs, international donor aid, development, local government, environment

This paper is an attempt to show the changing roles of NGOs in Chile and their role in the process of democratisation after the years of dictatorship. I spent 1983–1984 in Region X and XI carrying out fieldwork for a doctorate in Sociology where I examined the role of peasant cooperatives during the dictatorship of Pinochet. Later (1990 and 1995), I did more in depth studies of the situation in Chiloé and particularly an NGO, OPDECH (Oficina Promotora del Desarrollo Chilote — Office for the Promotion of Chilotan Development) which was formed in 1980 during the most difficult time of the dictatorship. OPDECH is used as an example in this paper to illustrate in practice what I am suggesting is happening in this sector after democratisation.

The focus of this paper is part exploration, part explanation and part exposé: (1) to explore what the NGOs were doing five years after restoration of democracy, (2) to explain what has happened to them, and what may or needs to happen and (3) to expose a small case study in the south where I looked at a consortium of environmental NGOs functioning in a new post-dictatorship context.

I have had the opportunity to observe Chile as a graduate student, a university researcher, and as representative of a donor agency. Different roles and views have permitted me to explore various aspects of the topic that has interested me: the rural sector, and the changes that have happened as a consequence of socio-economic and political developments in the last few decades.

Research (Lambrou, 1987) showed that cooperatives from 1973 to 1984 functioned as nuclei of democracy, keeping democratic principles and practices alive. They provided subsistence support for peasants and technical professionals alike. External agencies were very important in sustaining the cooperative movement by providing much needed financial assistance (Bebbington and Thiele, 1992). The continued existence of cooperatives permitted a middle class of professionals to find work and to be sheltered from persecution (Loveman, 1991).

The role of NGOs in the last five years also reflects the mood of Chile and the continuous adjustments to reality and compromises that are being made by everyone after years of extraordinary difficulties (Oxhorn, 1994; Lear and Collins, 1995). NGOs, like most other institutions, played a different role for 17 years that was peculiar to the situation that they found themselves in. They had the classic ideology and ethos of non-governmental organisations, in the sense that they kept their distance from the government and survived on this clear separation of ideology and *modus operandi*. Below I explain how NGOs operated then and how they are learning to operate now. My argument is that their new role and character entails having to leave behind some of the usual altruism associated with NGOs, and become more pragmatic, more effective, more opportunistic and certainly more efficient in terms that they would not have entertained before. Following a discussion of the NGOs' role since 1973, I examine the 5-year period of democratic rule using the example of the institutions that I worked with in Southern Chile (Lambrou, 1990).

NGOs DURING THE PINOCHET DICTATORSHIP

The state apparatus that had been set up during Allende's time, where the government was responsible for much of the assistance and investment in the countryside, was dismantled during Pinochet. Many of the people that had worked in research and for long-term rural development, lost their jobs and just tried to survive physically and economically. They sought alternatives in terms of physical and professional survival. The policies of the military government which neglected and discouraged local development, unintentionally encouraged the growth of a complex network of NGOs working in various projects, from human rights and legal services, to agricultural extension and rural or urban development. These institutions not only solved the problem of how to cope with the social needs of the poor who had seen the elimination of state services, but also provided a possibility of economic survival for a class of professionals who now had nowhere to go. The NGOs became a niche for progressive thinking, for informal anti-government networking and for the creative and analytical search for alternative solutions to the country's problems (Loveman, 1991).

OPDECH, and two other NGOs that now form the consortium (Corporacion para el Desarrollo Regional — Corporation for Regional Development) in the south of Chile, illustrate this shift. Given the distance from Santiago, it has always been easier to meet and to organise, to plan and to offer regionally-based solutions with less threat of interference from a harsh or neglectful government. The NGOs that emerged were formed by professionals who had been thrown out of INDAP (Instituto Nacional de Desarrollo Agropecuario — National Institute for Agricultural Development), or who had been persecuted or relegated to Chiloé. The *relegados* (internal exiles) legacy of Pinochet, where opponents of the regime were sent to extreme ends of the country cannot be easily forgotten or forgiven. It brought chaos and severe dislocation to individuals who had to leave their homes and communities to go to a totally different part of the country to live, often unable to exercise their skills and occupations. OPDECH was formed by a group of *tecnicos agricolas* (agricultural specialists) who had nowhere else to work. Besides the lack of professional opportunities, their political affiliation was often a serious impediment to their procuring jobs or having life opportunities. The original organisers of OPDECH were Communists and Socialists at a time when it was romantic, daring and totally dangerous to admit such affiliation. They were known to each other and they sought to consolidate through their ideology a style of work and a political opposition that would be kept in readiness for the anticipated overthrow of Pinochet. They believed in social equity, justice, regional development and a Chiloé that would be independent and thriving. Their youthfulness and romanticism served them well. Their altruism and their courage helped them to create an NGO that was dedicated to social change, to regional promotion and to a quality of work that would stand on its own and be useful for their future.

Altruism

OPDECH can be seen as a prototype of the altruistic NGO that I am arguing came into existence during this difficult period. There were other variations of course, and I examined several of them both in Southern Chile and in Santiago (Lambrou, 1987). In OPDECH, the degree of political awareness, regional commitment, opposition to the regime and professional capacity of its staff combined to create a powerful focus away from Santiago. In Santiago, many NGOs such as GIA, AGRARIA, SUR and FLACSO, also functioned with this type of general outlook. But they had to be more careful. They had to (appear to) tone down the political aspects of their work, as they were under more strict observation, and they had to give closer account for their activities to a more vigilant government presence.

External agencies

The role of external agencies during this period was crucial for the survival and regeneration of the NGOs and the grassroots movement. Given the existence of a military government which was bypassed and labelled an international pariah, donor agencies were falling over each other to find alternative channels for their development assistance. Their support helped create a large and multifaceted NGO network that offered many services previously unavailable from the government.

The role of the state in fomenting rural development came strongly and continuously under scrutiny by the research NGOs during the dictatorship (Levy, 1995). The state largely surrendered its role as provider of services. The exception was the poverty-alleviation assistance through-job-creation programmes (e.g. PEM — Programa de Empleo Minimo, and POJH — Programa Ocupacinal para Jefes de Hogar) targeted at the extreme poor, particularly after 1982 (Graham 1993). Pinochet's policies provided resources quickly to a great number of poor people, but they were carried out in an authoritarian manner, with no input from the population and with no long term job prospects (Graham, 1993). They left a legacy of stigmatised workers marginalised from formal sector employment and with little possibility of escaping the cycle of poverty. The poor could not participate in a process of development to solve their own problems. International donor agencies on the other hand, took up the task of investing in human capital rather than providing subsidies for basic needs programmes which did not deal with the longer term social development, especially in the countryside.

In Southern Chile the entire cooperative movement, the work in the countryside, and most of the various NGOs all owed their survival to external donors. Actually, a culture of 'projectitis' emerged where most of the rural poor saw their survival and salvation linked to having a project funded by an external foreign agency. OPDECH managed to put together an inspiring and arousing development plan for the region of Chiloé that was difficult to resist by agencies that were seeking to support and maintain a democratic movement in Southern Chile.

Difficulties with donor aid

There was a certain mystique and a glamour to be enjoyed by agencies such as OXFAM and NOVIB who braved the dictatorship and funded the poor and the *campesinos* of Chile. There were vast quantities of funds given to peasant organisations that were often unable to handle the influx of so many dollars. The IAF (Inter-American Foundation) inadvertently came close to destroying a set of cooperatives through the squabbles, corruption and in-fighting that resulted as thousands of dollars were donated to them that they could not possibly use wisely. The scrounging for resources, the experimentation with development alternatives, the pursuit of new organisational models and especially the experience of having to explain and justify their work to the outside world, forged a politically conscious NGO movement in Chile during the 1970s that sought to alleviate rural poverty. There were allowances made by donor agencies for inefficiency, and not much evaluation of results was done as would have been the case later. Accountability was not the foremost concern of agencies at this time. They were galvanised to help Chileans during the dictatorship, and that was the first priority.

OPDECH used its strong position as one of the few viable NGOs in Chiloé to assist other institutions such as peasant cooperatives, women's groups, and artesanal fishermen to put together their own development projects and to provide them with the needed technical assistance as well as to help them seek external funds. During the time of the dictatorship, when there was an equal amount of terror as there was a struggle for daily survival, NGOs learned to persist, to largely put aside their partisan political differences in opposition to the regime, and to work together (most of the time) for fundable results. They learned to read the international scene, to interpret how politics in Canada, the US, or Holland affected development aid, and then to adjust their needs accordingly. As a result, a middle class professional sector emerged that learned to speak the language of international NGOs, that frequented the same global agencies and knew how to present projects that would get funded. A clientelistic relationship was forged that had its ingratiating and corrupt side as well as its honourable and laudable goals.

Relationship with the state

The survival needs that pushed NGOs to become independent promoters of development *vis-à-vis* the state, was indeed an unusual situation for the Chilean left and progressive individuals. The majority had previously endorsed a positive and state-centred thrust to development. Pinochet privatised social services, introduced competition in health and social welfare provision, and made Chileans struggle with market forces in order to get what previously the government had provided.

The dis-involvement of the state apparatus in the welfare of its citizens opened a new chapter in NGO–government relations. NGOs became more innovative, more creative, and certainly more involved than the government bureaucracy in analysing and interpreting local development needs. What began as a survival mechanism became with time, a rationed and permanent response to democratic development and local initiative.

OPDECH was initially composed mostly by Communist professionals who had nowhere to go, but who were fiercely loyal to the locale, and committed to its people. Some of the initial OXFAM funded projects, for example, at first provided a way to be useful, to provide some relief, and to help local people at a time when the military regime was persecuting and exiling anyone daring to work with unions or peasants. With time, the attitude of just thinking of survival and resistance changed. Having survived the difficulties of living under a dictatorship, having learned on the job, and having successfully provided an alternative solution to the development problems, OPDECH and other NGOs in the region acquired a legitimacy and a wealth of experience.

Safekeeping democracy

When democracy was restored, NGOs had not just survived. In many cases they had thrived and also carved a new role for themselves which they had to renegotiate with the newly-elected democratic government. The accomplishments of NGOs during the Pinochet regime could not be swept away. It became clear during the dictatorship that the state was not the only possible promoter of development. Without the squabbling political parties to deflect attention from the task at hand, NGOs could muster more easily the energy, passion and enthusiasm to dream and execute projects of local and regional development. As a result, OPDECH and other southern NGOs gained experience and became a sustained representational and mobilising voice for democratic forces in the region. One of the most important contributions of NGOs and other institutions during this time, was their safekeeping of democratic practices and ideology. They incubated a leadership of local leaders and provided an outlet for democratic training of grassroots groups that had the opportunity to practice and to be involved in a participatory process of development (Lambrou, 1987).

DEMOCRATIC GOVERNMENTS, 1990–1995

The last five years of democratically elected governments (Aylwin, 1990–1994; Frei, March 1994–) saw an evolving pattern of NGO development and the establishment of a new relationship with the state (de la Maza, 1995; Sotomayor, 1995).

Re-insertion into society

After the 1990 election, NGO professionals immediately began to play a prominent role in government. Aylwin confirmed the autonomy of NGOs, their commitment to and participation in development, and the legitimacy of private channels of international cooperation. When he took office, he adopted a programme that focused on reconstructing democracy, dealing with human rights abuses, stimulating economic growth, attacking environmental degradation, and improving the living conditions of the five million poor. The programme was assembled by party leaders, professionals and intellectuals who had opposed the dictatorship. Most of these leaders had been linked to NGOs or academic research centres (Levy, 1995) and had had several years to think out alternative development programmes (Loveman, 1991). But what was also interesting in this period of re-insertion to society was the exit of hundreds of well trained NGO professionals who were invited to leave their NGOs and do the government's work: for example, Humberto Vega from PET (Programa de Economia y Trabajo — Programme of Economy and Work) became Treasurer General, and Alejandro Foxley of CIEPLAN (Corporacion para

Investigacion Economica en America Latina — Corporation of Economic Research for Latin America) became Minister of Finance.

After 1990, the social contract between the state and the different groups in civil society became redefined. Once a democratic government was at the helm, the majority of proposals for development that were produced envisaged a subordinate role for NGOs, whose new role was to implement the state-designed policies. Participation was at the implementation level, *not* at the decentralisation of these programmes and the involvement of NGOs in their design.

This is not the place to list all the agencies that emerged and the implications they had for NGOs, but some should be mentioned. The AGCI (the Agency for International Cooperation), and FOSIS (Fund for Social Solidarity and Investment) were created as key institutions to implement the government's international and socio-economic programme. MIDEPLAN (Ministry of Planning and International Cooperation) was among the first initiatives of the Aylwin government (Loveman, 1991). It was designed to coordinate networks of international cooperation with government agencies and NGOs developed after 1973. FOSIS was to be an instrument for the government's approach to investment in socio-economic development through NGOs and community organisations.

It was a new world, a new situation for NGOs as the above agencies led by capable ministers, assisted by ex-NGO professionals, took over the NGO and donor agency universe. There was immediately competition for access and influence to ministers, competition amongst NGOs and competition with the government agencies, such as FOSIS, for external funding.

During this early period many capable professionals left their NGO niches to return to universities, professions, unions and political parties. Partisan party competition had once again to be considered as it began to penetrate and influence unions, women's groups and local community organisations.

Situation in the south

During this first stage of the democratic regime, the southern NGOs had to begin reinventing a new role for themselves. With fewer funds available to them, with a new democratic state that wanted to do business with them, they sought to defend the space they had gained over several years of work. Not many survived (figures vary and are unreliable). They were decimated because they lost their *raison d'être* (opposition to the dictatorship), or because they could not shift from polemics to governance.

The intrusion of FOSIS in the field of fund generation created problems: NGOs did not exactly know what their role was in this new stage. For most of them, they became clearly executors of the various state programmes in very specific ways. In some cases FOSIS assumed that it could veto and vet projects to donor agencies. For example, the initial euphoria of a democratic government was replaced with an understanding of its bureaucratic nature, the demands of government jobs, and the lack of creativity and freedom that the NGO world had provided. As a result, many NGO professionals after a short time in government jobs, sought to return to NGOs.

However, the dilemma for OPDECH and the other NGOs remained: how to participate in the socio-economic and democratic process without succumbing entirely to the dictates of the neo-liberal state? How to maintain autonomy while taking advantage of the new opportunities?

Consolidation and maturity, 1993–1995

This stage, marked by 'consolidation and maturity' begins with the end of the Aylwin government in 1994, and continues under Frei as NGOs evolve under democratic rule (Sotomayor, 1995). It was now clear that there were openings for working with the government, but they were to be selected and evaluated. Many NGOs disappeared during this second stage; information about their numbers is confusing. They were unable to respond to the changed circumstances that involved a clearer definition of what role they could play, what speciality functions they could offer, and how to make their internal operations more efficient administratively. The spirit of opposition and solidarity for one overriding cause was removed. The political passion of belonging to a Socialist or Communist party during Pinochet was of little use now. It was actually a liability. A new sense of mission had to be found.

The NGOs in Southern Chile were composed of regional people who had thrived as a group in opposing Pinochet. They now looked for other jobs, joined the government, or sought to consolidate their NGOs. OPDECH and others had to redefine how to work with the social groups they had previously 'assisted'. It was not a question anymore of 'helping' the rural cooperatives, the fishermen, and the women's groups to survive, but more of working with them to become autonomous and for themselves to participate in the democratic order. These organisations could now directly communicate with their elected representatives. They did not need the NGOs to provide them with what was needed. From being teachers, tutors and protectors, NGOs now had to assume a service role. They began to take part in the technology transfer programmes and to execute locally state-financed technical training courses, or to function as consulting agencies. It became necessary to readjust their character in order to survive. Even though their role became diminished and subordinate to the state, there were still possibilities for providing useful services and assisting in drafting local development plans. The fierce competition for survival amongst NGOs prevented collaboration on local issues: some went alone, others sought niches for their programmes through direct external aid. Efforts were made to convince the government that the already existing framework could carry out its new programmes rather than duplicating the bureaucracy once again in the countryside by creating new government structures.

Municipal government

Historically, local government has acted largely as an agent of the central government in Chile (Nickson, 1995). Under Pinochet, local government was radically reformed to abolish local democracy by appointing government heads and replacing elected councils by CODECOs (Consejos de Desarrollo Comunal — Community Development Councils). The local administration was closely linked to the central government in a vertical hierarchical structure. Paradoxically however, a parallel process of de-concentrating service delivery also took place (Nickson, 1995). Local government became responsible for social expenditure (primary health care, basic education and social welfare). Municipalities were given new sources of local revenue and even a mechanism for redistribution from richer to poor municipalities. The Aylwin government accepted many of the reforms but also democratised the military regime's local administration in 1991, by granting legal autonomy to local government for the first time in Chilean history. First democratic elections of municipal officers were held in 1992, along with the introduction of a new structure of regional government able to coordinate regional activities and to manage a regional investment fund (Nickson, 1995).

The relationship with the municipal governments provides interesting insights in the case of Southern Chile. During the military regime, municipalities were devoid of any democratic facade. Mayors and councillors were appointed since local administration formed part of the national government apparatus. OPDECH avoided the local government, worked around it, and rarely sought to collaborate. After democracy was restored and municipal officers were elected, there was caution on both sides. Some NGOs and mayors began to seek the collaboration of NGOs in order to use the NGOs' skills and resources to make local programmes more effective. Initially the mutual doubts and the fragile nature of the cooperation led to some adjustments as a workable fit was sought between some local municipal activities and the type of work that local NGOs had been doing.

In 1995, I was able to investigate this newly forged partnership between municipal governments and NGOs in Southern Chile. After the last election, mayors were now elected officials. There was an emphasis to decentralise local programmes and pass on the responsibility of carrying them out to local NGOs. OPDECH, which invited two other NGOs to form a regional development corporation, very tentatively began exploring the nature of the new mayors, and the type of relationship that could be forged in this new democratic climate. Given the experience of this NGO and the king of track record it had in the region, it not only was able to interest the mayors but also to secure international funding to carry out some of its development work in association with the municipalities.

Continued aid from donors

International donors have continued to be interested in supporting NGOs directly. However, there is competition for the limited resources in a new more restricted donor universe and FOSIS has competed directly for the right to have resources shifted under its control. Efforts were made by OPDECH and others to collaborate on common projects but the 'top–down' directive approach of the government alienated some of the NGOs. The restricted international resources available to Chile that has become defined as a 'middle-income-country' if not a new tiger in South America (Hojman, 1995), has also detracted donors who are now shifting some resources to Eastern Europe. The southern NGO consortium was able to secure funding mainly on the basis of their past accomplishments and the promise of more participatory and community-oriented research that directly feeds to policy making at the regional level.

ENVIRONMENTAL CONCERNS

As the new democratic governments became committed to dealing with environmental degradation, a new mandate for environmental NGO action also emerged, partly in response to the state interest, and partly to the environmental shift in interest on the part of the international donors. Environment became a hot topic in the 1990s in Chile's democratic transition. Sustainable development became the cry of the 1990s. How to actually do it meant getting both state and private sector mutually committed to complimentary plans that were holistic.

The Chilean state was trying to define its role with regards to the environment. In 1995, it passed an Environmental Law that still lacked teeth because it was not heeded by large resource exporting companies, and because it was not grounded in community action and involvement. It is at this level that local NGOs could assist the government. They could play an informative, educational and policy-making role by providing their services and their experience of many years. Environmental education is unheard of, and there is a great dearth of environmental knowledge at the local level. Combined with the powerlessness of small communities to actually influence local environmental policy, environmental degradation is rampant and unheeded. In 1995, the municipalities were beginning to collaborate with OPDECH and other NGOs to design environmentally sustainable development plans that responded to the needs of the communities but did not sacrifice the local environment. It was only a small start and much ground had to be covered. There were also links being made (albeit with some caution) with other environmental NGOs in Santiago that could come to the south to help with such development plans. There were discussions about how to ensure community economic survival that did not destroy available forest and water resources. Community involvement was being sought.

The environmental agenda for the NGOs in the south is a relatively new addition to their development plans. They have done some research, as for example, on the effects of the salmon industries on lakes, on pollution downstream from the coastal industries, and on the loss of the native forests to wood chips bound for exports, etc. They were ahead of their time in the 1980s when they were pressing for controls on the foreign logging companies deforesting the interior of Region XI. Government agencies, particularly at the municipal level, are willing to use the NGO experience for informing their environmental policies. In addition, the preliminary environmental work these NGOs have done with communities in the past has already established a credibility that the government is anxious to take advantage of. The emphasis on participatory methods for research and action has enhanced their image. Because they are supposedly more flexible, honest, and generally efficient administratively they are seen as the most reliable agents for implementing local environmental development projects. In order to consolidate this new role, political party partisanship was largely set aside. Since 1990, OPDECH members have quietened or eliminated their Socialist/Communist ties, and have officially withdrawn from the parties. They have chosen to forsake isolationism due to ideology and instead throw themselves once more into the fray of trying to work for the development of the south. Their previous romantic devotion to altruistic causes has given way to a middle-aged pragmatism that seeks efficiency and results in areas such as the environment which needs urgent and new solutions. They are now becoming lobbyists, and in some cases opportunists. Some NGOs (particularly smaller ones in Santiago), have forsaken their anarchist revolutionary ideas, and are now simply executing projects regardless of the ideological slant. As yet the NGOs in the south have not become engaged extensively in this type of opportunism partly because they have been temporarily rescued by the continuous injection of foreign funds.

CONCLUSION

Chilean NGOs have undergone dramatic changes as social actors in the last twenty-five years. From intermediary, non-profit organisations working for economic and social development, in 1973, they abruptly changed to being defenders of democracy and agents of local development in the cities and in the countryside. They provided a safe haven for professionals committed to working for alternative, concrete, social change. They learned to operate without the state, to oppose its repressive actions vociferously, and finally to collaborate with it in a democratic climate. They learned to tap international goodwill and resources for local growth. Yet they also learned the perils of excessive funding and corruption. Their biggest contribution has been their commitment to the grassroots communities, the *campesinos*, the poor, and their capacity to interpret their needs to more distant agencies and governments. NGOs have contributed to shaping local and national policy. In many cases, they have greatly influenced their international donors' understanding of local needs by urging them to lobby international bodies and governments on their behalf. Thus, in many ways they have helped to shape the international development aid policies of developed countries.

Given the existing competitive and state-directed approach to development, what can be said about the role of NGOs in Chile? Are they still the advocates of the 'poor'? Can they be the voice of the poor when the government is at least officially responsible for them? (Poverty, however, remains ever-present in spite of the government's glowing statistics for foreign consumption). Can NGOs continue to maintain that they fight for the human, economic and cultural rights of poor women, peasants and cooperatives, when the state has committed itself to a more direct relationship with these groups? And what about the increasing autonomy of these groups? On the basis of their past work and commitment can NGOs now claim that they are more capable than government agencies to translate the demands of the grassroots into policy? Are they more effective at doing so? Why? Will they be able to reinvent themselves in a new role that combines their past altruism with the present day need for lobbying and technical excellence?

I am cautiously optimistic from my research of the NGOs in the south, that in spite of the opportunism and shift to more pragmatic approaches of development, NGOs have a role to play as partners with local governments. Their experience is an asset, as is their commitment to the grassroots, their adaptability to changing conditions and their willingness to change so as to better serve. It remains to be seen how this will actually evolve.

REFERENCES

Bebbington, A. and Thiele, G. (1992) *NGOs and the State in Latin America: Rethinking Roles in Sustainable Agricultural Development*. Overseas Development Institute, London.
Graham, C. (1993) From emergency employment to social investment: changing approaches to poverty alleviation in Chile. In *The Legacy of Dictatorship, Political, Economic and Social Change in Pinochet's Chile*, pp. 27–74. University of Liverpool, Monograph Series No. 17.
Hojman, D. E. (1995) Chile under Frei (again), the first Latin American tiger or just another cat? *Bulletin of Latin American Research* 14, 127–142.
Lambrou, Y. (1987) Peasant cooperatives in an authoritarian context: Chile 1973–1984. Ph. D. thesis, York University, Toronto, Canada.
Lambrou, Y. (1990) Peasants and social participation: the case of the Chonchi cooperative, Chile, 1973–1985. *Canadian Journal of Latin American and Caribbean Studies* 15, 30.
Lear, J. and Collins, J. (1995) Working in Chile's free market. *Latin American Perspectives* 84, 22 (1), 10–29.
Levy, D. C. (1995) Latin America's think tanks: the roots of non-profit privatization. *Studies in Comparative International Development* 30 (Summer), 3–25.
Loveman, B. (1991) NGOs and the transition to democracy in Chile. *Grassroots Development* 15(2), 8–49.
de la Maza, G. (1995) Las ONGs Chilenas y la nueva cooperacion. *Instituciones, Desarrollo, Cooperacion* 2 (Febrero–Marzo) 6.
Nickson, R. A. (1995) *Local Government in Latin America*. Lynne Reinner, London.
Oxhorn, P. (1994) Where did all the protesters go? Popular mobilization and the transition to democracy in Chile. *Latin American Perspectives* 82 (Summer), 49–68.
Sotomayor, O. (1995) Chile la experiencia del GIA entre 1990 y 1994. *Instituciones, Desarrollo, Cooperacion* 2 (Febrero–Marzo), 5.

Social Equity and Environmental Politics in Brazil

Lessons from the Rubber Tappers of Acre

Margaret E. Keck

For two decades, representatives of third world countries have argued in international fora that poverty pollutes more noxiously than does development.[1] From the IUCN's World Conservation Strategy in 1980 to the Brundtland Commission report and the 1992 UN Conference on Environment and Development, environmentalist manifestoes increasingly incorporated developmental concerns.[2] The notion of "sustainable development" linked environmental conservation with economic growth and later increasingly with social equity.[3] In practice, the connections have been difficult to sustain. As long as poor people were seen mainly as causes, however inadvertent, of environmental degradation, solutions were unlikely to be of their own making. At the end of the 1980s, however, in several well-publicized cases, including the one discussed here, advocates began to portray poor people as protagonists, even leaders, in seeking solutions. The story of how and why this inversion occurred is a fascinating example of the social construction of an issue and shows the relationship between strategic acts of image making, alliance building, and the seizing of institutional opportunities.

The political configuration of environmental and social conflicts and those attempting to address them vary considerably among and within countries. Connections are not always self-evident, nor are they self-activating. They are at least in part constituted by the social actors involved. When environmentalists began to call for growth with equity, they moved onto terrain already occupied by labor and social movement activists who were not sure what to make of them. The reinterpretation of long-standing struggles for social justice through an environmental lens has had profound implications for the resources and strategies available to their protagonists. Similarly, attempts to meld social and environmental agendas have been a major challenge for environmentalists. Although it is not unusual for social movements to adapt to new situations, blending old struggles with new and developing new strategies for approaching them, the approximation discussed here is unusual for two reasons. First, it involves sets of actors who normally espouse different visions of such fundamental questions as the relationship between humans and nature and the primacy of material and nonmaterial struggles. Second, it has involved a great deal of self-conscious negotiation, not only of alliances and strategies, but also of these fundamental conceptions.

Activists trying to build these relationships frequently rely on stories about struggles where environmental and equity considerations are joined. These stories help to build a frame in which apparently contradictory meanings and demands dissolve and diverse struggles become one. This process of frame "alignment" (in the sense that David Snow and his colleagues use the term) addresses not only participants and potential participants, but also broader publics who can be expected to respond to one or another element in the stories.

409

Snow et al. define frame alignment as "the linkage of individual and SMO interpretive orientations, such that some set of individual interests, values and beliefs and SMO activities, goals, and ideology are congruent and complimentary."[4] New actors and supporters become involved, sometimes new adversaries are identified, and new political opportunities become manifest. The stories thus become powerful metaphors through which activists can hope to influence policy. Deborah Stone has attributed to what she calls causal stories both an empirical role (they purport to demonstrate the mechanism by which one set of people brings about harms to another set") and a normative role ("they blame one set of people for causing the suffering of others"). "On both levels, causal stories move situations intellectually from the realm of fate to the realm of human agency."[5]

Of the metaphors intended to show the unity of environmental and equity struggles, the story of the rubber tappers in the western Amazonian state of Acre, Brazil, has been one of the most frequently invoked, especially in the United States. Other good examples are the stories of the Chipko Andolan in Uttar Pradesh, India, the Penan people in Sarawak, Malaysia, and more recently the movement to halt dam construction on India's Narmada river. In the retelling, as historical events are transformed into allegorical narrative, the meanings attached to these events come as much from the contexts in which they are invoked as from the contexts in which they took place. Yet, insofar as these stories are told not merely as allegory but also as models to be replicated, failure to keep the political context of historical events in view can frustrate those who would imitate them.[6]

In this essay I want to examine the political emergence of the Acre rubber tappers' movement as both history and myth, the relationship between the two, and the significance of both. In the late 1980s the Acre rubber tappers' movement and its leader Francisco (Chico) Mendes won international acclaim for their struggle to preserve traditional livelihoods against the encroachment of the ranchers who threatened to turn tropical forest into pasture. The movement's initial identity and goals were not explicitly environmentalist, and it had much closer relations with the Brazilian labor movement than it did with the self-described environmental organizations that had proliferated over the previous decade. That Chico Mendes' death made the front page of the *New York Times* astonished Brazilians, for whom he was merely another of the thousand-odd peasants and smallholders murdered because of land disputes over the previous decade.[7] Books and television documentaries made the rubber tappers' struggle into a metaphor for the struggle to save the Brazilian rain forest.[8]

Poor people's movements in the third world rarely achieve such visibility, and when they do rarely have the kind of lasting resonance that this one had. The resonance of this case was due to progressively broader framings of the conflict. Beginning as a local struggle by a traditional extractivist population over land use rights, it became part of a broader movement for social justice and finally part of a global environmental struggle. Each of these frames made sense of the story for a different audience. The expansion of the story's meaning had institutional and cognitive implications: it brought the rubber tappers access to new allies and new institutional arenas in which to wage their fight.[9]

A part of the interpretation offered here involves the history of the Acre rubber tappers' movement, the context in which it arose, and its strategic interaction with national and foreign nongovernmental organizations that targeted multilateral development bank policies in the Amazon. Both resource mobilization and political process approaches to the study of

410

social movements help to provide an account of the growth of the movement and its relative success in meeting some of its immediate goals. The first approach highlights organizational assets (members, communication networks, leadership, access, information, funds), while the second stresses historically specific conjunctural opportunities.[10]

But this kind of analysis does not fully penetrate the resonance of the rubber tappers' case. Organizational and political strategies were inseparable from the deliberate broadening of the way the struggle was portrayed; conflicts in this domain were quite sharp and always present just beneath the surface. International attention to the rubber tappers' case produced sometimes bitter controversy among Brazilian and foreign activists over the meaning of the rubber tappers' fight and over who had "rights" to appropriate it. Yet within a broader frame, to discuss whether Chico Mendes was primarily a trade union organizer, a political leader, or an environmentalist misses the point; clearly he was all of these at once. The story was powerful because it created an identity, and not merely a linkage, between a particular, localized struggle for social justice and global environmental goals. The social construction of this identity involved those who told the story and those who listened, all of whom had reasons, though not necessarily the same ones, to want it to be.[11]

If the controversy over the appropriation of the story involved a confrontation between "old" and "new" social movements, reframing the story evoked a third possibility, where elements of the old are reinterpreted in a new frame that joined environmental and other social movements and issues. This reframing was less difficult than it might otherwise have been because it followed upon a period during the last phase of the military regime when social movements with an unusually wide range of goals shared a common "oppositional" identity. The Brazilian environmental movement grew significantly during the transition from military to democratic rule in the late 1970s and 1980s. Such "new social movement" traits as participatory values and unconventional styles were widely shared during this period.[12] Even movements addressing material concerns were trying to break down vertical corporatist hierarchies. The "new unionism" in the labor movement and the Workers' Party with its stress on grass-roots participation were among the most visible.[13]

Democratization seemed to offer social movements an opportunity to affect state policy in positive ways. Brazilian environmentalists locate themselves along a left-right spectrum to an unusual degree, and an important segment of the movement hoped to bring environmental concerns into a national reform agenda. Although "ecosocialists" wanted to link social and environmental issues, few had a clear idea of how to accomplish this goal, and labor and other social movement activists were more concerned about growth and income redistribution than about the environmental costs of the Brazilian development model.[14] The rubber tappers' story provided a new language in which to renegotiate and redefine the relationship and incentives for both sides to do so. The environment became a lens through which long-standing social conflicts took on a new meaning. What had been isolated local problems gained a universal dimension.

History of Rubber Tapper Organization

The rubber tappers of Acre were initially brought to the western Amazon from the northeast by rubber barons anxious to profit from the rubber boom at the end of the nineteenth century.

411

They have a long history of fighting for survival, first against pervasive debt peonage, and later to eke out a living after the collapse of the rubber economy. Over time, they developed a diversified strategy for economic survival that mixed subsistence farming and sale of rubber and Brazil nuts. In the 1970s, a land boom fueled by government incentives and road building attracted investors from the south, desirous of obtaining large stretches of land for either cattle ranching or speculation. A process of concentration of landholdings ensued, with conflicts over dubious and often overlapping land titles. The rights of rubber tappers and other small farmers to the land they occupied came from long-standing possession rather than formal property titles; for the ranchers, these groups stood in the way of forest clearing and the consolidation of holdings. Around 1973 ranchers in Acre began to resort to violence to clear them off the land.

In 1974 rubber tappers began to organize to defend their livelihoods and their tenure on the land. Helped to organize by the Catholic church and by the arrival in 1975 of a delegate from the National Confederation of Agricultural Workers, CONTAG, the rubber tappers started in 1976 to use their signature tactic, the *empate*, or standoff,[15] in which they collectively expelled the work teams sent by the ranchers to clear forested areas. Although these expulsions did not involve violence against persons, they were considerable shows of force. Large groups of rubber tapper families surrounded teams of workers using chain saws to cut forested areas either where they were cutting or in their headquarters; they set fire to the headquarters and persuaded the work teams to leave the area.

The domestic political context in which rubber tappers organized contained favorable and unfavorable elements. The military government in power since 1964 began to liberalize the regime in 1974. The political opportunity structure was significantly more open than it had been just a few years earlier, and the rubber tappers could develop alliances with other social movement organizations springing up in Brazilian civil society during the 1970s. Over the same period, however, ranchers and other large rural landowners also became more organized. Fearing (correctly) that the transition to democracy would create greater pressure for agrarian reform, landowners in the 1980s increasingly resorted to violence to eliminate rural organizers they saw as threats to their interests.

The political liberalization that began in Brazil in 1974 sparked myriad forms of grass-roots organizing, many under the umbrella of the Catholic church. Catholic base communities multiplied during the second half of the 1970s. In 1975 the National Conference of Brazilian Bishops, CNBB, created the Pastoral Land Commission, CPT, whose first coordinator was the Acrean bishop Dom Moacir Grechi. A proponent of liberation theology, Dom Moacir supported early attempts to organize rubber tappers and small farmers in the state. The CPT played a major role in making land conflicts more visible, at considerable risk to its members. According to Dom Moacir:

> Until 1975 the land problem was not discussed in newspapers, on television, or in the media in general. After that we showed people in and out of the Church and also in government that we existed. So [the government] did all it could to demoralize us, even imprisoning priests who were linked to the CPT. . . . They saw that where unions didn't exist, the CPT got them started. Where serious injustices occurred, it denounced them to the newspapers. I mean, they considered it dangerous because it raised awareness among workers, leading to the formation of unions and workers' organization, while simultaneously exposing a whole world of crime, exploitation, land theft, where often high level authorities were involved.[16]

412

At the same time, the National Confederation of Agricultural Workers, CONTAG, grew rapidly, as a progressive leadership elected in 1968 used a new government policy to have rural welfare benefits (FUNRURAL) administered through unions to expand the base of rural organizing.[17] João Maia, a CONTAG organizer, arrived in Acre in 1975 and began to give the institutional support of the national rural labor movement to the struggles begun by rubber tappers and small farmers. CONTAG trained union organizers and brought a series of legal suits demanding just recompense for those being expelled from their land, many of which it won. The new landowners were not prepared to take this lying down. In João Maia's words:

> The ranchers who came to Acre had already opened ranches in São Paulo, Mato Grosso, Goiás and Rondônia, moving north, and they had never met with difficulties. Then they got to the end of the line and they came up against an organized union. So that's where the ranchers really began to react. Politically, they went to Brasília, to the National Security Council. We went too, via CONTAG. We explained the situation on the land and in the forest, and made an argument about rights of possession. This is a military area, and it was important to go about this carefully. We're an institutional organ, so we have to use institutional channels. Eventually, the ranchers began to feel they were up against a brick wall with the union, and realized that our lawyer could beat them in court. The workers were also getting organized and the practice of embargoing [physically preventing] deforestation was spreading, and we were starting to convince public opinion that intensive deforestation is a problem here in the Amazon and is going to be a serious problem for the future. So apparently they decided that the trick was to do something about the leadership, and in 1980 they killed the president of the Brasiléia union, the most combative one. It was to be a kind of warning so that people would be afraid and would stop the embargoes.[18]

The assassination of Wilson Pinheiros, president of the rural workers' union of Brasiléia, took place in the context of intensive political organization at the national level. The 1979 party reform eliminated the existing political parties; it both called for and made it possible to create new ones. The Workers' Party, PT, was organized in Acre based on precisely the same grass-roots initiatives that had helped to reinforce the rubber tappers' struggles at the end of the 1970s, drawing its base from church and union movements.[19] João Maia and many rubber tapper leaders were early proponents of the PT in Acre. At a rally to protest the assassination of Pinheiros, PT leaders Luís Inácio da Silva (known as Lula) and Jacó Bittar shared a platform with CONTAG president José Francisco da Silva, João Maia, and Chico Mendes, helping to give the incident national visibility. The day after the rally, a group of workers met the ranch foreman who was generally believed to have commissioned the assassination and killed him. Subsequently, the government used this act as a pretext to indict the speakers at the rally under the National Security Law for having incited the workers to violence. According to João Maia:

> The government wanted an excuse to curtail CONTAG's and the PT's activities nationally and in Acre, and to find a way to get at the Church people. This murder after a public rally provided a way of getting at all of them in one fell swoop. CONTAG and the Church in the rural area, and the PT too since our union supported the PT. It was really just a pretext, because this was the fourth time a foreman had been killed here in Acre. . . . But because it was a politicized moment and the government really had an interest in repressing the PT that was growing fast and also

413

repressing CONTAG, they took advantage of it. Indictment under the National Security Law is a political charge, so they took advantage of a pretext.[20]

These charges were finally dropped in 1983. Although the PT performed disappointingly in Acre in the 1982 elections, it established an important foothold in Acre from the beginning and helped bring the struggles of the Acre rubber tappers to national attention. The party's national research and cultural institute is named after Wilson Pinheiros.

Thus, the rubber tappers' struggle was heating up at precisely the moment when the climate for linkage with other forms of grass-roots organization was especially propitious. Many Brazilians saw this kind of organization as part of a wider struggle for democracy. Democratization was an uneven process. The military eased the strictures on political and social organization in fits and starts, and political opening was accompanied by frequent repressive measures intended to keep it within bounds. In particular, the military did not want political liberalization to bring social upheaval.

Even so, groups like the rubber tappers had a better chance of finding domestic allies than they would have had the Acre land boom begun ten years earlier. But although these allies were sufficient to reinforce the rubber tappers' struggle, they were insufficient to win it. CONTAG could help to negotiate between tappers and ranchers and could win for them in the courts recompense for livelihoods lost, but it could guarantee neither long-term tenure on the land nor a livelihood should tenure be won. The PT could help provide the tappers with a political voice, but it was still too weak electorally to give them access to the corridors of power. While the church could shelter organizing initiatives, its capacity to denounce injustice was far stronger than its ability to correct it. As Brazil's democratization progressed, violence against rural organizers increased, especially in the north and northeast, and civilian authorities proved unable or unwilling to control it.

In the early 1980s, the rubber tappers' movement began to seek alternatives that could insure their long-term survival. Soon after the 1982 elections, Chico Mendes said that he thought it was time to change course.

> Now I have to change the way I work. Before, I fought to defend land, even in the face of threats from hired gunmen. Now it's clear that wasn't enough, because we didn't take the time to establish priorities for what came next. That's what I'm thinking about now. The only solution I can see is to try a new kind of struggle within the union, for a popular education campaign in the countryside, and for medical care. We also need to open trails [*estradas*] for those who won the land through that union struggle, and to fight alongside these people for a way to transport their product. We need to try to organize an autonomous cooperative. These are the things I think we need to fight for. It's the only way to recover the space we've lost.[21]

The process had already begun. In 1980–81 Mendes with Paraná anthropologist Mary Allegretti and others designed *Projeto Seringueiro* (Rubber Tappers' Project) to include a cooperative, a literacy project organized on Paulo Freire's principles around the rubber tappers' experience, and training for health monitors. It was to be run by the Xapuri rural workers' union, to whose presidency Chico was elected in 1981. The project received funding from Oxfam, whose regional representative Tony Gross, like Allegretti, had initially come to Acre to work on a dissertation on the rubber tappers. It also won support

414

from the Brazilian organizations CEDI (Ecumenical Center for Documentation and Information) and CEDOP (Center for Documentation and Research of Amazonia).

The International Context

This phase of rubber tapper organization in Acre coincided with another process taking place in Washington, D.C., and the coming together of the two transformed both in fundamental ways. In 1983 a network of environmental activists, seeking a strategy to affect global environmental issues, began to map out a campaign around the environmental impact of multilateral bank loans.[22] The core group included Barbara Bramble of the National Wildlife Federation, Bruce Rich, then at the Natural Resources Defense Council and from 1985 at the Environmental Defense Fund, and Brent Blackwelder at the Environmental Policy Institute. They were joined in 1984 by Stephen Schwartzman, an anthropologist just back from dissertation fieldwork among the Krenakore Indians in Brazil, eventually also at the Environmental Defense Fund.

Schwartzman's Brazilian experience, coupled with the development of excellent sources of information in the field, made the World Bank's Polonoroeste project in Rondônia, next door to Acre, an ideal target. Intended to rationalize the chaotic and extremely rapid colonization process in Rondônia, the project seemed to have the opposite effect. The environmentalists convinced powerful congressional committee heads to hold hearings on the environmental impact of multilateral bank lending. Members of Congress then asked the treasury department to do its own review and instruct the U.S. executive director at the bank to pay more attention to the environmental impact of loans. In April 1985 the World Bank suspended for several months its share of Polonoroeste funding, on the grounds that the Brazilian government had violated major loan conditions concerning protection of wildlife and indigenous tribes. Disbursements resumed only after the government answered these objections, including the declaration of a 1.8 million hectare forest and indigenous reserve. In 1985 environmentalists began to monitor a proposed Inter-American Development Bank loan for paving the continuation of the BR-364 from Porto Velho, Rondônia, to Rio Branco in Acre. The Rio Branco-Porto Velho Road Improvement project was approved in March 1985.[23]

In this context, foreign environmentalists and representatives of the rubber tappers' movement in Acre finally met and established a relationship that filled important needs and provided important political resources for each of them. The rubber tappers had waged a moderately successful defensive struggle and had begun to deepen their organization with the formation of cooperatives and other self-help projects.[24] But they lacked the ability permanently to confront the powerful national and international forces likely to decide the fate of their region. The environmentalists, in turn, were making creative use of institutional political channels to push for more stringent conditions on big project loans regarding protection of the environment and indigenous rights. But they still lacked a credible response to those who argued that these considerations paled before Brazil's need for development projects capable of improving the lot of its desperately poor population.

Bridging these two groups was a diffuse international network composed primarily of anthropologists and representatives of development NGOs, who engaged in advocacy on

415

behalf of the populations with which they came into contact. Seeking international support for the rubber tappers, anthropologist Mary Allegretti and Tony Gross of Oxfam met with Schwartzman and other Washington environmentalists in May 1985, and the potential benefits of an alliance became apparent.[25]

Allegretti and Gross returned to Brazil and attempted to convince Chico Mendes and the rubber tappers to frame their demands for justice within an appeal to save the rain forest. Delegates to the first national meeting of rubber tappers, held in Brasília in October, discussed the PMACI loan and insisted that project planners should incorporate the experiences and needs of local people. This meeting also established the National Council of Rubber Tappers and began to formulate a proposal for extractive reserves in the Amazon. These reserves, to be held in the public domain, would guarantee rubber tappers the use of the land. The proposal also included measures to make rubber production economically viable, diversify economic survival strategies, and provide basic social infrastructure for those living on the reserves. It combined in a creative way the rubber tappers' struggle for a way of life with a recognition of the role that the preservation of such forms of livelihood could play in the survival of the forest.[26]

Stephan Schwartzman, who attended the meeting, took the proposal back to Washington with him and, as it evolved, worked to make it an integral part of the multilateral bank campaign. Simultaneously, the rubber tappers took it to the Brazilian special secretary of the environment, Paulo Nogueira Neto, reportedly meeting with a sympathetic response,[27] and developed closer relations with Brazilian environmentalists. In March 1987 the Environmental Defense Fund and the National Wildlife Federation brought Chico Mendes to Washington to speak with members of Congress and with World Bank and IDB staff and to go with Schwartzman to the annual meeting of the IDB in Miami. In the wake of this visit both the World Bank and the IDB formally endorsed the extractive reserves proposal.[28] In July 1987 the ministry of agrarian reform and development created a legal instrument for the establishment of such reserves.[29] The same month, Chico Mendes received the UN Environment Program's Global 500 award, presented to grass-roots activists, environmental organizations, and leading public figures for their contribution to environmental protection. The rubber tappers' movement, barely known by mass public opinion in Brazil, had already attracted a remarkable amount of international attention.

International attention was not enough. Although his growing renown may have helped to postpone his assassination, ranchers on the Acre frontier clearly understood who was powerful and who was not, and Chico Mendes was in the way. Justice, as envisioned in the faraway corridors of Washington or even Brasília, was an abstraction. The habitual passivity of authorities when faced with the assassination of rural organizers in Brazil (if not their collusion with ranchers) meant that Chico Mendes' killers had strong reasons to expect impunity when they shot him in his home on December 22, 1988. Ironically, Mendes did not live to see the first extractive reserves established by presidential decree as the last president to be elected indirectly by the military's rules, José Sarney, left office in early 1990.[30]

The international outcry over the murder of Chico Mendes came as a surprise to Brazilian authorities and to most Brazilians. Although he was well-known in rural labor and PT circles and in environmental organizations concerned with the Amazon, he was not known to the public at large.[31] In spite of the remarkable synergy created between the rubber tappers' movement and foreign environmentalists in the late 1980s, the stages on which they fought

416

their battles were relatively far from public view either in Brazil or abroad. The rubber tappers' struggles received domestic attention in Brazil through church, union, and party organizations, but their struggle was only one among many. The 1980s was a politically tumultuous decade in Brazil. New parties were created; five different sets of elections were held; a new constitution was written; urban and rural land occupations abounded; new labor organizations were formed, and new constituencies of workers became organized; and the military relinquished the presidency. The decade was also economically disastrous, with runaway inflation, the close succession of economic plans promising quick fixes, and the decline of per capita income. By the end of the decade income distribution was even more unequal than at the height of military rule.[32] Thus, for most Brazilians worried about more immediate problems, the fate of the forest and those who lived in it seemed very far away.

The scale of the international response to Mendes' death was also affected by contextual elements. In the summer of 1988 an unusually persistent heat wave in the northeastern United States coincided with the publication of satellite data about the extent of deforestation in the Brazilian Amazon. Brazil became the emblematic case for discussion of third world environmental problems. The assassination of Mendes appeared to confirm a spreading sense of Brazil's environmental "irresponsibility."[33] Spurred by increasingly public debates over climate change, the Amazon, hitherto of concern primarily to an obscure network of anthropologists, scientists, and environmentalists, became a popular cause, giving rise to countless books and television specials. U.S. and other foreign politicians sought photo ops in visits to the beleaguered rain forest. In a context that had appeared singularly lacking in heros, Chico Mendes became an ecological martyr.

Resonance

Although the alliance between rubber tappers and international environmentalists explains how they gained access to an international stage, it does not fully explain the symbolic reverberations of the case. This side of the story is captured much better if we see it as a vehicle for an ongoing attempt to meld together ethically and materially based arguments about social justice and environmental destruction. It announced the possibility of an environmentalism that was not an amenity but rather was part and parcel of a struggle around basic rights to subsistence. It inverted cause and solution: no longer was it necessarily the poor who (however unwittingly) degraded the environment and the better-off who wanted to save the poor from themselves. In this story, it was the opposite: the poor became the protagonists in seeking a solution rather than the objects of solutions imagined elsewhere.

For human rights and labor activists struggling for years to bring the assassination of rural organizers to public attention, it provided a welcome spotlight on an old problem. At a time when egalitarian values were increasingly labeled utopian, environmentalism was a new universal value on which many of the same claims could be grounded. For international publics, the case became an instant moral allegory; it gave substance to environmentalists' claim that preserving tropical forests was a universal good. Discussion of and response to the Acre example was thus important for environmental organizations, for nongovernmental

417

organizations formed to support poor peoples' movements of various kinds, for trade unions, for Catholic grass-roots groups, and for the left.

Although linking environmental and social questions was not a new idea, the Chico Mendes case linked them in a new way, transforming national struggles over social justice, over what kind of development should take place, into global concerns. It evoked a conception of sustainable development that not only considered basic human needs, but also championed the rights of specific populations to define their needs and formulate development alternatives. The translation of old issues into a new language and a new frame involved a redefinition of the stakes, of the constituencies affected, and of the strategies available and appropriate for affecting those questions. It was a highly political process. Increasingly, discussions of third world environmentalism identified the struggle to protect the environment with the struggles of poor people—particularly traditional peoples—rather than with self-declared environmental movement organizations. This process had international and national dimensions, involving a rereading both of "north-south" questions and (especially) of development and equity issues within nations.

Recognizing the social dimension of environmental problems (and vice versa) did not, of course, imply a consensus on how to approach them. Not all political and social actors who recognized a shared terrain wanted to share it. Both in Brazil and internationally labor leaders initially found it difficult to watch what they saw as a struggle by organized (and unionized) rural folk over land rights being appropriated by environmentalists as a fight to save the forest. Some of them accused Schwartzman and other Washington environmentalists of deliberately "sanitizing," that is, depoliticizing, the Chico Mendes story for self-serving reasons.[34]

Nonetheless, there is evidence that both sides ventured further on to the shared terrain. In March 1991 foreign environmental organizations involved in the multilateral bank campaign sent a strongly worded protest to the Brazilian government over the assassination of rural union leaders in Rio Maria, Pará, where environmental connections were much less direct than they were with rubber tapper organizations. They explicitly noted that the prosecution of Chico Mendes' murderers did not end their concern. Subsequently, they participated in a campaign to pressure Brazilian authorities to prosecute the cases. In 1990–91 many Brazilian unions held seminars on Amazonia and on the relationship between labor and environmental issues; CUT, the main central labor organization, formed working groups on the subject.

The preparatory process for the 1992 United Nations Conference on Environment and Development was also an important space for exchange between environmental organizations and other kinds of social movements in Brazil. From its first meeting in March 1990, the Brazilian NGO Forum sought to attract organizations working at the nexus of environmental and social issues. Its organizational secretariat was shared by SOS Mata Atlântica, probably Brazil's largest single environmental organization, and CEDI, an ecumenical NGO known for work around human rights, labor, and indigenous issues. The forum's coordinating body contained both environmental and social development organizations, including the National Council of Rubber Tappers, and the forum invited participation by trade unions, women's organizations, and a variety of other social movements. Often to the frustration of foreign environmentalist observers who wanted to see the forum more explicitly address the specific topics on the agenda of the 1992 conference,

418

a significant amount of time and energy in forum assemblies was devoted to a process by which environmental and other social movement organizations were learning how to talk to each other.

International environmental NGOs also strengthened their ties with local development organizations that provide support to a variety of social movements. Bramble and Porter note that the international linkages of environmental NGOs in the north with third world organizations tend more often to be with nongovernmental social development institutes than with environmental groups. Part of the reason for this is instrumental; organizations like CEDI in São Paulo and IBASE and FASE in Rio de Janeiro, most of whose activities are financed from abroad, are accustomed to and equipped for international information exchange. In a country where most environmental organizations can barely afford a telephone, international E-mail and fax communication is still out of reach. Whatever the reasons, these linkages help to keep the social dimension of environmental issues in the forefront of international NGO attention. Greenpeace recruited people with a history of activity in a variety of social struggles, not just explicitly environmental ones, to organize its Brazilian section in the early 1990s.

The discussion of environment and development taking place among members of these organizations, and increasingly among international environmental NGOs as well, is diverging from the environmental management perspective most often found in intergovernmental fora. The lessons of the rubber tappers' case and others like it seem to call into play a conception of the environment that is inextricably linked with the survival, not just of humanity or of the planet, but also of specific populations and ways of life.[35] They place a high value on indigenous knowledge, often above technical-scientific knowledge, and want to encourage such populations to demand that their knowledge and needs be considered. They contend that the universal good contained in environmentalism has a multitude of locally specific variants. While not negating the role of technical knowledge, this perspective relegates it to the status of one form of knowledge among many.

Why did the Acre story have the kind of resonance it had with populations whose life worlds were so distant from that of the protagonists? Snow and Benford suggest that the resonance of a particular way of framing issues and events depends, among other things, on its fit with the belief system and the experiential life world of the target audience.[36] At first glance, the Acre case would seem an unlikely contender for attention. The rubber tappers' role as stewards of the forest spoke to some important values within the belief system of northern sympathizers, but not the most central ones. However, Chico Mendes' murder joined a story about stewardship with one about rights. Their combined appeal was much more powerful, especially in the U.S., where the language of rights has traditionally carried a great deal of weight. Snow and Benford also suggest that a frame's ability to bridge different life worlds depends on its credibility, experiential commensurability, and narrative fidelity. The latter they define as the fit with "the stories, myths, and folk tales that are part and parcel of one's cultural heritage and that thus function to inform events and experiences in the immediate present."[37] In this respect, the rubber tappers' story becomes a modern version of a vast western folk repertoire in which poor people in the forest confront powerful interlopers and defeat them against impossible odds.

Within such a perspective, the relationship between environmental and development issues involves a process of recognition as well as one of linkage. Although not all

419

environmental conflicts fit easily into such a model, the rubber tappers' example has been evoked in attempting to think strategically about such conflicts in widely disparate contexts. Some use it instrumentally, thinking that to call something "environmental" makes it more politically attractive, but even this approach helps stimulate debate. At a meeting I attended in October 1990 in Santo Amaro in the southern zone of the city of São Paulo, it was brought up in a discussion of the problem of occupation of watershed areas by low income people seeking places to build affordable housing. Such occupations are clearly forbidden by the state's Watershed Protection Law, and the reservoir near which they were taking place supplies around a quarter of São Paulo's drinking water. Nonetheless, the housing shortage in the region is so critical that public authorities are reluctant to expel the occupiers. Several of those present evoked the example of Chico Mendes and the rubber tappers to suggest that the housing movement begin to recast its appeal to the city as a whole in environmental terms, translating the local need for affordable dwellings into an element of the more general need for potable water. This kind of linkage is obviously much more difficult to make; the occupiers are a problem for the watershed, while the rubber tappers were potentially a solution for the forest. Although several environmental groups took up the demand for housing as part of their fight to protect the watershed, they were not very successful.

The murder of Chico Mendes and the case of the rubber tappers' movement came to public attention at a moment when global environmental change was an increasingly salient issue on the international agenda. This context provided opportunities, in the form of an alliance with foreign environmental NGOs, to translate their struggle for survival from a local arena, where the balance of power was distinctly unfavorable, to an international arena, where it was more favorable. Its power as a metaphor lay in its ability to make concrete in human terms the rather abstract notion of sustainable development. Also, it forced a sharper recognition of the social content of environmental change and of the degree to which struggles over environmental issues may recapitulate in a new form long-standing social conflicts. As far as this awareness spreads, it should help to expand the still fragile dialogue between environmental and other social movements, domestically and internationally.

The Limits of Social Construction

Although the Acre case has become almost a paradigm for discussions of the need to involve local populations and indigenous knowledge in promoting sustainable development, there are some dangers in overgeneralizing from the Acre example. Although the stories that make social problems resonate in the experience of people far from their situation can legitimately be said to have a life of their own, those who use these stories as a basis for strategies would do well to look closely at the contexts from which they emerged. It is important to remember that the movements about which the stories are told continue to have a life of their own as well, and over time they may come to diverge considerably from the symbolic identity attributed to them. Well before their struggle was noticed internationally, the Acre rubber tappers had attained a fairly high degree of organization and visibility locally. They had built alliances with other local movements, unions, and the Catholic church during a political conjuncture that favored such links. By the time they met the environmentalists involved in

420

the Multilateral Bank Campaign, they were in a good position to evaluate the advantages of the proposed linkage. Similarly, for the bank campaign contact with the Acre rubber tappers came at a time when a specific lever was available for influencing the situation: the IDB loan on the Rio Branco-Porto Velho road improvement project.

This kind of conjuncture is rare. Few indigenous and rubber tapper populations in the Amazon are so well organized, and such a powerful form of international leverage is rarely present. In the absence of leverage, international attention to the plight of indigenous populations in tropical forests is unlikely to have the same impact. Consider, for example, the case of the struggles of the Penan and other indigenous peoples of Sarawak, where international media attention and pressure from such organizations as Friends of the Earth and Survival International have been much less successful in slowing the rate of deforestation. In the absence of a preexisting web of organization, the transposing of the Acre "paradigm" to new areas can lead international NGOs to make erroneous assumptions about how indigenous populations "ought" to be organized.

Interpreting the lessons of the Acre case requires that we take these cautionary notes into account. Even as we recognize the universalizing power of the case as a metaphor that merges concerns with social justice and the natural environment, we must also recognize its historical specificity. International linkages may be a powerful political resource for third world movements of this kind, but they are most valuable as a supplement to, not a replacement for, the development of political resources locally. The international attention span, after all, is short.

Nonetheless, insofar as third world countries have stressed the development side of the environment and development relationship, they have (perhaps unwittingly) facilitated the reinterpretation of a whole range of local struggles, particularly over land use, through an environmental lens. This reinterpretation widens the field of potential allies for such struggles, as well as the number of arenas relevant for their adjudication, and in the process reconfigures the power relations around them. The Acre case is a powerful illustration of the degree to which defining an issue as environmental is a political process.

NOTES

1. This paper is part of a study of environmental politics in Brazil that has received support from the Yale Center for International and Area Studies, the Howard Heinz Endowment, the Social Science Research Council, and the John D. and Catherine MacArthur Foundation. Several interviews cited were done in 1982 during earlier research on the Workers' Party, partly financed by a grant from Columbia University's Institute for Latin American and Iberian Studies. On "the pollution of poverty," see, for example, João Augusto de Araujo Castro, "Environment and Development: The Case of the Developing Countries," *International Organization*, 26 (Spring 1972).

2. International Union for the Conservation of Nature and Natural Resources, *World Conservation Strategy: Living Resource Conservation for Sustainable Development* (Gland: IUCN, 1980); World Commission on Environment and Development, *Our Common Future* (Oxford: Oxford University Press, 1987).

3. Margaret E. Keck, "Sustainable Development and Environmental Politics in Latin America," in Colin I. Bradford, Jr., *Redefining the State in Latin America* (Paris: OECD, 1994).

4. See David A. Snow, E. Burke Rochford, Jr., Steven K. Worden, and Robert D. Benford, "Frame Alignment Processes, Micromobilization, and Movement Participation," *American Sociological Review*, 51 (August 1986), 464–81. By SMO they mean social movement organization. The framing concept comes from Erving Goffman, *Frame Analysis* (Boston: Northeastern University Press, 1986). Goffman, pp. 10–11, defined framing as the process by which

421

"definitions of a situation are built up in accordance with principles of organization which govern events—at least social ones—and our subjective involvement in them."

5. Deborah A. Stone, "Causal Stories and the Formation of Policy Agendas," *Political Science Quarterly*, 104 (1989), 283. On the importance of metaphor and analogy in political reasoning and policymaking, see Deborah A. Stone, *Policy Paradox and Political Reason* (Glenview: Scott, Foresman, 1988).

6. Murray Edelman argued that the construction of problems "is as much a way of knowing and a way of acting strategically as a form of description; and it is often a way of *excluding systematic attention to history and to social structure as well*" (my emphasis). Murray Edelman, *Constructing the Political Spectacle* (Chicago: University of Chicago Press, 1988), p. 36.

7. See Amnesty International, *Brazil: Authorized Violence in Rural Areas* (London: Amnesty International Publications, 1988).

8. See, for example, Susanna Hecht and Alexander Cockburn, *The Fate of the Forest* (London: Verso, 1989); and Andrew Revkin, *The Burning Season* (Boston: Houghton Mifflin, 1990).

9. The relationship proposed here between cognitive frame and institutional resources is similar to the one between image and venue discussed in Frank R. Baumgartner and Bryan D. Jones, "Agenda Dynamics and Policy Subsystems," *The Journal of Politics*, 53 (November 1991), 1044–74.

10. For an overview of the development of these approaches, see Doug McAdam, John D. McCarthy, and Mayer N. Zald, "Social Movements," in Neil Smelser, ed., *Handbook of Sociology* (Newbury Park: Sage, 1988), pp. 695–737, and the review article by Sidney Tarrow, "National Politics and Collective Action: Recent Theory and Research in Western Europe and the United States," *Annual Review of Sociology*, 14 (1988), 421–40. A useful compendium of recent work in this tradition is Aldon D. Morris and Carol McClurg Mueller, eds., *Frontiers in Social Movement Theory* (New Haven: Yale University Press, 1993).

11. Edelman, pp. 32–35.

12. These traits included emphasis on quality of life and cultural issues, a participatory ethic, diffuse value rather than group based appeals, expressive rather than instrumental motivations to participate, fluid organizational structures, and unconventional political styles. See Russell J. Dalton, Manfred Kuechler, and Wilhelm Burklin, "The Challenge of New Movements," in Russell J. Dalton and Manfred Kuechler, eds., *Challenging the Political Order: New Social and Political Movements in Western Democracies* (Cambridge: Policy Press, 1990), pp. 10–16; and Scott Mainwaring and Eduardo Viola, "New Social Movements, Political Culture, and Democracy: Brazil and Argentina in the 1980s," *Telos*, 61 (Fall 1984), 17–52.

13. See Margaret E. Keck, "The New Unionism in the Brazilian Transition," in Alfred Stepan, ed., *Democratizing Brazil* (New York: Oxford University Press, 1989); and Margaret E. Keck, *The Workers' Party and Democratization in Brazil* (New Haven: Yale University Press, 1992).

14. Eduardo J. Viola, "The Ecologist Movement in Brazil (1974–1986): From Environmentalism to Ecopolitics," *International Journal of Urban and Regional Research*, 12 (June 1988), 211–28.

15. It is interesting that the first translation offered for *empate* in the *Novo Michaelis* is "act or effect of being or becoming equal, equality." Others, besides stalemate, are "unprofitable investment of capital" and "obstacle, hindrance." I use "standoff" rather than the more habitually used "stalemate," as it seems to capture the confrontational nature of the action.

16. Author's interview with Dom Moacir Grechi, Rio Branco, Acre, December 19, 1982.

17. See Alan Biorn Henning Maybury-Lewis, "The Politics of the Possible: The Growth and Political Development of the Brazilian Rural Workers' Trade Union Movement, 1964–1985" (Ph.D. diss., Columbia University, 1991).

18. Author's interview with João Maia, Rio Branco, Acre, December 18, 1982.

19. See Keck, *The Workers' Party and Democratization in Brazil*, ch. 5.

20. Author's interview with João Maia, Rio Branco, Acre, December 18, 1982. The National Security Law could be used widely in Acre because virtually the whole state was designated a national security area, either by a decree dating from the time of Juscelino Kubitschek so designating areas within 150 km from the national border or by a 1970 decree establishing national security areas for 100 km on each side of a national road in the Amazon region.

21. Author's interview with Chico Mendes and Nilson Morão, Rio Branco, Acre, December 18, 1982.

22. This campaign followed close on the heels of a successful campaign by environmentalists in Washington, D.C., to influence AID policy in the third world. See Ronald Brownstein, "Success Story: Environmentalism Amid the Ruins," *The Amicus Journal* (Fall 1983); and Thomas B. Stoel, Jr., "Protecting the Global Environment: The Need for Citizen Action and Advocacy," *The Amicus Journal* (Summer 1985). On the multilateral development bank campaign, see Pat Aufderheide and Bruce Rich, "Environmental Reform and the Multilateral Banks," *World Policy*

422

Journal, 5 (Spring 1988), 301–21; Bruce Rich, "The Emperor's New Clothes: The World Bank and Environmental Reform," *World Policy Journal* (Spring 1990), 305–29; and Barbara J. Bramble and Gareth Porter, "Non-Governmental Organizations and the Making of US International Environmental Policy," in Andrew Hurrell and Benedict Kingsbury, eds., *The International Politics of the Environment* (Oxford: Oxford University Press, 1992), pp. 313–53.

23. The IDB loaned around $52 million for the project, including around $8 million for a Project for the Protection of the Environment and Indigenous Communities (*Projecto de proteção do meio ambiente e das comunidades indígenas*, PMACI). As a result of lobbying by U.S. environmentalists, the U.S. executive director of the IDB abstained from the vote on environmental grounds, and it was clear that the Brazilian government would be under pressure to produce a serious plan for implementing the project.

24. According to Candido Grzybowski, between 1975 and 1988 forty-five *empates* took place, of which fifteen were successful and helped to preserve 1.2 million hectares of forest, but as a result of which some 400 rubber tappers were imprisoned for participation in the movement. See Candido Grzybowski, "Rural Workers' Movements and Democratization in Brazil" (Boston: Center for International Studies, Massachusetts Institute of Technology, Working Paper, 1989), p. 14. A version of this paper was published in *Journal of Development Studies*, 26 (July 1990).

25. For an account of this meeting, see Revkin, *The Burning Season*, p. 193. Gross and Allegretti were looking for an international representative for the indigenous peoples' program of INESC, a Brasília-based NGO, and recruited Schwartzman for this task. The rubber tappers came up in the context of a discussion of development projects and the bank campaign, especially concerning how to protect the rights of indigenous peoples. Personal communication from Stephan Schwartzman, February 20, 1992.

26. Grzybowski, p. 15; see also Stephan Schwartzman, "Extractive Reserves: The Rubber Tappers' Strategy for Sustainable Use of the Amazon Rainforest," in John O. Browder, ed., *Fragile Lands of Latin America: Strategies for Sustainable Development* (Boulder: Westview Press, 1989), pp. 150–63.

27. "Rubber Tappers Bounce Back," *Development Report* (May 1986), 10.

28. See Stephan Schwartzman, "Deforestation and Popular Resistance in Acre: From Local Social Movement to Global Network," *Centennial Review*, 35 (Spring 1991).

29. Portaria 627, July 30, 1987. See Schwartzman, "Extractive Reserves," p. 152.

30. As Schwartzman reminded me in his comments on an earlier draft, the first such reserve (in Seringal Cachoeira) was created, not under Sarney's 1990 decree establishing the *Reserva Extrativista* under the authority of IBAMA, but earlier under the MIRAD category of "*projeto de assentamento extrativista.*" Its creation resolved a conflict over that area in favor of the rubber tappers against Darly Alves, later convicted for masterminding the assassination of Chico Mendes. Placing extractive reserves under IBAMA had political-institutional significance in making it possible for organizations demanding their creation to bypass INCRA opposition. Schwartzman, personal communication, February 20, 1992.

31. Some 2,000 people attended his funeral in Xapuri, including environmentalists, labor leaders, and politicians from all over Brazil. See "Thousands in Brazil Attend Slain Ecologist's Funeral," *The Washington Post*, Dec. 26, 1988.

32. The National Household Survey published in 1990 showed that between 1981 and 1989 the top decile of the population increased its income share from 46.6 to 53.2 percent, while the share of the lower 50 percent fell from 13.4 to 10.4 percent. "Trancos e barrancos," *Veja*, Nov. 21, 1990, pp. 42–45.

33. See, for example, the *New York Times* editorial on December 28, 1988, entitled "Brazil Burns the Future," protesting the continued burning of the rain forest and casting doubt upon the Sarney government's ability to prosecute Mendes' murderers. The story of Mendes' assassination received prominent coverage in the *New York Times*, *The Washington Post*, *The Boston Globe*, and other papers, and protests were read into the *Congressional Record* of January 3, 1989 by Senator Robert Kasten and Representative David Obey.

34. See in this respect the article by Susanna Hecht and Alexander Cockburn, "Defending the Rain Forest and Its People," *The Nation* (May 22, 1989), 686, 695–702; and the exchange between Stephan Schwartzman and Bruce Rich and the authors in "Letters," *The Nation* (September 18, 1989), 262, 291–92. The memorial service for Chico Mendes in Washington, D.C., which occasioned some of these accusations, initially also outraged at least one Washington, D.C. trade unionist, active around Brazilian labor issues. In the latter case, the conflict was attenuated by the need recognized on both sides to work together around the rubber tappers' case. In Brazil, Márcio Souza's polemical *O Empate contra Chico Mendes* (São Paulo: Marco Zero, 1990) accused the EDF, together with Mary Allegretti's *Instituto de Estudos Amazonicos* (IEA), of "collecting money abroad, using them in Acre to divide and attack the work of the Workers' Party, the unions, and the Church. While Chico Mendes led the struggle, he was politically capable of keeping anything from destroying the unity and perseverance of the workers in Acre. But his death, with the resulting

423

power vacuum, and his transformation into a myth as a green leader, an ecologist, who defended plants and butterflies, brought confusion and uncertainty to the movement" (p. 150). And indeed, some of the international coverage of the story has ignored the rubber tappers' political associations.

35. The Chipko movement in Uttar Pradesh, India, is one of the best known examples. See Vandana Shiva, "Ecology Movements in India," *Alternatives*, 11 (1986), 255–73; Thomas Weber, *Hugging the Trees: The Story of the Chipko Movement* (New Delhi: Penguin Books, 1989); and Ramachandra Guha, *The Unquiet Woods: Ecological Change and Peasant Resistance in the Himalaya* (Berkeley: University of California Press, 1989).

36. David A. Snow and Robert D. Benford, "Ideology, Frame Resonance, and Participant Mobilization," in Bert Klandermans, Hanspeter Kriesi, and Sidney Tarrow, eds., *From Structure to Action: Comparing Social Movement Research across Cultures* (Greenwich: JAI Press, 1988).

37. Ibid., p. 210.

424

Adding Collective Actors to Collective Outcomes

Labor and Recent Democratization in South America and Southern Europe

Ruth Berins Collier and James Mahoney

The study of late twentieth century democratic transitions has become a major topic in comparative politics, and one particular analytic framework, which gives primacy to elite strategic choice, has become virtually hegemonic.[1] Despite a number of critiques, this approach continues to shape scholarly understandings of the recent process of democratization. Yet a single framework can not possibly embrace the whole panoply of issues raised by these transitions. An alternative line of analysis not easily accommodated within the dominant account is the role of collective actors. *Contra* the dominant paradigm, the present study explores the role of one particular collective actor, the organized labor movement, in recent democratic transitions in South America and southern Europe.

Focusing on collective action undertaken by unions and labor-affiliated parties, we argue that the labor movement often played an important role in recent transitions. Labor was not limited to an "indirect" role, in which protest around workplace demands was answered through cooptive inclusion in the electoral arena. Rather, the labor movement was one of the major actors in the political opposition, explicitly demanding a democratic regime. In some cases union-led protest for democracy contributed to a climate of ungovernability and delegitimation that led directly to a general destabilization of authoritarian regimes. Moreover, continual protest, rather than creating an authoritarian backlash, kept the transition moving forward. Finally, while the protest of other groups also put the regime on the defensive, labor-based organizations went further in two ways: they often won a place in the negotiations, and they expanded the scope of contestation in the successor regime.

The dominant paradigm has built upon the founding essay by O'Donnell and Schmitter, which emphasizes the role of leadership and elite interaction. While that essay suggests that "the greatest challenge to the transitional regime is likely to come from . . . the collective action of the working class," it also emphasizes the ephemeral nature of the "popular upsurge" and the subsequent "decline of the people."[2] Other comparative analyses and theoretical accounts, focusing more exclusively on elite interaction, have not picked up on this theme. This article argues that union-led protest was much more central to the democratization process than implied by an elite-centric perspective, which sees labor's role primarily as altering the strategic environment of elite negotiators and theoretically underrates the role of mass opposition, labor protest, and collective actors generally.

Three related points can be made about the overall perspective of this "transitions literature." First, it has emphasized leadership and crafting, thus signaling the importance of individual rather than collective actors. Second, it tends to define actors strategically (for example, hardliners and softliners) with respect to their position in the "transition game," thus sidelining questions about class-defined actors. Third, despite an emphasis on government-opposition negotiations, it has tended to be state-centric, thus subordinating social actors; scholars have tended to classify transitions either as initiated and to some degree controlled by incumbents or as resulting from regime collapse seen in terms of a state-centric image of implosion.[3] Therefore, the dominant framework is not very useful for present purposes because its basic theoretical assumptions and orienting concepts almost preclude the problematization of the labor movement and collective action in the first place.

Exploring five of the eleven recent South American and southern European transitions, those which have become particularly important points of reference in the literature, we elaborate two patterns of democratization that depart from the standard account (see Table 1). Both patterns suggest that the labor movement was more central to the politics of democratization than has been recognized and that its role often began earlier and continued to the end. The first pattern is the biggest departure in terms of the countries it groups together and the characterization of the transitions: in the pattern of destabilization/extrication, collective protest, within which labor protest was prominent, destabilized and delegitimated the authoritarian regime. Authoritarian incumbents adopted no transition project prior to this

Table 1 Patterns of Democratization

	Destabilization/Extrication	**Transition Game**
Authoritarian Incumbents	No Project; Defensive Exit	Limited Democracy Project; Negotiated Exit
Labor Movement	Destabilizes Authoritarian Regime; Triggers Transition	Derails Incumbent Project; Advances Transition
Cases	Spain 1977 Peru 1980 Argentina 1983	Uruguay 1984 Brazil 1985

286

destabilization, and, instead of elite negotiation, the transition is better characterized as forced retreat. In the second pattern, transition game, the incumbents adopted a legitimation project, but this project was derailed. Subsequently, collective protest, in which the labor movement had a prominent role, helped to reshape the transition and keep it moving forward. In both patterns, collective action secured the legalization of labor-affiliated parties, which otherwise might have fallen victim to elite negotiation.

The present analysis adopts a different temporal conceptualization from the prevailing framework, which starts with divisions in the state and ensuing rule changes. That conceptualization reinforces the emphasis on state and elite actors and effectively makes questions about the origins of state divisions exogenous. By contrast, this article explores the origins of these divisions. Furthermore, analyses within the dominant framework concentrate on the final stage of the transition. We see this stage as a closing end-game, necessarily dominated by elites establishing rules for the actual transfer of power and designing the institutions of new democracies. Our emphasis is again on an earlier period, on the decision of authoritarian actors to exit and on the effective ceding of control to opposition or elected authorities, even if the outgoing incumbents still attempt, sometimes successfully, to exert influence.

Destabilization/Extrication

In Peru, Argentina, and Spain, union-led protests were crucial in destabilizing authoritarianism and opening the way for democratization. Authoritarian incumbents had not formulated a reform project when labor took the offensive in strikes and protests against the regime. Incumbents were unable to ignore such opposition or formulate a response to these challenges. In each case, the regime was destabilized, and incumbents made the decision to relinquish power, clearly pursuing a defensive extrication in which the goal was ultimately to step down and salvage whatever terms they could. These terms varied. The Peruvian and particularly the Argentine military incumbents came away with much less than the Spanish civilians, who were able to transform themselves into democratic actors. In Peru, labor protest propelled the regime into crisis, and following a successful general strike in 1977 the government moved quickly to announce elections for a constituent assembly which assumed direction of the transition. In Argentina, the human rights movement helped galvanize opposition to authoritarianism. But the issue of union power had divided the military from the beginning, and labor protest was important in preventing the consolidation of the military regime. With the failure of the Malvinas invasion, intended to forestall the regime crisis, the government quickly called for the elections that marked the regime transition. In

287

Spain, labor protest produced a severe challenge to the regime even before the death of Franco and undermined the initial Francoist and post-Franco responses. Suárez then came to power and immediately built a consensus for a transition election. In all these cases, negotiations between the authoritarian government and the prodemocratic opposition parties continued after the extrication decision, and these discussions included left and labor-affiliated parties.

Peru Unlike most cases, the authoritarian regime in Peru did not initially engage in the systematic repression of labor.[4] Rather, during the government of General Velasco (1968–1975) Peruvian authoritarianism had a distinctly "populist" character in which labor organizing was strongly encouraged. Nevertheless, by 1973 organized labor moved increasingly into opposition in conjunction with several factors—the onset of a severe economic downturn, increasing attempts to replace the Communist-led union federation (CGTP) with a state-controlled one (CTRP), and the grave illness of General Valasco. In that year strikes increased substantially (roughly double the average for the previous five years), creating a climate of instability and facilitating the fall of Velasco's government in August 1975.[5]

Under the subsequent government of Morales Bermúdez, state-labor relations quickly became antagonistic, and organized labor emerged as the major antiauthoritarian actor. The new administration moved sharply away from Velasco's populism, adopting antilabor policies and carrying out repression more characteristic of other authoritarian regimes. In the second half of 1976 the labor movement responded with a series of strikes, which symbolized a new posture of direct and confrontational opposition against the authoritarian regime.

The single most important event in triggering the transition of 1980 was the general strike of July 19, 1977 (the first since 1919 and the largest strike in Peru's history). This strike united nearly all trade union bodies and paralyzed industrial activity in Lima. In addition to workplace concerns, the strike demanded basic democratic freedoms. "The 1977 strike carried the unmistakable message that attempts by the military to slow or avoid a transfer of power to civilians would result in only greater turmoil that would further undermine the military's already weak credibility."[6] The general strike reflected labor's leadership of the antiauthoritarian opposition; other opposition groups generally mobilized later when they joined with unions to form a fractious coalition known as the "popular movement."

In the aftermath of the strike, members of the traditional political parties and economic elite argued that a return to democracy was necessary to restore political order and economic growth. Indeed, as a result of the strike "Morales Bermúdez was obligated to announce a timetable for the return to civilian rule."[7] In August 1977 the government lifted the state of emergency and announced constituent

288

assembly elections for June 1978. Thus, the military decided to extricate itself and proceed with a transition. Until the assembly elections of June 1978, strikes and popular mobilization continued, including further general strikes in February, April, and May 1978.

During the final phase of transition, mobilization declined "because the assembly marked an important step in the military's road back to the barracks—the one aim which united the fragile coalition of groups which made up the 'popular movement.' "[8] Nevertheless, labor unions and labor-affiliated parties continued to play a role. APRA, the party with historic ties to the labor movement, won 35 percent of the vote to the constituent assembly. More important, with the shift in partisan affiliation of the labor movement that occurred during the military regime, the left won 33 percent. Further, the constituent assembly solicited advice from many social groups, including union leaders, and during this period the military government kept up contacts with party leaders, especially APRA's but also including the left. In July 1979 all citizens over eighteen years of age were enfranchised, and elections in May 1980 completed the transition.

Argentina While it is true that the democratic transition in Argentina in 1983 followed the regime's collapse after military defeat in the Falkland Islands/ Malvinas war, the standard characterization ignores the factors that brought on the military expedition in the first place. The still limited research on this topic reveals two points at which labor may be interpreted as playing a key role. First, labor protest contributed to the division in the military between hardliners and softliners which the invasion of the Malvinas was intended to overcome. Second, some analysts maintain that labor protest directly prompted the generals to carry out the Malvinas invasion. Either way, evidence suggests that this military regime, like the one a decade earlier (1966–1973), was destabilized by labor protest.[9]

The labor question had long been at the core of Argentine politics, and it remained crucial throughout the period of military rule from 1976 to 1983. The 1976 coup was itself partly a response to worker activism, and within a month of coming to power the military government considered a new labor law to deactivate the labor movement. Early military factionalism was closely linked to divisions over how to handle the labor question. One faction favored a direct assault on unions, while another favored an older pattern of state-labor relations in which labor moderation was bought with concessions granting a still limited but more positive role for unions. Under the leadership of General Videla, the hardline faction emerged dominant within the government and executed the harsh policies of political repression associated with the "dirty war," a policy of economic liberalization that constituted an attack on labor interests, and a labor law that has been described as completing the unprecedented onslaught against labor.[10]

Despite government repression, "defensive strikes" were mounted after the

289

coup. While unions willing to cooperate with the military coalesced around the CNT, by early 1977 some unions formed the Commission of 25 to oppose the government and its project for a new labor law. In 1979 union opposition accelerated, starting with the first general strike under the military dictatorship. Centered primarily on wage policy, the strike did not yet constitute a prodemocratic movement. Soon after, however, in reaction to the new labor law, the labor movement united in the CUTA, which undertook overtly oppositional activities on multiple fronts. It announced a plan to fight the new law through "national plebiscites" in the workplace; it initiated contact with political parties, labor lawyers, and the ILO; and it developed its organization in regional labor groupings. Individual unions also stepped up their activity. Although the CUTA soon split, the oppositionist CGT "displayed growing boldness, worked to develop thicker organizational networks through contact with various actors within society, and made direct calls for a change in labor policy and of the regime itself."[11] Thus, the unions took the lead in mobilizing opposition and attempting to coordinate other social sectors, at the same time that the political parties rejected the initiative and business groups were divided.

Open divisions within the ruling authoritarian regime emerged in this context of labor protest, accompanied by economic deterioration. With growing social instability, the succession to the presidency of the softliner General Viola in March 1981 became the focus for ideologically based antagonisms among top officers. The discontent of the navy was particularly pronounced since, in addition to having been cut out of "its turn" in the succession, it was identified with a hardline approach and opposed Viola, who favored a more pragmatic economic policy and more normalized relations with conciliatory unions.

Labor opposition contributed to Viola's inability to consolidate power. Initially divided over cooperation with Viola, the union movement reunited in an overtly oppositionist and prodemocratic stance when it became clear that Viola's promised conciliation would not be forthcoming. In July 1981 the CGT mounted another general strike, and under its leadership the opposition fostered a climate of instability and a sense that "civil society was getting out of control" so that opposition to Viola grew even within his own branch of the military.[12] On November 7, 1981, the CGT called another mass mobilization, and two days later Viola was forced to resign.

The removal of General Viola exposed deep divisions that compromised the military's institutional control of government. With the defeat of the softliners, the new president, General Galtieri, returned to a hardline authoritarian stance and launched the Malvinas invasion to placate the navy, which favored the venture.

According to the first argument, then, "diverse views on how to deal with society produced internal divisions within the Armed Forces."[13] Labor's prodemocratic opposition prevented the military regime from consolidating power

290

and led to its destabilization by reinforcing and intensifying splits within it, which the disastrous military adventure was intended to repair.

According to the second argument, labor protest directly prompted the decision of the generals to invade the Malvinas. As Ronaldo Munck put it, "the military adventure of the generals cannot be explained in purely 'military' terms. . . . It was the constant level of working-class resistance since 1976, which was moving from a defensive to an offensive phase by 1982, which alone explains [the] bizarre political gamble by the armed forces."[14]

Opposition and protest increased after the ouster of Viola. The CGT took steps to coordinate joint action with the parties, now organized in the *Multipartidaria*, and on March 30, 1982, along with human rights groups and political parties, it staged the largest demonstration since the 1976 coup. By this time "the CGT's massive demonstrations were threatening the stability of the government and appeared to have pushed the military rulers to take a desperate step. . . ."[15] Three days later, Argentina invaded the Malvinas islands. In this account, in order to shore up support in the face of the opposition's offensive, Galtieri activated plans for the invasion. By reviving a long-standing nationalist cause he hoped to rally the country behind the regime.[16]

In either interpretation, the invasion was a desperate move to preserve a regime already in deep trouble, and pressure from the CGT was, directly or at a step removed, a major source of the problem. The invasion was launched either to address splits within the military exacerbated by labor protest or to deal with the challenge of accelerating popular mobilization in opposition to the authoritarian regime in which the CGT played a central initiating and coordinating role.

The military gamble failed. Not only did Argentina lose the ensuing war against Britain, but the invasion failed to defuse labor protest. Though the labor movement supported the military campaign, it remained active in opposition to the regime throughout the war. By mid June 1982, with the loss of the war and ongoing massive mobilization, the discredited military quickly moved to extricate itself by installing a "caretaker" government and announcing that general elections would be held in October 1983.

The labor movement was an important player in the remaining phases of the transition. The interim government attempted to negotiate the military's extrication more extensively than is generally recognized, but three successive plans to shape the subsequent government were rejected by the *Multipartidaria*, in which the union movement was a prominent influence. Throughout, "the junta made a special effort to negotiate the transition with Peronist union leaders."[17] Though all these attempts came to naught, it is noteworthy that labor was the major interlocutor in these efforts. The victory of Raúl Alfonsin in the 1983 elections completed the transition.

291

Spain   According to most authors, Spain is a prototypical case of democratization by elite negotiation.[18] The dominant interpretation of Spain sees the democratization process as beginning roughly with the death of Franco in November 1975 and points to adept elite leadership in the ensuing uncertain environment to explain successful democratization. Particularly important was the skill of regime moderates, most notably Adolfo Suárez, in pursuing democratic negotiations simultaneously with both the moderates from the "democratic opposition" and the *continuistas* of the Franco establishment. Further, by pursuing these negotiations and reforms incrementally, Suárez garnered support for this carefully crafted democratization.

This interpretation misses the crucial role played by labor.[19] First, by the early 1970s, even before the death of Franco, labor pressures for an end to authoritarian rule set off a deepening regime crisis. Second, dramatic labor protests undermined attempts to establish a system of "Francoism without Franco." Finally, once the regime was destabilized, elements of the labor movement helped define a more moderate opposition strategy that enabled Suárez to negotiate the final agreements leading up to the democratic elections of June 1977. As Maravall states:

> popular pressure "from below" played a crucial part in the transition, especially that coming from the workers' movement. It was a causal factor in the Francoist crisis, in the non-viability of any mere "liberalization" policy, in the willingness on the part of the "democratic right" to negotiate the transition and carry through reform up to the point of breaking with Francoism, and in the initiative displayed by the Left up to the 1977 elections.[20]

The labor movement was in a unique position to open space within the authoritarian regime. In 1948 the Communist Party decided to use union elections to penetrate the official, corporative structure, eventually facilitating the emergence of the parallel, more oppositionist Workers' Commissions. In different but symbiotic ways, both the legal unions and illegal Commissions became important sites of opposition and channels for undermining authoritarianism. By the 1960s it was clear that the official unions were not functioning as integrative mechanisms; the Commissions mounted sustained working-class protest; and the per capita strike rate became one of the highest in Europe. Toward the end of the decade the labor movement's agenda increasingly turned from workplace demands to demands for broad political liberties. Its orientation also shifted toward mobilization aimed at toppling the regime; Communist Party and labor leaders began to discuss openly the possibility of a *ruptura democrática* (democratic rupture). With the failure of its labor project, the government was forced to choose between repression and democratic opening.

In part as a consequence of labor opposition, serious divisions emerged within

292

the regime. Hardliners were initially dominant, and repression increased from 1967 to 1973. Franco decided to insure the future of authoritarianism through a Francoist monarchy with Juan Carlos as king. Yet repression was ineffectual in reducing social protest. During 1970 labor strikes rose to over 1,500,[21] nationalist terrorism also accelerated, and "the government had no political answer to this increasing level of conflict."[22] Softliners became increasingly vocal in pressing for a change of policy. In late 1972 and early 1973 Franco and his prime minister, Carrero Blanco, responded in speeches that suggested that some type of political opening would be forthcoming.

Sustained labor protest in 1973 helped keep the government on the defensive in search of a new formula for stability. After the assassination of Carrero Blanco in December 1973, Franco appointed a moderate, Carlos Arias Navarro, whose strategy was to establish a *dictablanda,* or softer dictatorship, but labor activism prevented its stabilization. Strikes increased dramatically under Arias to the largest number in Spanish history in 1974. The strike record was again broken in 1975. In reaction to this labor protest, the hardliners retrenched, favoring a severe crackdown and driving a deeper wedge in the regime. "When the news of Franco's illness broke . . . everything seemed to show that the regime was in crisis."[23] In the opening months of 1976 labor strikes and demonstrations once again reached unprecedented levels, but in the face of this offensive "the ministry remained impotent."[24] Labor protest thus undermined the strategy of limited liberalization pursued by Arias. When he resigned in July 1976, it had become clear that, "if a catastrophic clash between the irresistible force of the left and the immovable object of the right was to be avoided, it was essential that rapid progress be made to the introduction of democracy."[25]

By the time Suárez became prime minister, then, the labor movement had done much both to destabilize the authoritarian regime and to reject government attempts to respond in ways that fell short of democracy. It seemed clear that the government had to find some means of effecting a speedy transition. Suárez accomplished this task in about two months. He won the cabinet's approval of a transition project that committed the government to elections within a year. Within another two months, the project was approved by the Cortes (legislature).

These events are worth pondering. The task—and triumph—of Suárez, as many have emphasized, involved nothing less than convincing the Cortes to agree to its own replacement in a very short time. How was he successful? The key question is not whether Suárez was a skilled negotiator. Rather, can what he did be seen as an extrication? Did Suárez, in other words, negotiate an extrication, even though he did it very well, with ultimately positive implications for democratic consolidation? It is difficult to imagine that an entrenched Cortes would participate so quickly in its own demise without the high level of pressure of oppositional mobilization and regime crisis. Even analysts like Linz and Stepan, who emphasize the agency of

293

Suárez, refer to the "fear of a vacuum of authority, of a sudden transfer of power to the then quite radical opposition forces," in prompting Suárez and the reformers to act.[26]

Beyond its role in provoking the transition, labor opposition also shaped the way it unfolded. Even before Suárez came to power, the democratic opposition, led by the Communist Party, affiliated trade unions, and the Socialist Party, recognized that it could not directly overthrow the government and abandoned the strategy of *ruptura democrática* in favor of *ruptura pactada* (negotiated rupture), which envisioned a provisional government and a constituent Cortes to determine the successor regime. The reform project that Suárez proposed in October and that the Cortes passed in November 1976 paralleled this project by providing for the election of the constituent assembly, but it rejected a provisional government. Once Suárez engineered a consensus behind the transition project, the rest followed quickly according to the adopted timetable. In June 1977 free elections were held to choose the democratic Cortes, which wrote a constitution and provided the institutional structure of the new democracy.

Although in the final months of the transition labor and the left opposition lost power to the more moderate opposition, their role in bringing about and shaping the transition should not be underestimated. They precipitated the transition, and in many ways their *ruptura pactada* strategy gave the transition its particular form. Indeed, discussions and negotiations took place between the government and left parties, including the Communist Party, which was legalized during the transition. The argument here is not that labor single-handedly brought about the demise of authoritarianism or constructed the new democracy. Nor is it that labor was the most important of an array of players (including industrialists, students, Basque and Catalan nationalists, and the king). Nevertheless, labor exerted constant pressure on the regime for about ten years, and this pressure continued during the years of the transition itself. Despite the widely noted "moderation" of labor in these years, Pérez-Díaz notes the "explosion" in the level of industrial conflict and collective action in 1976–79 and a rise in real wages at a rate almost double the OECD average in 1973–79.[27] Certainly, Suárez used the legal instruments of the Francoist system to bring about its liquidation and demonstrated impressive leadership skill in negotiating a broad consensus around the transition. Yet to begin the story of Spanish democratization from this point is to focus on the final step of a longer process and to miss the important role of labor. Labor protest destabilized the authoritarian regime, made impossible a reform that stopped short of democratization, and thus forced incumbents to undertake a rather speedy extrication.

294

Transition Game

Two traits of the Uruguayan and Brazilian transitions more closely fit the standard model. First, elite strategic games involved a protracted series of moves and countermoves and formal and informal negotiations among military incumbents and party leaders. These strategic games arose in a particular context in which from the very beginning the military sought legitimation through a façade of civilian rule operating through chosen groups of politicians and a restricted electoral arena. These regimes thus embraced an incumbent project which defined a game between government and leaders of selected political parties, whether long-established (Uruguay) or newly formed under government guidance (Brazil). Second, collective action by labor organizations appeared relatively late in a larger process of civic activation and rejuvenation and followed the action of party leaders, who were the first on the scene and figured centrally in the government's legitimation project from the beginning.

Nevertheless, this account understates the role of mass popular opposition in general and of labor protest in particular. Legitimation projects adopted by both military governments were undermined by popular opposition expressed in the limited electoral arena. A 1980 plebiscite marked the first failure of the government project of Uruguay, and opposition gains in the 1974 elections portended the failure of the government project in Brazil. Henceforth both regimes were thrown on the defensive; incumbents continually scrambled to alter their project and change the rules of the political game in the face of an opposition increasingly on the offensive. Given the pattern and target of repression, the space for social movements, and particularly for the labor movement, opened later. Once it emerged, however, labor activity was forceful in the final transition stage.

Furthermore, the activities of labor opposition undermined government attempts to control and limit the party system, created room for the entry of a political left, and were particularly important where formal (Uruguay) and informal (Brazil) negotiations between government and major party leaders could have led to an agreement to exclude left parties. Indeed, in both cases the Communist party remained banned. Nevertheless, in Brazil labor protest gave rise to a new socialist party based in the new union movement, and in Uruguay the reconstitution of the labor movement and its protest activities provided an outlet for the banned *Frente Amplio,* its participation in various opposition fora, and finally its legalization and participation in the final negotiations, thus allowing the stalled transition to proceed.

Brazil In Brazil, movement toward a democratic regime was initiated autonomously by the authoritarian incumbents, who came to power in a 1964 military coup.[28] At the onset the military sought legitimation through a controlled

295

two party system operating in a very restricted electoral space. In 1974, after a more repressive interlude, military softliners regained the upper hand and during the presidency of General Geisel reinstituted a period of "decompression."

With decompression, leaders of the officially recognized opposition party found space for more autonomous action and made electoral gains in 1974 and again in 1976. With the failure to engineer a political opening that would favor the progovernment party and the rise of many groups in civil society calling for a democratic transition, the military closed congress and further manipulated the electoral law to reestablish some control.

At this point, in the late 1970s, the labor movement burst onto the political scene. The more limited process of liberalization was transformed into one of democratization, in which the party and electoral systems were opened. This process ultimately culminated in the (indirect) election of a civilian president in 1985. It is difficult to determine how decisive the activities of the labor movement were in these developments, given inroads already made by the opposition party and other social groups. Nevertheless, they fundamentally shaped the transition process.

Repressed following a 1968 strike, the labor movement developed a new form of resistance in the early 1970s. By 1978, especially in the multinational automobile plants, it crystallized in the new unionism, which "signaled the existence of massive, organized discontent with the regime, and . . . constituted powerful evidence that democratization was necessary to resolve the potential for social conflict."[29] The metalworkers' strike of 1978 spread to more than one-half million workers.[30] One of the largest strike waves in Brazilian history followed it in 1979, as over three million workers participated in more than one hundred strikes.[31]

This dramatic resurgence of the labor movement placed it at the forefront of a broad spectrum of social movements then emerging in opposition to the authoritarian regime. Though many of its actions began as worker demands, the protests quickly became more overtly political. Initially factory based, the movement led by labor spread in two complementary directions. The first went beyond the union sector to the larger working-class neighborhoods and communities, where labor protests won the active involvement and material support of church groups and the larger community. Second, the labor movement moved beyond narrower workers' issues to champion the demands and concerns of the lower classes more generally. Though many groups already expressed antiauthoritarian sentiment, the labor movement identified itself with a broad constituency and played an important role in building and leading a more unified, prodemocratic mass movement.[32] In addition, labor leaders became important national political figures who articulated broad political demands.

When the government, defensively scrambling to divide the opposition, abandoned its two party project, unions organized an avowedly socialist Workers'

296

Party, further frustrating the government's attempt to exorcise the left. This party served as an "instrument of struggle for the conquest of political power" by embracing an overtly political strategy predicated on the attainment of a democratic regime.[33] Thus, labor leadership expanded from union-based activity not only to a broader social movement, but also to a political organization. By 1983 labor mobilization culminated in a strike of over three million workers, and the following year workers participated in a massive campaign for direct presidential elections. Though the campaign was not successful in its immediate goals, it helped deepen the succession crisis faced by the regime and force the government to allow an opposition victory when the electoral college chose the first civilian president in 1985.

Hence organized labor played an important role in the Brazilian transition. It provided more than the mass pressure used by traditional party leaders in pursuing their own strategies. Labor protest and mobilization were directly responsible for expanding political and electoral space to include a new force on the left and for securing the legality and participation of the union-based Brazilian Workers' Party.

Uruguay Uruguay's authoritarian regime did not originate in a definitive military coup but rather in a two-sided process in which democracy eroded and the military gradually increased its autonomy and took over as it conducted an "internal war" against urban guerrillas. The military-dominated regime thus continued to seek electoral legitimation and the collaboration of political parties. As in Brazil, the Uruguayan military committed itself to regularly scheduled elections and developed projects for a new regime. At the same time, the labor movement was an important prodemocratic actor in the transition process and figured prominently in the events leading up to the installation of a democratic regime in 1985.[34]

The "gradual coup" was completed by 1973, though the military initially continued to rule behind the civilian façade of the elected president and retained its commitment to holding the elections scheduled for 1976. As the elections approached, the military abandoned that commitment and devised a new plan for "limited redemocratization" under military control and created a civilian-military body charged with drafting a constitution, which would be submitted to a plebiscite in 1980.[35] When the plebiscite was held, voters defeated the constitution, throwing the government project off track. Once again relying on party collaboration, the military initiated conversations with the traditional parties and proposed a transition in 1985 according to a new constitution it would negotiate with the parties. To rehabilitate the parties, a new law, written in collaboration with party leaders, called for primary elections in 1982. The primaries dealt the military another defeat: instead of the intended purge of the parties in favor of the collaborating factions, factions less friendly to the government were victorious.

The following years have been analyzed in terms of the "coup poker" strategies

297

89

of the parties, the alternating harder and softer lines of the government, and the moves and countermoves of an elite strategic game. With stops and starts, formal negotiations took place between the military and party leaders, culminating in the 1984 Naval Club Pact, signed by the participants, who in the end included the left parties except for the Communists. In accord with the agreements laid down in the pact, elections were held later that year, and a new democratic government took power in 1985.

This standard account misses an additional story from below in which the labor movement played an important part. That organized labor was an avid prodemocratic actor can be seen in its initial resistance. The day the military made the final move to assure its political control by closing the legislature in 1973, workers began a general strike against the dictatorship, thereby emerging as the only group to register its opposition publicly. For two weeks thousands of workers occupied factories, perpetrated acts of sabotage, and closed down the economy until the strike was broken. If the labor movement was not heard from in the following years, it was due to the ensuing repression in which unions were dismantled and many leaders were arrested or forced into exile.

Mass actors reemerged in connection with three developments. The first was the stunning defeat dealt the military in the 1980 plebiscite, not because of opposition parties, which hardly had an opportunity to mobilize, but because the electorate used the vote to reject the military's project. It has been suggested that, although unions were also severely repressed at the time, workers played an important clandestine role in mobilizing for the "no" victory.[36] Despite the appearance of "surrogates" for the exiled or imprisoned political leaders of the noncollaborating parties and factions, the plebiscite was clearly a case of mass action and victory from below.

Second, the outcome of the 1982 party primaries may have been significantly affected by union activity. A law of the previous year authorized unions at the enterprise level. Though the law was very restrictive, in a contested decision workers decided not to reject it but to use it both to organize openly and to gain some legal protection. From the outset, these enterprise unions had a democratic political program, so that the primaries took place in a period of increasing labor mobilization.

Third, and more definitively, the limited liberalization following the plebiscite created space for the opposition to mobilize. Along with the cooperativists, the union movement began to revive in 1982, first at the enterprise level and then at the national level when the Inter-Union Plenary of Workers (PIT) was formed. Linked with the grass-roots, the PIT had a special capacity for mass mobilization. On May Day 1983 the PIT carried out the first major demonstration since 1973, attracting an estimated 100,000 to 200,000 people, and explicitly called for the immediate return of democratic liberties.[37] The May Day demonstration catapulted the PIT to

298

the leadership of the social movement and, according to Caetano and Rilla, represented a qualitative change in the politics of transition.[38]

For the next year, collective actors, especially the PIT, set the pace and led the prodemocracy opposition. In the face of constant pressure from mass protest, the military was ultimately forced to retreat. In the beginning of 1983 the military attempted to write yet another new constitution, but by the end of the year important sectors of the military dropped the idea and began to focus instead on finding "the best exit."[39]

The general strike called by the PIT in January 1984 gave a decisive impetus to the military's retreat. Previously, it had responded to growing mobilization with increased repression. After the strike it lifted censorship and allowed the Communist leader of the left-wing *Frente Amplio* to return to the country. The strike also changed the relationship between the traditional parties and the social movement. Sanguinetti, the leader of the opposition faction of the Colorado Party, in effect apologized to the PIT for his party's opposition to the successful January strike and proposed a reorganization of the democratic opposition to coordinate the activities of the parties (including the left) and the PIT in a new *Multipartidaria*.

During the next months the *Multipartidaria* entered prenegotiations with the government, while it kept up the pressure by calling a series of symbolic one day strikes. These strikes succeeded in pressuring the government to make concessions, including, at the end of July 1984, legalization of the *Frente Amplio* and its constituent parties, except for the Communist Party and the Tupamaros. Negotiations came to a rapid conclusion in the Naval Club Pact, signed in August, in which the military got very little (the most popular Blanco candidate as well as some *Frentistas* were excluded from running in the November transition elections). The PIT's protests were thus important not only in pushing the transition forward, but also in forming the *Multipartidaria* as a more inclusive democratic opposition that negotiated the end of authoritarianism.

Conclusion

Although it would be wrong to treat labor organizations as *the* principal force behind democratization at the end of the twentieth century, the literature as a whole has erred in the other direction in portraying transitions as primarily an elite project, a conversation among gentlemen, with labor protest having relatively little consequence. It has done so even though case study analyses by country experts have regularly pointed to the key role of collective action in general and labor protest in particular. Hence there is a disjuncture between the evidence presented in case study material and the general interpretations offered in the literature on transitions.

299

Why have scholars who study transitions from a comparative theoretical perspective failed to recognize the importance of workers and other collective actors? Empirical oversight on the part of comparative theorists is not the reason. Our disagreement is not over the facts: we have relied on the same secondary literature as proponents of the dominant framework and, where relevant, have even used their own original research. Rather, we disagree over analytical framing. In necessarily privileging some facets of reality over others, frameworks can be useful in illuminating particular questions, but they should not be made hegemonic.

The original framework was appropriate in problematizing a leader-based strategy for achieving democratization. However, this framework does not travel well to other analytic concerns. When adopted more generally, it becomes a conceptualization of democratic transitions as fundamentally driven by and ultimately "about" intraelite dynamics and politics within the state, while it ignores other important questions. Scholars working within the assumptions of the dominant framework lack the means to conceptualize the role of social opposition adequately, even when they clearly want to acknowledge its importance. Linz and Stepan, for example, acknowledge that Spanish political reform occurred in a "context of heightened societal pressure for, and expectations of, change" and that "popular pressure kept the transition going forward." Yet they resist situating the role of mass pressure and collective action theoretically on a level equal to elite negotiation and designate Spain "a 'regime initiated transition' *although* under the pressure of society."[40]

In sum, our analysis has supplemented the focus on elites with one on collective action by paying particular attention to the labor movement. In initial stages of democratization, labor mobilization in the pattern of destabilization/extrication contributed to divisions among authoritarian incumbents, who previously had no transitional project. During relatively early stages in the transitions game labor protest for democracy helped to derail the legitimation projects of incumbents.

In later stages of the transition labor mobilization had two effects. First, depending on the pattern, protest provoked or quickened the transition and kept it on track. These effects were the consequence of pressure exerted to the very end. Our case evidence thus calls into question the perspective that labor restraint during the final transition phase contributes to democracy by convincing elites that democracy can lead to social and political order, thereby facilitating elite negotiations.[41] In fact, unprecedented levels of labor mobilization occurred in Spain up through the elections of 1977; labor protest in Peru continued until the constituent assembly elections; the pressure of collective action, including labor protest, accelerated in Brazil in the final stage; and the labor movement in Uruguay continued to flex its muscles through a series of one day strikes.

Second, mobilization and protest won labor-based parties a place among the negotiators and also in the successor regimes. The Peronists in Argentina, the

300

Ruth Berins Collier and James Mahoney

Spanish Communist Party, the Peruvian left, and to some degree Uruguay's *Frente Amplio* all won such a place. Even in Brazil, where no negotiating role was attained, collective action underpinned the founding of the socialist Brazilian Workers' Party. The collective action of labor movements thus played a key democratic role not only in propelling a transition, but also in expanding political space and the scope of contestation in the new democratic regime.

NOTES

Ruth Berins Collier would like to acknowledge the support of the Center for Advanced Study in the Behavioral Sciences and the National Science Foundation (Grant No. SBR-9022192). The authors would also like to thank David Collier, Giuseppe Di Palma, Robert Fishman, Guillermo O'Donnell, Gabriela Ippolito-O'Donnell, and Philippe Schmitter for their comments.

1. The exemplar of this framework is Guillermo O'Donnell and Philippe C. Schmitter, *Transitions from Authoritarian Rule: Tentative Conclusions about Uncertain Democracies* (Baltimore: The Johns Hopkins University Press, 1986). See also James Malloy and Mitchell Seligson, eds., *Authoritarians and Democrats: Regime Transition in Latin America* (Pittsburgh: University of Pittsburgh Press, 1987); Enrique Baloyra, ed., *Comparing New Democracies: Transition and Consolidation in Mediterranean Europe and the Southern Cone* (Boulder: Westview, 1987); Giuseppe Di Palma, *To Craft Democracies: An Essay on Democratic Transitions* (Berkeley: University of California Press, 1990); John Higley and Richard Gunther, eds., *Elites and Democratic Consolidation in Latin American and Southern Europe* (Cambridge: Cambridge University Press, 1992).

2. O'Donnell and Schmitter, pp. 52, 55.

3. On the elaboration of Linz's initial distinction between transition by *reforma* and transition by *ruptura*, see Juan Linz, "Some Comparative Thoughts on the Transition to Democracy in Portugal and Spain," in Jorge Braga de Macedo and Simon Serfaty, eds., *Portugal since the Revolution: Economic and Political Perspectives* (Boulder: Westview, 1981); Donald Share and Scott Mainwaring, "Transitions through Transaction: Democratization in Brazil and Spain," in Wayne Selcher, ed., *Political Liberalization in Brazil: Dynamics, Dilemmas, and Future Prospects* (Boulder: Westview, 1986); Samuel Huntington, *The Third Wave: Democratization in the Late Twentieth Century* (Norman: University of Oklahoma Press, 1991); J. Samuel Valenzuela, "Democratic Consolidation in Post-Transitional Settings: Notion, Process, and Facilitating Conditions," in Scott Mainwaring, Guillermo O'Donnell, and J. Samuel Valenzuela, eds., *Issues in Democratic Consolidation* (Notre Dame: University of Notre Dame Press, 1992).

4. This analysis is based primarily on Nigel Haworth, "The Peruvian Working Class, 1968–1979," in David Booth and Bernardo Sorj, eds., *Military Reformism and Social Classes: The Peruvian Experience, 1968–1980* (London: Macmillan, 1983); Julio Cotler, "Military Interventions and 'Transfer of Power to Civilians' in Peru," in Guillermo O'Donnell, Philippe Schmitter, and Laurance Whitehead, eds., *Transitions from Authoritarian Rule: Latin America* (Baltimore: The Johns Hopkins University Press, 1986); Nigel Haworth, "Political Transition and the Peruvian Labor Movement," in Edward Epstein, ed., *Labor Autonomy and the State in Latin America* (Boston: Unwin Hyman, 1989); Henry Pease García, *Los caminos del poder: Tres años de crisis en la escena política* (Lima: DESCO, 1979); Cynthia McClintock, "Peru: Precarious Regimes, Authoritarian and Democratic," in Larry Diamond, Juan Linz, and Seymour M. Lipset, eds., *Democracy in Developing Countries: Latin America* (Boulder: Lynne Rienner, 1989); Latin American Bureau, *Peru: Paths to Poverty* (London: Latin American Bureau, 1985); Henry Dietz, "Elites in an Unconsolidated Democracy: Peru during the 1980s," in

301

Higley and Gunther, eds.; Julio Cotler, *Democracia e integración nacional* (Lima: Instituto de Estudios Peruanos, 1980).

5. David Scott Palmer, *Peru: The Authoritarian Tradition* (New York: Praeger, 1980), p. 114.

6. Dietz, p. 241.

7. Latin American Bureau, p. 70.

8. Haworth, "The Peruvian Working Class," p. 76.

9. This analysis is based primarily on Gerardo Munck, "State Power and Labor Politics in the Context of Military Rule: Organized Labor, Peronism, and the Armed Forces in Argentina, 1976–1983," (Ph.D. diss., University of California, San Diego, 1990); Andres Fontana, *Fuerzas armadas, partidos políticos y transición a la democracia en Argentina* (Buenos Aires: Estudios CEDES, 1984); Ariel Colombo and V. Palermo, *Participación política y pluralismo en la Argentina contemporánea* (Buenos Aires: Centro Editor de América Latina, 1985); Edward Epstein, "Labor Populism and Hegemonic Crisis in Argentina," in Epstein, ed.; Ronaldo Munck, *Argentina: From Anarchism to Peronism* (London: Zed Books, 1987); James McGuire, "Interim Government and Democratic Consolidation: Argentina in Comparative Perspective," in Yossi Shain and Juan Linz, eds., *Interim Governments and Transitions to Democracy* (Cambridge: Cambridge University Press, 1996).

10. G. Munck, pp. 268–84.

11. Ibid., pp. 305–6.

12. Ibid., pp. 318–19.

13. Ibid., p. 326.

14. R. Munck, pp. 78, 79.

15. G. Munck, p. 327.

16. R. Munck, p. 79.

17. McGuire, p. 189.

18. See, for example, Huntington, pp. 125–27; Share and Mainwaring; Linz, "Some Comparative Thoughts"; Kenneth Medhurst, "Spain's Evolutionary Pathway from Dictatorship to Democracy," in Geoffrey Pridham, ed., *New Mediterranean Democracies: Regime Transition in Spain, Greece, and Portugal* (Totowa: Frank Cass, 1984); Di Palma, pp. 6–8; Richard Gunther, "Spain: The Very Model of the Modern Elite Settlement," in Gunther and Higley, eds.; Terry Lynn Karl and Philippe Schmitter, "Modes of Transition in Latin America, Southern and Eastern Europe," *International Social Science Journal*, 128 (May 1991); Juan Linz and Alfred Stepan, *Problems of Democratic Transition and Consolidation: Southern Europe, South America and Post-Communist Europe* (Baltimore: The Johns Hopkins University Press, 1996).

19. In addition to the sources in the previous note, this discussion is based primarily on José Maravall, *The Transition to Democracy in Spain* (London: Croom Helm, 1982); José Maravall, *Dictatorship and Dissent* (London: Tavistock, 1978); Raymond Carr and Juan Pablo Fusi Aizpurua, *Spain: Dictatorship to Democracy* (London: George Allen & Unwin, 1979); Paul Preston, *The Triumph of Democracy in Spain* (London: Methuen, 1986); Robert Fishman, *Working-class Organization and the Return of Democracy in Spain* (Ithaca: Cornell University Press, 1990); Victor Pérez-Díaz, *The Return of Civil Society: The Emergence of Democratic Spain* (Cambridge, Mass: Harvard University Press, 1993); Joe Foweraker, "The Role of Labor Organizations in the Transition to Democracy in Spain," in Robert Clark and Michael Haltzel, eds., *Spain in the 1980s: The Democratic Transition and a New International Role* (Cambridge: Ballinger, 1987); José Félix Tezanos, Ramón Cortarelo, and Andrés de Blas, eds., *La transición democrática española* (Madrid: Sistema, 1989).

20. Maravall, *The Transition to Democracy*, p. 14.

21. Maravall, *Dictatorship and Dissent*, p. 33.

22. Car and Fusi, p. 192.

23. Ibid., pp. 205–6.

24. Ibid., p. 210.

Ruth Berins Collier and James Mahoney

25. Preston, p. 91.
26. Linz and Stepan, *Problems of Democratic Transition*, p. 92.
27. Pérez-Díaz, pp. 238–39, 242.
28. This analysis is based primarily on Thomas Skidmore, *The Politics of Military Rule in Brazil, 1964–1985* (New York: Oxford University Press, 1988); Maria Helena Moreira Alves, *State and Opposition in Military Brazil* (Austin: University of Texas Press, 1985); Gay Seidman, *Manufacturing Militance: Workers' Movements in Brazil and South Africa, 1970–1985* (Berkeley: University of California Press, 1994); Margaret Keck, *The Workers' Party and Democratization in Brazil* (New Haven: Yale University Press, 1989); Maria Helena Moreira Alves, "Trade Unions in Brazil: A Search for Autonomy and Organization," in Epstein, ed.
29. Keck, p. 42.
30. Alves, *State and Opposition*, pp. 194–97.
31. Ibid., p. 199.
32. Seidman, p. 197.
33. Ibid., p. 169.
34. This analysis is based primarily on Gerardo Caetano and José Rilla, *Breve historia de la dictadura (1973–1985)* (Montevideo: CLAEH/Ediciones de la Banda Oriental, 1991); Luis González, *Political Structures and Democracy in Uruguay* (Notre Dame: University of Notre Dame Press, 1991); Charles Gillespie, *Negotiating Democracy: Politicians and Generals in Uruguay* (Cambridge: Cambridge University Press, 1991); Juan Rial, *Partidos políticos, democracia y autoritarismo* (Montevideo: CIESU/Ediciones de la Banda Oriental, 1984); Gerónimo De Sierra, *El Uruguay post-dictadura: Estado-política-actores* (Montevideo: Facultad de Ciencias Sociales, Universidad de la República, 1992); Martin Gargiulo, "The Uruguayan Labor Movement in the Post-Authoritrian Period," in Epstein, ed.; Jorge Chagas and Mario Tonarelli, *El sindicalismo Uruguayo bajo la dictadura, 1973–1984* (Montevideo: Ediciones del Nuevo Mundo, 1989).
35. Rial, vol. 1, pp. 73–74.
36. De Sierra, p. 218.
37. Ibid., p. 220; Gillespie, p. 131.
38. Caetano and Rilla, p. 91.
39. Ibid., p. 95.
40. Linz and Stepan, *Problems of Democratic Transition*, p. 88 (emphasis added).
41. In addition to O'Donnell and Schmitter, see especially J. Samuel Valenzuela, "Labor Movements in Transitions to Democracy: A Framework for Analysis," *Comparative Politics*, 21 (July 1989).

303

The Institutional Roots of Popular Mobilization: State Transformation and Rural Politics in Brazil and Chile, 1960–1995

PETER P. HOUTZAGER

Institute of Development Studies, University of Sussex

MARCUS J. KURTZ

Ohio State University

The past thirty years in Latin America have produced tremendous transformations of the state's role in society, both in the scope of its activities and the extent of its presence. Sometimes this has led to the state's unprecedented expansion into the far reaches of economic and social life, other times to its retreat from direct institutional presence in favor of indirect market-mediated linkages to society. The impact of these transformations on associational life and the quality of political participation has to some extent been obscured in recent scholarly work on democratic transition and consolidation, important as these issues are.[1] This paper explores how the transformations in the deeper "structural linkages" between state and society have affected political organization and mobilization in rural Brazil and Chile. In so doing, we contend that institutions not normally seen as central to democratic politics are in fact crucial to understanding political participation and mobilization.

What are these institutional patterns and why do they matter? By structural linkages we mean the gamut of productive, social, and regulatory functions of the state that help define the boundaries between public and private, including the systems of labor relations, social welfare, and land tenure.[2] These deep linkages help shape interests in society and provide (or deny) resources to contending social actors. Unlike political linkages, they need not change with regime transitions. Democratization changes the institutional mechanisms through which elites are selected and opens up new avenues through which social groups can make claims on the state. But, especially in cases of pacted or negotiated transition, transformations at the regime level are attained precisely by freezing other state institutions created under authoritarianism.[3]

0010-4175/00/2629-0446 $9.50 © 2000 Society for Comparative Study of Society and History

We argue that new structural state-society linkages forged under military rule shaped political participation and mobilization in the post-authoritarian countrysides of Brazil and Chile (after 1985 and 1989, respectively). In particular, we argue that the different forms these structural linkages took in the two countries contributed decisively to distinct political outcomes—the dramatic increase in popular mobilization in Brazil, which succeeded in placing agrarian issues at the center of national debate, and the virtual collapse of a formerly potent rural union movement in Chile. We elaborate precisely how military-era state reorganization of labor relations, land tenure, and social provision contributed to these very different political outcomes after democratization.

Scholars have by and large taken one of two positions on the more general question of how state structures and policy initiatives affect civil society. The first holds that a "large" or vigorous state can disrupt the bases for associational life and "crowd out" civil groups. State-society relations are a zero-sum game from this perspective, and gains for one come at the expense of the other.[4] The second position holds that state and society are "mutually constitutive" and reinforce each other. Proponents of this position suggest that a strong state can, under certain circumstances, foster associational activity and help create the bases for a dense civil society, which in turn increases the efficacy of state action. The central concern of these scholars is to identify the conditions under which state-society relations lead to a strengthening of democracy or development.[5] Our position is closest to the second group of scholars.

Brazil and Chile offer a particularly good paired comparison through which to explore these issues. The military governments in Brazil (1964–1985) and Chile (1973–1989) both carried out extensive agricultural modernization projects that in each case succeeded in creating internationally competitive agroexport sectors. Both countries experienced a significant reengineering of state institutions in rural areas and agrarian change. Upon democratization, the Brazilian countryside experienced an unprecedented level of mobilization, and new rural movements succeeded in forcing agrarian issues to the forefront of political debate. In contrast, the Chilean countryside was quiescent and politically invisible. Yet it was Chile in the pre-authoritarian period, not Brazil, that had one of Latin America's most highly-organized and politicized agrarian sectors, and therefore had a strong social and institutional legacy of popular mobilization on which to build. By comparison, few regions in Brazil had a tradition of popular mobilization prior to military rule.

How do transformations in state-society structural linkages help us account for the scope of popular organization in Brazil and its collapse and irrelevance in Chile? The different paths to economic modernization pursued by the military in Brazil and Chile—developmental and neoliberal, respectively—created very different parameters for agrarian mobilization in the post-authoritarian period. Specifically, the developmental and neoliberal models produced different state structures and systems of labor relations, which had polar effects on the bases of rural associational life and collective action. The developmental model in Brazil established an interventionist state in rural areas, which included a corporatist system of labor relations, a broad-based program of social provision, and increased state regulation of land. This institutional configuration facilitated the expression of collective identities around new issues brought into the public domain, and provided rural social groups with critical material and organizational resources. In contrast, neoliberalism in Chile produced a minimalist state heavily reliant on market forces, including a pluralist and highly decentralized system of labor relations, a privatized pension system, and an efficient new land market. The state's retreat from economic and social spheres eroded vital material and organizational resources in rural communities and undermined collective identification by taking many agrarian issues off the political agenda and "privatizing them."

The new structural linkages forged under military rule—a time when each state enjoyed a high degree of autonomy from popular pressures—were carried over into the democratic regimes in both Brazil and Chile. The transition pacts negotiated by political elites left intact the development models pursued under military rule. As a result of this institutional carryover, Brazilian rural movements found urban allies who competed for rural support around the new agrarian issues, while in Chile agrarian issues continued to be excluded from the political agenda and urban parties did not bid against each other for rural support. In both cases the rural sector remained important in national political dynamics. In Brazil, rural issues were forced onto the national political agenda. In Chile, the absence of rural mobilization was crucial to the stability of democratic politics.[6]

AN INSTITUTIONAL APPROACH TO POPULAR MOBILIZATION

The institutional approach we take in this paper focuses on the impact of different patterns of structural state-society linkages on popular mobilization. We suggest that the form of state "penetration" of society and the types of structural linkages created to different sectors influence whether and how movements organize. The state's role in economic regulation and social provision influences three critical dimensions of collective action. These are: the bases for group solidarity and identity formation, the level of material and organizational resources available to rural actors, and the availability of urban allies. We contrast our explanation with approaches that focus on regime dynamics and the social legacies of past mobilization.

The state's influence on popular mobilization occurs through several mechanisms. The state provides a target for mobilization, favors and protects particular forms of political actions while discouraging others, and plays a key role in delimiting the range of issues around which social groups organize. For example, the legal framework it establishes and the specific policy initiatives it undertakes bring certain issues into the public sphere, but not others. As it advances into or retreats from policy areas, the national political agenda widens or narrows, in effect defining and redefining critical parameters of the political arena itself. In so doing, the state defines the issues around which rural social groups may coalesce, and delimits the bases on which rural movements can forge alliances with urban political actors.[7]

More concretely, the provision of physical infrastructure (roads, telephone service, railways) and public transportation reduce the cost of collective action and contribute importantly to organizing efforts on a regional, and especially national, scale.[8] Finally, direct state support for local organizing efforts can have a critical impact. State elites have frequently encouraged and subsidized a variety of associational forms in order to create new political allies or enhance the efficacy of state action. States have offered organizational support, access to resources and subsidies, and even a degree of protection from repression by local political elites. Corporatist labor regimes, with varying degrees of state control, have been an extreme example of such efforts in Latin America, but a variety of other forms outside the system of labor relations can be identified as well.[9]

Our attention to state institutions does not imply that regime change does not have an important impact on popular mobilization in developing countries. Numerous studies have shown how the easing of repression and opening of political space with democratization contributed to the emergence of new social movements. However, the cases of Brazil and Chile suggest that democratization is only a piece of the puzzle, and alone cannot account for which social groups mobilize, around what claims, and in what types of movements. For example, the comparatively greater vitality of the post-transition Chilean political parties does not explain our outcome; it is in Brazil, with its inchoate party system, that mobilization emerges. We therefore focus on how the new institutional arrangements created with the modernization of agriculture affected the ability of social groups to coalesce and engage in collective action.

In the analysis that follows each case begins with a brief overview of the pre-coup period, then goes on to examine the political and institutional framework the two militaries erected to implement their respective development models. We look at how changes wrought in the areas of land reform, labor relations, and social provision affected the capacity of rural social groups to organize and mobilize. We pay particular attention to their impact on peasant access to resources and local organization, group solidarity, and the availability of elite allies. The analyses culminate with an interpretation of the interplay between the new political environment in the transitions to democracy and the reemergence of rural popular movements.

BRAZIL: DEVELOPMENTALISM AND POPULAR MOBILIZATION

The military in Brazil (1964–1985) pursued a developmentalist model that established a highly interventionist state in rural areas. The new model represented a shift from the previous import-substitution strategy to a protected but export-promoting approach that sought to redefine the country's insertion into the international economy and foster national integration. In the countryside, the new developmental model had three prongs: the creation of an export-oriented agro-industrial sector, national territorial integration, and the incorporation of formerly excluded rural social groups. While the developmental state had been firmly implanted in urban areas in the 1930s and 1940s, in the countryside the traditional pattern of oligarchic domination had remained in place up until the coup. The new model therefore brought profound changes in the role and structure of the state in rural areas. These changes laid the foundation for the emergence of several national rural movements and an unprecedented popular mobilization in the democratic regime. The new movements in turn sought to expand the role of the state in the countryside, enhance its capacity to deliver services and regulate rural labor relations, and strengthen its agencies responsible for agrarian reform.

On the one hand, the military's effort to institutionalize state control over rural labor through a corporatist labor regime created a new institutional space within which rural groups could organize and gain access to unprecedented resources. On the other hand, the state's expanded role in rural social and economic life, along with agrarian legislation enacted in the early 1960s, brought an array of agrarian issues into the public domain, creating new bases on which movements could build collective identities transcending regional specificities. In addition, during the democratic transition, political actors from the far left to the far right, including prominently the progressive wing of the Catholic Church, sought to mobilize rural allies around these new issues, placing them at the center of national political debate.

Brazilian rural movements entered the democratic period with an extensive organizational base and important political allies and, in contrast to Chile, rapidly emerged as national political actors. By the time Brazil held direct presidential elections in 1989, several national rural movements had organized a series of agricultural strikes and mass protests over such diverse issues as agrarian reform, agricultural credit and prices, social security, and health care.[10] The largest of the new movements was the corporative Movimento Sindical dos Trabalhadores Rurais (Rural Workers' Union Movement), with over eight million members and thirty-two hundred unions. Smaller but often more highly mobilized movements, such as the new unionism movement associated with the labor entity Central Única dos Trabalhadores (CUT), the Movement of the Landless (MST), and the Rubber Tappers' Movement, represented hundreds of thousands more.

The countryside of the pre-coup period provides a benchmark from which to examine the changes wrought under military rule and their impact on rural political activity. The political alliance that sustained the state prior to the coup was built on an accommodation between modernizing urban sectors and the locally hegemonic rural oligarchies. The regulation of land and rural labor relations, as well as agricultural policy, resided in the hands of regional oligarchies ensconced in state-level government. Existing rural labor legislation, which allowed for unions and set a minimum wage, was not enforced. Instead, rural social relations were regulated by various forms of clientelism, superimposed on a wide array of land tenure arrangements. Social security and public health care, access to which urban workers had gained in the 1930s, also did not reach the countryside.[11] The structural linkages between the national state and the countryside therefore remained tenuous, and the post-war developmentalism did not reach far beyond urban centers.

In the years immediately prior to the 1964 military coup this picture changed somewhat. The political polarization in urban areas spilled over into the countryside, and the state, fearing that the archaic agrarian sector posed a critical bottleneck to economic development and a breeding ground for agrarian radicalism, sought to extend its authority into rural areas. A limited agrarian reform initiative was stymied by conservative rural elites, but regulation of rural labor advanced with the Rural Workers Statute (ETR) of 1963, which extended the urban corporatist labor regime to the countryside.[12] Fueled in part by these initiatives, a small number of regionally-based peasant mobilizations developed. At the time of the military coup, however, only an estimated half million people had joined unions, roughly four percent of the agricultural labor force.[13] There was only one significant (sector-wide) strike in agriculture in 1963, in the northeast's sugar industry, and it rigorously followed the letter of the new labor legislation.[14] The famous peasant leagues were already in decline. Unlike Chile during the same period, the movements that developed in Brazil therefore were limited in size, regional in scope, and generally moderate in their demands and ideological orientation.[15]

Military Rule and Agrarian Developmentalism (1964–1985)

The Brazilian military oversaw a vertiginous expansion of the state's role in the countryside. The post-1964 alliance among the military state-elite, national, and international business sectors led to a basic shift in the previous ISI development model. The first four years of military rule were consumed by efforts at inflation control and economic stabilization, but after 1968 the state took a lead role in redefining Brazil's entry into the global economy.[16] A cornerstone of this effort was the expansion of the developmentalist state into the countryside to foster the modernization of agriculture. The specific form this expansion took, and its efficacy, varied by region and sector, but the regulation of land and labor, and the provision of social welfare and agricultural credit, were brought into the state's purview for the first time.[17]

The foremost concern of the state-elite was the development of a competitive and diversified export-oriented agro-industry that could help redefine Brazil's insertion into the international economy and fuel a new cycle of economic growth. The expansion of the agricultural frontier into the Amazon region was expected to result in additional gains in agricultural production, as well as exploitation of its untold mineral wealth. Provision of ample and heavily subsidized credit, the federalization and expansion of agricultural research and extension services, and investment in physical infrastructure such as highways all underwrote the modernization of agriculture. Agricultural policy, however, was inevitably intertwined with national integration—that is, with the economic integration of sparsely settled regions and the extension of the national state's reach across national territory, including areas where the authority of local and regional oligarchies prevailed. The military therefore attempted, with varying levels of success, to centralize authority out of the hands of the oligarchies and create new bureaucratic machinery in rural areas to circumvent existing state and local government.

The incorporation of rural workers, broadly defined, into an institutionalized relationship with the state, and the regulation of rural labor relations, were central components of the military's agrarian policies. The military stimulated rural unionization, which it saw as a means of diffusing the potential threat from the left, slowing the flow of rural-to-urban migration, and strengthening the national state in rural areas where it had heretofore been largely absent. The military used the labor legislation enacted prior to the coup, the ETR, to extend the corporatist labor regime to rural areas. The law created a new legal category—*rural worker*—which included wage laborers, sharecroppers, and small farmers, and allowed for two types of territorially-based unions: "rural worker unions" (*sindicato dos trabalhadores rurais*) and "employer unions" (*sindicatos rurais*). In return for extensive state control, the legislation provided a stable revenue source—the union tax—and a representational monopoly, which greatly facilitated unionization.[18] It also extended a number of new labor and social rights to rural labor. The military expected unions, on the one hand, to deliver a social wage in the form of social security and health services and, on the other, to teach members their rights under national law, thereby creating citizens, and petition for the implementation of legislation through the labor courts.

A central component of the military's strategy to draw the rural population into the state-sanctioned union movement was the expansion of social security and health care. Social security had been extended to the countryside by law in 1963, but, as with most previous rural legislation, had not been implemented. In 1971, the military created PRORURAL, a program that gave rural workers a limited form of social security, health care, and other social benefits such as funeral-service subsidies (a major expense for the rural poor) for the first time. Benefits were hardly generous—retirement pensions, for example, were half the minimum wage—but, when combined, medical and dental care, retirement and disability pensions, and other services amounted to a substantial social wage. Rural unions played a prominent role in delivering the new benefits, by the early 1980s holding half of all the medical contracts and a large number of dental contracts. Within two years of its implementation almost a million people were receiving pensions, and by the early 1980s three million received some form of benefit from the program.[19]

State regulation of land expanded almost immediately after the coup with passage of the Land Statute of 1964. The statute's primary concern was the modernization of agricultural production, and it substantially expanded the state's authority over land titles and land tenure contracts, making them public and national decisions rather than the private concern of local elites. In addition, the Land Statute called for agrarian reform, providing a critical legal benchmark that different groups would later invoke in their claims for reform.[20] For the state-elite, asserting federal control over land was critical not only to the rationalization of land tenure, but also to the integration of the final and greatest frontier region—the Amazon, which covers over a third of national territory. The National Institute of Agrarian Reform and Colonization (INCRA) became the state's bureaucratic instrument for land matters in the 1970s, and would henceforth be a common target of rural movements making land claims and demanding agrarian reform.

Organizing under Authoritarian Rule

Several national, rural, popular movements emerged under authoritarian rule. The largest of the movements was the Rural Workers Union Movement, which was built within the confined institutional space created by the developmental state and corporatist labor regime, which together provided both an extensive organizational infrastructure and resources, as well as a coherent ideological framework. The movement focused primarily on rural wage labor issues, such as wage levels and enforcement of labor legislation, and on the expansion of the new social welfare system. Labor legislation specified in detail how unions should be organized, who could be members, and through what channels they could make claims. The union tax and PRORURAL contracts provided unprecedented resources.

The movement reinforced its multiple linkages to the state in several ways. It built an inclusive class-based identity around the legal category of 'rural worker' in order to replace an array of regional identities and link together diverse rural strata. At the core of the identity was the struggle for massive and immediate agrarian reform, a demand carefully formulated to match the language of the Land Statute of 1964. Barred from mobilizing in the 1968-1978 period, the movement sought to draw the state into mediating rural labor relations, fighting the arbitrary power of landowners by bringing cases before the labor courts and petitioning for implementation of national legislation. As the level of state control diminished after 1979, the movement expanded its repertoire and emphasized the use of strikes in the context of well-organized wage campaigns. The strikes also sought to activate the movement's linkages to the

103

state—the strikes rigorously followed the restrictive law enacted by the military in 1964 (changed only in 1988), and aimed to provoke state intervention and arbitration of the collective bargaining process.[21]

The movement grew rapidly, and by 1980 had 2,254 unions and twenty-one state federations (see Table 1). Membership reached almost seven million.[22] The strength of the movement and the extent of its mobilizational capacity were considerably smaller than its size suggests, however. The movement had a progressive national leadership with strong support in a number of regions, but a majority of rural unions were primarily concerned with delivering services on behalf of the state.[23] The movement's resource dependence on the state left it vulnerable as well.

A number of important social movements emerged alongside the corporatist union movement in the 1979–1985 period. Most of these movements emerged out of the popular organizing work of the progressive wing of the Catholic Church. The church's organizing work was shaped in basic ways by the new structural linkages binding the developmental state and rural communities, including the legally sanctioned channel for small farmer and agricultural worker representation—the existing corporative rural workers' movement. The Church became deeply involved in popular organizing in part as a reaction against the military's agrarian developmentalism, and especially the violent process of national integration of the Amazon region. Highly critical of the state-regulated union movement, the clergy focused much of their energy on organizing opposition movements to win control over local unions; this step was seen as the first of a series that would help rebuild the left and lead to the radical transformation of Brazilian society from below. They created a radical political-religious identity that nonetheless drew on the legal definition of rural workers. As the transition to democracy advanced during the 1980s, various social movements grew out of these Church efforts, including the new unionism affiliated with CUT, the Movement of the Landless, and the Movement of Families Affected by Dams. These movements organized around a variety of issues, but small farmers' and landless families' access to land stood out, and agrarian reform was a central demand.

Socio-economic Change and Mobilization. Much of the literature on peasant movements links mobilization to either disruptive socio-economic changes accompanying the modernization of the agrarian sector or a decline in standards of living. In Brazil neither explanation can account for the pattern of mobilization. First, popular mobilization followed a national pattern, and occurred both in regions where there was significant change and in ones where there was not. Second, mobilization occurred across a variety of social groups, from wage laborers to capitalized small farmers to landless families, which experienced the modernization of agriculture in very different ways. Groups that had gained and lost with the modernization all mobilized. Third, although there was a remarkable demographic shift from rural to urban areas, leaving only thirty-two per-

TABLE 1
Rural Unionization in Brazil, 1960–1990

	Unions* (legally recognized)	Union Membership** (in thousands)	Union Density***
1963	270	—	—
1970	1,066	1,500	9.4%
1980	2,254	6,898	40%
1990	2,811	8,314 (1988)	43%

*The number of unions comes from IBGE Sindicatos: Indicadores Sociais. Vol. 4 (Rio de Janeiro, 1990), and Pearson, "Small Farmer," n. p., and represents a conservative estimate.
**The numbers for 1970 and 1980 come from estimates by Maybury-Lewis, based on CONTAG reports. The 1990 figure is from IBGE (1990). There is considerable discrepancy between the two sets of numbers—Maybury-Lewis, The Politics of the Possible, 219, for example, puts union membership in 1986 at 9,929,538.
***Union density calculations are based on the Agricultural Census. Using the Demographic Census the rate increases substantially: eleven percent in 1970, fifty-four in 1980, and fifty-nine in 1990.

cent of Brazilians in rural areas by 1980 (down from fifty-five percent in 1960), income for rural wage laborers and small farmers in the countryside rose during this period and poverty declined.[24] Between 1964 and 1980 the average family income in rural areas rose from eighty percent of the minimum wage in 1960 to 160 percent in 1980.[25] Finally, although land concentration increased during the 1960–1980 period, different regions experienced widely divergent patterns of change, and the relationship to rural mobilization is tenuous. Two important areas for the corporative union movement—the states of Pernambuco and São Paulo—experienced a decrease in land concentration as the number of small and large properties fell. Two important poles of Church-supported movement activity—Rio Grande do Sul and Pará—experienced land concentration, but in very different ways. In the former, the subdivision of medium-sized properties led to a rise in small holdings; in the latter to an increase in large holdings' average size (even though the share of medium-sized farms increased and that of small ones fell).[26]

Rural Mobilization in the Democratic Regime (1985–1995)
The developmentalist model entered into crisis in the 1980s, a victim of oil shocks and the debt crisis. But the political pact that guaranteed the transition to democracy did not revise the state's role or alter its new institutional linkages to the rural sector. Hence, issues brought into the public sphere under the military regime became part of the new democratic political arena, as movements organized around them and national political actors competed for the new movements' support. As a result, the rural movements that emerged during

the 1970s and early 1980s were almost immediately integrated into the political alliances forming within the reemerging left. These alliances helped movements to establish themselves as significant political actors and to keep the rural issues around which they organized on the national political agenda.[27] Prominent among the issues around which movements mobilized and forged alliances were agrarian reform, labor relations, and social security.[28]

The Rural Workers' Union Movement entered the democratic transition with an impressive organizational network and, despite important weaknesses, represented a desirable ally to political elites. The movement joined a diffuse center-left block that included among others the traditional left (including what was left of the communist parties) and the progressive wing of the Party of the Brazilian Democratic Movement (PMDB). The movement negotiated its support with the Democratic Alliance—the broad coalition that oversaw the transition and elected the first civilian president—in return for government support for a national agrarian reform program and the consolidation of a form of liberalized state corporatism similar to that which prevailed in urban areas in the pre-coup period. The movement's national leadership also defined an important role for itself within the labor movement. It was a critical actor in the process leading to the creation of the two rival national labor organizations, the CUT and CGT (Confederação General dos Trabalhadores).[29]

Movements in the Church camp allied with the more sharply defined and militant left that created the labor central CUT and the Workers' Party (PT). In contrast to the Rural Workers Union Movement, this segment of the left refused to participate in the transition pact and stood in opposition to the new civilian (but conservative) government. Participation in the labor central and the party enabled the movements to place their demands in the political arena at the national level, including in Congress, and gave leaders national exposure.[30] In addition, various movement leaders were elected to local and national public office on the Workers' Party slate. In the case of the new unionism, the CUT played a critical role in unifying local and regional Church-sponsored groups into a single, ideologically coherent, national movement. Rural unionists had a significant presence in CUT as a result.[31] In addition, after the Constituent Assembly of 1988, the Movement of the Landless (MST) emerged as the principal force behind agrarian reform, and has proven to be one of Latin America's most visible and successful popular movements. It has obtained significant concessions from both national and state governments.[32]

Of the three areas of debate that we analyze, agrarian reform has been the most prominent and polemical in what was quickly dubbed the New Republic. The National Campaign for Agrarian Reform organized by CONTAG and various center and center-left politicians and civil associations succeeded in placing the issue in the AD's platform. As a result, one of the first acts of the new civilian government was to announce the National Agrarian Reform Plan in 1985. A strong conservative countermobilization succeeded in blocking the government's initiative, but the issue remains high on the national agenda to this day.[33] It was one of the most hotly contested items in the Constituent Assembly in 1988, where pro-reform forces submitted popular amendments—later defeated—proposing national agrarian reform with 1.2 million signatures. Despite the legislative reversals, the MST has since 1988 succeeded in pushing the government into expropriating significant tracts of land for redistribution. Between 1985 and 1996 the government redistributed 8,715,531 hectares of land to 219,386 families.[34]

The mobilization of rural movements around the issue of agrarian reform has had an important impact on how parts of the state are constituted in rural areas. The alliance between the Rural Workers' Union Movement and the Democratic Alliance, for example, led to the creation of the Ministry of Agrarian Reform (MIRAD) and a revival of the National Institute for Agrarian Reform and Colonization (INCRA). At the end of the 1980s INCRA was abolished and authority for carrying out agrarian reform was transferred to the conservative Ministry of Agriculture. Continued mobilization and political pressure by pro-reform movements and allies, and particularly by the MST, led in the early 1990s to the resurrection of INCRA and the creation of a new Extraordinary Ministry for Land Policy, which became responsible for agrarian reform. These two entities have led to an ad hoc but growing role for the state in land redistribution.

The systems of labor relations, health care, and social welfare were also important arenas of popular organizing and mobilization. The rural union movement has focused primarily on the defense of rural labor rights and wages, and used the corporatist labor regime to force the state to intervene on its behalf in labor disputes.[35] Strike activity has been substantial, especially when compared to pre-1964 levels. Only a year after the military's exit from power, rural strike activity reduced production by five million person-days.[36] There were strikes in Pernambuco's sugar zone in every year during the 1980s but two, and in São Paulo a wave of strikes that began in 1984 paralyzed a significant part of that state's sugarcane plantations, and later spread to orange growers.[37] Health care and social welfare, which in the 1960s neither existed nor were on the national agenda, became central demands of rural movements during the 1980s and 1990s and contentious issues in national politics. Tens of thousands of people took to the streets during the 1980s, particularly in the south of Brazil, to demand the expansion of health care services, extension of social security to women, and parity in benefits with urban workers.[38] The height of this campaign came with the 1988 constitution and its implementing legislation in the 1990s, which finally gave male and female rural workers the same level of benefits as urban workers, and created a truly universal social insurance program for the first time. The number of people who received welfare support grew from zero in the 1960s to six million in 1993.[39]

The rural movements in Brazil experienced serious crises at the end of the democratic transition in 1989, but nonetheless survived into the 1990s and succeeded in keeping their issues on the national agenda. The new unionism movement recently merged with the Rural Workers' Union Movement, which affiliated with CUT. With support from the Movement of the Landless, they have succeeded in reversing some of the previous losses in agrarian reform and at least temporarily stymied government efforts to reduce rural social provision. The movements have also increased their representation in Congress and local government. What impact the current process of state reform under President Fernando Henrique Cardoso will have on the rural movements is not yet clear.

CHILE: NEOLIBERALISM AND DEMOBILIZATION

The Chilean military regime (1973–1989) imposed a neoliberal development model that dramatically reduced the state's direct role in the regulation and organization of the rural economy and society. Like Brazil, the agrarian component of authoritarian development strategy was geared toward entry into the global economy, a marked departure from the import-substitution path Chile had pursued since the Great Depression. In the process of transformation, export agriculture blossomed, while the direct ties between peasants, rural unions, and the state were severed. The transformation of the structural linkages between state and society from direct institutional presence to indirection market mediation changed the national political dynamics around which rural politics was constructed. In the countryside, despite sharp declines in living standards, this change prompted the atrophy of peasant organization and protest, and narrowed the scope of political contestation. As state-society linkages became indirect and market-based, both the capacity of the state to act in the countryside and of peasants to mobilize against the state declined.

The imposition of the neoliberal model required a redefinition of the state's role, rather than a simple retreat from former developmental and social functions. New institutions were created to govern land and labor markets, as well as to provide old-age security. With respect to land tenure, many provisions of the former agrarian reform law were replaced by a system of well-defined individual and alienable land titles, creating the legal and physical infrastructure of an efficient land market de novo. In the arena of labor relations, the former semi-corporatist peasant labor law was replaced with a pluralist labor code that at once fragmented peasants into distinct strata, weakened the ability of unions to bargain, and removed the state from the adjudication of labor conflicts. It was a legal framework designed to individualize workers. Finally, the military replaced the former entitlement-based public welfare system with a private pension scheme and narrowly-targeted anti-poverty relief, a change that led to marked decline in rural coverage.

These institutional changes dramatically reduced the bases for collective action in what had been one of the best-organized and most militant peasantries on the South American continent. The reorganization of land and labor markets disrupted resources internal to the peasantry, while former publicly-provided supports for mobilization were withdrawn. Changes in the structure of state institutions also fragmented the interests of the peasantry by heightening regional and socioeconomic differences. Furthermore, neoliberalism changed the very boundaries of the national political agenda, removing issues of historic importance to peasants such as agrarian reform, water rights, the availability of inputs and credit, and crop prices from the post-transition debate. This altered the dynamics of national partisan competition in the transition to democracy, reducing both the salience of democratic politics for peasants, and the availability of allies. Efforts to spark organization—often by the very same leaders from the earlier period of mobilization, and with outside and NGO support—have been unsuccessful in this new political terrain. Bereft of allies and lacking internal resources, rural social groups were unable to reconstitute even a shadow of the militant movements of the 1960s and early 1970s. Ironically, after the democratic transition in Chile, peasant politics became a markedly quiescent and elite affair.

In the case of Chile, the benchmark from which to assess the impact of the military's development model on rural mobilization is markedly different from that of Brazil. During the 1960s and early 1970s successive reformist governments dramatically expanded state presence in rural areas. In response to stop-go spurts of growth and accelerating inflation, governing elites sought to enlarge internal markets for import substitutes by increasing peasant production and living standards. Serious agrarian reform, the expansion of social security to rural areas, and state regulation of rural labor relations brought the national state to the countryside in an effort to meet domestic food needs, expand markets, and save foreign exchange. [40]

The entry of the state into the countryside produced a highly competitive political dynamic that encouraged rural mobilization.[41] First, the Peasant Unionization Law (Ley 16.625) of 1967 established important connections between the state and rural workers.[42] The law set out the basic organizational structure of the union movement and funded it through a two percent tax on wages, levied on employers. The tax revenue was then channeled to the competing peasant union confederations—two leftist and two Christian Democrat—in proportion to their membership. Importantly, all categories of rural worker—landless and landholding, permanent and temporary alike—were under its terms simply "agricultural workers," and were grouped together within a single geographic area, the *comuna* (roughly equivalent to an American county). The state actively encouraged the organization of the rural working class by providing access to unprecedented resources and facilitating the formation of collective identification across geographic regions and social categories. It also became directly involved through unionization drives run by the agricultural extension service (INDAP).

Second, agrarian reform legislation aimed at widening the internal market was passed in 1967 (Ley 16.640), virtually without peasant pressure, and became a key institutional resource that, coupled with the availability of urban allies, played a central role in the ensuing mobilization.[43] The legislation raised expectations on the part of peasants, who, in response to the law, launched waves of direct action in an attempt to force expropriation. These mobilizations were supported by competing political parties (and their affiliated unions) as a way of expanding their rural support base.[44]

Chilean peasants, as one of a very few politically-unattached voting blocs in a highly competitive electoral arena, became central actors in the dynamics of national political competition. Agrarian issues—from agricultural modernization to land reform—became central to national political conflicts.[45] Three distinct political forces courted peasant support—Christian Democrats, a left-wing splinter from the Christian Democrats, and a Socialist-Communist alliance.[46] Chilean peasants therefore organized and mobilized in unprecedented ways because of the ready availability of allies, the manner in which crucial institutions encouraged collective identification, and because of the state's presence and support for rural unions. Unionization, strikes, and land invasions rose dramatically (See Table 2).

Authoritarianism, Neoliberalism, and Demobilization (1973–1989)

In the period of military rule in Chile (1973–1989) a dramatic reorientation of national developmental strategy was imposed, eventually coalescing into one of the most extensive and coherent free market models found in the contemporary world. At the same time, mobilizational politics was severely repressed in rural areas (as well as urban). Many scholars have assumed that the lack of mobilizational activity in the succeeding years was a function of the harshly repressive policies imposed by General Pinochet. But the fact that unionization rebounded substantially in urban areas after democratization but not in rural ones points to the partiality of this account. We contend that rural demobilization was achieved in part through a decidedly different mechanism—the neoliberal transformation of the structural linkages between state and rural society.

Chilean neoliberalism targeted export markets as the fundamental source of domestic economic dynamism. As a consequence, national production was reoriented toward primary products salable in foreign markets, and away from the costly and low-quality manufactured goods produced by protected Chilean industry.[48] In addition to traditional copper exports, this reorientation crucially included a substantial focus on nontraditional agro-exports (especially fruits, wines, and forestry products). To produce internationally-competitive products, the free importation of chemical inputs and/or productive technology was required, and former state monopolies on these goods were abolished and privatized. Similarly, the tariff barriers that had supported both manufacturing and traditional agriculture were reduced to a uniformly low ten percent level by 1979. Finally, state marketing boards for agricultural products were abolished. As a consequence, nontraditional agricultural output surged, and became an important component of foreign exchange earnings by the 1980s.[49]

TABLE 2

Unionization, Strikes, and Land Invasions in Chile

Year	Union Density[47]	Strikes	Land Invasions
1964	0.7%	n.d	0
1967	n.d.	693	9
1968	24.3	648	26
1969	31.2	1127	148
1970	33.9	1580	456
1971	38.1	1758	1278

SOURCES: For union density, 1964–1969, data are from Patricia Provoste and Wilson Cantoni, *Descripción numérica de la organización sindical campesina chilena 1968–1969* (Santiago, Chile: Fondo de Educación y Extensión Sindical [FEES], 1971), 21–38; For 1970–1971, see Gobierno de Chile, *Segundo mensaje del Presidente Salvador Allende ante el congreso pleno* (Santiago, Chile: Gobierno de Chile, 1972), 278, 858; Scully, *Rethinking the Center: Party Politics in Nineteenth and Twentieth Century Chile* (Stanford, CA: Stanford University Press), 156; Banco Central de Chile, *Indicadores económicos y sociales* (Santiago, Chile: Banco Central de Chile, 1989). For land invasions: Juan Carlos Marín, *Las tomas* (Santiago, Chile: ICIRA, 1972), 16, and Loveman, *Chile*, 286. For strikes, see Cristóbal Kay, "Agrarian Reform and the Transition to Socialism in Chile, 1970–1973," *Journal of Peasant Studies* 2, no. 4 (July 1975), 424.

The transition to a free market agricultural model also required lowering the cost of labor and guaranteeing the security of private property. It was the way in which land and labor markets were transformed that dismantled state institutions, fragmented the peasantry as a class, and narrowed the political agenda in such a way as to exclude most rural issues, thereby closing peasants off from urban allies.

Unlike the situation in Brazil, where agricultural modernization brought with it improvements in living standards, Chilean neoliberalism was an economic calamity from the peasant perspective. From a comparatively low level of twenty-five percent in 1970, rates of rural poverty rose to 53.5 percent toward the end of military rule.[50] We will see below that this impoverishment was accompanied by an increase in land concentration. Of our two cases, the objective bases for peasant grievances and mobilization are strongest in Chile. But mobilization actually occurred in Brazil. The explanation lies in the way agroexport orientation was imposed and how these policies transformed the structural linkages between state and rural society.

The Land Market, Agrarian Counter-Reform, and Demobilization. The first step in the reorientation of agriculture was the creation of a substantial private agro-export sector. At the time of the coup, however, nearly forty percent of the best agricultural land in the country was held in state-owned land reform coops. The pre-coup agrarian reform had abolished corporate land ownership and severely restricted the size of private land holdings (Ley 16.640). The central issue, then, was how to get the sixty-three percent of agricultural land held by peasants—in the form of smallholding or on the coops—into capitalist hands (see Table 3). The process began with a distribution of coop lands among peasants, former landlords, and sale at auction.[51] Most of the land then slipped through peasant hands, as market forces reconcentrated it in efficient-sized capitalist farms. Thus, the land market for peasant parcels became the key mechanism in the transformation of the distribution of agricultural property.

It was the process of creating land markets themselves that weakened the bases for peasant collective action—it placed them in competition with each other, and created a serious fragmentation of interests. Importantly, the legal infrastructure necessary to support a private market in land had to be created from scratch, a process that was hardly politically neutral. The agrarian reform "normalization"—the transfer of collective property to individual hands—required the state to: (1) define and assign definitive title to collectively owned property; (2) provide the mechanisms under which it could be transferred from one individual to another; and (3) remove individuals who did not receive land from their former residences, as rights to dwellings and usufruct on the old haciendas were incompatible with a strong regime of individual private property. These rules provoked a dramatic change in rural social structure and geography, adding physical disarticulation of communities to the already fragmented rural social world.

The privatization of reform sector lands was based on a point system, subject to an exclusion of all individuals who had participated in land invasion (Decreto Ley 208 of 1973). But since at least seventeen hundred land invasions had occurred between 1970 and 1972, an enormous number of peasants found themselves dispossessed for political reasons.[52] Thus, the first social differentiation introduced during the "normalization" of land tenure was the assignment of land only to "apolitical"—read conservative—peasants.

The data in fact confirm what could readily have been predicted. By 1978, only a few years into the privatization, nearly thirty-seven percent of land reform beneficiaries had wholly or partially ceded their land.[53] This was not, however, a process of social differentiation among peasants. Rather, only 6.5 percent of these sales were to other peasants. Indeed, 89.3 percent of the sales went to the emergent capitalist sector, consisting of marketers, capitalist farmers, urban professionals, and public functionaries.[54] This group began to constitute the new capitalist, agro-export class fragment (see Table 3).

The building of land markets also changed the set of issues on the national political agenda. Accessory privatizations absolved the state of responsibility for the provision of vital productive inputs. These were now to be supplied "equally" (meaning at the same price for all) by the private sector. As much as ISI had forced agrarian issues onto the national political agenda, neoliberalism worked to take them off. Privatization of trade, production, and services made what had formerly been crucial public institutions and resources for peasants into private transactions. Just as importantly, it transferred to individual hands the shared goods of the land reform cooperatives, removing the final concrete reason for

TABLE 3

The Reorganization of Land Tenure under Military Rule
(Percent of agricultural land in basic irrigated hectares.)

Farm Size Stratum	1965	1973	1976	1979[a]	1986	1990s
Minifundio	9.7	9.7	9.7	13.3	14.0	
Family Labor Farm	12.7	13.1	24.9	29.0	26.0	
Reform Sector	0.0	40.6	18.1	4.0	3.0	
PEASANTS	22.4	63.4	52.7	46.3	43.0	37.0
Capitalist Farms	22.2	36.6	43.4	36.3	31.0	
Large Agribusiness	55.4	0.0	2.9	16.9	26.0	
CAPITALIST	77.6	36.6	47.3	53.2	57.0	61.0

[a]These data were calculated by Jarvis working backward from property tax assessments, making the assumption that the value of a basic irrigated hectare was seventy-eight thousand pesos. For a justification, see Jarvis, *Chilean Agriculture*, 1021.
SOURCES: Adapted in part from Kurtz, "Free-Markets," 281. For 1965, see Instituto Nacional de Estadística. *IV Censo Nacional Agropecuario* (Santiago, Chile: INE, 1965). For 1973, see Luz Eugenia Cereceda and Fernando Dahse, *Dos décadas de cambios en el agro chileno* (Santiago, Chile: Instituto de Sociología. Pontificia Universidad Católica de Chile, 1980), 135. For 1976, see INE, *V Censo Nacional Agropecuario* (Santiago, Chile: INE, 1975). For 1979, see Lovell Jarvis, *Chilean Agriculture under Military Rule: From Reform to Reaction, 1973-1980* (Berkeley: Institute of International Studies, 1985), 10. For 1986 see Lovell Jarvis, "The Unravelling of the Agrarian Reform." in Cristóbal Kay and Patricio Silva eds., *Development and Social Change in the Chilean Countryside: From the Pre-Land Reform Period to the Democratic Transition* (Amsterdam: CEDLA, 1992), 199. For 1990s, see World Bank, *Chile: Estrategia para elevar la competitivdad agrícola y aliviar la pobreza rural* (Washington, DC: World Bank, 1995), 35.

peasant producers to organize collectively—to manage these cooperatives. Alternatives to the market-provided inputs were systematically eliminated.

The establishment of land markets also definitively removed even the distribution of land—perhaps the archetypal agrarian issue—from the political arena by allowing land to pass through peasant hands. As a result, long-run reconcentration of holdings would be much harder to challenge. Reestablishment of the old hacienda-oriented patterns of land tenure would have kept the issue of land reform alive in future political debates. Instead, the military brought the process of land reform to its "natural" conclusion—it distributed the remainder of the land technically in compliance with many of the terms of the 1967 agrarian reform law. Having done so, future changes in land tenure would be "legitimate"; any reconcentration would simply be the result of voluntary market transactions.

Thus, the creation of institutions supporting agricultural private property and land transactions, in the Chilean context, provoked peasant differentiation, changes in social geography, and a serious fragmentation of interests. The creation of institutions of private property created individuals, just as the creation of collective property had created meaningful social collectivities during the agrarian reform.

The State and Labor Relations: Restructuring and Demobilization. The creation of a flexible labor market in rural Chile first and foremost required a set of pluralist institutions to structure the contracting of labor and the organization of unions. The 1979 Labor Code provided the institutional framework for a pluralist replacement of the 1967 Peasant Unionization Law. These new institutional rules disrupted rural organization by: (1) undercutting the bases for collective identification; (2) dramatically reducing the efficacy, and therefore appeal, of unionization; and (3) removing the resources that formerly supported organization—in terms of both social and physical capital. When this was coupled with high levels of un- and underemployment, the fate of rural labor mobilization was sealed.

While peasant unionization did reemerge with legalization in 1979, the fragmentation and weakness of this movement mimicked the institutional fragmentation embodied in the new labor law. The rural labor movement was a declining shadow of its former self; as locals became disconnected from national confederations, membership consistently declined, unions divided by region and subsector, and, most critically, rarely managed to negotiate collective contracts.

How were existing interests and identities undermined by the changing labor institutions? Under the 1967 Peasant Unionization Law, the lowest level of organization was the comuna, and cultivators of any type—the sole exception was employers—would be joined in a single organization (Artículo 3). This was the only form of peasant union, and it was entitled to engage in collective bargaining with any of the employers within the comuna. In contrast to this very broad-based unionization of all rural cultivators under the catch-all phrase "agricultural worker," the 1979 Labor Code produced dramatic fragmentation in organization and interest formation. First, it replaced the single geographic union local with three different forms of organization: enterprise unions, including only the workers on a single farm; inter-enterprise unions for linking workers employed by two or more different employers; and independent unions for workers not directly dependent on any employer.[55]

Substantial additional distinctions between unions and types of members accompanied this fragmentation of organizational structures. First, of the three legal forms of unions, only enterprise unions were entitled to bargain collectively. Second, temporary workers—the newly dominant form of wage labor in the countryside—were not permitted to become members of enterprise unions and hence were excluded altogether from collective bargaining. Moreover, noncontiguous plots of land owned by the same individual constituted separate enterprises for unionization purposes (and a minimum of eight year-round employees was required for legal organization). Finally, open shops were compulsory, and any number of competing unions could be created within a single enterprise. Legal structures heightened distinctions between permanent and seasonal workers, between unionized and nonunionized workers on a single farm, and between the landed and landless (the former typically entering "independent" unions, the latter enterprise and inter-enterprise unions).

The new legal structure also radically reduced the resources available for organization. While the 1967 law provided for generous compulsory funding of unions via a tax levied on employers, the 1979 law provided only for dues paid voluntarily and directly by union members. Direct governmental support—formerly coming from the agricultural extension agency (INDAP) and the union outreach and education fund (FEES)—was abolished. While the 1967 law even required employers to provide union halls (Art. 12), finding locations in which union activists could physically meet with workers became quite difficult after 1979.

Finally, changes in the labor code shattered the bargaining power of the unions. While under the 1967 law it became illegal for a firm to operate during the course of a legal strike (except for emergency tasks), the 1979 law put a sixty-day limit on strike action (this limit has since been abolished). Similarly, after 1979 unions no longer had exclusive jurisdiction. Employers are now permitted to bargain individually or with arbitrary groups of workers in hopes of dividing their labor forces, even on unionized farms (Libro III, Art. 90). They can also prevent legal strikes during the harvest, the only time such strikes are likely to be effective.

When this highly restrictive organizational structure was linked with the socioeconomic background conditions prevalent in Chilean agriculture, fragmentation and demobilization resulted. One critical aspect has been the emergence of a very large seasonal labor force.[56] When such an inherently unstable labor market was combined with a fragmented labor relations system, the vulnerability of rural workers surged. In particular, the liberalization of the labor market was accompanied by the closing-off of the escape valve rural-to-urban migration had provided since the 1940s—urban unemployment reached catastrophic levels in the early 1980s. Rural labor markets themselves became extremely competitive.[57] Individuals were divided from each other by variations in property ownership, type of employment, and access to the few remaining institutional resources (which favored permanent employees). Interests fragmented, and the bases of collective organization evaporated.

The generation of a new, mobile, employment-seeking stratum was not politically neutral. It is important to remember that a large proportion of those not receiving land reform parcels were expelled because of Decree Law 208, which excluded anyone who had previously participated in a land invasion. Rural employers were well aware of this, and considered these former coop members politically dangerous, frequently refusing to hire them.[58] ICIRA shows that only 22.4 percent of these ex-reform sector peasants found year-round employment: a further 25.1 percent found seasonal employment, with the remainder in various conditions of disguised or open unemployment.[59] At the same time the cash shortage and low output levels prevented the new, individual peasant parcels from generating substantial levels of non-family employment.

This fragmentation, resource deprivation, and disempowerment is apparent in an examination of what little remains of the peasant union movement. Presently, organized workers are affiliated with five different national federations and confederations—two centrist and three leftist—with the majority of their membership attached to the moderate confederations.[60] Further, in a dramatic break with past practice, fully thirty-six percent of union members are unaffiliated with any national confederation at all, nor does any single confederation represent even twenty thousand workers.[61]

Social Provision and Interest Disaggregation. The final area of special importance in the rural sector was the privatization of social welfare and pensions. The private provision of pension services is depoliticizing because it makes the level of pension benefits a function of personal investment, which cannot be altered in obvious ways as a result of political pressure on the state. This is in marked contrast to the operation of the previous public defined-benefit system. In rural areas, political action was historically essential to the access of peasants to such state-provided social services. Such pressure, for example, was frequently used in order to force landlords to make their legally-required contributions to the former social security service. As such, political parties and unions were important mediators in the obtaining of pension benefits for rural workers.[62] In general, the pension system was divided into separate funds, with different benefits according to broad occupational classifications. This provided an obvious incentive for broad-based collective organization around shared interests shaped by the structure of this state welfare institution. With the destruction of these institutions, both the incentive for collective organization and the facilitating conditions for collective identification were eroded—inequality and social fragmentation increased.[63]

Despite the fact that employers are not responsible for paying for social security benefits, the privatized pensions system does build in strong dependencies on one's employer in the countryside. Participation is compulsory (and common) only for those with access to a year-round job, as suggested by the low coverage for temporary workers. But agricultural work, unlike most industry, is an inherently seasonal affair, and modern export agriculture much more so than traditional agriculture.[64] These permanent jobs are reserved for the most loyal workers, particularly since most of the protections against unfair dismissal have been removed from the labor law.[65] As a consequence, the low level of alternative employment helps employers transform economic power into political power in the countryside.

Given the low and uneven rural coverage rates and the "freedom" to choose between different pension plans, it is likely that most of the workers in any agricultural enterprise will not be covered by a pension plan, and those that are affiliated may be tied to different private funds. Thus, any conflicts that arise about pensions will involve only a fraction of the workers in a firm. And the sorts of issues that will be considered important will vary. In any event, the conflict will never be of a clearly collective character, as the employer is not the entity responsible for social provision. Whereas in the earlier period there was a homogenizing dynamic in the productive enterprises, under the current system there is an increasing degree of social differentiation.[66]

Rural Politics and the Democratic Regime (1989–1995)

The transition to a democratic regime in 1989 did not bring dramatic changes to the countryside. There was little resurgence in rural unionization, and issues important to peasants were left off the national agenda. Even though the remaining peasant organizations—through their umbrella organization, the Comisión Nacional Campesina (CNC)—were mostly directly linked to the reformist Concertación alliance, which won the three post-transition Presidential elections, little response was made to peasant demands. This was due in part to an implicit understanding among the opponents of military rule that the fundamental elements of neoliberalism would remain undisturbed as part of the pact securing the transition to democracy.[67] The agenda-constricting impact of the neoliberal model therefore carried over into the democratic regime and severely constrained competition for rural support. Linked to this was a remarkable conversion of formerly reformist and radical parties—from the Christian Democrats to the Socialists—to orthodox policy positions.[68] Consequently, the state transformations imposed under military rule were largely unaffected by the democratization process.

By 1992, peasant unions represented a mere forty-four thousand workers, less than six percent of the agrarian labor force. While attempts were made to unify the constituent confederations at the national level—a broad alliance emerged spanning the spectrum from the Communists in the confederation El Surco to the Christian Democrats in the Confederación Nacional Campesina—they were unable to place any of their goals on the national political agenda. They demanded that their Concertación allies initiate: (1) the restitution of land lost by peasants during the military regime; (2) dramatic changes in the labor code, to change the organizational base of rural unions and bring temporary workers within their purview; and (3) a return to state ownership of processing and marketing industries for domestic food crops.[69] None of these issues attained anything like the importance they had in Brazil.

Instead, in agriculture, post-transition governments have been largely content with status quo policies inherited from the military. President Aylwin's (1990–1993) Agriculture Minister, Juan Agustín Figueroa, placed firm limits on the policies that the center-left Concertación would pursue in rural areas. While he recognized the importance of political participation via peasant unions, he was unwilling to propose changes in the labor code giving collective bargaining rights to temporary workers. This was by far the largest segment of the labor force in the dynamic agro-export sector. Similarly, he deflected calls for greater stability of employment by arguing that agricultural modernization would correct that problem by itself. With respect to land reform, no return to expropriation was contemplated. Instead a small fund was set up to purchase and redistribute some land to peasants harmed under Decree Law 208 of 1973.[70] President Aylwin was similarly evasive on issues of importance to peasants.[71] Peasant unions, despite their ties to governing parties, were unable to force the discussion of rural issues, much less the implementation of any serious reform.

Why are even reformist political parties unwilling to consider substantial changes in agrarian policy? The answer here is twofold. On the one hand, they are hemmed in by the constitutional provisions that were negotiated as part of the process of democratic transition. Most important here are considerations of property rights. While expropriation (e.g., land reform) is legal, in general full compensation must be made within five years—ten if the national interest is at issue—at an interest rate of eight percent, in addition to full readjustment for inflation.[72] Given that legal challenges can intercede at many stages of the process, a return to substantial agrarian reform is politically impracticable, and fiscally impossible. Similarly, strong central bank autonomy prevents substantial deviation from liberal orthodoxy on the part of elected officials. On the other hand, the national-level success of market-oriented policies in generating growth has inhibited changes in the rural sector that would threaten market principles—most importantly in terms of the granting of subsidies, fixing prices, directly providing inputs, or raising tariffs. Since the introduction of most "rural" issues carries with it direct challenges to neoliberal principles, placing such issues on the national agenda raises negative political externalities that the Concertación government has no interest in facing.

With a dearth of political allies and a disrupted rural environment, peasant political mobilization has nearly disappeared. Peasant unions, long the principal mechanism for economic and political participation among cultivators, were devastated and have not recovered with democratic transition. The repression attendant upon the military coup brought the level of rural unionization down to 14.8 percent by 1981. By 1985, six years *after* unionization was legalized and repression was eased, rural union density had *fallen* to 7.1 percent of the labor force.[73] Nor did democratic transition reverse the decline. In 1992, after three years of democratic rule, only 5.4 percent of the agricultural labor force was enrolled in a union. This contrasts markedly with the urban experience, where legalization in 1979 stemmed the decline in unionization, and democratic transition brought with it a wave of union resurgence, returning organization in 1992 to the level it had reached in 1969. Non-agricultural union density was 14.7 percent in 1969, it fell to 8.8 percent by the mid-1980s, and returned to 14.7 percent after democratization.[74] Rural strikes, numbering over a thousand by the early 1970s, dropped to single digits by the mid-1980s, where they remained into the 1990s. In the cities, however, strike activity expanded from roughly forty per year to over two hundred between 1985 and 1992.

Peasant unions were unwilling or unable to press their demands through strikes, while their urban counterparts managed to do this, at least at a reduced level, especially after the democratic transition. Organizational efforts continued—often led by the same leaders who had been so successful in the 1960s and 1970s. And outside resources were also sometimes provided from domestic NGOs and international sources. Nevertheless, in a context of social atomization and an unfavorable structure of political opportunities, rural leaders were unable to halt the persistent decline in organization.

CONCLUSIONS

Post-transition politics in the Brazilian and Chilean rural sectors have diverged dramatically. In Brazil, agrarian issues have taken center stage in national political debates and significant, mobilized peasant movements have emerged. In Chile, rural issues have lost their former political prominence, and what had been one of the most organized and mobilized peasantries on the continent lapsed into atomism and quiescence. We have sought to account for this transformation of rural politics with an explanation that focuses on state institutions and the structural linkages to societal actors. These linkages were largely unaffected by the transition to democracy, having been born in the developmental projects of the earlier military periods.

Military rulers in each country pursued an export-oriented economic strategy—a neoliberal one in Chile and a statist, developmental one in Brazil. The consequent changes to state institutions—particularly the expansion or contraction of the state's welfare role in the countryside, the regulation of land tenure, and the transformation of labor law—defined the resources and opportunities available to peasant leaders in important ways. The developmentalist state in Brazil provided the infrastructure that would undergird a very substantial expansion in peasant unionization and later, after corporatist controls were weakened, mobilization. The withdrawal of the state and its replacement by market forces in Chile removed key resources from an already-mobilized peasantry. The importance of such resources is highlighted by the rapidity with which the movement collapsed, and its continued decline after repression was ended. But the developmental model also affected the availability of urban allies and political resources for rural movements. The commitment to free markets by all major political actors in post-transition Chile dramatically narrowed the agenda of national politics in ways that excluded many formerly important agrarian issues. Bereft of issues to bring to rural electoral competition, reformist parties did not seek alliances with peasant organizations. The political costs of such alliances—attacking fundamental tenets of the neoliberal model—were seen as prohibitive. In Brazil, no such commitment existed. With the state deeply involved in the economy, competing reformist parties had much to offer peasant voters. Agrarian issues took center stage as the left attempted to make inroads into a countryside long dominated by conservative, clientelistic elites.

Thus the constitution of state-society structural linkages is for us central to the understanding of mobilizational outcomes. In Chile from 1964 to 1973, the penetration of the state into the countryside at once increased its capacity to impose its will, but also served as a spur to mobilization from below that eventually pushed the state well beyond its initial goals. Under the military, state-society relations took on a more mutually deconstitutive character—as the state withdrew, it lost its former control over rural life (to the market), but also provoked the disarticulation of a formerly strong peasant movement. The story is similar in Brazil. When the state's linkages to rural society were weak before 1964, so was mobilization. But the state's efforts to impose control over the sector and expand formal citizenship ironically also opened up new incentives and resources, which led to an outpouring of popular mobilization during the democratic transition. While the new movement faced defeat over land reform in the 1988 Constituent Assembly, it did succeed in strengthening the progressive rural bureaucracy—INCRA—and accelerating the pace of land expropriation.

By highlighting the importance of state structures for the fate of popular movements, the institutional approach to popular mobilization we have developed in this paper advances our understanding of the broader relationship between democracy and strategies of development. In particular, it helps expose instances when state action strengthens civil society, supporting the formation of what some scholars have called "social capital," and when it undermines that civil society by eroding local networks and the bases for solidarity. In a very important way, the type of developmental approach taken by the state bounds the level of organization and political participation possible for popular sector actors.

NOTES

1. There is an extensive literature that examines the ways in which the institutional organization of democracy shapes the stability and character of post-transition politics. See, for example, Juan Linz and Alfred Stepan, *Problems of Democratic Transition and Consolidation: Southern Europe, South America, and Post-Communist Europe.* (Baltimore: The Johns Hopkins University Press, 1996); Juan Linz, "The Perils of Presidentialism." *Journal of Democracy* 1 (1990), and contributions to Scott Mainwaring and Timothy Scully, eds., *Building Democratic Institutions: Party Systems in Latin America* (Oxford: Oxford University Press, 1995); and Jorge Domínguez and Abraham Lowenthal. eds. *Constructing Democratic Governance: Latin America and the Caribbean in the 1990s* (Baltimore: The Johns Hopkins University Press, 1996).

2. Important contributions that have taken similar starting points are Jonathan Fox. "The Difficult Transition from Clientelism to Citizenship: Lessons from Mexico." *World Politics* 46 (January 1994); and Margaret Weir and Theda Skocpol, "State Structures and the Possibilities for 'Keynesian' Responses to the Great Depression in Sweden. Britain, and the United States," in Peter Evans. Dietrich Rueschemeyer, and Theda

Skocpol, eds., *Bringing the State Back In* (Cambridge, UK: Cambridge University Press, 1985). Charles Tilly, "Social Movements and National Politics," in Charles Bright and Susan Harding, eds., *Statemaking and Social Movements: Essays in History and Theory* (Ann Arbor: University of Michigan Press, 1984), and *Popular Contention in Great Britain, 1758–1834* (Cambridge, MA: Harvard University Press, 1995); Sidney Tarrow, *Power in Movement: Social Movements, Collective Action and Politics* (Cambridge, UK: Cambridge University Press, 1994). Tilly and Tarrow both emphasize the influence of the modern nation-state on collective action. In this paper we seek to advance this line of thought, examining how specific forms of nation-state are connected to different patterns of collective action.

3. Preservation of important state institutions during democratization is often conceived in the democratization literature as the "price" to be paid for transition. See, for example, Guillermo O'Donnell and Philippe Schmitter, *Transitions from Authoritarian Rule: Tentative Conclusions about Uncertain Democracies* (Baltimore: The Johns Hopkins University Press, 1986), 62–63.

4. Alexis de Tocqueville, *Democracy in America* (New York: Harper and Row, 1969), e.g., 513, was an early critic of state presence in associational life. See also pluralists like Robert Dahl, *Democracy and Its Critics* (New Haven: Yale University Press, 1989), 221, and Seymour Lipset, "The Social Requisites of Democracy Revisited," *American Sociological Review* 59 (February, 1993). Both scholars make the autonomy of groups in civil society from direct state influence a defining characteristic of a democratic polity. Others, as politically disparate as Charles Lindblom, *Politics and Markets: The World's Political-Economic Systems* (New York: Basic Books, 1977), 238–39, and Carl Friedrich and Zbigniew Brzezinski, *Totalitarian Dictatorship and Autocracy* (Cambridge, MA: Harvard University Press, 1956), Ch. 17, worried about increasing state control over economic activity and how it interfered with the autonomy of associational life. Some social capital theorists make similar arguments. See Robert Putnam, *Making Democracy Work: Civic Traditions in Modern Italy* (Princeton: Princeton University Press, 1993), and James Coleman, *Foundations of Social Theory* (Cambridge, MA: Belknap, Harvard University Press, 1990). In another work Putnam does suggest the possibility of state and society reinforcing each other. Robert Putnam, "The Prosperous Community," *American Prospect* 13 (Spring 1993), 35–42. In Latin America the surge of social movement activity during the late 1970s and 1980s has been linked by some scholars to the crisis of the "developmental state"—the decline of the state opens up new political space where autonomous social groups can organize. See Arturo Escobar and Sonia E. Alvarez, eds., *The Making of Social Movements in Latin America: Identity, Strategy, and Democracy* (Boulder: Westview Press, 1992).

5. See for example Joel S. Migdal, Atul Kohli, and Vivienne Shue, eds., *State Power and Social Forces: Domination and Transformation in the Third World* (Cambridge, UK: Cambridge University Press, 1994); Francis Hagopian, *Traditional Politics and Regime Change in Brazil* (New York: Cambridge University Press, 1996); Peter Evans, *Embedded Autonomy: States and Industrial Transformation* (Princeton: Princeton University Press, 1995); Judith Tendler, *Good Government in the Tropics* (Baltimore: The Johns Hopkins University Press, 1997); and the essays on "state-society synergy" in *World Development* 24, no.6 (1996).

6. On this point, see Marcus J. Kurtz, "Free-Markets and Democratic Consolidation in Chile: The National Politics of Rural Transformation" *Politics & Society* 27, no. 2 (June 1999).

7. Tarrow, *Power in Movement*, 66. See also J. Craig Jenkins, "Social Movements, Political Representation, and the State: An Agenda and Comparative Framework," in J. Craig Jenkins and Bert Klandermans, eds., *The Politics of Social Protest: Comparative Perspectives on States and Social Movements* (Minneapolis: University of Minnesota

Press, 1995), 16–17; Alfred Stepan, "State Power and the Strength of Civil Society in the Southern Cone of Latin America," in Evans et al., eds., *Bringing the State Back In*, 339.

8. Peter B. Evans, "Government Action, Social Capital and Development: Reviewing the Evidence on Synergy," *World Development* 24, no.6 (1996), 1119–32.

9. Examples can be found in the U.S. extension service's role in the emergence of the Farm Bureau early in the twentieth century, discussed in Patrick H. Mooney and Theo J. Majka, *Farmers' and Farm Workers' Movements: Social Protest in American Agriculture* (New York: Twayne Publishers, 1995), 68–74. This was clearly the case in Chile between 1967 and 1973, when the government's Union Extension and Outreach Fund (FEES) provided material resources to peasant organizations, and the agricultural extension service (INDAP) directly promoted unionization. More recent examples include the Brazilian extension service's support for agricultural cooperatives in Brazil examined by Tendler, and the food councils of state agency CONASUPO in Mexico discussed by Fox. See Tendler, *Good Government in the Tropics;* Jonathan Fox, "How Does Civil Society Thicken? The Political Construction of Social Capital in Rural Mexico," *World Development* 24, no. 6, 1089–103.

10. In 1980 for example an estimated seven hundred thousand small farmers took to the streets to protest government agricultural policy, and close to a quarter million agricultural workers in the sugar industry went on strike. CONTAG, *As Lutas Camponesas no Brasil—1980* (Rio de Janeiro: Marco Zero, 1981); Candido Grzybowski, *Caminhos e Descaminhos dos Movimentos Sociais* (Petropolis: Vozes, 1987).

11. Rural labor gained the right to organize unions in 1944, but the law was rendered a dead letter by rural elites. In the ensuing twenty years there was little or no enforcement of the labor code provisions that applied to rural labor. Neale J. Pearson, "Small Farmer and Rural Worker Pressure Groups in Brazil," (Ph.D. Dissertation, Department of Political Science, University of Florida, 1967), 63; Robert E. Price, "Rural Unionization in Brazil" (mimeo, University of Wisconsin Land Tenure Center, 1964).

12. Peter Flynn, *Brazil: A Political Analysis* (Boulder: Westview Press, 1978), 245.

13. Price, "Rural Unionization" (1964), 69; Shepard Forman, "Disunity and Discontent: A Study of Peasant Political Movements in Brazil," *Journal of Latin American Studies* 3, no. 1 (1971), 9; IBGE, *Censo Agropecuário, 1960* (Rio de Janeiro: IBGE).

14. The level of mobilization was significant only in northeastern Brazil, and particularly in the state of Pernambuco, where around a quarter million people joined rural worker unions and peasant leagues. The important state of São Paulo, for example, had an average of seven strikes in the eleven years preceding the coup, and most stoppages were of a single plantation. Cynthia Hewitt, "Brazil: The Peasant Movement of Pernambuco, 1961–1964," in Henry A. Landsberger, ed., *Latin American Peasant Movements* (Ithaca: Cornell University Press, 1969), 396–97; Clifford A. Welch, "Rural Labor and the Brazilian Revolution in São Paulo, 1930–1964" (Ph.D. Dissertation, Department of History, Duke University, 1990), 325.

15. See Hewitt, "Brazil: The Peasant Movement"; Welch, "Rural Labor and the Brazilian Revolution"; Clodomir Moraes, "Peasant Leagues in Brazil," in R. Stavenhagen, ed., *Agrarian Problems and Peasant Movements in Latin America* (New York: Anchor Books, 1970); José de Souza Martins, *Os Camponeses e a Política no Brasil* (Petropolis: Vozes, 1981).

16. Peter Evans, *Dependent Development: The Alliance of Multinational, State, and Local Capital in Brazil* (Princeton: Princeton University Press, 1979); Thomas Skidmore, "Politics and Economic Policy Making in Authoritarian Brazil, 1937–71," in Alfred Stepan, ed., *Authoritarian Brazil* (New Haven: Yale University Press, 1973) and "The Political Economy of Policy Making in Authoritarian Brazil, 1967–1970," in Philip O'Brien and Paul Cammack, eds., *Generals in Retreat: The Crisis of Military Rule in Latin America* (Manchester, UK: Manchester University Press, 1985).

17. Brazil's profound regional variation meant that the project took on different faces in different regions: in the southern half of the country, it was the capitalization of production and creation of agro-industry; in the center-west and north, the incorporation of new land into cultivation; in the northeast, the structural transformation of the archaic and uncompetitive sugar industry. See Skidmore, "Politics and Economic Policy Making," 12–13, and "The Political Economy of Policy;" David Goodman, "Rural Economy and Society," in Edmar L. Bacha and Herbert S. Klein, eds., *Social Change in Brazil, 1945– 1985: The Incomplete Transition* (Albuquerque: The University of New Mexico Press, 1986); Stephen Bunker, *Underdeveloping the Amazon: Extraction, Unequal Exchange, and the Failure of the Modern State* (Chicago: University of Chicago Press, 1985).

18. Price, "Rural Unionization in Brazil," 11–12, 66; Shepard Forman, *The Brazilian Peasantry* (New York: Columbia University Press, 1971), 20. Social security, an important part of the corporatist regime, was legally extended to rural workers in a separate law later that same year but only became effective during the 1970s, under military rule.

19. It was funded in such a manner as to transfer income from urban to rural areas, and rural workers did not pay into the program directly. Ministério do Trabalho e Previdencia Social, *Informativo do Funrural* (Brasilia, Brazil, 1973), 2, 7–8, Table 1; Ruda Ricci, "CONTAG e a Crise de Representação no Campo (1979–1985)" (Master's thesis, Department of Political Science, UNICAMP, São Paulo, 1993), 84; and James Malloy, *The Politics of Social Security in Brazil* (Pittsburgh: University of Pittsburgh Press, 1981).

20. Joe Foweraker, *The Struggle for Land* (Cambridge, UK: Cambridge University Press, 1981), 84–87, 90.

21. Almost without exception these ended with labor courts imposing new collective contracts. Anthony W. Pereira, *The End of the Peasantry: The Rural Labor Movement in Northeast Brazil, 1961–1988* (Pittsburgh: University of Pittsburgh Press, 1997), 67–8.

22. The share of dues paying members was significantly lower. Novaes, "CONTAG e CUT" (1991), 178–79; Maybury-Lewis, *The Politics of the Possible*, Appendix A; Tavares, "CONTAG."

23. A reasonable estimate places the share of such unions at over two-thirds of all unions in 1979. Peter P. Houtzager, "State and Unions in the Transformation of the Brazilian Countryside, 1964–1979," *Latin American Research Review* 33, no. 2 (1998); Grzybowski, *Caminhos e Descaminhos*.

24. Agriculture's share of economically active persons dropped from fifty-four to thirty-two percent, but it nonetheless remained the largest employment sector in the 1980s.

25. The median income, which is an indicator more sensitive to inequality of income distribution, went from fifty-eight to ninety-two percent. These figures do underestimate income levels because the census does not include subsistence production (for own consumption) and people often underdeclare their true income. The number of poor households fell from seventy-three percent in 1970 to sixty percent in 1987. Poor households are those with incomes below twice the cost of a "basic food basket;" indigent households below one basket. Because of the extraordinary level of inequality to start off with, the share of poor remained far higher than in much of Latin American. Rodolfo Hoffmann, "Vinte Anos de Desigualdade e Probreza na Agricultura Brasileira," *Revista de Economia e Sociologia Rural* 30, no.2 (April/June 1992), 98; Rodolfo Hoffman, "Distribuição de Renda na Agricultura," in Antonio Salazar P. Brandão, ed., *Os Principais Problemas da Agricultural Brasileira: Análise e Sugestões* (Rio de Janeiro: IPEA, 1992), 22; ECLAC, *Social Panorama of Latin America, 1994 edition* (Santiago: ECLAC, November 1994), 140; *Statistical Yearbook for Latin America and the Caribbean, 1994 edition* (Santiago, Chile: CEPAL, 1995), 46.

26. IBGE, *Censo Agropecuário*, 1960 and 1980.

27. This claim is made by Leôncio Martins Rodrigues as well: "As tendencias políticos na formação das centrais sindicais," in A. Boito Jr., ed., *O Sindiclaismo Brasileiro nos Anos 80* (tao Paulo: Paz e Terra, 1991), 13–14.

28. Small farmers also mobilized around agricultural policy issues. In 1980, for example, an estimated seven hundred thousand soybean producers took to the streets in southern Brazil to protest a new export tax. In 1987 and 1988 tens of thousands of small farmers participated in impressive mass demonstrations and caravans to Brasilia to protest the government's economic policy.

29. It participated in the founding of the CGT in 1986, though it later abandoned that entity. At the founding congress, rural unions represented twenty-six percent of the total participating entities, and sixteen of twenty-two state-level federations affiliated to the CGT. Longtime president of the National Confederation of Agricultural Workers, José Francisco da Silva, became the vice-president of the CGT.

30. The peasant-worker alliance was an important and integral part of the founding logic of both the party and labor central, and both embraced various agrarian issues, such as radical agrarian reform (under the control of the workers), agricultural policy favoring small farmers, and parity in social benefits with urban workers. The Workers' Party was formed in 1979, the CUT in 1983.

31. In the labor entity's three national congresses during the 1980s, rural leaders represented over a third of the delegates. The vice-president of CUT has been a rural unionist from its founding in 1983 up until 1997. See Ricardo Antunes, *O Novo Sindicalismo* (São Paulo: Pontes, 1995).

32. João Pedro Stédile, ed., *A Reforma Agrária e a Luta do MST* (Petrópolis: Vozes, 1997); Zander Navarro, "Democracy, Citizenship and Representation: Rural Social Movements in Southern Brazil," *Bulletin of Latin American Research* 13, no. 2 (1994), 129–54.

33. Landowners organized their own popular movement, the UDR (União Democratica Ruralista), and a lobby in Congress called the Frente Ampla, which succeeded in blocking the government's national agrarian reform plan.

34. Sérgio Leite, "Assentamentos Rurais no Brasil: Impactos, Dimensões, e Significados," in João Pedro Stédile, ed., *A Reforma Agrária e a Luta do MST* (Petrópolis: Vozes, 1997), 158–59.

35. To force state intervention, strikes aimed to paralyze entire agricultural sectors (such as sugar and orange production) in a region, rather than specific employers. Unions in several states developed their own forms of wage campaigns, with varying degrees of militancy and compliance with the corporatist legal requirements.

36. Ministério do Trabalho, UFRJ, *O Mercado de Trabalho Brasileiro: Estrutura e Conjuntura* (Brasilia: MTb, 1987).

37. As a result, by the 1990s rural workers in over half-a dozen states had some form of rural collective contract; the number of agricultural workers with labor contracts (*carteira assinada*) reached 1.3 million, double that of 1979 (though still only twenty-six percent agricultural wage laborers). IBGE, *Anuário Estatístico, 1991* (Rio de Janeiro: IBGE, 1991).

38. Social welfare and health care were the two principle issues around which the powerful Agricultural Workers' Federation of Rio Grande do Sul (FETAG-RS), in Brazil's southern most state, mobilized. Union involvement declined significantly over the course of the 1980s as a result of the unification of rural and urban welfare systems.

39. Guilherme da Costa Delgado, "Agricultural Familiar e Política Agrícola no Brasil" (Working Document, IPEA, Rio de Janeiro, June 1994), 19. IBGE, *Anuário Estatístico, 1994* (Rio de Janeiro: IBGE, 1994).

40. Brian Loveman, *Chile: The Legacy of Hispanic Capitalism* (New York: Oxford University Press, 1988), 211.

41. Arturo Valenzuela, *The Breakdown of Democratic Regimes: Chile* (Baltimore: The Johns Hopkins University Press, 1978), 13, points out that Chile was at the time the single most statist economy in the hemisphere, with the exception of Cuba.

42. The Peasant Unionization Law replaced the earlier peasant labor law, whose terms were so restrictive as to effectively block any peasant unionization. Cristóbal Kay, "Political Economy, Class Alliances, and Agrarian Change in Chile," *Journal of Peasant Studies* 8, no. 4 (1981).

43. Solon Barraclough and Almino Affonso, "Diagnóstico de la reforma agraria chilena (noviembre 1970–junio 1972)," *Cuadernos de la Realidad Nacional* 16 (April 1973), 73, makes it clear that the promotion of peasant organization was a crucial element of the Allende administration's political strategy.

44. Loveman, *Chile*, 280.

45. On the importance of peasants to political competition in the 1960s, see Timothy Scully, *Rethinking the Center: Party Politics in Nineteenth and Twentieth Century Chile* (Stanford: Stanford University Press, 1992), 108; James Petras, *Politics and Social Forces in Chilean Development* (Berkeley: University of California Press, 1969), Chapter 7, especially 256–58.

46. See Loveman, *Chile*, 280; and Emilio Klein, "Tipos de dependencia y obreros agrícolas en Chile," *Boletín de Estudios Latinoamericanos y del Caribe* 16 (June, 1974).

47. Proportion of agricultural wage-workers enrolled in a peasant labor union. Calculated as a percentage of the economically active population in agriculture.

48. Oficina de Planificación Nacional [ODEPLAN], *Chilean Economic and Social Development, 1973–1979* (Santiago, Chile: Imprenta Calderón y Cía., 1979), 33–35.

49. See Oficina de Estudios y Políticas Agrarias [ODEPA], *Síntesis agro-regional* (Santiago, Chile: Ministerio de Agricultura, 1992).

50. Arturo León, "Urban Poverty in Chile: Its Extent and Diversity," Working Paper #8, Democracy and Social Policy Series, Trans. Judy Lawton (Notre Dame, IN: Kellogg Institute, 1994), 10–11.

51. Departamento de Economía Agraria [DEA], *Panorama económico de la agricultura* (Santiago, Chile: Departemento de Economía Agraria, Pontifica Universidad Católica de Chile, 1980), 25. Roughly 51.6 percent was distributed as peasant parcels, with the remainder divided roughly equally between returns to landlords and auctions.

52. Marín, *Las tomas.*

53. Instituto de Capacitación e Investigación en Reforma Agraria [ICIRA], *Análisis de la situación de los asignatarios de tierras a junio de 1978* (Santiago, Chile: Ministerio de Agricultura, 1979), 116.

54. Cereceda and Dahse, *Dos décadas,* 117.

55. *Código de Trabajo de 1992.* Libro III, Artículo 5.

56. There are, of course, exceptions to this rule. But given the climatic and technological characteristics of Chilean agriculture, there is widespread consensus that substantially more seasonal labor than permanent (year-round) is employed.

57. Lovell Jarvis, *Chilean Agriculture,* 89, suggests that fifteen percent would be a realistic unemployment rate for the agricultural sector. Carlotta Olavarría, *La asignación de tierras en Chile (1973–1976), sus efectos en el empleo agrícola* (Santiago, Chile: PREALC, 1978), 14, points to a typical combined level of un- and underemployment of between twenty and thirty-seven percent. Indeed, the mass expulsion of coop members during the counterreform probably renders these very conservative estimates.

58. Ibid., 32.

59. This includes residing with friends or relatives who were able to obtain a parcel, work in the minimum employment program, retirement, open unemployment, etc. See ICIRA, *Análisis,* 22.

60. Before the coup, roughly twice as many peasants were associated with leftist unions as with centrist ones.

61. The logic of finance and resource allocation virtually required affiliation to a national federation or confederation in the 1967–1973 period. Unpublished data from the Ministry of Labor, 1992.

62. For an example, see Loveman, *Struggle in the Countryside: Politics and Rural Labor in Chile, 1919–1973* (Bloomington: Indiana University Press); such political mediation is exemplified by the actions of Deputy Andrés Aylwin, *Carta informe sobre experiencias sindicales campesinas* (Santiago, Chile: Cámera de Diputados, 1967).

63. Pilar Vergara, "Market Economy, Social Welfare, and Democratic Consolidation in Chile," in William Smith, Carlos Acuña, and Eduardo Gamarra, eds., *Democracy, Markets, and Structural Reform in Latin America* (New Brunswick: Transaction Publishers, 1994), 244.

64. Daniel Rodríguez and Sylvia Venegas, *De praderas a parronales: Un estudio sobre estructura agraria y mercado laboral en el valle de Aconcagua* (Santiago, Chile: GEA, 1989), 151–52.

65. *Código de Trabajo 1992*, Título V, Art. 3.

66. Sylvia Venegas, *Family Production in Rural Chile: A Socio-Demographic Study of Agrarian Changes in the Aconcagua Valley, 1930–1986* (Ph. D. dissertation, Department of Sociology, University of Texas at Austin, 1987), Ch. 12.

67. See Kenneth Roberts, "From the Barricades to the Ballot Box: Redemocratization and Political Realignment in the Chilean Left," *Politics and Society* 23, no. 4 (December 1995).

68. See Paul W. Drake and Iván Jaksić, "Introduction: Transformation and Transition in Chile, 1982–1990," in Paul W. Drake and Iván Jaksić, ed., *The Struggle for Democracy in Chile* (Lincoln, NE: University of Nebraska Press, 1992), 15.

69. The complete analysis of the crisis of the peasantry and its political demands as expressed by the unions can be found in Comisión Nacional Campesina [CNC], *Renace la esperanza democrática en el campo* (Santiago, Chile: CNC, 1990), 13–17.

70. See an interview conducted by peasant union leaders with the Minister, transcribed in *Tierra: La revista del trabajador del campo* (1990), 7–11.

71. See *Tierra* IX, no. 2 (May–June 1991), 4–7.

72. *Ley Orgánica Constitucional de Expropriaciones*, No. 18.932, February 10, 1990. See especially Title IV, Articles 16–19.

73. Luís Salinas, *Trayectoria de la organización sindical campesina* (Santiago, Chile: AGRA Ltda, 1985).

74. For 1969 see Kay, "Agrarian Reformism," 424. For the mid-1980s, calculated from Ministerio de Trabajo y Previsión Social, *Estadísticas de la negociación colectiva* (Years 1992, 1991, 1990, and 1989) (Santiago, Chile: unpublished data). Agricultural labor force data (used in calculating union density) were taken from ODEPA, *Sintesis*, and Banco Central de Chile, *Indicadores económicos y sociales regionales* (Santiago, Chile: Banco Central de Chile, 1991).

Associations and Activism:
Mobilization of Urban Informal Workers
in Costa Rica and Nicaragua

Charles L. Davis
Edwin E. Aguilar
John G. Speer

The wave of democratization that swept through Latin America and Eastern Europe in the past decade renewed scholarly interest in the study of the role of civil society in democratic transitions and consolidation.[1] As Edwards and Foley explain,

> Latin American conceptions [of civil society] reflected both the struggle against the military dictatorships of the 1970s and 1980s and a widespread conviction that conventional party politics had failed these societies. Latin American activists and thinkers thus framed civil society not only as "society against a repressive state" but also as society in place of the parties. The leftist orientation of many antimilitary activists led to an identification of civil society with the so-called popular sector—including a wide variety of lower class and leftist groupings under this umbrella but generally excluding even those sectors of the business and professional classes who eventually joined in the opposition. (Edwards and Foley 1998, 125; see also Foley and Edwards 1996, 45–46).

The scholarly literature has generally emphasized civil society rather than political parties as the key to democratic transition and to deepening democracy in Latin America (see, for example, Oxhorn 1995; Dietz 1998). Autonomous, decentralized popular organizations, not political parties, were most often in the forefront of opposition to authoritarian regimes. During the transition to civilian government and since, however, political parties have often weakened and displaced popular organizations (for Chile, see Oxhorn 1995, 1998; for Uruguay, see Cañel 1992). These organizations, nevertheless, have continued to pose challenges to traditional top-down, corporatist, and clientelist linkages between state and citizen. They have, moreover, presumably contributed to a more politically conscious and active citizenry.

Booth and Richard (1998a, 1998b) have shown that civil society activism (involvement in unions, civic associations, cooperatives, professional groups, and community self-help groups) in six Central American countries has led more to the acquisition of political capital than social

35

capital. "Social capital includes interpersonal trust, networks, and norms that aid in mutual cooperation. . . . Political capital consists of civic norms that support democratic governance . . . and conventional participation" (Booth and Richard 1998a, 35).[2] The forms of political capital they investigated included commitment to democratic norms, voting, campaign activism, and contacting public officials. While recognizing that civil society activism might also stimulate confrontational political activity, Booth and Richard were particularly interested in how much cooperative attitudes and behaviors supportive of democratic institutions were being promoted.

What is not clear from their study is whether civil society promotes a different type of citizen political involvement than do political parties. Some analysts of contemporary civil society in Latin America argue that political mobilization through civil society is likely to be fundamentally different from mobilization through political parties. Jelin (1997, 79–97), for example, links less-institutionalized modes of political mobilization to popular organizations and social movements in civil society and controlled electoral mobilization to institutionalized party systems (see also Oxhorn 1995). Certainly, popular-sector organizations in civil society become involved in electoral politics, but the argument is that they also sustain collective mobilization that extends beyond electoral politics.

If that argument is true, we would expect to find that political parties promote what O'Donnell (1994) calls "low-intensity citizenship," in which citizen political activity is largely limited to periodic voting; while popular organizations in civil society would promote "high-intensity" citizenship, characterized by more sustained, often less institutionalized forms of political participation that require more time, energy, and resources. Moreover, we might find that civil society plays "a major role, if not *the* major role, in building citizenship skills and the attitudes crucial for motivating citizens to use their skills" (Foley and Edwards 1998, 11–12). Political parties, in contrast, might shun this role, focusing their resources instead on short-term electoral mobilization.

The general literature on mass political participation suggests that parties have an incentive to mobilize citizens only for electoral purposes; political mobilization outside the electoral arena will be either self-generated (that is, through what has been called "cognitive mobilization") or else generated by organizations outside the party system (see Verba et al. 1978).[3] The literature on Latin American civil society suggests a similar de facto division of labor. Even though political parties have an obvious incentive to appeal for the electoral support of popular organizations, they have, in some cases, sought politically to demobilize the popular sector so as to preserve elite-negotiated transitions to democracy and to maintain political stability and order (for Chile, see Oxhorn 1995). Less-institutionalized, high-intensity forms of political activism presumably occur primarily through popular organizations and social movements located in civil society, not through political parties.

Taking the comparison further, Williams (1994) has identified two levels of democratization. One level involves "the revitalization of the political arena" in which competitive elections and regime accountability are restored (1994, 171). The other level involves "expanding the space available for autonomous social organization and mobilization." At this level, according to Williams, "typically marginalized groups are granted greater opportunities to organize and express their interests in a collective fashion" (1994, 171). The potential is thus created for, as Jelin says, "less institutionalized collective means of expressing old and new social demands" (Jelin 1997, 79), opening up new avenues for more activist forms of citizenship. The civil society literature has typically viewed these two levels of democratization as operating independently of each other, with political parties being the primary agent of electoral mobilization and civil society the primary agent for higher-intensity forms of political participation (for exceptions, see Barnes 1998; Williams 1994).

This study addresses all these theoretical issues by examining political parties and popular organizations, or civic associations, as agents of political mobilization among urban informal workers in Nicaragua and Costa Rica during the early 1990s. Using survey data collected in Nicaragua in 1991 and Costa Rica in 1993, it explores the relative influence of these two groupings in promoting various types of political activity.

Certainly the focus on these two countries does not provide the leverage to generalize any findings to the region as a whole. Costa Rica and Nicaragua, however, do provide contrasting institutional settings in which civil society is differentially embedded (see Seligson and Booth 1993). The differential embeddedness of civil society in these two countries has developed out of their different historical experiences. In Costa Rica, a consolidated democratic regime with a stable two-party system and a relatively autonomous civil society dates back to 1948.[4] In many ways, political development in Costa Rica more closely parallels that of the advanced industrial democracies than that of other Central American countries. Nicaragua, by contrast, resembles other countries in Latin America and Eastern Europe that have achieved significant democratization since the early 1980s. A latecomer to democratization, Nicaragua experienced a long period of U.S.-supported dictatorship under the Somoza dynasty, which lasted from the 1930s until the triumph of the Nicaraguan revolution in 1979. The current regime developed out of the revolutionary struggle and an era of domination by the leftist Sandinista Front of National Liberation (FSLN) that lasted until the party's electoral defeat in 1990.

These two cases allow us to examine whether mobilizing processes vary between civil society and political parties in these two "most different" countries of Central America. Do political parties in both countries focus on electoral mobilization, leaving more demanding forms of mobilization to civil society, as the literature suggests? There are reasons to believe that this simple dichotomy may not hold in countries where post-Marxist parties on the left have embraced concepts of popular or participatory democracy, in contrast to electoral democracy. Such parties usually form close linkages with relatively autonomous popular organizations. The revolutionary FSLN in Nicaragua is such a party. It has been committed not only to mobilizing electoral support but also to enhancing opportunities for popular organizations to engage in collective mobilization (Williams 1994). Other class-based political parties on the left, such as the Labor Party in Brazil or Causa R in Venezuela, have exhibited similar propensities. Thus the nature of the party may matter for mobilization.

The Nicaraguan case illustrates how loyalty to the FSLN, a party that is formally committed to popular democracy, affects people's propensity to join civic associations and to engage in high-intensity citizenship. The Costa Rican case, by contrast, provides an example of an established two-party system in which parties have functioned almost exclusively as vehicles for electoral mobilization. Here we would expect weaker relationships between party loyalty and participation outside the electoral arena. We would not expect party loyalties to relate to associational involvement, as party activity in Costa Rica is largely limited to elections. Similarly we would expect that loyalty to the National Opposition Union (UNO) in Nicaragua would exhibit relationships similar to those in Costa Rica, because that right-of-center party coalition does not share the FSLN's commitment to popular democracy.

In Nicaragua, the vanguard revolutionary party could be more important in mobilizing both voters and political activists than the recently resurrected civil society has been. By contrast, political parties may be more confined to their traditional role of mobilizing voters in Costa Rica's established two-party system, while political activists are mobilized largely through civil society. If so, we would expect to find in Costa Rica that involvement in civic associations is more strongly related to more demanding forms of political activity than is partisan loyalty. Conversely, partisan loyalty ought to be more closely linked to electoral participation than is associational affiliation. In brief, the presumed division of labor between political parties and civil society may depend on the political context.

CIVIL SOCIETY AND THE URBAN INFORMAL SECTOR

The study focuses specifically on the informal sector of the economy in the cities. Enterprises in this sector are characterized by several factors:

- Low capital requirements for entry into the market
- Reliance on locally available resources
- Family ownership
- Small-scale production
- Labor-intensive technology
- Acquisition of skills outside of formal schooling
- Unregulated markets (Hart 1973, 61–89)

There are theoretical reasons to believe that the structural position of the urban informal sector in Latin American countries might militate against virtually any efforts at collective mobilization or high-intensity forms of citizenship. As Roberts has suggested, structural conditions confronting the urban informal sector "foster individualism" rather than social cooperation (1996, 49–50). The sector's heterogeneity generates conflicting economic interests, and the marginal economic situation of many workers fosters a household survival strategy that seeks "to increase the number of household members in the labor market, either from within the nuclear family or by adding members to the household" (Roberts 1996, 50). These conditions could foster a clientelistic orientation to politics that may undercut any interest in collective engagement to exert political pressure or influence from the bottom up (Roberts 1996).

The literature suggests, nevertheless, that a relatively democratized civil society can be an effective agent of politicization among traditionally demobilized groups, such as the informal sector (see, for example, Oxhorn 1995). Neoliberal reforms have hurt the urban informal sector throughout Latin America, albeit not to the same degree in every country (Itzigsohn 1996). The sector has expanded as the economically active lower-class population has been displaced from the formal sector since the debt crisis of the 1980s (see Tardanico 1997). Therefore, civil society organizations in the urban informal sector could conceivably become a major source of opposition to neoliberal reforms, as well as a source of advocacy for new or expanded government services and benefits. It is important to keep in mind, however, that the informal sector is heterogeneous in terms of income level, economic security, social background, and even political ideology and belief (see Roberts 1996; also Aguilar 1995; Speer 1997, 270).

In Costa Rica, wage levels and living conditions for the lower classes generally improved by 1990 as the economy recovered from the worst effects of the debt crisis (see Gindling and Berry 1992; Morley 1995, 134–50; Castiglia et al. 1994; Tardanico and Lungo 1997, 95–141). Most of the improvement came in rural rather than urban areas, however, while the number of people living in poverty in urban areas actually increased (see

131

Korzeniewicz 1997, table 5; Morley 1995, 134–50). Increasing urban poverty in Costa Rica partly reflects the precarious employment situation of the informal sector.

The urban informal sector in Nicaragua has faced an even more precarious situation, partly as a result of neoliberal restructuring of the economy and the devastation of the civil war. As Speer notes, "Economic adjustment policies in the late 1980s and early 1990s meant severe austerity for most Nicaraguans" (1997, 266). One consequence has been an increasing "informalization" of the Nicaraguan economy. According to Speer, "It is entirely possible that by 1995 upwards of 50 percent of urban Nicaraguans earned most of their income in the informal sector" (1997, 266). An increasingly crowded informal sector combined with the government's austerity measures has led to a general deterioration of living conditions for workers dependent on this sector for employment (Speer 1997). It is clear that informal workers in Costa Rica have been far more economically advantaged than their Nicaraguan counterparts. Still, both would have reasons to challenge government economic policies and to press for greater government responsiveness to their needs.

Nicaragua

Civil society in each country, and in the urban informal sector in particular, has developed within a distinct political context and institutional frame-work. In Nicaragua, a relatively autonomous civil society first emerged under the auspices of the revolutionary FSLN during the struggle against the Somoza dictatorship in the 1970s. During this period, "the organized popular sectors—peasants, labor, women, and youth—served as the FSLN's mass base of support in both rural and urban areas" (Polakoff and La Ramée 1997, 185). Urban informal workers also joined FSLN mass organizations at this time (Booth 1982, 114).

After coming to power in 1979, the FSLN attempted to implement its "version of democracy, which at the beginning was seen as participatory and economic with only limited priority given to aspects of electoral democracy" (Hoyt 1997, 44). The associational infrastructure that developed under FSLN tutelage, however, did not give the mass organizations full autonomy (Polakoff and La Ramée 1997; Williams 1994, 174–75). Contradictory Leninist tendencies became most pronounced during the period of the counterrevolutionary war and the economic downturn in the middle and late 1980s (see Polakoff and La Ramée 1997; Hoyt 1997, 50–53). Some revolutionary organizations operated as instruments of the state for the implementation of policy, while others, like the taxi driver cooperatives, guarded their autonomy more jealously. Even the most state-controlled associations, though, "did offer to the people some real space for participation" (Hoyt 1997, 55). Following the end of the Contra War and the FSLN's electoral defeat in 1990, popular organizations linked to the FSLN gained more autonomy, and they have continued as a source of opposition to the neoliberal reforms of Violeta Barrios de Chamorro (1990–97) and Arnoldo Alemán (1997-present) (Hoyt 1997, 97; Polakoff and La Ramée 1997; Babb 1998).[5]

Nicaragua's party system currently is highly fractionalized, with seven identifiable "party families," each made up several separate parties. Coleman and Stuart (1997) identify them as liberal, conservative, revolutionary, Christian democratic, social democratic, Central American integrationist, and counterrevolutionary. Very few of these parties register much political support in national elections; some are actually nothing more than vehicles for the personal ambitions of Nicaraguan political figures. Most Nicaraguans have scant awareness of the many splinter factions on the political scene. Even among the few parties with significant ties to civil society, the urban informal sector has not been the primary target of organizing efforts, nor has the well-being of this sector been a primary concern of any party in power. This situation was also true in 1991 at the time of interviewing for this study. As the Jesuit publication *Envío* that year explained, "The urban informal sector has been one of the most controversial in Nicaragua. Some call it the 'apron bourgeoisie'; for others, it is a popular sector that neither the Sandinista nor the UNO economic policies have taken into account" (1991, 41).

The FSLN stands out nevertheless as the only political party to have made any concerted efforts toward organizing networks within the urban informal sector. Such was not the case with the National Opposition Union (UNO), a coalition of opposition parties whose candidate, Violeta Chamorro, captured the presidency from the FSLN in the 1990 election.

Mass organizations such as the Sandinista Defense Committees (CDS), the Sandinista Youth (JS), and the women's organization AMNLAE were not the only vehicles used by the revolutionary government to organize in the informal sector. Initially, the FSLN showed an interest in organizing the urban informal sector into cooperatives. These workers were encouraged "to produce and sell needed goods in small, independent associations of fewer than a dozen individuals" (Babb 1998, 112). The cooperatives, in turn, were encouraged to join the National Chamber of Medium-sized and Small Industry (CONAPI) to receive training and subsidized prices for primary goods (Babb 1998, 112).

Many cooperatives among artisans, street vendors, small repair shops, and homefront stores in Managua and elsewhere, however, did not survive the economic retrenchment associated with the war economy of the mid- and late 1980s. The decline of cooperatives continued under the Chamorro government as it sought to promote microenterprise to replace Sandinista cooperatives (see Babb 1998, 117–19).

The efforts to organize the informal sector had their most lasting effects among market stallkeepers and taxi drivers. In the early 1980s, the government built dozens of new markets around Managua alone, vastly improving working conditions but also imposing new regulations on trade practices and creating channels for tax collection. At the same time, the FSLN organized cooperative trade associations within the city's major markets. It is ironic that even before the FSLN's electoral defeat in 1990, these associations sometimes acted as channels for protest against government policies (Collinson and Broadbent 1990, 61–64).

Much more combative were the taxi cooperatives formed by the revolutionary government. Licensed taxi drivers in Managua were fully integrated into cooperatives by the mid-1980s. The cooperatives carried the names of revolutionary heroes or historic dates important to the popular uprising against the Somoza dictatorship. Nevertheless, taxi cooperatives became well-known bastions of civic opposition to the revolution. Contrary to conventional wisdom, though, taxi drivers were not simply reactionary. Taxi drivers had engaged in transportation strikes against each of four successive governments: those of Somoza, the Sandinistas, Chamorro, and Alemán.

Among the various occupational groups in Managua's informal sector, then, the market trade groups and taxi cooperatives emerged from the turmoil of the 1980s with the strongest associations. Their organizational strength and effectiveness were attributable, more than any other factor, to the characteristics of the occupations themselves. Unlike most informal occupations, with practitioners far-flung around the city, market workers and taxi drivers spend time in close proximity to fellow workers. For most street vendors, owners of small roadside workshops, and other informal sector workers, such opportunities are less readily available.

Aside from mass organizations and occupational associations, religious associations have helped shape the character of Nicaraguan civil society, including the urban informal sector. Since the time of the popular struggle against Somoza, when Christian base communities played a key role in consciousness raising among the poor, religious association has been an important basis of political cleavage in Nicaragua. Although the progressive Catholic church has been associated with the Sandinista revolution while the traditional Catholic church and the evangelical Protestant movement have maintained a hostile stance toward Sandinismo, religion's influence on the political beliefs of the urban poor is complex. As Davis (1997) has shown, religious conflict has had less influence on partisan cleavages among informal sector workers in Nicaragua in comparison to the influence of other political, economic, and historical factors.

A broad view of civil society within Nicaragua's urban informal sector shows a population that has matured in the midst of social, political, and religious turmoil. Daily struggle with economic necessity has not allowed much leisure for civic activities. The characteristics of informal sector work have likewise mitigated against the formation of strong occupational associations for most workers. Nevertheless, experience with revolutionary mass organizations, workplace cooperatives, and religious groups has shaped a civil society that has frequently proved itself willing to challenge the incumbent government.

The FSLN moreover, has never been simply a mechanism for mobilizing voters, like political parties in many consolidated democratic systems (see Verba et al. 1978). From the beginning, the party has attempted to create and maintain space for the emergence of decentralized, grassroots civil society. Some of the party's actions were contradictory, as commitment to popular democracy conflicted with the demands of a war economy and of drastic structural readjustment. Still, the linkages that developed between the FSLN and civil society distinguished the party from many other political parties in the region and in Nicaragua itself.

Costa Rica

In Costa Rica, one of the major contributors to the stabilty of the country's democracy in the post-1948 era has been the state's capacity to limit and control lower-class political mobilization (Peeler 1985; Yashar 1997). Ironically, the Costa Rican state has still been one of the more responsive and progressive of Latin American states in implementing various social welfare measures and social reforms, despite the lack of a militant civil society among the lower classes. The Bismarckian character of the Costa Rican state has continued to some extent even with the neoliberal reforms of recent years (see Gindling and Berry 1992). As Yashar explains, "the Costa Rican regime after 1948 consolidated the welfare state, created during the reform period, with the intention of providing social services for and preempting demands by urban and rural popular classes" (1997, 190).[6]

The preemptive nature of social reforms since 1948 does not mean that civil society in contemporary Costa Rica is politically inert and powerless (see Booth 1998, 95–98). Interest articulation, however, is usually carried out through the established parties—the National Liberation Party (PLN) and the Social Christian Unity Party (PUSC)—and in ways that do not threaten the coalitional foundations of the state (see Yashar 1995, 95–99).

Costa Rica's working class is affiliated with a variety of community-level organizations. These include community development organizations and other organized groups, both urban and rural, which have demanded policy changes and improved services (see Booth 1998, 97–98). In addition, a substantial number of the working class are probably active members of either Costa Rica's generally conservative Catholic church or its recently emergent Protestant sects (see Booth 1998, 89–91). All these organizations in civil society could potentially be agents of politicization. Costa Rica, however, does not have a tradition of militant labor unions in the post-1948 era. Indeed, as Backer (1978) has noted, the strongest period of union organization in Costa Rica occurred between 1942 and 1948, before the establishment of the current democratic regime. Between 1948 and 1965, unions lost significant membership and saw their political influence fade almost to the vanishing point. The weakening of the union movement was largely orchestrated by post-1948 governments, partly through restrictive labor laws that curbed the unions' political activity and collective bargaining power (Yashar 1997, 187). At the same time, those governments sought to consolidate support for the established parties by adopting popular social reforms (see Peeler 1985). Only since 1965 have unions started a meager turnaround in their membership and their political influence (Backer 1978, 13).

In contrast to the fate of unions, solidarity associations and cooperatives have emerged as the leading forms of collective organization among workers in Costa Rica. Unlike unions, these organizations have been embraced by the Costa Rican government as preferred methods of labor organization. Solidarity associations are set up in individual firms to provide loans and other services to workers through profit-sharing arrangements. Business and the state both prefer these nonconfrontational associations as an alternative to unions. Not surprisingly, they have weakened the Costa Rican union movement (Booth 1998, 97; also Yashar 1997, 187, 268–69).

The Costa Rican state's acceptance of the cooperative movement has been so complete that a government institution was created in 1973 to promote the creation of cooperatives for a variety of economic activities. INFOCOOP (the National Institute for Cooperative Development) provides seed money for creation of new cooperatives and also extends them credit. It supplies technical expertise for newly created organizations, from help with setting up the organizational structure to accounting procedures. This assistance has contributed to the growth of cooperatives throughout the Costa Rican work force. Vargas (1992) estimates that by the late 1980s, some 30 percent of the economically active population belonged to a cooperative.

The reason the state favors cooperatives and solidarity associations as a form of labor organization is related to their decentralized, fragmented, and apartisan structure, which poses virtually no threat to political stability and the continuing hegemony of the two-party system. These associations, along with unions, remain largely independent entities politically and do not march in lockstep with any political party. Depending on the political issue, some support government positions while others oppose the government. In recent decades, these organizations have often found themselves in opposition to neoliberal policies that Costa Rican governments have adopted. This was particularly true during the presidency of the PLN's José María Figueres (1994–98). During this period, the economic situation in Costa Rica worsened dramatically, and the state deepened its neoliberal policies.

THE SURVEY DATA

To trace the relationship between civil society and political mobilization in the urban informal sector, this study began with two surveys of characteristics of the urban informal sector, a different survey from each country. The data on Nicaragua come from a January 1991 survey of 480 informal sector workers in Managua. The survey instrument was designed for a longer study of the motivational basis of regime support among the urban informal sector in Managua (Speer 1999). The survey was conducted by a research firm in Managua, ITZTANI-INOP.

ITZTANI-INOP interviewed 80 members from each of 6 occupational groups selected to reflect the heterogeneity of the urban informal sector: taxi drivers, street vendors, market vendors, owners of homefront stores (*pulperías*), mechanized workshops, and more labor-intensive workshops. Taxi drivers were interviewed at five different cooperatives and market stallkeepers at three open markets. The other occupational practitioners were interviewed in 20 randomly selected *barrios* of the city. Each enterprise employed five or fewer workers (for further discussion, see Speer 1997, 1999).

The Costa Rican data come from a July 1993 survey of 504 informal sector workers in San José (N = 403) and Limón (N = 101). The survey instrument was designed for a longer study of this sector's political attitudes and behavior (Aguilar 1995). The survey was conducted by the market research firm UNIMER of San José. Random sampling techniques were applied as much as possible to street vendors, licensed and unlicensed taxi drivers, cobblers, market vendors, and *pulpería* owners. As in the Nicaraguan sample, these groups were selected to reflect the heterogeneity of the informal sector, from street vendors, the group most clearly exhibiting informal sector characteristics, to licensed taxi drivers, a group on the boundary between the informal and formal sectors.

For example, as both Speer (1999, chap. 5) and Aguilar (1995, 23–62) show, taxi drivers in both countries fit four of the criteria of informality as identified by the International Labor Office (see Hart 1973, 61–89): family ownership, small production, labor-intensive technology, and dependence on informally acquired skills. *Piratas* (unlicensed taxi drivers) in the Costa Rican sample work in unregulated markets, another characteristic identified with the informal sector. Even though taxi drivers operate on the boundary of the formal and informal economies, their income level in these samples is not out of line with the incomes of other occupational groups more clearly identified with the informal sector (see tables 1 and 2).[7]

Table 1. Income of Informal Sector Workers by Occupation: Nicaragua (in U.S. dollars)

	Income on a good day				Income on a bad day				Income on a typical day			
	Mean	Median	Standard Deviation	N	Mean	Median	Standard Deviation	N	Mean	Median	Standard Deviation	N
Street vendor	$11	$6	$11	73	$3	$2	$3	71	$6	$4	$6	73
Traditional workshop	$13	$7	$19	67	$3	$1	$7	67	$7	$3	$13	68
Pulpería	$22	$9	$31	54	$6	$3	$8	54	$11	$6	$14	54
Market seller	$16	$12	$15	59	$3	$3	$3	59	$8	$6	$8	59
Nontraditional workshop	$33	$18	$45	62	$6	$1	$10	62	$17	$8	$25	62
Taxi driver	$21	$22	$11	76	$6	$6	$6	76	$13	$12	$8	76
Total sample	$19	$12	$25	391	$4	$3	$7	389	$10	$6	$14	392

N = 480
Note: Respondents self-reported income in millions of córdobas. Dollar figures calculated at current exchange rate on survey date: 3,274,000 córdobas to US$1.
Source: Speer survey data 1991.

Table 2. Income of Informal Sector Workers by Occupation: Costa Rica (in U.S. dollars)

	Income on a good day				Income on a bad day				Income on an average day			
	Mean	Median	Standard Deviation	N	Mean	Median	Standard Deviation	N	Mean	Median	Standard Deviation	N
Taxi driver	$28	$21	$21	84	$10	$8	$7	84	$19	$15	$13	84
Pulpería	$113	$106	$81	84	$49	$35	$48	84	$81	$70	$66	84
Cobbler	$21	$17	$22	84	$6	$7	$8	84	$14	$10	$12	84
Unlicensed taxi driver	$33	$28	$28	84	$13	$10	$8	84	$23	$21	$15	84
Market seller	$69	$56	$58	83	$20	$14	$17	83	$45	$35	$35	83
Street vendor	$24	$22	$60	84	$11	$7	$16	84	$25	$16	$37	84
Total sample	$51	$28	$26	503	$18	$10	$61	503	$34	$19	$42	503

N = 504

Note: Respondents self-reported income in colones. Exchange rate at time of survey: approx. 141.50 colones to US$1. "Average day" income derived from average of "good" and "bad" days.

Source: Aguilar survey data 1993.

While sampling procedures in both cases may have not produced representative samples of the urban informal sector, these stratified samples do reflect its heterogeneity.[8] Tables 1 and 2 show measures of central tendency (mean and median) for respondents' self-reported income "on a good day" and "on a bad day." In addition, self-reported income "on a typical day" is shown for the Nicaraguan sample (table 1), while an estimate of average daily income of Costa Rican respondents is reported in table 2. For the Costa Rican sample, this figure is obtained by averaging expected income on a good and bad day.

For both samples, income levels vary significantly by occupational groups. In the case of the Nicaraguan sample, "typical" daily median income levels range between US$3 for workers in traditional (labor-intensive) shops to US$12 for taxi drivers (see table 1).[9] As expected, income levels are significantly higher in the Costa Rican sample but also vary by occupational category, between a median income of US$10 on an "average day" for cobblers to a median income of US$80 for *pulpería* owners (see table 2). Income levels are higher for unlicensed than for licensed taxi drivers, possibly because the routes, hours, and prices of unlicensed drivers (*piratas*) are not regulated (see Aguilar 1995, chap. 1). Moreover, relatively high standard deviations in some cases indicate significant variation in income within some occupational groups. The wide variation between incomes on "a good day" and "a bad day" for all occupational groups indicates the vulnerable economic position of the informal sector in both countries.[10]

Educational levels are roughly comparable in the two samples; the average in both is above the sixth grade. The gender composition differs. In the Nicaraguan sample, 45 percent of the respondents are female, while only 12 percent of the Costa Rican sample is female. Therefore the composition of the samples differs significantly in regard to gender and income. This compositional variation is important to remember in analyzing the effects of associational involvement and party loyalty on political mobilization.

PREDICTORS OF POLITICAL INVOLVEMENT

The analysis of the survey data focused on the relative importance of associational affiliations compared to demographic variables and party loyalty as predictors of various forms of political mobilization, both cognitive and behavioral. The first task, though, was to gauge the frequency with which respondents engaged in various modes of political participation, ranging from low-intensity voting to higher-intensity activities like petitioning government authorities, protest, engagement in political discussions, and campaign involvement. The analysis also looked at frequency distributions for associational affiliations, along with the determinants of associational affiliation.

The first issue addressed was the extent to which respondents in both countries joined various types of civic associations. Respondents in both samples were asked about current membership in a variety of organizations as well as about membership in any organization in the past (table 3). Both samples make it clear that these respondents are not joiners. For all organizations, less than 20 percent of the sample report membership. It is also clear in both samples that respondents are more likely to be members of occupational organizations than of other types of organizations. Occupational organizations include cooperatives and unions in both samples, along with solidarity and professional associations in the Costa Rican case. This finding probably reflects the centrality of economic concerns to workers whose economic situation is precarious.

Cooperatives are clearly the most common venue by which these informal sector workers seek collective solutions to their economic problems. These organizations in both samples draw disproportionately from licensed taxi drivers. In both samples, a larger number of respondents report membership in the past than in current organizations (table 3). This finding suggests that organizational membership in both countries is transitory.

Further insight might be gained into these workers' organizational propensities by focusing on the number of organizations to which they belong or used to belong. Table 4 groups the number of their affiliations into none, one, and two or more, counting present along with reported past affiliations. Table 4 also shows membership affiliation by country and party loyalty. Attention to party loyalty gives some insight into the role of political parties in stimulating mass involvement in civil society. Comparing the two total columns reveals very similar profiles. Party loyalists in both samples are somewhat more likely to affiliate with civic organizations than are independents.

The most striking finding of table 4, however, is the much greater propensity of FSLN loyalists to engage in civil society activities than that of UNO loyalists or loyalists of Costa Rica's two centrist parties. Were FSLN loyalists excluded, the Costa Rican sample would exhibit significantly higher levels of engagement than the Nicaraguan sample. This finding suggests that the FSLN, more than the other parties, has served as an agent of collective mobilization beyond the electoral arena.

In addition to partisanship, individual socioeconomic characteristics that might also be expected to correlate with engagement in collective organizations are considered. To examine these predictors of associational membership, an ordinary least squares (OLS) regression analysis was used (see appendix). People of higher socioeconomic status, older citizens, church attenders, and males in Latin American societies might be expected to be more active in civil society; such relationships have been found elsewhere in Latin America (see, among others, Verba et al. 1978). Table 5

Table 3. Association Membership (percent of sample)

	Nicaragua			Costa Rica		
	Yes	No	Unreported[a]	Yes	No	Unreported[a]
Neighborhood association	3.1	96.9	0.2	7.0	93.0	0.6
Cooperatives	16.1	83.9	0.2	16.2	83.8	0.8
Union	1.5	98.3	0.2	3.8	96.2	0.6
Other organizations	0.2	99.8	0.0	4.5	95.5	3.2
Past membership	18.1	81.9	0.0	16.8	83.2	6.0
Christian base community	1.3	98.8	0.0	—	—	—
Solidarity association	—	—	—	2.4	97.6	0.08
Professional association	—	—	—	2.6	97.4	1.0

[a]Percent unreported calculated separately from frequency distributions.
Source: Speer survey data 1991 (N = 480); Aguilar survey data 1993 (N = 504).

shows that such individual characteristics do matter in both Costa Rica and Nicaragua. Age and socioeconomic status are associated with greater involvement in civic associations. More economically secure members of the informal sector and older workers may feel less constrained by family and job pressures and, therefore, may take on more organizational involvements. A clear difference between the two countries is that gender bias in organizational membership appears to be more prevalent among Nicaraguans than among Costa Ricans. Perhaps this finding reflects a greater diffusion of the women's movement in the more economically advanced countries of Latin America.[11]

Here again is evidence of the influence of loyalty to the Sandinista party on engagement in civil society. With the exception of gender, FSLN loyalty is the strongest predictor of organizational involvement in the Nicaraguan sample. By contrast, loyalty to the PLN, while statistically significant, is a weaker predictor of organizational involvement than either age or socioeconomic status in the Costa Rican case. Loyalty to the PUSC does not obtain statistical significance as a predictor of organizational involvement. Clearly, age and socioeconomic status are better predictors of this variable than is party loyalty.

Unfortunately, the samples lack similar indicators of political participation, with the exception of campaign activism. Still, available indicators of what we have labeled high-intensity forms of participation provide insight into the political activities that require a substantially greater

Table 4. Association Membership and Party Loyalty (percent of sample)

	Nicaragua				Costa Rica			
	FSLN	UNO	Ind.	Total	PLN	PUSC	Ind.	Total
Number of organizations								
None	45.3	67.1	75.1	66.3	58.5	62.5	74.1	64.2
1	44.2	23.1	16.9	24.6	25.2	25.0	19.0	23.4
2+	10.5	9.8	7.9	9.1	16.4	12.5	6.9	12.4
N	86	143	189	418	159	136	116	411
Contingency coefficient			0.24	0.15				
Significance level			0.0001	0.07				

Note: Sample includes present and past affiliations.
Source: Speer survey data 1991 (N = 480); Aguilar survey data 1993 (N = 504).

investment of individual energy, skills, resources, and time than does voting. In the aggregate, levels of this type of political participation among respondents in both samples were low. In the Nicaraguan case, fully 90.3 percent of respondents reported almost never attending political meetings, while 87.7 percent indicated that they almost never discussed politics within an organization. Similarly, 86.7 percent of the Nicaraguans reported almost never participating in campaign activities. Similar patterns were found in the Costa Rican case. Only 14.2 percent of the respondents reported ever participating in a political protest, while only 18.0 percent had ever joined in presenting a demand or petition to the government, and only 28.2 percent had participated in campaign activities. As found elsewhere (see, among others, Verba et al. 1978), mass publics exhibit a limited involvement in politics beyond voting, and even less might be expected from the urban informal sectors of Latin American countries.

As expected, voting was a far more common activity. Among Costa Ricans, the data show that 73.1 percent of respondents reported voting in the 1990 presidential election, while 75.8 percent expected to vote in the 1994 presidential election. Data on voting were not available from the Nicaraguan survey. It is likely, however, that voter turnout in the 1984 and 1990 presidential elections was also high in the informal sector. According to one study (Barnes 1998), national turnout was about 69.0 percent of the voting-age population in the 1984 presidential election and about 78.0 percent in the 1990 presidential election.[12] It is safe to assume that turnout rates for the Nicaraguan informal sector are substantially higher than rates for high-intensity political activities.

Reported campaign activism was considerably higher in the Costa Rican sample than in the Nicaraguan (28.2 percent versus 13.3 percent). We would hesitate to conclude on this basis alone that participation in

Table 5. Predictors of Membership in Civic Associations

	Nicaragua		Costa Rica	
	B	Beta	B	Beta
Socioeconomic variables				
Socioeconomic status (SES)	0.07*	0.15*	0.13*	0.20*
Age	0.07*	0.12*	0.01*	0.14*
Church attendance	0.00	0.00	0.01	0.03
Gender[a]	0.38*	0.29*	0.10	0.04
Party loyalty				
FSLN	0.26*	0.17*		
UNO	0.02	0.02		
PLN			0.17*	0.11*
PUSC			0.11	0.07
Adjusted r2	0.14		0.07	
F value	11.96*		4.98*	

[a]Male = 1, female = 0
Note: Sample includes present and past affiliations.
*The F value, or regression coefficient, is statistically significant at the .05 level or beyond.

high-intensity activities is higher among the urban informal sector in Costa Rica. Findings from the Booth and Richard study (1998a), however, suggest this possibility. Those data show that in urban, cross-sectional samples from these two countries, Costa Ricans were more likely to be active in voting, campaign activities, and contacting public officials than were Nicaraguans (see Booth and Richard 1998a, table 1, p. 37).[13] Unfortunately for the purposes of the present research, Booth and Richard do not report data on the informal sector. Theoretically, at least, we might expect the informal sector in Costa Rica to be more politically active because of a longer history of democratic government and a more open civil society.

The next question in the analysis is the relative influence of civic association membership and party loyalty on the likelihood of these informal sector workers' engaging in high-intensity political particpation and, for the Costa Rican sample, in voting. In addition, the relative effects of associational affiliation and party loyalty on the degree of cognitive mobilization are considered. Respondents' party loyalty, church attendance, and various individual socioeconomic characteristics are analyzed as alternative explanatory factors.

For the Nicaraguan case, OLS regression coefficients were derived for the dependent variables of attendance at political meetings, participation in campaign activities, and engagement in political discussions in an organization, plus a summative measure of all three. As shown in table 6, none of the socioeconomic indicators is statistically significant as a predictor of high-intensity participation, nor is church attendance. Perhaps this finding reflects the characteristic that the great majority of church attenders do so at traditional Catholic or Protestant churches, rather than at progressive ones where political issues are more directly confronted.[14]

The data show that these types of political participation can be linked primarily to membership in civic associations and party loyalty (table 6). Workers who belong to organizations are more likely to engage in each of these political activities.[15] In the Nicaraguan case, however, loyalty to the FSLN is even more important. Except for the variable of discussing politics in an organization, the beta weights, or standardized coefficients, are substantially higher for loyalty to the FSLN than for associational affiliation.

Table 6 also shows that loyalty to the UNO is a statistically significant predictor of participation in campaign activities but not of the other forms of high-intensity participation. Verba et al. report similar findings in their seven-nation study (1978), which found party loyalty in some cases related to electoral forms of participation, such as voting or campaign activities, but not to nonelectoral forms of participation. Presumably, political parties have an incentive to mobilize voters and campaign activists but not other types of political activists. By contrast, the FSLN has stimulated a higher-intensity mobilization among its supporters that extends beyond the electoral arena. This finding can be explained by the party's demonstrated commitment to mass mobilization both inside and outside the electoral arena.

The Costa Rican case reveals some similarities with the Nicaraguan sample (table 7). Individual socioeconomic characteristics exert minimal influence on the likelihood of engaging in high-intensity political activities, including petitioning, campaign participation, and political protest. Only one of the regression coefficients achieves statistical significance. There is a slight tendency for younger workers to participate more in electoral campaigns. This finding is somewhat surprising and contrary to conventional wisdom; it should be kept in mind that this is a modest relationship. Also as in the Nicaraguan case, associational affiliation is a statistically significant predictor. It is interesting that church attendance significantly relates to campaign participation but not to the other two indicators. Therefore, involvement in civil organizations does lead to a more politically active informal sector in both Costa Rica and Nicaragua. But are civil associations or political parties more important mobilizing agents in Costa Rica?

The data show that loyalty to the PLN and the PUSC is a statistically significant predictor of campaign activism but not of the two nonelectoral forms of participation (table 7). By contrast, petitioning and protest

Table 6. Predictors of High-Intensity Political Activities: Nicaragua

	Attend Political Meetings		Participate in Campaign Activities		Discuss Politics in an Organization		Summative Measure (Factor Scale)	
	B	Beta	B	Beta	B	Beta	B	Beta
Socioeconomic								
SES	-0.03	-0.05	0.00	0.00	-0.04	-0.09	-0.04	-0.06
Age	-0.02	-0.05	-0.03	-0.05	-0.02	-0.04	-0.04	-0.05
Gender	-0.02	-0.02	0.08	0.06	0.11	0.08	0.09	0.05
Associational Church attendance	-0.04	-0.05	0.03	0.05	0.00	0.00	-0.02	-0.02
Membership in civic associations	0.10*	0.11*	0.21*	0.20*	0.29*	0.28*	0.37*	0.23*
Partisan								
FSLN	0.45*	0.33*	0.49*	0.31*	0.48*	0.30*	0.91*	0.39*
UNO	0.05	0.04	0.15*	0.11*	0.04	0.03	0.15	0.07
Adjusted r2		0.12		0.13		0.28		0.21
F value		7.08*		7.83*		11.18*		12.77*

*The F value, or regression coefficient, is statistically significant at the .05 level or beyond.

engagement are influenced more by associational membership than by party loyalty. The impact of party loyalty becomes much more apparent in relation to voting (table 8). Whether these respondents turn out for elections depends far more on their attachment to one of the two major parties than on their affiliation with civil associations. Without those party ties, the likelihood of not voting increases substantially. Unlike the FSLN and more like the UNO in Nicaragua, Costa Rica's two major parties engage in electoral mobilization but do not facilitate collective mobilization outside the electoral arena. In sum, the relative influence of political parties and civic associations on political participation in Costa Rica depends on whether the mode of participation is electoral or nonelectoral.

The next consideration is the relative influence of associational involvement and partisan loyalty on cognitive mobilization. Two different dimensions of cognitive politics are available from the data sets used for this study.[16] In the Costa Rican data set, this factor is political efficacy, a person's sense of empowerment to influence the political process. In the Nicaraguan data it is political interest, the extent to which the person pays attention to the political world (see appendix). Both attributes would

Table 7. Predictors of High-Intensity Political Activism: Costa Rica

	Petition		Participate in Campaign Activities		Protest		Summative Measure (1+2+3)	
	B	Beta	B	Beta	B	Beta	B	Beta
Socioeconomic								
SES	-0.03	-0.07	0.01	0.03	-0.02	-0.05	-0.02	-0.03
Age	0.00	-0.03	-0.01*	-0.13*	0.00	-0.08	-0.01*	-0.12*
Gender	0.01	0.01	0.10	0.07	0.02	0.02	0.11	0.05
Associational								
Church attendance	0.01	0.02	0.03*	0.12*	0.02	0.09	0.06*	0.11*
Membership in civic associations	0.06*	0.11*	0.06*	0.09*	0.09*	0.18*	0.20*	0.18*
Partisan								
PLN	-0.01	-0.01	0.20*	0.22*	0.03	0.04	0.18*	0.11*
PUSC	0.08	0.10	0.17*	0.18*	0.06	0.07	0.30*	0.17*
Adjusted r2		0.01		0.07		0.03		0.06
F value		1.57		5.56*		2.93*		4.81*

*The F value, or regression coefficient, is statistically significant at the .05 level or beyond.

presumably enable a person to engage in self-directed political action without the external guidance that has traditionally been provided through Latin America's corporatist and clientelist systems of representation.

Table 9 shows that membership in civic associations in both samples is a statistically significant predictor of these cognitive dimensions of politics. Membership in these organizations increases the likelihood that informal sector workers will acquire the cognitive capacities necessary for activist citizenship. Although comparing two different cognitive dimensions must be done carefully, the contrast in the influence of partisanship across these two samples is striking. Loyalty to the FSLN emerges as the strongest predictor of political interest in the Nicaraguan case (compare the beta weights in table 9). By contrast, loyalty to the two major Costa Rican parties is negatively associated with political efficacy. This finding suggests that these parties might well mobilize support among the least politically engaged of the informal sector. In general, these findings support the argument that the functions of political parties in Latin America are not necessarily limited only to periodic mobilization of voters. The case of the

Table 8. Predictors of Voting: Costa Rica

	B	Beta
Socioeconomic		
SES	0.03	0.02
Age	0.01*	0.15*
Gender	-0.08	-0.03
Associational		
Church attendance	0.01	0.02
Membership in civic associations	0.10*	0.10*
Partisan		
PLN	0.99*	0.64*
PUSC	0.99*	0.62*
Adjusted r2		0.44
F value		47.01*

*The F value, or regression coefficient, is statistically significant at the .05 level or beyond.

FSLN shows that certain parties actually facilitate the acquisition of cognitive attributes necessary for self-directed participation.

Two other findings deserve comment. The gender bias noted among Nicaraguan respondents is also apparent in relation to political interest; males are likely to be more attentive to politics. By contrast, there is no evidence of such bias in the distribution of responses in the Costa Rican efficacy scale. The other finding is that church attenders in Costa Rica tend to feel more politically empowered than nonattenders. By contrast, church attenders in Nicaragua tend to be less interested in politics than are nonattenders. Unfortunately, the Costa Rican data do not allow us to explore the type of churches that respondents attend or the nature of their interaction within churches. As noted, Nicaraguan respondents tend to identify with traditional Catholicism, which might discourage an interest in the secular world of politics. Costa Rican churches, on the whole, might provide more opportunity for the acquisition of civic skills and the motivation necessary for activist citizenship, as found for churches in the United States (Brady et al. 1995).

The final question for analysis is how the independent variables influence alienation from or allegiance to the currently established political order. Costa Rica provides an example of a consolidated competitive democratic regime; Nicaragua, a competitive democratic regime in the process of consolidation. As such, the legitimacy of the latter regime is still contested. The effect of engagement in civic associations on system support appears to be largely neutral in both samples; that is, it has

Table 9. Predictors of Cognitive Mobilization

	Nicaragua: political interest		Costa Rica: political efficacy	
	B	Beta	B	Beta
Socioeconomic				
SES	0.07*	0.10*	0.04	0.07
Age	-0.06	-0.06	0.01	0.06
Gender[a]	0.35*	0.16*	0.04	0.02
Associational				
Church attendance	-0.10	-0.09	0.06*	0.14*
Membership in				
civic associations	0.28*	0.16*	0.11*	0.11*
Party loyalty				
FSLN	0.23*	0.22*		
UNO	0.20	0.09		
PLN			-0.20*	-0.14*
PUSC			-0.05	-0.03
Adjusted r2	0.14		0.04	
F value	8.45*		3.29*	

[a]Male = 1, female = 0
*The F value, or regression coefficient, is statistically significant at the .05 level or beyond.

essentially no relationship with diffuse support for the regime (see table 10; appendix). Perhaps the explanation is that citizens use civic associations primarily to work toward more immediate economic goals but not for addressing larger issues regarding the quality or merits of the political regime or public policy. The short-term instrumental purposes of these associations, however, still do not prevent them from also becoming agents of politicization and mobilization.

Political parties clearly exert a more powerful influence on this basic political orientation. In Costa Rica, supporters of the two dominant parties are more likely to exhibit regime support. This finding might be expected from partisans of long-established political parties in a consolidated regime. Similar findings have been reported for partisans of the Democratic and Republican parties in the United States (Ginsberg 1986). For Nicaragua, Sandinista supporters tend to be more negative and supporters of the UNO more positive toward the regime.[17] This finding perhaps reflects an alienation among Sandinista supporters, brought on shortly before the 1991 survey by what Williams (1994) calls the demise of "popular" democracy in the transition to electoral democracy in Nicaragua. This

Table 10. Predictors of Diffuse Regime Support

	Nicaragua		Costa Rica	
	B	Beta	B	Beta
Socioeconomic				
SES	0.15*	0.16*	0.05	0.05
Age	0.08	0.06	0.00	0.05
Gender[a]	-0.16	-0.05	0.00	0.00
Associational				
Church attendance	0.01	0.00	0.02	0.02
Membership in				
civic associations	-0.08	-0.05	0.05	0.08
Party loyalty				
FSLN	-0.57*	-0.16*		
UNO	0.64*	0.21*		
PLN			0.25*	0.12*
PUSC			0.29*	0.13*
Adjusted r2	0.11		0.02	
F value	6.82*		2.14*	

[a]Male = 1, female = 0
*The F value, or regression coefficient, is statistically significant at the .05 level or beyond.

finding indicates that at the time of the survey, soon after the FSLN's 1990 electoral defeat, FSLN partisans were less willing to accord legitimacy to the post-Sandinista regime than were other partisan groups.

CONCLUSIONS

Democratic theorists from Tocqueville to Robert Putnam have maintained that involvement in the face-to-face organizations and associations of civil society promotes civic responsibility and engagement in ways that promote democracy. While analysts of civil society in Latin America note the conflictive nature of much popular participation through this means (Foley and Edwards 1998, 11–14), they generally argue that civil society promotes a more engaged form of citizenship than does the institutionalized party system. Within the institutionalized framework of political parties and elections, citizens are largely engaged in a low-intensity form of participation that is often elite-directed and makes only minimal demands on them. In the literature from Latin America, electoral participation is at least implicitly linked to traditional clientelist politics. Civil society, by contrast, presumably promotes a more sustained, committed type of civic engagement. This study has examined these assumptions in the case of the urban informal sector in Nicaragua and Costa Rica.

To summarize the major findings, the level of associational involvement among both samples was found to be low. This finding is consistent with what has been found elsewhere: that the organizational resources of most societies tend to be heavily concentrated among the economically and educationally advantaged (see Verba et al. 1978; Brady et al. 1995). The dispersion and economic vulnerability of the urban informal sector do not facilitate collective organization. To the extent that informal sector workers affiliate, it is most likely with occupation-based organizations. Given their high degree of economic vulnerability and insecurity, this type of organizational focus is hardly surprising.

The data analysis makes clear that the organizational milieu of the urban informal sector contributes to a more activist type of citizenship than is generally encountered among this sector as a whole. Organizational involvement in both samples fosters both greater cognitive engagement with politics and high-intensity forms of participation. These effects are observed among people who are presumably among the least politicized and least motivated to participate. Thus these findings are fully consistent with other studies showing that emergent civil societies in Latin America can be a significant source of popular sector mobilization that extends beyond electoral participation (Booth and Richard 1998b; Oxhorn 1995; Dietz 1998).

The civil society literature suggests that the nature of political engagement in electoral politics is fundamentally different from political engagement that develops from civil society. The findings of this study only partially support that argument. In Costa Rica, fundamentally different forms of citizen political engagement were found in these two arenas. Within the institutionalized framework of political parties and elections, citizens are largely engaged in voting, an activity that is largely elite-directed and makes only minimal demands on citizens. The only exception is the promotion of some campaign activism by party elites (see table 7). By contrast, the main impetus to more demanding forms of participation come from the associations of civil society.

The Nicaraguan case does not fit this pattern. Similar to the Costa Rican case, associational involvement in Nicaragua is related to high-intensity participation and to cognitive mobilization. One party, the FSLN, however, also is linked to political activism that extends beyond electoral participation. To understand why this party differs both from the Costa Rican parties and the UNO in this respect, we must understand the party's origins. The FSLN did not simply emerge from new societal, factional, or value cleavages, as new parties might do in established party systems. It emerged instead as a fountainhead for a revolutionary transition from a repressive authoritarian government. The party needed to mobilize civil society to succeed in its struggle against the Somoza dynasty. Its commitment to popular democracy continued after coming to power, albeit within limits (Williams 1994; Hoyt 1997).

This study helps to explain why activist citizenship is not significantly lower in the new democracy of Nicaragua than in the more established democracy of Costa Rica. The FSLN contributed to the formation of a relatively autonomous civil society and, along with the popular sector, helped to create a more activist citizenry. Thus the participatory gap between this and a more established democracy could be closed. To exclude FSLN loyalists from the sample would create a significantly larger participatory gap between the two samples. In Nicaragua, a political party has played a far larger role in promoting democratic citizenship than the civil society literature generally recognizes. Indeed, this study cautions against facile assumptions about either civil society or political parties in promoting citizen participation. The mobilizational capabilities of each may depend far more on the national context than has been generally recognized.

APPENDIX: MEASUREMENT TOOLS

Ordinary Least Squares Regression Analysis (OLS)

This type of analysis assumes a linear relationship between each independent variable and the dependent variable. The B coefficients are the unstandardized regression coefficients that measure the amount of change in the dependent variable that is produced by a unit change in the independent variable, holding the other independent variables constant. Beta coefficients are standardized regression coefficients in which all independent variables have been standardized to faciltate comparison. The F value tests whether a linear relationship exists between the dependent variable and the entire set of independent variables. The adjusted r2 value measures the amount of variance in the dependent variable explained by each set of independent variables. For more on regression analysis, see Berry and Feldman 1985.

Socioeconomic Status (SES)

For the Nicaraguan sample, SES was measured by a standardized index of reported average daily income and number of years of formal education. For the Costa Rican sample, SES was measured by a factor scale using per capita family income, formal education, and interviewer assessment of socioeconomic condition (above poverty line, basic needs not met, extreme poverty).

Political Interest

This factor scale was formed for the Nicaraguan sample from four items in which respondents were asked about the frequency with which they discussed politics at home, discussed politics at work, read political news in the newspapers, and paid attention to broadcast news.

Political Efficacy

This factor scale was formed for the Costa Rican sample from three items: the respondent's ability to link what the respondent had identified as the most serious problem in the city to an origin, the respondent's perceived capacity to do something to help solve this problem, and the respondent's perception of the likelihood that the government would pay attention to respondent's suggestions for solving the problem.

Diffuse Support for the Regime

For the Nicaraguan sample, a standardized measure of diffuse support was formed with two indicators: whether respondent felt pride in the Nicaraguan political system and whether respondent thought the political system should be changed or left alone. For the Costa Rican sample, a six-item factor scale was used: respondent's assessment of fairness of courts, assessment of protection of human rights, pride in Costa Rican political system, feeling toward Costa Rican political system, opinion of the degree to which citizens ought support the Costa Rican political system, and adequacy of representation in the political system.

ACRONYMS

AMNLAE .... Asociación de Mujeres Nicaragüenses Luisa Amanda Espinosa
CDS .... Comités de Defensa Sandinista
CONAPI .... Cámara Nacional de Mediana y Pequeña Industria
INFOCOOP .... Instituto Nacional de Fomento Cooperativo
FSLN .... Frente Sandinista de Liberación Nacional
JS .... Juventud Sandinista
PLN .... Partido Liberación Nacional
PUSC .... Partido Unidad Social Cristiana
UNO .... Unión Nacional Oppositora

NOTES

The authors thank Kenneth M. Coleman for his useful comments on an earlier version of this article. Professors Speer and Aguilar gratefully acknowledge financial support from the National Science Foundation for the surveys used in this study.

1. Interest in civil society has emerged on multiple fronts, including the left in Western Europe, the right in the United States, and the "neo-Tocquevilleans" who have evolved out of Robert Putnam's work. As a consequence, different conceptions of civil society have developed; see Foley and Edwards 1998, 5–11.

2. Their concept of social capital draws from Putnam 1993, 163–85.

3. As defined by Dalton, "Cognitive mobilization means that citizens possess the level of political skills and resources necessary to become self-sufficient in politics. Instead of depending on elites and reference groups (external mobilization), citizens are now better able to deal with the complexities of politics and make their own political decisions" (1988, 18).

4. See Ameringer 1982 and Biesanz et al. 1979 for discussions of the founding of the modern Costa Rican state.

5. For a more detailed discussion of the FSLN since 1990, see Prevost 1997, 149–64.

6. Paige (1997, 244–50) argues that the creation of the welfare state during the reform period of the 1940s cannot be explained as a preemptive response on the part of the coffee oligarchy but instead was caused by pressures from below, particularly from popular organizations, the Catholic church, and the Communist Party.

7. For further discussion of Costa Rican sample, see Aguilar 1995, chap. 1; for the Nicaraguan sample, see Speer 1999, chap. 5.

8. It is impossible to determine how representative these samples are of each country's informal sector because accurate estimates of population parameters are not available for each occupational group. In achieving greater heterogeneity of occupational groups, moreover, these samples may well be biased toward the upper income level of the informal sector.

9. The median is the value at the midpoint of the distribution, such that half the sample is above and half below the median value. This measure of central tendency is a more useful measure of income than the mean, which can be distorted by extreme cases.

10. The reader is cautioned about annualizing these income figures because on many days, workers may earn very little or no income. Caution should also be exercised in comparing the annual income of urban dwellers to per capita GDP in countries where rural income is so much lower and the rural population so large.

11. Women's issues have not been a high priority with the FSLN, which might help to explain the relationships with gender. See Polakoff and La Ramée 1997, 191–93. The finding that the Nicaraguan taxi drivers, who are all male, are among the most organized also is a contributing factor in gender differences.

12. Barnes (1998) estimates that registration rates exceeded 90 percent for the 1984, 1990, and 1996 presidential elections, despite a difficult registration process.

13. The surveys for Booth and Richard's study were done in the early 1990s in Costa Rica, El Salvador, Guatemala, Honduras, Nicaragua, and Panama.

14. The Nicaraguan data show that only 65 out of 480 respondents identified with the progressive Catholic church. By contrast, 285 respondents identified with either the traditional Catholic church or with Protestantism. See Davis 1997, 183–212 for these data and further evidence that religion does not play a strong role in the politicization of the Nicaraguan informal sector.

15. It should be noted that the influence of civic associations on participation is independent of party loyalty. It is not the case in Nicaragua that the influence of civil society is simply an artifact of prior loyalty to the FSLN.

16. Ideally we would have preferred to use the same dimension for both samples. Unfortunately, a common indicator of cognitive mobilization was not available. Multiple-item indicators and multiple dimensions of cognitive mobilization also would have been preferable but were not available.

17. Speer (1997, 272–76) has shown that in regard to a diffuse support dimension that he identifies with the social contract (that is, the Constitution and human rights protections), those respondents in this sample who identify with the FSLN are more likely to be positive than other respondents.

REFERENCES

Aguilar, Edwin. 1995. *El sindicato nos tiene con vida aquí:* Informal Labor, Occupational Organization, and Political Behavior in Costa Rica. Ph.D. diss., University of North Carolina, Chapel Hill.

Ameringer, Charles. 1982. *Democracy in Costa Rica.* New York: Praeger.

Babb, Florence E. 1998. From Cooperatives to Microenterprises: The Neoliberal Turn in Postrevolutionary Nicaragua. In *The Third Wave of Modernization in Latin America,* ed. Lynne Phillips. Wilmington: Scholarly Resources. 109–24.

Backer, James. 1978. *La iglesia e el sindicalismo en Costa Rica.* San José: Editorial Costa Rica.

Barnes, William A. 1998. Incomplete Democracy in Central America: Polarization and Voter Turnout in Nicaragua and El Salvador. *Journal of Interamerican Studies and World Affairs* 40, 3 (Fall): 63–101.

Berry, William D., and Stanley Feldman. 1985. *Multiple Regression in Practice.* Beverly Hills: Sage.

Biesanz, Mavis H., Richard Biesanz, and Karen Z. Biesanz. 1979. *Los costarricenses.* San José: Editorial Universidad Estatal a Distancia.

Booth, John A. 1982. *The End and the Beginning: The Nicaraguan Revolution.* Boulder: Westview Press.

———. 1998. *Costa Rica: Quest for Democracy.* Boulder: Westview Press.

Booth, John A., and Patricia Bayer Richard. 1998a. Civil Society and Political Context in Central America. *American Behavioral Scientist* 42, 1 (September): 33–46.

———. 1998b. Civil Society, Political Capital, and Democratization in Central America. *Journal of Politics* 60, 2: 780–800.

Brady, Henry, Sidney Verba, and Kay Lehman Scholzman. 1995. Beyond SES: A Resource Model of Political Participation. *American Political Science Review* 89, 2 (June): 271–94.

Cañel, Eduardo. 1992. Democratization and the Decline of Urban Social Movements in Uruguay: A Political-Institutionalist Account. In *The Making of Social Movements in Latin America: Identity, Strategy, and Democracy*, ed. Arturo Escobar and Sonia E. Alvarez. Boulder: Westview Press. 276–90.

Castiglia, Miguel, Daniel Martínez, and Jaime Mezzera. 1994. *Sector informal urbano: su contribución al producto*. Cuadernos de Ciencias Sociales no. 73. San José: FLACSO.

Coleman, Kenneth M., and Douglas Stuart H. 1997. The Other Parties. In Walker 1997. 165–84.

Collinson, Helen, and Lucinda Broadbent. 1990. *Women and the Revolution in Nicaragua*. London: Zed Books.

Dalton, Russell J. 1988. *Citizen Politics in Western Democracies: Public Opinion and Political Parties in the United States, Great Britain, West Germany, and France*. Chatham, NJ: Chatham House.

Davis, Charles L. 1997. Religious Transformations and Partisan Polarization in Latin America: The Case of the Urban Informal Sector in Nicaragua. *Journal of Developing Areas* 31 (Winter): 183–202.

Dietz, Henry. 1998. *Urban Poverty, Political Participation, and the State: Lima, 1970–1990*. Pittsburgh: University of Pittsburgh Press.

Edwards, Bob, and Michael W. Foley. 1998. Civil Society and Social Capital Beyond Putnam. *American Behavioral Scientist* 42, 1 (September): 124–39.

Envío (Managua). 1991. The Rich Get Richer. March: 41–47.

Foley, Michael W., and Bob Edwards. 1996. The Paradox of Civil Society. *Journal of Democracy* 7, 3 (July): 38–52.

————. 1998. Beyond Tocqueville: Civil Society and Social Capital in Comparative Perspective. *American Behavioral Scientist* 42, 1 (September): 5–20.

Gindling, T. H., and Albert Berry. 1992. The Performance of the Labor Market During Recession and Structural Adjustment: Costa Rica in the 1980s. *World Development* 20, 11: 1599–1616.

Ginsberg, Benjamin. 1986. *The Captive Public: How Mass Opinion Promotes State Power*. New York: Basic Books.

Hart, Keith. 1973. Informal Income Opportunities and Urban Employment in Ghana. *Journal of African Studies* 11, 1 (March): 61–89.

Hoyt, Katherine. 1997. *The Many Faces of Sandinista Democracy*. Athens: Ohio University Center for International Studies.

Itzigsohn, José. 1996. Globalization, the State, and the Informal Economy: The Limits to Proletarianization in the Latin American Periphery. In *Latin America in the World Economy*, ed. Roberto Patricio Korzeniewicz and William C. Smith. Westport: Greenwood Press. 101–16.

Jelin, Elizabeth. 1997. Emergent Citizenship or Exclusion? Social Movements and Non-Governmental Organizations in the 1990s. In *Politics, Social Change, and Economic Restructuring in Latin America*, ed. William C. Smith and Roberto Patricio Korzeniewicz. Coral Gables: North-South Center Press. 79–104.

Korzeniewicz, Roberto Patricio. 1997. The Deepening Differentiation of States, Enterprises, and Households in Latin America. In *Politics, Social Change, and Economic Restructuring in Latin America*, ed. William C. Smith and Roberto Patricio Korzeniewicz. Coral Gables: North-South Center Press. 215–50.

Morley, Samuel A. 1995. *Poverty and Inequality in Latin America: The Impact of Adjustment and Recovery in the 1980s.* Baltimore: Johns Hopkins University Press.

O'Donnell, Guillermo. 1994. The State, Democratization, and Some Conceptual Problems. In *Latin American Political Economy in the Age of Neoliberal Reform: Theoretical and Comparative Perspectives for the 1990s*, ed. William C. Smith, Carlos H. Acuña, and Eduardo A. Gamarra. Coral Gables: North-South Center Press. 157–80.

Oxhorn, Philip D. 1995. *Organizing Civil Society: The Popular Sectors and the Struggle for Democracy in Chile.* University Park: Pennsylvania State University Press.

————. 1998. Social Inequality, Civil Society, and the Limits of Citizenship in Latin America. Paper presented at the 1998 Meeting of the Latin American Studies Association, Chicago, September 24–26.

Paige, Jeffery M. 1997. *Coffee and Power: Revolution and the Rise of Democracy in Central America.* Cambridge: Harvard University Press.

Peeler, John A. 1985. *Latin American Democracies: Colombia, Costa Rica, and Venezuela.* Chapel Hill: University of North Carolina Press.

Polakoff, Erica, and Pierre La Ramée. 1997. Grass-Roots Organizations. In Walker 1997. 185–202.

Prevost, Gary. 1997. The FSLN. In Walker 1997. 149–64.

Putnam, Robert D., with Robert Leonardi and Raffaella Y. Nanetti. 1993. *Making Democracy Work: Civic Traditions in Modern Italy.* Princeton: Princeton University Press.

Roberts, Bryan. 1996. The Social Context of Citizenship in Latin America. *International Journal of Urban and Regional Research* 20, 1: 38–65.

Seligson, Mitchell A., and John A. Booth. 1993. Political Culture and Regime Type: Evidence from Nicaragua and Costa Rica. *Journal of Politics* 55, 3 (August): 777–92.

Speer, John G. 1997. The Urban Informal Sector. In Walker 1997. 265–79.

————. 1999. The Motivational Bases of Political Support Among Urban Informal Sector Workers in Transitional Nicaragua. Ph.D. diss., University of Kentucky.

Tardanico, Richard. 1997. From Crisis to Restructuring: Latin American Transformations and Urban Employment in World Perspective. In *Global Restructuring, Employment, and Social Inequality in Urban Latin America*, ed. Tardanico and Rafael Menjívar Larín. Coral Gables: North-South Center Press. 1–46.

Tardinico, Richard, and Mario Lungo. 1997. Continuities and Discontinuities in Costa Rican Urban Employment. In *Global Restructuring, Employment, and Social Inequality in Urban Latin America*, ed. Tardanico and Rafael Menjívar Larín. Coral Gables: North-South Center Press. 95–142.

Vargas, R. Jorge. 1992. El cooperativismo en los años ochenta: balance de una decada. In *El nuevo rostro de Costa Rica*, ed. Juan Manuel Villasuso. San José: CEDAL. 191–202.

Verba, Sidney, Norman H. Nie, and Jae-On Kim. 1978. *Participation and Political Equality: A Seven-Nation Comparison.* Cambridge: Cambridge University Press.

Walker, Thomas W., ed. 1997. *Nicaragua Without Illusions: Regime Transition and Structural Adjustment in the 1990s.* Wilmington: SR Books.

Williams, Philip J. 1994. Dual Transitions from Authoritarian Rule: Popular and Electoral Democracy in Nicaragua. *Comparative Politics* 26, 2 (January): 169–86.

Yashar, Deborah J. 1995. Civil War and Social Welfare: The Origins of Costa Rica's Competitive Party System. In *Building Democratic Institutions: Party Systems in Latin America,* ed. Scott Mainwaring and Timothy R. Scully. Stanford: Stanford University Press. 72–99.

———. 1997. *Demanding Democracy: Reform and Reaction in Costa Rica and Guatemala, 1870s–1950s.* Stanford: Stanford University Press.

New Social Movements in Latin America: The Dynamics of Class and Identity

HENRY VELTMEYER

This essay provides a counterpoint to the postmodern interpretations of social movements in Latin America. Its purpose is to argue for the necessity of a class analysis of these movements. The main focus of this argument is on the emergence of what has been labelled 'new peasant movements', which, it is argued, constitute the most dynamic forces of resistance to neoliberal capitalism in Latin America. Postmodernism in this context is viewed as a deficient intellectual approach, premised as it is on an idealist conception of reality.

INTRODUCTION

The Mexican peasant insurrection in Chiapas on the first of January in 1994 has had a profound impact. It put an end to the ruling class's illusion of social peace and stability, bringing on centre-stage not only the long and hard struggles of indigenous peoples in Mexico and elsewhere, but also what we could term the sociology of social movements – the way in which movements of resistance and social change are conceived. In the immediate context, the uprising seriously undermined and tarnished the glow that surrounded the government's neoliberal policies of structural adjustment, which just a month earlier had been lauded by president Clinton at a summit of Latin American heads of state as a model for other governments in the region. In the same context, it raised serious questions about the feasibility of armed struggle, a tactic that had all but been abandoned by the Left as a result of the repeated failures and the destruction of the many organisations that had taken up arms in the 1960s and 1970s.

Department of Sociology, Saint Mary's University, Halifax, NS., Canada. For his collegiality and critical reading of the manuscript the author thanks Raul Delgado of the Maestria en Ciencia Política de la Universidad Autónoma de Zacatecas, Mexico, where the author is currently on a visiting appointment. The author also acknowledges the valuable critical and extensive stylistic comments made by Tom Brass on the various drafts of this article.

The Journal of Peasant Studies, Vol.25, No.1, October 1997, pp.139–169
PUBLISHED BY FRANK CASS, LONDON

159

The flood of studies and interpretations that have been produced in the wake of the initial insurrection and the subsequent process of political transition and transformation can be placed into two categories. First, there are all those studies (and published reflections) that have focused on and debated the politics of armed struggle. The obvious and clear 'success' of the uprising in placing the demands of indigenous people on the political agenda, and in forcing the government to seriously negotiate these demands as well as its relations with and treatment of these people, revalidated the tactic as a form of resistance and struggle. In fact, similar organisations to the Zapatista Army of National Liberation (EZLN) have formed and appeared in several places where subsequently similar conditions to Chiapas exist.[1] However, the left wing of what in Mexico is termed 'the political class' (referring to the intelligentsia and the PRD, the major centre-left political party in the country) was manifestly shaken and generally gave the EZLN an ambiguous response, sympathising with its aims but objecting to its methods. Critically important support within the country for the EZLN came from other quarters, including some intellectuals associated with a plethora of community-based or national organisations of Mexico's vibrant civil society that, in the end forced the government to reject its policy of armed confrontation and enter into a process of negotiations with the EZLN.

A second category of more widely ranging and internationally scattered studies have tended to focus on what is 'new' and distinctive about the EZLN's organisation and its internal dynamics with respect to the social movement of indigenous peoples – a movement that has ramifications and resonance well beyond Chiapas and Mexico.[2] The theoretical perspective of these diverse studies is diffuse and has numerous permutations, but in its critical dimensions is based on what has come to be known as 'postmodernism', a perspective that in the 1980s displaced Marxism as the dominant approach to the sociological study of peasant communities and their social and political dynamics. The essence of this perspective is that the Chiapas uprising, like the 'new social movements' that emerged throughout Latin America in the 1980s, represents a radically new form of organisation and politics that highlights the postmodern condition: a radical subjectivity of experience and the self-constitution of a new social subject, a social actor seeking to define and express him/herself on a largely self-constructed stage.[3]

With reference to these two bodies of literature, the purpose of this essay is (i) to identify and cut through what is at issue in the emerging (or by now well-established) debates; and to argue that (ii) the Chiapas uprising constitutes or represents not so much a 'new social movement', as conceived by proponents of postmodernism, but a resurgence of class-based social movements in Latin America; (iii) that this latest wave of social movements, the third in the post-Second World War Latin American context, is led by peasants and revolves around their struggle for access to land and other productive resources, freedom or democracy, and social justice – eminently 'modernist' and class demands predicated on the need to establish a new relationship with existing society and its state; and (iv) that, in the context of these peasant-based and led movements, the tools of class analysis need to be validated and reconstituted. It is argued that, despite its constitution of a number of salutary principles, postmodernism does not provide a useful theoretical perspective or analytical framework for understanding and explaining the dynamics of social and political struggles in Latin America. What it contributes, and its major effect, is intellectual immobilisation and political demobilisation. The dynamics of the ongoing and new social struggles in Latin America require a reconstituted form of class analysis.

This argument is as follows. Part I reconstructs the critical elements of the postmodern perspective as they relate to an analysis of new social movements in Latin America.[4] Part II provides several counterpoints to this perspective, with specific reference to class formation and social movements in the rural sector of Mexican society. Fragments of class analysis are introduced here. Part III places these processes in a broader Latin American context and identifies the class dynamics of an emergent social movement of peasants and indigenous peoples. This social movement is shown to be 'new' in a number of respects, representing the most dynamic force in Latin American society to the neoliberal agenda. The essay concludes with lessons that can be drawn from our exploratory analysis.

The Postmodern Agenda: A New Pivot of Social Analysis

The sociology of development, like its counterparts in economics and politics, is the product of intellectual (and political) developments in the post war period, but can be traced back to an intellectual project of the eighteenth century Enlightenment: modernism. The process associated with this project (modernisation), and reflected in the eighteenth century idea of 'progress', has three critical dimensions: *economic* – the expansion of society's productive forces, the growth of output, and on this basis an improvement in the standards of living of the population;[5] *political* – liberation from oppressive and restrictive structures and institutions, increased freedom for the individual (the institution of democracy) and thus greater capacity for self-realisation;[6] and *social* – the creation of a society which, in Rousseau's words, 'creates conditions equal for all', or that provides equity and social justice (in the distribution of society's resources).[7] The process involved in the realisation of this project and its conditions[8] is alternatively conceptualised as (i) industrialisation (the shift from agriculture to industry and the associated transformation of the structure of production) and capitalist development (the institution and spread of wage labour and the market), the 'motor' of the development process; (ii) modernisation (the transformation of a system whose functioning is based on n 'traditional' values into one based on 'modern' values);[9] and (iii) democratisation (the institution of a democratic system of government). No matter how conceived, or what aspect and dimension is emphasised in analysis, modernisation is the essence of the project involved, the object or goal of the associated process of change and development.[10]

In the late 1950s, faith in the idea of 'progress' (and the notion of a development process), either was lost or gave way to the notion that the process of modernisation was at an end, that it had exhausted its limits and was giving way to a new 'post-industrial period', in which, as C. Wright Mills among other sociologists argues, all the historic expectations that have characterised 'Western culture' are no longer relevant and the Enlightenment faith in the united progress of reason and freedom, together with the ideologies grounded in that faith (liberalism, socialism) 'have virtually collapsed as adequate explanations of the World and ourselves'.[11]

Not all sociologists at the time shared this notion of an emerging post-modern, post-industrial, or post-capitalist society. Indeed, the sociology of development and its theory of modernisation was still in its infancy. Over the next two decades sociological analysis was divided among those who, like C.W. Mills and Daniel Bell, sought to analyse the post-industrial condition, and those who continued to believe in the fundamental process of modernisation, or capitalist development.[12] However, by the 1980s, sociological theory – and development theory more generally – reached an impasse and by a number of accounts went into crisis [*Booth*, 1985; *Corbridge*, 1990; *Schuurman*, 1993].

Within the specific though interdisciplinary field of development studies this impasse or crisis took the form of an incapacity of the theorists and practitioners in the mainstream to withstand the attacks made on their postulates and propositions by, on the Left, proponents of Marxist-oriented theories of dependency and imperialism, and, on the right, by proponents of neo-classical economics and neoliberal policies of structural adjustment. One resolution of this crisis was what has amounted to a 'counter-revolution' in theory and policy [*Toye*, 1987], resulting in the formation of a new 'Washington consensus' on correct thinking and policy.[13] There were several other attempted resolutions, most notably by exponents of a search for an alternative form of development that is predicated on neither the agency of the state nor the functioning of the market but on community-based, human scale, people-led participatory action.[14] As for sociological analysis more generally, there were a number of critical theoretical issues, but the most salient revolved around the question of historical determination – whether human agency, the actions and projects of individuals or particular social groups and classes, were determining factors of historical development, or whether these developments were determined by objectively given conditions, by the working (the 'laws' of) of the economic system on individuals.

The debate on this issue has taken numerous forms with many permutations that cut across the theoretical – and political – divide between liberal and Marxist sociologists and between advocates of materialism (structuralism) and idealism (subjectivism) in social analysis, or between a society's 'political economy' and its 'culture'. One of the more critical and intellectually influential (although, we will argue, wrong-headed) forms of this debate revolved around French post-structuralist discourse-analysis and an associated critique of structuralism, particularly in its Marxist form of class analysis.[15] The main object of this critique was the structuralist belief in the capacity to represent in thought (and reflected in the textual discourse) conditions that are real in their effects, conditions generated by underlying deep structures that are invisible in themselves, manifest only in their effects.[16] The radical idea introduced by these post-structuralists was that the human mind has no way of determining the correspondence between the real and its representations – of 'knowing' or accessing the 'real'; and that the observed patterns and regularities captured in thought and reflected in theoretical discourse (the 'text') were determined internally, imposed by the mind (that is, had no empirical referents), and did not necessarily – or at all – represent conditions that are 'real' in themselves; and that the 'real' is largely subjective, determined by and reflective of the particular standpoint of the particular 'historical subject'.

This form of analysis,[17] which to some extent can be traced back to the nihilist philosophy of Nietsche and a long sociological tradition of idealist critiques of science (including the Frankfurt school of critical theory that emerged in the 1920s and 1930 but was transplanted and reworked at the New York School for Social Research)[18] had a significant impact on the form that analysis – and theorising – could and would take. In its most radical form, it implied a disbelief, scepticism or agnosticism with respect to the possibility of scientific knowledge – of structural determination, and of the relevance of meta-theories predicated on structural determination or the working of a system – of objectively given, and determining, conditions.[19] It presupposes a radical heterogeneity and subjectivity – the standpoint of the historically situated individual, able socially to construct – and thus determine – her/his own reality.

How is this post-structuralist analysis/critique and post-modernist perspective applied in practice; that is, in social analysis? It is clear enough that it has had a significant impact on the analysis of certain issues in specific fields, such as international development and peasant studies, and on the explanation of the internal dynamics of what have been defined as 'new social movements'. For the most part these movements have been analysed in the context of societies in what are customarily regarded as industrialised, capitalist democracies in Europe and North America. However, new social movements have also been identified in Latin America, the conditions of which, in the 1980s, generated a spate of studies into social movements as well as the internal dynamics of peasant communities and behaviour.[20] Despite some obfuscation on the issue, this analysis was – and is – explicitly designed as a rejection and replacement of the Marxist structural discourse and class analysis that had hitherto dominated these fields.

The postmodernist perspective underlying and derived from the post-structuralist critique of structuralism and Marxism is reflected in and has taken the form of several concepts and principles enunciated as a new framework of analysis. The central concept is that of a self-constituted subject or social actor, who is able to draw up a script, construct an identity, improvise a corresponding role or line of action, and act it out on a stage set up in the particular setting in which participants in the action find themselves.[21] Its major principles, variously and broadly applied (as we will see) to the dynamics of social movements and peasant communities in Latin America, can be formulated as follows: (i) subjectivity – the idea that conscious experience is predominantly subjective in nature and as such both the source of social identity and the constituent (or determinant) component of social action;[22] (ii) heterogeneity – the idea that the form of consciousness and action cannot be viewed as simply the effect of some underlying cause, of a deeply embedded structure that is invisible and manifest only in its effects on behaviour (consciousness and action)[23] and (iii) contextuality – the idea that forms of social action should be related to (explained in terms of) their meaning, arising in historically specific contexts, rather than their cause.

Postmodernism and New Social Movements in Latin America

On the basis of these ideas – with reference to the associated principles (which were sometimes enunciated, sometimes not) – the study of peasants in Latin American societies and the emergence of new social movements in the urban sector of these and other societies have been placed in a postmodernist perspective, all but displacing Marxism, which in the 1960s and 1970s had dominated these fields. At the centre of Marxism was the concept of class, defined in terms of the individual's objectively defined relationship to the means of production, and applied with reference to the idea that the structure of this relationship was based on the division between the owners of the means of production and the direct producers or workers; under capitalism, this social relation was structured by the exploitation of labour and the extraction of surplus value, a process which produced both the objective and subjective conditions of social change, the revolutionary transformation of the capitalist system. The working class is the active agent of this transformation, and thus the historical subject of the revolutionary project.

In the context of Latin America and elsewhere in the 1980s, these propositions were generally and specifically rejected by a new (and a converted old) generation of scholars, who counterposed a series of alternative propositions that placed political developments in the region in a very different perspective. The notion of a structurally specific mode of production that generates objective conditions for different classes of individuals was accordingly jettisoned. The notion of coercive and exploitative social relationships such as debt peonage and wage labour was replaced with the notion of diverse social actors more or less in control of their lives, depending only on the success of their performance – on their ability to construct and project in their action a specific social identity. In this context, for example, the subjugated are widely portrayed as holding power over their exploiters [Brass, 1991]. Social relations like peonage, once thought to rely heavily on coercion, are viewed as symbiotic, even in the best interests of the peons themselves [Knight, 1988].

Seen through the prism of postmodernist concepts and ideas (discourse, experience, agency, and contextuality), powerful peons dominate the hapless hacendados; and exploitative class relations are replaced by notions of a moral economy, where patron and client, hacendado and peon, patron or employer and employee, are bound together by relations of mutual benefit, community spirit, and notions of fairness. The World Bank, for example, in its 1995 report on world labour views the jobber, who has long figured on the historical stage as a brutally exploitative self-serving middleman or class agent, as an efficient (and honest?) broker who smoothes the useful mechanism of social exchange in rural communities.[24] In this and other contexts, the objectively given conditions of class exploitation and oppression are seen as figments of mechanistic structuralism and are reconstructed as a play of diverse actors searching for and actively constructing their social identity. In this process, mundane manifestations of social discontent and resistance are seen to alter class relations cumulatively and fundamentally.

New Social Movements in Latin America: The Construction of Social
Identity versus the Politics of Class

If one were to describe in terms of 'objective' social conditions what the
1980s meant for Latin America it would be possible to do so in terms of four
elements: (i) debt crisis, economic stagnation, and the decline of economic
conditions for the majority of the population (in some cases deterioration to
a level achieved in 1970);[25] (ii) the retrenchment of military and authoritarian
regimes and their replacement with constitutional democratically-elected
civilian regimes;[26] (iii) the widespread implementation of the Structural
Adjustment Program (SAP), an amalgam of stabilisation and austerity
measures (currency devaluation, anti-inflation) and 'structural' economic
reforms (liberalisation, deregulation, privatisation, downsizing) designed by
the International Monetary Fund and the World Bank;[27] and (iv) the
reaffirmation of the capital accumulation process based on a radical change
in the capital–labour relationship and the associated class structure.[28]

These four sets of objective conditions, associated with and generated by
a far-reaching economic and social restructuring process, undergone and
experienced to different degrees by every country in the region in the
1980s,[29] provide the context in which 'new social movements' have been
identified and analysed. Take, for example, the retreat of the generals to
their barracks and the reinstitution of liberal democracy throughout the
region. In virtually every case, this process was preceded and accompanied
by an explosive combination of newly formed popular social organisations
and political demands for the restoration of democracy as well as specific
(economic and political) demands by particular social groups. The feature
of these struggles is protagonists from 'civil society' – popular organisations
that had displaced the traditional organisations (political parties and unions)
which had hitherto dominated the contested terrain of politics. In effect,
these newly formed popular sector organisations were constituted –
constituted themselves – as the he 'subjects' of an unfolding political
process.[30]

Although to date there exists no systematic comparative study of social
movements constituted by these popular sector organisations,[31] it is possible
to identify their salient features in terms of four criteria: their social base,
their demands, the arena and specific form of struggle, and, in
postmodernist terms, the identity assumed or constructed by participants in
the course of struggle. And we could add a fifth criterion: the political or
ideological issues of the targeted adversary, or what in Marxist discourse
used to be defined as 'the enemy'.

In terms of the first two criteria, we can identify at the base of these new
social movements (NSMs) various marginalised groups of the urban poor,
protesting against government economic policies and the lack of

democracy, and demanding legalisation and title to the plots of land which they had occupied, as well as support in constructing houses and access to utilities and services, plus middle-class organisations protesting against the violation of human rights and demanding respect for these rights [*Calderon and dos Santos*, 1987; *Sondereguer*, 1985];[32] women protesting against the impact of government policy on their households and lives, and joining the demand for democracy [*Barrig*, 1987; *Jelin*, 1990];[33] indigenous populations and communities struggling to recover and define their ethnic and cultural identity;[34] youth, who joined and led protests against government austerity measures and the lack of democracy, as well as their exclusion from school or the workplace [*Vila*, 1985; *Valenzuela*, 1985];[35] family members of persons imprisoned or 'disappeared' by the retreating military regimes or murdered for political reasons;[36] and new working-class organisations formed in the burgeoning informal sector, as well as a few established workers' centres, to demand of government authorities the right to occupy the physical space needed to conduct their 'work' (in the streets) and access to the licences which governments distributed to regulate economic activity [*Calderon and dos Santos*, 1987)][37]

As indicated, the proliferation of 'new social movements' in Latin America in the 1980s requires a more detailed and synthetic study of the identity assumed by each, their internal dynamics, and the conditions that gave rise to them, as well as the form and direction of the struggles involved. However, the displacement of political parties, unions, and other traditional instruments of class struggle (and of what in Latin America is referred to as the 'political class') from the contested terrain of politics has been enough to convince an entire generation of sociologists and anthropologists of the constitution and existence of a *new* complex of social actors, the 'subjects' of the current struggle for social change.[38]

From this perspective, the emergence of 'new social movements' had a double effect on progressive social thought in Latin America. On the one hand, it tended to invalidate a strict class analysis or, in postmodernist discourse, class essentialism. On the other, it raised serious questions about the viability or relevance of the vanguard party and other Marxist or Leninist forms of political organisation which had achieved a virtual hegemony in the social movements of the 1960s and 1970s. In this context it was a given that the axis of struggle, and of the construction of social movements for change, had shifted towards and was based on a new 'subject' that was at the same time more politically diverse and heterogeneous than that identified and defined in terms of the Marxist concept of class [*Hunter*, 1995]. If the industrial proletariat, which had figured so centrally in Marxist class analysis had more or less disappeared from the political scene (as argued by Laclau), the intellectual search for a new historical subject confronted (and ended with) the resurgence of popular sector organisations that expressed both the political potential of the oppressed (as well as the exploited and the marginalised) and the highly diverse contextually specific demands, concerns, and actions of different groups and categories of citizen.

The most critical and defining feature of these new social movements, from this point of view, was the social identity constructed in each case. The actions, of popular community-based organisations were seen to reflect the diversity of their subject positions, localised experiences and forms of consciousness. Thus, a series of movements led and organised by women in different urban contexts expressed their self-awareness as women and their efforts to construct for themselves a social identity as women which would (and did) allow them to act on the basis of collectively-shared experience of discrimination (and oppression) experienced in different spheres of their lives – the family, the workplace, and in the public sphere of politics [*Jelin*, 1990; *Waylen*, 1993]. Likewise, indigenous peoples throughout Latin America struggled to recover and express their cultural and national identity [*Chiriboga*, 1985; *Van Cott*, 1994].

These new social movements also shared a common form of resistance, which expressed the subjective and heterogeneous conditions of self-awareness, and took the form of a search for survival on a day to day basis as well as the demand for enough political space and participation in decisions that affected people's everyday lives.[39] In this context, the demand for social transformation, characteristic of class-based movements, was transmuted into demands for democracy, for more political space within which to project their social action, which in turn was transformed into more specific demands to meet the immediate needs of and address the concerns of people in their communities. In this process resistance no longer took the form of explosive encounters with the guardians of the existing order or large-scale mobilisations for social transformation. It took the form of a day-to-day struggle for survival – to control the conditions of their particular situations [*Borja et al.*, 1989; *Herzer et al.*, 1986; *Scott*, 1985].

Postmodernism in Perspective

With hindsight, it is now possible to place in perspective this postmodernist approach to new social movements. First, it is clear enough that it does indeed identify a characteristic feature of the diverse movements: the limited scope of their demands for change, the politically limited and economically defensive actions, as well as search for cultural identity. However, at a different level, this theory of NSM profoundly misunderstood the nature and dynamics of these movements and miscast their participants.

As observed and argued by de la Cruz, Calderon, Laserna and others (in

Camacho and Menjivar [1989]), it is clear enough that very few of these movements exhibited or operated with a class-conscious awareness of their objectively-shared position *vis-à-vis* the economic system or government neoliberal policies that created objectively similar conditions for them. In terms of these 'objective' conditions, therefore, it should be possible to analyse the social basis of the new social movements in class terms, the major elements of which constitute what could be loosely defined as the 'new working class' that has evolved in a radically different form from that analysed and theoretically constructed in traditional Marxist analysis.

Counterpoints of Class: Fragments of an Alternative Form of Analysis

Not all sociological studies of peasant communities and social movements in Latin America have been trapped in the rather sterile debate between an economistic form of class analysis that ignores the subjective aspects of class formation on the one hand, and an overly subjectivist and idealist postmodernist interpretation on the other. Some of these studies will be briefly summarised so as to illustrate the complexities and nuances of what amounts to a reconstituted form of class analysis that takes into account gender, ethnic, and development issues.

In the context of Chiapas, Mexico, Benjamin [1989], an historian, examines the dynamics of the way in which a landowning class managed to consolidate and preserve ownership and control over the state's considerable economic resources and political destiny, and in the process transform itself over time into government agents or bankers, and to acquire both wealth and power. According to Benjamin, this included the appropriation of the best tracts of arable land (for the production of cacao, coffee, cotton, sugar, mahogany), monopoly control over capital and other productive resources, effective political control of the state and local governments (the legislature, judiciary, police), the subjugation of the largely indigenous (Mayan) peasant population and their conversion into *jornaleros* (daily wage labourers); and the marginalisation of their communities, a function not of their geographic isolation, as is so often argued, but of an actively directed process. As Benjamin reconstructs it, these developments were based on the pre-existing relationship of different social groups to the means of production, and also entailed a symbiotic relationship between the holders of political and economic power, defined by him as two interconnected elites constituting a dominant, and ruling, class.

In Chiapas, the political upheavals of 1910–20 had little impact on the structure of economic and political power, although they did lead to the mobilisation of social forces of opposition and resistance, the emergence of a socialist movement, and, in the 1930s, the formation of the Confederación Nacional de Campesinos (CNC) and the Confederacion de Trabajodores Mexicana (CTM), both of which ultimately were accomodated within the corporatist structure set up by the governing party. In the 1960s and 1970s, another round of social upheaval and mobilisation led to the formation of left-wing, class-based political organisations that launched and waged a long series of disconnected and ultimately unsuccessful political and armed struggles to settle demands for land and higher wages, and beyond these for control of the state and social transformation. These struggles in Chiapas were part of region-wide wave of social and political movements that formed the organisational roots of the armed insurrection of the EZLN on the first of January in 1994. They also constituted the political context to a process of capitalist penetration of marginalised peasant and indigenous communities, a process which converted large tracts of *ejido* or communal property into *de facto* private plots that were bought and sold within the indigenous community, generating – according to an account given by Greenberg [1989] – class divisions and an upsurge of intra-communal conflict, and converting large numbers of peasants into landless workers or *de facto* wage labourers, a process that was consciously accelerated by the constitutional reforms of the federal government in 1992.[40]

Another study that highlights some of the subtleties of an emerging reconstituted class analysis is that by Gavin Smith [1989] of a rural community in Peru. Smith develops a complex and provocative argument that the determination of class relations should not begin with an analysis of property relations and their objective conditions, to which forms of consciousness, the experience of struggle and political relations are added on; rather, the interplay of experience and consciousness, which so often in postmodernist discourse constitutes a vaguely defined subjective agency, is shown to be integral to the formation and transformation of productive or property relations; that is, it is a constituent, and thus determinant, element of class formation, as critical as are the objective conditions of this formation. At one level, Smith only makes more precise what Marx had argued as a methodological principle in the 19th Brumaire. But his contribution is a welcome relief from the intellectual posturing of so many postmodernists who rarely, as it happens, leave the ethereal world of their conceptualisations to experience 'reality' in its objectively given conditions. After all, concepts have no empirical reference points in the 'world out there'.

What is most useful in Smith's analysis is his examination of the relationship between community and class, the Scylla and Charybdis of social analysis and of the debate (or divide) between Marxism and postmodernism. In his study Smith establishes the complimentarity of the two concepts, viewing the object of his analysis (the community) as a complex of diverse class relations and not – as in so much sociological analysis – a vaguely defined organic whole held together and constituted by a sense of belonging and shared social identity. Smith shows how members of a community can unite in a common struggle even though the interests, aims and objectives of the different classes that comprise it – and that connect it to the wider society – diverge. In the struggle of the Huasicanchinos for land, a form of commonality was produced on the basis of a shared discourse, but this did not mean that class differences were subsumed or replaced by community ties. Again and again he shows that divergent class interests both within and outside the community threaten to destroy the community and to undermine the commonality of its struggles [*Smith*, 1989: 233].

In this context, Smith provides an illuminating theoretical commentary on the process of social transformation within a peasant community. At this level, his analysis has much to recommend it, a corrective to the excessive objectivism and economism of traditional class analysis and the excessive subjectivism of postmodernist discourse analysis. However, Smith's focus on the internal dynamics of class and community also contains a problem, one that is shared by many anthropologists and sociologists in their study of 'peasant communities'. The problem is that the connection of the community to the wider society – and to its economic and political systems – is not brought into a clear focus. This could be posed (and in the literature it often is) as a question of the penetration of economically and politically marginal and geographically remote (often indigenous) communities by outside forces. The dynamics of this penetration also have a class dimension which needs to be both conceptualised and analysed, as they are to some degree by the studies on Mexico discussed or referenced above (Benjamin, Greenberg, Schryer). However, these studies are not immune from the ambiguity that characterises so many academic studies in this field when it comes to the marginal status of so many traditional indigenous communities.[41] On the one hand, many of these communities are geographically isolated as well as marginal in economic, social and political terms, leading many studies to view the conditions of their marginality (deprivation, poverty) as the result of geographic isolation or as self-imposed, rather than as the result of social and political exclusion, discrimination, and the nature of the relationship that these communities have with the broader society, its culture, and its economic and political institutions. In these terms, these studies evoke the need of these communities to overcome their isolation and to integrate into the wider society – to be incorporated into its institutionalised practices and structure. On the other hand, the conditions encompassed by the term 'marginality' are correctly viewed as the product not of the marginal status of indigenous communities but of the specific form of their relationship with the broader society.

Take the case of Chiapas, one of Mexico's richest states in terms of natural resources, and one of the poorest in terms of the incidence of marginality, the objective conditions of which correspond to the large number of communities of peasant producers and the large size and distribution of the indigenous population. It has been estimated that at least 60 per cent of these peasants are, in fact, *jornaleros*, or wage labourers for the large *hacendados,* ranchers and *caciques* who own most of the arable land, commercial operations and productive resources in the region and also control the political system.[42] And a large number of peasants, dispossessed of their land, have migrated to the Lacandon forest in search of wage employment in the country's largest petrochemical plant, hydroelectric complex, oil fields, and logging operations.[43] As Benjamin and others [*La Botz*, 1994] have documented, this process of 'primitive accumulation' (the separation of producers from their means of production), which has converted many peasant producers into landless workers, a super-exploited semi-proletariat, or what Marx had conceptualised in a different context as 'an industrial reserve army' has been a long time in the making, at least decades and in some cases centuries. The conditions and dynamics of this historical process make it difficult to conceive of the 'marginal' peasant community as isolated from the wider society, disconnected from its economic structure. Moreover, the largely self-sufficient base of the peasant economy, constructed within the institutional and legal framework of the *ejido* system of community landholding, is also part of Mexico's national economy. Not only does it serve to reproduce the incredibly cheap labour that so many *casmpesinos* are compelled to offer to the *hacendados* and capitalists across the country, but, as a result of Mexico's entry into NAFTA, it is also subject to competition from US producers that has crippled the local economy.[44]

It is clear that the complex of peasant communities, constituting the economic and cultural basis of Mexico's indigenous peoples and society, is very much a part of a national – indeed global – economy and deeply affected by its workings.[45] Thus it is that *subcomandante* Marcos, in the immediate wake of the *Zapatista* uprising, could speak of NAFTA as 'a death sentence' for the indigenous people of Chiapas and the country. However, the uprising and the subsequent process of negotiations – and transition of the EZLN from an army of national liberation into a new political force – make it just as clear that there is a significant 'political' dimension to the relationship that the country's indigenous peoples have with Mexican society. One of the central issues in the prolonged negotiation process is precisely the need to fundamentally change the constitutionally defined political relationship of the country's indigenous peoples to the government and to the state – to meet thereby the Zapatista movement's crucial demands for 'liberty, independence, and democracy – and social justice'. At issue in these clearly modernist demands[46] is the struggle of Mexico's indigenous peoples to escape the objectively given (and experienced) conditions of their exploitation and oppression; and to do so not in the subjectivity of experience (the construction of a social identity), nor even by changing their position within the operating economic system (neoliberal capitalism) and its political adjunct, but to change the system itself.[47] This is the challenge faced by the EZLN. The issue, as we will argue, is fundamentally that of class in its interconnected objective and subjective conditions.

The Latin American Peasantry: The Emergence of a New Force for Social Change

The discursive turns and opportunism of many political leaders on the left in Latin America have led in many parts to confusion and an absolute distrust of the 'political class' and their favourite political instrument – the party. In this context, many citizens have left the class struggle to devote themselves to the problems of every-day life, seeking at this level to survive the conditions created by austerity measures and to make a living. Some intellectuals, as we have noted, armed with a postmodernist perspective, misinterpreted this trend, seeing in it the constitution of new social subjects and the emergence of new social movements based on the politics of everyday life and the generation of non-class identities.[48]

Despite the dual trend of an escape into the politics of everyday life and the election of neoliberal parties to national power, in many Latin American countries movements of resistance and opposition to the neoliberal policies were formed, more often than not in the immediate context of having just constituted a neoliberal regime. This resistance and opposition to neoliberal policies took different forms, but it had an undoubted class basis, postmodernism notwithstanding. This can be seen in Bolivia, for example, in the widespread and mounting protests of the miners and the *cocaleros* (miners turned coca farmers), teachers and public sector workers, and a new form of union linked to the social movements, but coordinating their actions with an amalgam of social organisations instead of the parties on the Left. Above all, it is evident in the emergence of new struggles in the countryside – the centre and axis of the new insurgence.[49]

A good example of these new class-based movements is the Movement of Landless Workers (MST) in Brazil, formed on the basis of hundreds of organisations and hundreds of thousands of activists and supporters in the countryside. The MST has generated a nation-wide political discussion about the issue of land, and according to observers is the most dynamic social movement in the country, the best organised, and the most effective, with a record of concrete achievements and considerable support.[50] In Bolivia, the closing of the mines, the import of inexpensive commodities has weakened the hitherto powerful mining and industrial unions. In their place have been formed peasant organisations, particularly among the *cocaleros* (many of whom are ex-miners) who are currently leading the struggle against neoliberalism, with large demonstrations, marches, and general strikes that have paralysed the country.[51] In Paraguay, the National Federation of Peasants is the principal force behind the massive mobilisations that are currently shaking the country, placing the land issue on the political agenda and at the forefront of the struggle against the neoliberal regime.[52] Also in Mexico (in Chiapas, Guerrero, Oaxaca) confrontations between peasants and the State are an almost daily occurrence.[53] In Ecuador, Colombia, El Salvador, and other countries in the region, peasants have likewise constituted themselves as the principal subject of the class struggle. In many contexts peasants are of indigenous origin, giving their struggle a national and ethnic character, but the cause of the struggle can be found in their relationships to the means of production and to the State.

In short, the epitaph for the peasantry intoned by analysts and historians such as Eric Hobsbawn [1994] is premature and misinformed. The demographic argument in terms of their diminishing number in the labour force does not translate into good political analysis, at least with respect to Latin America. First, millions of families continue to live in the countryside – over six million families just in Mexico. Second, the urban crisis and unemployment do not provide peasant youth with a promising avenue for escape. Third, in the current context of land occupations in Brazil, Paraguay, El Salvador and other countries in Latin America there is evidence of a movement that runs counter to the traditional pattern of migration from the countryside to the city. Fourth, neoliberal policies have battered small producers all across the region with low prices, unequal competition and an unpayable debt, creating in the process social and family ties with the sons and daughters of the landless workers. And fifth, apart from structural considerations, there has emerged a new generation of peasant leaders with a notable capacity for organisation, a sharp understanding of international and national politics, and a deep political commitment to changing their life situation.[54]

Clearly we are not speaking of traditional peasant movements. First, in many cases the peasants are not divorced from urban life. In some cases they are ex-miners or displaced workers.[55] In other cases, the militants had a religious formation but abandoned the church to enter the struggle for agrarian reform as leaders of the movement of landless workers and peasants.[56] In many cases they are daughters of small peasant producers with a primary or secondary level education who decide to join (and sometimes end up leading) the movement instead of migrating to the cities to work in domestic service.[57] The new peasant leaders often travel to the city to attend seminars and training schools and to participate in political discussions. In short, although they have their roots in the rural struggle, and are agricultural producers, they tend to have a cosmopolitan view. The number and quality of these peasant intellectuals vary from country to country. In Brazil, the MST has invested considerable resources and energy in the training of leadership cadres, with hundreds of peasants participating annually in a national training program.[58] In other cases, as in Paraguay, Bolivia and El Salvador, the movement depends on a small number of leaders with savvy. In any case, what distinguishes these new peasant movements is the quality, militancy and democratic character of their leadership, which is reflected in the stated position of subcomadante Marcos that he leads by obeying ('mando obedeciendo').[59]

The second crucial point about these New Peasant Movements (NPMs) is that they are independent of political parties. The MST, for example, has cordial relations with the PT, as does the ADC in El Salvador with the FMLN. But the strength of both movements is in the direct struggle – land invasions, the blocking of highways, marches and demonstrations, and the occupation of public buildings. Their strategy and tactics are decided by ideological discussions within the movement, and not subject to any party line. Much rather the contrary, it is these movements that provide the dynamism for the political struggles of the parties of the left, and ensure the commitment of the latter to the rural struggle. At present, the NPMs in many cases constitute the catalyst of resistance to and protests against neoliberal policies. In Bolivia, for example, the peasant organisations have broken their ties with political parties, and are actively engaged in debating whether or not to form their own political organisation. In Paraguay, many leaders of the Peasant Federation have launched their own revolutionary socialist movement. In Ecuador, the National Confederacion of Indigenous Peoples (CONAIE) has called for a new 'national indigenous uprising' and has formed its own political organisation, even launching its own Presidential candidate in the last elections.

Third, the NPMs as a rule are involved in direct struggle and not in the electoral process. As in Chiapas, they have tended to disregard the latter as a form of political action. They prefer to confer and negotiate directly with the representatives of the State, or to coordinate activity (such as strikes, or support for legislation) with unions, NGOs or political parties directly. They are careful to retain control of the pace and the direction of the principal form of struggle – massive mobilisations and direct action.

Fourth, the NPMs are influenced by a mixture of classic Marxism and – in various contexts – by ideas related to ecology, ethnicity and nationality. In Paraguay, and in particular Bolivia, the class struggle of peasants and rural workers is closely tied to issues of ethnic identity, indigenous culture, the rights of indigenous peoples, and the demand for national autonomy. In this context, internal debates are characterised as a rule by a close connection between the issues of class and nation.[60] And in a number of contexts the latter are combined with gender issues. In Brazil and Bolivia, for example, groups have örganised within the NPM for the purpose of obtaining better representation and equality for women in the power structure, and ensuring that gender issues are put on the political agenda. In such contexts, women tend to think and work politically within the framework of gender-class, discarding both a bourgeois-feminist class-less perspective and an economistic form of class analysis.

Fifth, the NPMs are generally coordinated, and to a certain point united, on the basis of regional organisations such as CLOL and increasingly international forums such as Via Campesina, which debate and exchange relevant experiences related to rural struggles —struggles that are increasingly shared and viewed as the same. Through these kinds of experiences and links an internationalist orientation and practice is emerging. Thus, the militants of PT in Brazil frequently join with their counterparts in Paraguay and, to a lesser degree, in Argentina and Uruguay. And the same is occurring in the Andes, among the indigenous peoples and peasants of Bolivia, Peru and Ecuador, and also in Central America.

To summarise, the resurgence of NPMs in the 1990s is not simply a return to 1960s and 1970s. In many cases the successes and the failures of those experiences have been studied and debated by the intellectuals of the NPM in a search for lessons that can be drawn from them. There are also elements of continuity with those struggles, at the level of the surviving militants, their sons and daughters. In addition, there are critical differences in terms of strategy, tactics, and organisation that separate the earlier movements from the new wave of peasant movements. These new movements are much more aware of and oriented by an understanding of the existence of a new world order and of the associated workings of neoliberal economic policies. They are also generally more united by an awareness of the need to fight this system, to do so on the basis of a united front among indigenous peoples and peasants, and the need to join with other forces organised in opposition to the neoliberal economic and social order.

CONCLUSIONS

The conditions that gave rise to the Chiapas rebellion and uprising were clearly structural in origin and objective in their effects on a population that responded actively and with a clear theoretical awareness of their own social identity as an exploited class and an oppressed people.[61] In the organised and active response to these conditions, the Zapatistas (the EZLN) were (and are) part of a new wave of social movements sweeping the region.[62] Although the Chiapas rebellion generated a serious (and ongoing) debate as to political methods and appropriate (and viable) forms of struggle, the outbreak and the subsequent process of struggle[63] is part of a history being constructed by peasants and indigenous people across Latin America. Resistance and opposition to the neoliberal agenda and the underlying capitalist system is forming and mounting in other popular sectors of civil society, including a restructured working class, but we can conclude that the peasantry in its various forms and sectors is the most dynamic force for change. Its actions, as Marx argued in 1844 with respect to a striking group of Silesian weavers,[64] bear the 'superior quality' of consciousness – theoretical awareness of what it is and represents – and the willingness and ability to act on it.

The actions of the peasantry also allow us to address an ongoing academic debate as to the objective and the subjective dimensions of social movements and the question of their class character and basis. In this respect, we conclude that the indigenous people and peasants in Chiapas and elsewhere in the region are constituted as a class, under the objectively given conditions of their relationship to the means of production, and to the state, the guarantor of this relationship. At the same time, these peasants and indigenous people have constituted themselves as a class in subjective terms, with reference to actions based on a clear awareness of themselves as a class and a people – seeking to liberate themselves (and others in the process) from the exploitative and oppressive structures of neoliberal capitalism in its Latin American form.

Under these conditions of class formation, there is no question of a radical heterogeneity or the specificity of a localised context for the Zapatista uprising. The rebellion resonated throughout the region, particularly among the peasantry and indigenous peoples who have experienced similar or comparable conditions, and who are essentially engaged in the *same* political process of resistance and opposition to neoliberal capitalism in Latin America.[65]

In this context, the conditions of which require class analysis, the Zapatistas (and other peasant-led social movements) have posed a major challenge for other forces of resistance and opposition to the existing economic and social order. Whether or not these forces – including those that progressive intellectuals on the Left can muster – are up to this challenge remains to be seen. The political Left in Latin America and elsewhere have yet to resolve their own crisis: a lack of organic connection to the ongoing struggle for social change [*Petras*, 1990]. They are at a crossroads of history – a history constructed by (among others) the peasantry and indigenous people of Latin America. It is to be hoped that they will choose the right road leading, as comandante Marcos has stated, to a new world in which there is life, not death, and where the modernist aspirations of economic progress, liberty, democracy and social justice exist for all.

NOTES

1. In Guerrero, there have surfaced at least three groups that have resorted to armed struggle The most important of these is the ERP, which appeared on the first anniversary of a massacre of 17 peasants by government police forces. The ERP also builds on a long tradition of armed struggle in the state.

2. This literature is voluminous, much of it focusing on statements by sub-comandante Marcos and the series of declarations made on behalf of the EZLN, all of which were made available nearly instantaneously through the medium of electronic communication and a number of computer-networks that provided a broad international audience with almost day-to-day accounts and interpretations of the process that the EZLN was engaged in. With respect to this electronic communication and networking of scholars and supporters all across the world, the Chiapas rebellion is seen by some as the most novel social movement to have appeared, and the bearer of the form that social struggles will take in the twenty-first century, at least with respect to the international support and solidarity networks among people all over the world able to intellectually engage with the Zapatista struggle through laptops and desktops in their offices. For a suggestive analysis of this aspect of the uprising see Cleaver [1994].

3. For an overview and analysis of a range of these new social movements in Latin America see Calderon [1995], Assies *et al.* [1990] and Escobar and Alvarez [1992].

4. Many studies with a postmodern perspective focus on social movements in the industrialised capitalist democracies of Europe and North America. The implications and analysis of these studies are outside the scope of this essay.

5. In the analysis – and 'grand theory' – provided by the pioneers of development economics (see Meier and Seers [1984]), economic progress or 'growth' is generally associated with the process of accumulation of physical (and social) capital, on the basis of increasing the rate of savings (to a critical or 'take-off' point), and investing these savings in capital-intensive industry, inducing a process of industrialisation (and an associated structural transformation), modernisation and capitalist development (the institution of wage labour and the market, regulated or freely operating). On the postulates and propositions – the body of grand theory – produced in the immediate post-war period (the 1950s and 1960s) and the subsequent period of reworking and a counter-revolution in theory and policy, see inter alia Meier and Seers [1984] and Hunt [1989].

6. Whereas the strictly economic dimension of modernisation is reflected in the indicator of growth in per capita output (see the World Bank's annual World Development Report), this dimension of 'development' or 'modernisation' has both an economic and a political aspect, the conditions of which are reflected in the concept of 'human development' formulated by the UNDP (see its annual Human Development Report) as an 'increased capacity to make

choices, to realise the individual's human potential, a concept that in turn reflects the Enlightenment ideal of 'freedom' and the need to be freed from limiting or oppressive conditions.

7. While economists and political theorists have tended to focus on the economic and political dimensions of the modernisation process, Sociologists have tended to focus on this dimension of the process, with reference to the idea of 'equality' (in the context of the nineteenth century labour struggles against exploitation and of women and other groups of individuals for the suffrage and political participation) or 'equity' (in the context of contemporary development).

8. Although these developments are conceived of, and taken up, as an intellectual and political project, that is, as the result of specific actions taken to a pre-defined end, most scholars view them as the product of a 'processs'. That is, the workings of a 'system', 'objectively given structural conditions', which operate on people in terms of their position within the system on the basis of its 'laws', which are grasped by scientific analysis. Whether these 'laws' (and the objectively given conditions which they specify) are determining factors in historical developments or whether actions of individuals on the basis of ideas and ideals are determining has always been – and remains – a central theoretical problem of sociological analysis.

9. Analysis of this aspect of the modernisation process was the specific contribution of sociology, made within the theoretical perspective and analytical framework of structural-functionalism established in particular by Talcott Parsons. On this contribution, and specifically the theory of modernisation, see *inter alia* Hoogvelt [1984] and, in particular, Frank [1972].

10. In the analysis of this process in different contexts it is often assumed that there is fundamentally but one road to modernity (industrialisation technological transformation, capitalist development, social and cultural transformation, and democratisation), with lots of variations, paths and sidetracks (see, for example, Hobsbawn [1994]). However, Therborn [1995], establishes the specificity of various alternative roads to modernity, especially the one taken by Western Europe.

11. Cited in Meiksins Wood [1995: 1]. See also Daniel Bell [1960] in *The End of Ideology*, subtitled: 'On the Exhaustion of Political Ideas in the 1950s'. As Bell saw it: 'all universalistic, humanuistic ideologies of the nineteenth century, especially Marxian socialism, are exhausted'. In this initial formulation of a transition to a 'postmodern era' the central focus of sociological analysis was on the formation of a post-industrial or post-capitalist form of society. Unlike the postmodernists of the 1980s, the central concern of sociologists like Mills, Bell and Dahrendorf was not with the process of economic development itself but with the possibility that this might lead to socialism.

12. The sociology of development, by definition, was advanced by those who fundamentally believed in the existence of a process of development – of incremental change and the accumulation and unfolding of conditions of social transformation. Of course, theorists and practitioners were divided paradigmatically between those whose point of departure was a theory of modernisation and those whose analysis was predicated on variants of a theory formulated by Marx. Variants of these two schools of thought dominated the sociology of development throughout the 1960s, the 1970s and the 1980s.

13. This consensus (see Williamson [1990]) took the form of a programme of stabilisation and structural adjustment measures (liberalisation, privatisation, deregulation, austerity and downsizing/modernisation of the state), formulated by the economists of the World Bank and the IMF as loan conditionalities imposed on borrowing countries. On these measures, the thinking behind them and their impacts, see *inter alia* Bello *et al.* [1994], Korten [1995], Veltmeyer and Petras [1997], Woodward [1992].

14. For some unknown reason, there does not yet exist a systematic review and examination of this wide-ranging and multifaceted intellectual movement of 'Another Development', although there exists a marxist critique, dating from Lenin, of its populist strand. A more radical resolution of this crisis within development theory is expressed in W. Sachs [1992], contributors to which more or less share the view that development, as a concept, as an intellectual project, and in practice, is a misbegotten enterprise that, as Deepak Lal and other

neoliberal critics of development economics argued from a radically opposed perspective, is 'bad' for 'developing countries'. In this respect, there is little to distinguish the proponents of the existence of a theoretical impasse in the study of economic development from the standpoint taken and arguments advanced by postmodernists. On this point see Brass (1995).

15. Post-structuralism, like its main object of criticism, structuralism, and the currently dominant form of political economy, regulationism, is a French school of thought, with both philosophical and sociological formulations that have become intellectually fashionable. See in particular Baudrillard [1988], Derrida [1982] and Lyotard [1984], and more ambiguously, Michel Foucault. As far as far as Marxism and the identification and analysis of 'new social movements' is concerned, of particular importance are the reflections of Ernesto Laclau [1989, 1990], a former exponent of structural Marxism in the form of a modes of production approach, which in the late 1970s was the major Marxist alternative to Latin American dependency theory.

16. Among the clearest expositions of the logic of structural analysis in its Marxist form are the writings of Louis Althusser, the object of intense debate and criticism in the 1970s. On this debate see *inter alia* Banet [1989] and Veltmeyer [1974, 1978].

17. The tendency of this form of analysis to dissolve in thought conditions that are 'real' is clearly and dramatically reflected in a remark by Gayatri Chakravorty Spivak, a translator of Derrida, at a seminar at the Pembroke Center for Teaching and research on Women, at Brown University (March 1988) (cited by Nugent [1995: 124–5]): 'class is the purest form of signifier', implying that class is but a linguistic symbol with no concrete referent in the material world. In this post-structuralist discourse, the idea of class as a structure is just that: an idea imposed on but no basis in the immediacy of lived or experienced reality.

18. The intellectual antecedents and the range of ideas encompassed by 'postmodernism' is subject to debate and interpretation, but it has basically two centres of reference: a set of conditions associated with the culture of late-capitalist society – postmodernism as condition [*Harvey*, 1989; *Jameson*, 1991], and as a new form of knowledge and analysis (Derrida, Lyotard, Baudrillard, Foucault) based on what I would interpret as an idealist epistemology that in social analysis can be traced back to some extent to the Frankfurt School and beyond that to German historicism (Dilthey, etc.), Nietzchian nihilism and irrationalism, the Early Works of Marx and a philosophy enunciated in different ways by Kant and Hegel. On this see Veltmeyer [1978].

19. Postmodernism in this form [*Lyotard*, 1984; *Baudrillard*, 1988] not only rejects the 'grand narratives', 'totalising' ideas or 'meta-theories' – reflected in liberal and socialist ideologies and appeals to universal standards such as progress, freedom, humanity, justice, and equality – but gives up any idea of an intelligible historic process and causality, and with it any idea of 'making history'. There is no structured process accesible to human knowledge; there are only, as Derrida [1982] emphasises, disconnected, anarchic, and inexplicable 'differences'.

20. See, for example, Escobar and Alvarez [1992], Scott [1985], Slater [1985], Camacho and Menjivar [1989].

21. There are diverse formulations of this concept, which can be, and in analysis is, contrasted with the central concept of Marxist analysis – class. *Inter alia* see Touraine [1987, 1989], whose formulations have been absorbed by or are central to the analysis of many Latin American sociologists (see, for example, Tironi [1991].

22. This principle is diametrically opposed to the first principle (objectivity) of Historical materialism, formulated by Marx as the idea that 'in the process of social production, people enter into relations that are indispensable and independent of their will ... that correspond to stages in the development of the material forces of society...and to which correspond certain forms of consciousness ... which, in general, are determined by the form [objective conditions] of [people's] social existence.' In this context, despite the protestations or obfuscation of some, and of other attempts to actually combine materialism and postmodernism (see, for example, Marchand and Parpart [1995]), postmodernism, we would argue, is fundamentally idealist in its epistemology and form of analysis, denying the objectivity of the conditions of social existence and of class relations generated by the workings of a system.

23. This principle of structural determination, which is critical to Marxism as social science, is

fundamentally antithetical to postmodernism, the main object of its theoretical and methodological critique of Marxism.

24. For a critique of this appropriation by the World Bank of the concept of a moral economy developed by Scott [1976, 1985] see Breman [1996].

25. These conditions, reflected in a trend towards increased disparities in the distribution of income and an extension of various forms and degrees of poverty, have been extensively documented and analysed in the Latin American context. *Inter alia* see Kliksberg [1993], Lustig (1995), Veltmeyer and Petras [1997], Vuskovic [1993] and Woodward [1992].

26. On this redemocratisation process, which in the Latin American context can be dated precisely from 1979 (Ecuador) to 1989 (Chile), see *inter alia* Stepan (1988), Petras and Vieux [1994], and Touraine [1989].

27. The literature on the SAP in Latin America, in terms of its implementation and social impacts, is voluminous. *Inter alia* see Veltmeyer and Petras [1997].

28. The objective conditions of this development are reflected in a dramatic shift in the relative shares of labour and capital in national income and value added in the production process, and further reflected in a significant transformation of the working class. For some reason, the objective conditions of this shift and transformation although well understood, have been documented only with respect to changes in forms of labour and working conditions, and have not been systematically analysed either in macro-economic terms (changes in the structure of production and the shift in income participation shares) or in sociological terms (changes in the class and social structure).

29. On this process see *inter alia* Veltmeyer and Petras [1997].

30. *Inter alia* see Escobar and Alvarez [1992] and Hunter [1995].

31. Fairly well documented and systematic case studies of these movements can be found in Eckstein [1989] and Dominguez [1994]. However, neither discuss the theoretical issues involved in the construction of new social movements. Escobar and Alvarez [1992] does, but in its focus on the new cultural dimensions of Latin American social movements ignores (theoretically rejects) the resurgence of class-based social movements. Theoretically, the most ambitious comparative study of new Latin American movements is Assies *et. al* [1990], although like most studies of new social movements the focus is entirely on the urban question.

32. In the worst phase of the Pinochet dictatorship in Chile, the *colonos* of the *poblaciones*, the shantytowns formed on the periphery of Santiago and other cities, confronted the military police in direct street action and led the political struggle of resistance and opposition abandoned by the political parties and unions that had been banned, broken up or placed in recess by the regime [*Petras and Leiva*, 1986; *Tironi*, 1991]. At the beginning of the 1980s, in Argentina the pobladores of Gran Buenos Aires organised themselves in the form of mutual- or neighbourhood associations to demand the legalisation of occupied land and help in the building of houses and accessing electricity, water, sewage and other public services. Soon thereafter, the urban poor took to the streets in the very centre of Buenos Aires to press these demands in the form of direct action and confrontation with the police and the army which the government had called into service. In Chile and Peru, and elsewhere, similar popular economic organisations were formed to set up communal soup kitchens, and survival and defense systems, as well as organisations to press political demands of various sorts, including the restoration of democracy, and to do so on the basis of direct action. On these struggles of the urban poor see *inter alia* Garcia Delgado and Silva [1985], Fara [1985], Petras and Leiva [1986], Jacobi [1985], Moises and Kowarick [1981], Espinosa [1985], and Tovar [1985]. A more global view of this process can be found in Hardoy and Portes [1984].

33. Together with the urban poor generally, women were the major protagonists of these urban local struggles. On this and the self-constitution of women as a new social actor, see *inter alia* Barrig [1987], del Carmen Feijoo and Gogna [1985], Saffioti and Ferrante [1985], Escobar [1985], Prieto [1985], Molina [1986], Prates and Rodriguez [1985]. On these diverse struggles see also Garcia Delgado and Silva [1985] and Zambrano [1987].

34. See, for example, Rufino dos Santos [1985]; Vives [1985]. These ethnic struggles can be placed into two categories: oriented towards the demand for cultural and ethnic 'identity', mostly within an urban context (see Calderon [1987]) and those oriented towards social and

national liberation, the vindication of their economic rights and demands. Many of these struggles took place in the countryside and more often than not were combined with the peasant movement and its class organisations. See *inter alia* Chiriboga [1985] and Calderon and Jelin [1987].

35. Rodriguez [1985]; Vila [1985]; and Valenzuela [1985], *inter alia*. As analysed by Vila [1985], the politics of resistance practised by youth often took a cultural form – expressed, for example, in music. However, although rarely analysed in these terms, youth constituted a major element of the street and neighbourhood struggles of the urban poor for local democracy throughout the 1980s..

36. A year after the 1976 military coup in Argentina, las Madres de la Plaza de Mayo (still active 20 years later on the basis of a now generalised highly radical and militant opposition to the neoliberal economic model as well as demand for the redress of human rights violations, political immunity, and corruption) provided the first marches against the dictatorship at a time when neither parties or unions had the capacity or were able to muster the resources to combat the military regime, to resist its hardline policy of repression, assassination and 'disappearances' – up to 30,000, according to Human Rights organisations.

37. One of the more obvious and critical changes wrought by conditions and government policies in the 1980s was in the form, organisation and conditions of work related to a change in the structure of the urban working class. Salient features of this change include the growth and proliferation of informalisation, characterised by the predominance of work 'on one's own account' (self-employment), payment on commission, the lack of or short-term contracts, and the absence or inoperability of government regulation or social protection. Numerous studies by CEPAL, the ILO, various generations of sociologists (as well as a few economists) have determined that in the 1980s jobs in the industrial sector (manufacturing and construction) as well as government service, the backbone of the 'traditional' working class – and what have been labelled 'good Jobs' (well-paying, offered on indefinite full-time contracts) – suffered an absolute decline and that the 'informal sector' accounted for the vast bulk if not 100 per cent of the job growth. At a regional level, in 1980 the informal sector constituted but 10 per cent of all jobs; by the end of the 1980s, they constituted close to 40 per cent – an incredible growth, with considerable social – and political – ramifications. The critical structural – and political – feature of these changes is the shift from the factory and office to the streets. As far as political conflict and acts of protest are concerned, the demands of the the 'new' working class no longer are concerned with wages and working conditions but have tended to revolve around the issues of physical space, the right of *vendedores callejeros* or *ambulantes* to work the streets, and the distribution of licenses to sell goods or operate taxis or buses, etc. These demands have also formed the nucleus of the struggles of plumbers, electricians, shoemakers, and the producers of such ' traded services', Apart from such 'work-related issues, this new urban working class, who make up the bulk of the 'new urban poor' (the 40 million or so that have been added to official register of the poor in Latin America since 1982), tends to mobilise around consumption-issues (the price of fuel, public transportation, food, etc., affected by government policy – austerity measures, etc.

38. On these new social movements see *inter alia* Slater [1985]; Escobar and Alvarez [1992], and the bibliography of this essay.

39. On this aspect of new social movements see *inter alia* Herzer *et al.* (1986), Borja *et al.* [1989], Palermo and Gonzales Bombal [1987], Perez and Piedra Cueva [1986], Tovar [1987].

40. By official accounts, over 60 per cent of 'peasants' have been converted into *jornaleros*, which is to say, a semi-proletariat, dependent on both access to land and some form of wage labour. A similar penetration of indigenous communities and society by capitalism, and with it the state, occurred in other parts of Mexico and throughout the region. Another anthropologist, Frans Schryer, has studied the impact of such penetration in Hidalgo, with reference in this case not to coffee-growing but cattle-raising. As in Greenberg's account of developments in Chiapas, the penetration of capital and capitalism, the institutions of money and the market, is seen by Schryer as a source of intra-community conflict that combined with equally rampant inter-community forms of conflict. In the context of these conflicts, Schryer's study, like those of Greenberg and Benjamin, demonstrates that although class is

modified by a complex matrix of other factors within a peasant community, it remains a primary consideration in examining how and why people resist and rebel. The process of conversion of peasants into wage-labourers or landless workers was greatly accelerated by the agrarian reform initiated by Salinas in 1992 in order to modernise the agricultural sector, that is, expel surplus peasant labour and production, and concentrate arable land into larger-scale internationally competitive units of profitable and efficient production.

41. In Mexico, for example, at least 70 per cent of the country's indigenous peoples live in what are officially characterised as 'marginal zones', areas characterised by higher than average indices of low income, malnutrition, illiteracy, and other conditions of poverty such as high rates of child mortality and lack of access to adequate housing, electricity, potable water and other services.

42. Although Chiapas is home to the largest hydro-electric and petrochemical plants in the country, the basis of the state and regional economy is ownership and productive use of the land, most of which is controlled by a small number of ranchers and *hacendados*. In the 1930s, during the presidency of Lazaro Cardenas millions of hectares of land was redistributed, raising the number of families on *ejidos*, or collective communal farms, in Chiapas from 71,0000 in 1950 to 148,000 in 1970. Nation-wide there were more than 3 million 'beneficiaries' of the land distribution program arising out of a commitment of the Mexican Revolution and constitutional response to the revolutionary demands of peasants for 'tierra y libertad' in the form of article 27 of the 1917 constitution which promised land reform and the protection of communal landholding. By 1992, on the eve of the constitutional repudiation by the Salinas regime of this revolutionary commitment, opening up the *ejido* to the free market), the 'social sector' of Mexican agriculture controlled more than half of the country's total stock of arable land and accounted for 55 per cent of total domestic production of maize, the subsistence staple of Mexican society. However, in many places, the land so distributed had the poorest soil, and without financial support the productivity of the *ejido* system remained very low, generating a species of agrarian production crisis which motivated the neoliberal regime of Salinas to begin a 'modernisation' programme that entailed the expulsion of the inefficient small producer and the conversion of the *ejido* into large export-oriented farms and commercial operations. The indigenous peasant had no role to play in this modern world, creating intense pressures for their very survival, and these pressures were at their most intense in Chiapas, where nearly half of the total land area was controlled by just 6,000 ranchers, less than 1 per cent of the population; and these ranchers, together with the big landlords, hired thugs to intimidate the Indians and make them relinquish what remained of their land and either drive them out or convert them into wage labourers. These conditions clearly were 'objective' in their effects, helping to generate the Chiapas uprising.

43. In 1960 the Lacandon forest was home to 12,000 people, but, unable to make a living on the land thousands of peasants were driven into this forest. Today the forest, an important centre of the Chiapas rebellion, has 3,000,000 people [*La Botz*, 1994: 6–8], mostly indigenous *jornaleros*.

44. This economy is based on the production and local marketing of corn (maize), the economy of which has been devastated as a direct result of the deregulation of imports from Texas produced under very different technological conditions, with a much higher rate of productivity, lower per unit costs, and considerable government subsidies, allowing, in fact, Texan producers to dump their surplus product even on the local markets in Chiapas, with devastating effect. Similar problems exist in other sectors of the economy, such as coffee production, much of which, in the case of Chiapas is in the hands of highly vulnerable small producers (the large producers control the export sector of the country's coffee production, the bulk of which is found in Chiapas) and cattle-raising both in Chiapas, central states like Zacatecas and the northern states.

45. Unlike Roger Burbach [1994], who has interpreted the Zapatista uprising as history's 'first postmodernist political movement', the Zapatistes are painfully aware of the systemic and structural basis of their struggle. For the Zapatistas there is no question of cultivating their subjectivity, or constructing their identity; the issue for them is how to do battle against a 'system' (defined by them as capitalism in its neoliberal form) and its conditions which are

very much experienced as objective in their effects. On this point, see the First Declaration from the Lacandon jungle and subsequent declarations as well various encounters and forums organised in 1996 'against neoliberalism ... and for humanity'.

46. The characterisation by Burbach [1994] of the Zapatista uprising as 'a postmodernist political movement' is made with reference to the 'fact' that (although postmodernists, like Nietzsche, would tend to argue that 'facts do not exist, only interpretations') unlike traditional guerrilla armies of national liberation the EZLN did not 'seek state power' or social transformation, but only 'an authentic or fuller democracy' (which, oddly enough given the illogic of his argument, is one of the defining characteristics of the modernisation paradigm and the modernist project). In his postmodernist interpretation Burbach also makes an unspecified reference to the 'new forms of making politics', which is as unilluminating. To speak of 'facts' *vis-à-vis* the EZLN it is clear that there is nothing contextually specific about the Zapatista uprising; it is universalist in its key demands for democracy, freedom, and social justice, and both its organisation and politics bespeaks of the structural forces operating not only on indigenous peoples in Chiapas but on indigenous – and other classes of – people all over Latin America and the world. The only possibly meaningful reference to postmodernism in the social movement of the EZLN is its effective use of electronic computer-based communication, which allows for instantaneous transmission all over the world, the same 'postmodern condition' that led the *New York Times* to characterise the December 1994 financial crisis and meltdown in Mexico as 'the first postmodern financial crisis in history'. Most unilluminating, not to say more.

47. In the context of its transition from an armed force into a new political force able to speak and negotiate demands on behalf of all indigenous peoples in the country, the EZLN's political demands have also been transmuted from a call for social transformation into a call for full democracy. However, this shift reflects the Zapatistas' effort to open up a political space for civil society, which, it is hoped, will be able to create the conditions for social transformation. That is, the Zapatistas recognised that in its limited organisation it did not have the resources and the force needed to take over the state, let alone induce a process of social transformation.

48. See, for example, the essays collected by Escobar y Alvarez [1992] and Slater [1985]. This line of interpretation of Latin American NSMs through its theoretical formulations seek to resolve the theoretical impasse of which Schuurman [1993] and others speak. The movement in search for Another Development has its origins in the impasse reached by proponents of liberalism and structuralism, the two dominant lines of theory and analysis in the field. But the proponents of Another Development are also unable to explain the dynamics of international development and resolve the theoretical crisis, which as Booth [1985] has argued, also, and in particular, has affected Marxist thought. In this connection Booth, Schuurman and others have in effect 'constructed' a 'theoretical crisis' as a means of staging and launching an attack on structuralist forms of analysis and on Marxism in particular. As in the field of social movements, this entire approach to development needs to be taken up and critiqued, as has Brass [1995].

49. The following analysis makes reference to and is based in part on an as yet unpublished essay by James Petras, whom the author accompanied on a series of visits to Bolivia and Brazil to interview the leaders and rank and file members of these peasant unions and social movements. Reference to the peasant movement in Paraguay is directly taken from Petras's essay.

50. The history of the MST can be found in Stedile and Sergio [1993] and MS [1994]. As for the internal dynamics of the MST see chapter nine in Veltmeyer and Petras [1997].

51. A brief history of the MST can be found in Stedile and Sergio [1993].

52. *Informativo Campesino* (Asunción), No.91, April 1996.

53. For some documentation of these struggles see *La Jornada*, 10 Agosto 1996: 3; *Chiapas*, No.2 (Mexico, 1996); *La Jornada*, 10 Octubre 1996.

54. According to Petras, who has interviewed the leaders and activists of the most dynamic peasant organisations in Brazil, Bolivia, and Paraguay, the leadership of these new peasant social movements is a critical factor that distinguishes them from the peasant movements of the 1960s and 1970s. They are characteristically unbureaucratic and informal in their form

of work and relationship with the rank and file. They have few resources and are accustomed to traveling long distances on the bus or by pick-up to attend meetings. They also tend to maintain close ties with the peasant communities that form the base of the movement.

55. Interview by Petras of leader of the *cocaleros*, Evo Morales, 10 June 1996.
56. Interview of regional leaders of the MST taking the first block of the leaders training course, 19–29 March 1995 (Instituto Cajamar, São Paulo).
57. Interview by Petras of women landless workers at a conference on Peasant Struggles in the Countryside, Cajamar, São Paulo, 22 June 1996
58. MST [1991, 1994]. The author has accompanied Petras in a number of visits and short courses offered at the National Leaders Training School at Caceres, Santa Catarina.
59. Hernandez [1992] and Mejia and Sarmiento Silva [1987], among others have noted the profoundly democratic character of the leadership in Latin America peasant movements, which is also reflective of indigenous values and forms of organisation.
60. In Bolivia, in a seminar held in June 1996 with Petras and the author, the leaders and militants, in their majority cocaleros and participants in a leadership training school in La Paz, the central theme of debate was the relation of class to nation. Many spoke of left intellectuals and parties in a disparaging way, with respect to their inability or unwillingness to take seriously or to come to terms with what for them was the central issue – ethnicity and the nation. In the current political context, there is clearly a strong awareness of indigenous identity. Nevertheless, discussants at the seminar were by and large agreed on the need to combine the concepts of class and nation in an analysis of their reality..
61. The conditions in question (they are not at issue) are reflected in the well-known facts of the state's high incidence of marginality and poverty, that correlate with the relatively high proportion of indigenous peoples in the population and dependence on agriculture, in both cases the highest in the country. As for these conditions – which are not at al specific to the state, merely more concentrated – 19 per cent of the economically active population receive no income at all, another 40 per cent earn less than the federally mandated minimum wage of $3.30 a day, and another 15 per cent earn only twice this amount, resulting in an average per capita income that is a little more than 50 per cent of the national average. A third of the population is illiterate, without access to health care or electricity (in a state that accounts for more than 25 per cent of the countryry's source of electric power); and the conditions of poverty are endemic and widespread. Samuel Ruiz, the bishop of San Cristobal estimates that in the year leading up to the rebellion over 15,000 'indios' died poverty-related of hunger, disease and violence [Roberts, 1994: 10–11].
62. Petras [1997] argues that these peasant-led movements constitute the vanguard of a reconstituted political Left, and as such are part of a third wave of Left politics: the first, in the 1960s and 1970s, was based on class organisations (unions, parties) and actions, the second was based on of social organisations and social movements in the 1980s.
63. The phase of armed struggle was over after about a week of encounters. Subsequently, the EZLN has constructed and entered a path of negotiations with the government, has appealed to civil society for active support in the struggle for democracy, and converted itself into a new political force able to operate on behalf of the country's indigenous peoples at a national level. In this context, the most critical contribution made by the *EZLN* in the process of its conversion from an armed force into a new political force able to operate at a national level is the formation in 1996 of the Congreso Nacional Indigena (CNI), a forum with the capacity of uniting the diverse forces of Mexico's indigenous peoples and pressing their collective demands. On the dynamics of this process see *inter alia* La Botz [1994].
64. Prior to this 1844 strike of Silesian weavers Marx was at one with his colleagues (self-proclaimed young or Left Hegelians) in thinking that the 'subject' or 'active force' of social revolution (the emancipation of 'man') was constituted by 'philosophy', the intellectuals like himself, armed with theoretical awareness of what the working class (the proletariat) represented (the alienation or practical negation of the human essence), and that the proletariat constituted its 'object' or material basis. However, in the strike Marx discovered a working class that combined within itself, its own action, the objective and the subjective conditions of social revolution; that was theoretically aware of itself and what it represented (class conscious), leading Marx to formulate his theory of proletarian self-determination,

reformulated some 50 years later by Georg Lukacs in his conception of the working class as 'the identical subject-object of history. On this issue, relating to a relatively unknown manuscript of Marx ('Marginal Notes to ... the King of Prussia') see Veltmeyer [1978].

65. Without a doubt, the major significance of the Zapatista rebellion has been to (i) place on the national agenda the long established demands of indigenous people for 'freedom, democracy, and social justice; (ii) to force the government to negotiate a new relationship with the indigenous peoples not just of Chiapas but of the whole country; and (iii) creation of the conditions for the formation of the Congreso Nacional Indigena, a forum for concerted political action; and (iv) the creation of a new way of 'doing politics' based on a radical direct internal democracy, which is (reflected in among other developments the subordinate relationship of the military arm of the movement to the civilian arm (the Clandestine Revolutionary Indigenous Committee) composed of representatives from each ethnic community involved in the struggle. However, the rebellion has resonated widely and deeply in the rural sectors of different Latin American societies. For example, In Brazil, a leader of one of the MST's largest operations (the invasion and occupation by over 300 families of Hacienda Formosa in Curionpolis in West Amazonia), said that they had adopted 'Zapatista characteristics' and that 'there ais a similarity between us and the Mexican guerrillas in that we are also fighting for social justice' (a highly modernist and universalist demand, we could add) (*Latinaamerica Press* Vol.28, No.10, 22 March 1996, p.7).

REFERENCES

Assies, Willem *et al.*, 1991, *Structures of Power, Movements of Resistance: An Introduction to the Theories of Urban Movements in Latin America*. Amsterdam: Center for Latin American Research and Documentation.

Baudrillard, Jean, 1988, *Selected Writings* (edited by Mark Poster), Stanford, CA: Stanford University Press.

Banet, E. T., 1989, *Structuralism and the Logic of Dissent*, London: Methuen.

Barrig, Maruja,' 1987, 'Democracia emergente y movimiento de mujeres', in Eduardo Ballon (ed.). *Movimientos sociales y democracia: la fundación de un nuevo orden*. Lima: DESCO.

Bell, Daniel, 1960, *End of Ideology: On the Exhaustion of Political Ideas in the 1950s*. Glencoe, IL: Free Press.

Bello, Walden, with Shea Cunningham and Bill Rau, 1994, *Dark Victory: United States, Structural Adjustment and Global Poverty*, London: Pluto Press.

Benjamin, Thomas, 1989, *A Rich Land, A Poor People: Politics and Society in Modern Chiapas*. Albuquerque, NM: University of New Mexico Press.

Borja, Jordi *et al.*, 1989, *Poder Local y descentralización en América Latina*, Santiago de Chile: CLACSO-SUR.

Booth, David, 1985, 'Marxism and Development Sociology: Interpreting the Impasse', *World Development*, Vol.13, No.7.

Brass, Tom, 1991, 'Moral Economists, Subalterns, New Social Movements and the (Re)Emergence of a (Post) Modernised (Middle) Peasant', *Journal of Peasant Studies*, Vol.18, No.2.

Brass, Tom, 1995, 'Old Conservatism in "New" Clothes', *Journal of Peasant Studies*, Vol.22, No.3.

Burbach, Roger, 1994, 'Roots of the Postmodern Rebellion in Chiapas', *New Left Review* 205.

Calderon, Fernando, 1995, *Movimientos sociales y politica*. Mexico: Siglo XX.

Calderon, Fernando, 1987, 'Movimientos etnicos y cultura', in *El desafio de la étnidad en en el siglo XXI: auto-determinacion, gobierno y estado*, Paris: Asociacion Internacional de Ciencia Politica' (mimeo).

Calderon, Fernando y Mario dos Santos (eds.), 1987, *Los conflictos por la constitucion de un nuevo orden*. Buenos Aires: CLACSO.

Calderon, Fernando y Jose Reyna (eds.), 1996, *La irrupción encubierta*. Mexico: CIIH, UNAM.

Calderon, Fernando y Elizabeth Jelin (eds.), 1987, *Clases y movimientos sociales en America Latina, Perspectivas y realidades*, Buenos Aires: Cuadernos CEDES.

Camacho, D and R. Menjivar (eds.), 1989, *Los movimientos populares en America Latina*, Mexico City: Siglo XX.

Centro de Estudios y Promoción del Desarrollo, 1981, *America Latina 80: democracia y movimiento popular*, Lima: DESCO.

Chiriboga, Manuel, 1985, *Crisis Economica y movimiento campesino y indígena*. Quito: CERLAC (mimeo).

Cleaver, Harry, 1994, 'The Chiapas Uprising', *Studies in Political Economy*, No.44.

Corbridge, Stuart, 1990, 'Post-Marxism and Development Studies: Beyond the Impasse'. *World Development*, Vol. 18, No. 5.

Corcoran Nantes, Yvonne, 1990, 'Women and Popular Urban Social Movements in Sao Paulo', *Bulletin of Latin American Research*, Vol.9, No.2.

Del Carmen Feijoo and Monica Gogna, 1985, 'Las mujeres en la transición a la democracia', Buenos Aires: Buenos Aires: CEDES (mimeo).

Derrida, J, 1982, *Margins of Philosophy*. Chicago, IL: Chicago University Press.

Dominguez, Jorge, 1994, *Social Movements in Latin America: The Experiernce of Peasants, Workers, Women and the Urban Poor, and the Middle Sectors*, New York: Garland Publications.

Eckstein, Susan, 1989, *Power and Popular Protest: Latin American Social Movements*. Berkeley, CA: University of California Press.

Escobar, Cristina, 1985. *Movimientos de mujeres*, Bogota: CINEP.

Escobar, Arturo, 1995, *Encountering Development: The Making and the Unmaking of the Third World*, Princeton, NJ: Princeton University Press.

Escobar, Arturo and Sonia Alvarez (eds.), 1992, *The Making of Social Movements in Latin America: Identity, Strategy, and Dermocracy*, Boulder, CO: Westview Press.

Espinosa, Vicente, 1985, *Los pobladores en la politica*, Santiago de Chile: ILET,

Fara, Luis, 1985, *Luchas reivindicativas urbanas en una contexto autoritario*, Buenos Aires: CEDES.

Frank, Andre Gunder, 1972, 'The Development of Underdevelopment', in Cockcroft *et al.*, *Dependence and Underdevelopment: Latin America's Political Economy*, New York: Doubleday Anchor.

Garcia Delgado, Daniel and Juan Silva, 1985, *El movimiento vecinal y la democracia. Participación y control en el Gran Buenos Aires*, Buenos Aires: CEDES.

Greenberg, James, 1989, *Blood Ties: Life and Violence in Rural Mexico*. Tucson, AR: University of Arizona Press.

Hardoy, Jorge and Alejandro Portes (eds.),1984, *Ciudades y sistemas urbanos*, Buenos Aires: CLACSO.

Harvey, D, 1989, *The Condition of Post-Modernity*, Oxford: Blackwell.

Helman, Judith, 1990, 'The Study of New Social Movements in Latin America and the Question of Autonomy', *LASA Forum* 21.

Hernandez, Luis, 1992, 'La UNORCA: doce tesis sobre el nuevo liderazgo campesino en Mexico', in J. Moguel Botey and L. Hernandez (eds.), *Autonomia y nuevos sujetos sociales en el desarrollo rural*. Mexico.

Herzer, Hilda *et. al.* 1986, 'Poder local e instituciones', *Revista Mexicana de Sociologia*, No.4.

Hobsbawn, Eric, 1994, *The Age of Extremes*. London: Weidenfeld & Nicolson.

Hoogvelt, Ankie, 1984, *The Third World in Global Development*. London: MacMillan Press.

Hunt, Diana, 1989, *Economic Theories of Development*. Hertfordshire: Harvester Wheatsheaf.

Hunter, Allen, 1995, 'Los nuevos movimientos sociales y la revolución', *Nueva Sociedad*, Vol.136, Nos.3–4.

Jacobi, Pedro, 1985, *Movimentos sociais urbanos e a crise: da explosao a participacao popular autonoma*, São Paulo: FESP.

Jameson, F, 1991, *Postmodernism, or, The Cultural Logic of Late Capitalism*, London: Verso.

Jelin, Elizabeth, 1987, *Movimientos sociales y consolidacion democratica en la Argentina actual*. Buenos Aires: Sudamericana.

Kliksberg, Bernardo (ed.), 1993, *Pobreza: Un Tema Impostergable*, Mexico DF: Fondo de Cultura Economico.

Knight, Alan, 1988, 'Debt Bondage in Latin America', in L.J. Archer (ed.), *Slavery and Other*

Forms of Unfree Labour, London/New York: Routledge.

Korten, David, 1995, *When Corporations Rule the World*, New York: Kumarian Press..

La Botz, Dan, 1994, *Chiapas and Beyond: Mexico's crisis and the Fight for Democracy*.

Laclau, Ernesto, 1989, 'Politics and the Limits of Modernity', in A. Ross (ed.), *Universal Abandon? The Politics of Postmodernism*, Edinburgh: Edinburgh University Press.

Laclau, Ernesto, 1990, *New Reflections on the Revolution of our Time*, London: Verso.

Lustig, Nora (ed.), 1995, *Coping with Austerity: Poverty and Inequality in Latin America*, Washington DC: The Brookings Institution.

Lyotard, J F., 1984, *The Postmodern Condition: A Report on Knowledge*, Manchester University Press.

Marchand, Marianne and Jane Parpart (eds.), 1995. *Feminism/Postmodernism/Development*, London: Routledge.

Meier, G. M. and D. Seers (eds.), 1984, *Pioneers in Development.*, Washington, DC: World Bank.

Meiksins Wood, Ellen, 1995, 'What is the 'Postmodern' Agenda?: An Introduction', *Monthly Review*, Vol.47, No.3.

Mejía Piñeros, Maria Consuelo and Sergio Sarmiento Silva, 1987, *La lucha indígena: un reto a la ortodoxia*, Mexico.

Molina, Natacha, 1986, 'Movimiento de mujeres en Chile', in Fernando Calderon and Jose Reyna (eds.), *La irrupción encubierta*. Mexico: IIH-UNAM.

Moises, Jose and Lucio Kowarick *et al.*, 1981, *Cidade, povo e poder*, São Paulo: CEDEC-Paz e Terra.

MST (Movimiento Sin Tierra), 1991, *Como Organizar a la Masa Sao Paulo*, São Paulo: MST National Office.

MST, 1994, *Documento Basico do MST*, São Paulo: MST National Office.

Nugent, Daniel, 1995, 'Northern Intellectuals and the EZLN', *Monthly Review*, Vol.47, No.3.

Otero, Gerardo, 1990, 'El nuevo movimiento agrario: autogestion y producción democrática', *Revista Mexicana de Sociologia*, Vol.5, No.2.

Palermo, Vicente and María Gonzalez Bombal, 1987, 'La politica local', in Elizabeth Jelin (ed.), *Movimientos sociales y consolidación democrática en la Argentina actual*, Buenos Aires: Sudamericana.

Petras, James, 1977, 'Latin America: The Peasantry Strikes Back', *New Left Review*, No. 223.

Petras, James, 1990, 'Retreat of the Intellectuals', *Economic and Political Weekly*, New Delhi, 22 Sept.

Petras, James and Fernando Leiva, 1986, 'Chile's Poor in the Struggle for Democracy', *Latin American Pespectives*, Vol.13, No.4.

Petras, James and Steve Vieux, 1994, 'The Transition to Authoritarian Electoral Regimes in Latin America', *Latin American Perspectives* 83, Vol.21, No.4.

Prieto, Mercedes, 1985, *Notas sobre el movimiento de mujeres en el Ecuador*, Quito: CERLAC (mimeo).

Prates, Susana and Silvia Rodriguez, 1985, *Las movimientos sociales de mujeres en la transicion a la democracia*, Montevideo: CIESU (mimeo).

Roberts, Martin, 1994, 'Revolt of the Other Mexico', London: *New Stateman and Society*, January 7.

Rodríguez, Eduardo, 1985, *La juventud como movimiento social. Elementos para el estudio del caso uruguayo*, Montevideo; CIESU.

Rufino dos Santos, Joel, 1985, *O movimento negro e a crise brasileira*, San Paulo: FESP.

Sachs, Wolfgang (ed.), 1992, *The Development Dictionary*, Zed Press.

Saffioti, Meileth and Vera Ferrante, 1985, *Formas de participacao da muljer em movimentos sociais*, San Paulo: FESP (mimeo).

Schuurman, Frans (ed.), 1993, 'Modernity, Post-Modernity and the New Social Movements', in F.J. Schuurman, *Beyond the Impasse: New Directions in Development Theory.*,London: Zed Books.

Scott, James, 1976, *The Moral Economy of the Peasant*, New Haven, CT/London: Yale University Press.

Scott, James, 1985, *Weapons of the Weak: Everyday Forms of Peasant Resistance*, New Haven, CT: Yale University Press.

Slater, David, 1985, *New Social Movements and the State in Latin America*, Amsterdam: CEDLA.

Sondereguer, Marla, 1985, *El movimiento de derechos humanos en Argentina (1976–83)*. Buenos Aires: CEDES (mimeo).

Smith, G., 1989, *Livelihood and resistance: Peasants and the Politics of Land in Peru*. Berkeley, CA: University of California Press.

Stedile, Joao Pedro and Frei Sergio, 1993, *A luta pela terra no Brasil*, São Paulo: Editorial Pagina Alberta Ltda.

Stepan, Alfred, 1988, 'Caminos hacia la redemocratización: consideraciones teóricas y análisis comparativos', en *Transiciones desde un gobierno autoritario*, vol.3. Buenos Aires: Paidós.

Therborn, Goran, 1995, *European Modernity and Beyond*. Beverly Hills, CA: Sage.

Tironi, Eugenio, 1991, 'Pobladores en Chile: protesta y organización', in J. Schatan *et al.* (ed.), *El sector informal en America Latina*. Mexico DF: Fundacon Neumann-CIDE.

Touraine, Alain, 1987, *Actores sociales y sistemas políticas en America Latina*, Santiago: PREALC/ILO.

Touraine, Alain, 1989, *América Latina. Política y sociedad*, Madrid: Espasa.

Tovar, Teresa, 1987. 'Barrio, ciudad, democracia y politica', in Eduardo Ballon (ed.), *Movimientoz sociales y democracia: la fundación de un nuevo orden*, Lima: DESCO.

Tovar, Teresa, 1985, *Vecinos y pobladores en la crisis (1980–1984)*, Lima: DESCO.

Toye, J. 1987, *Dilemmas of Development*, Oxford: Blackwell.

Tucker, Kenneth (1991). 'How New Are the New Social Movements?' *Theory, Culture and Society*, Vol.8, No.2.

Valenzuela, Eduardo, 1985, *Los jóvenes y la crisis de la modernización*, Santiago de Chile: ILET.

Van Cott, Donna Lee (ed.), 1994), *Indigenous Peoples and Democracy in Latin America*, New York: St. Martin's.

Veltmeyer, Henry and James Petras, 1997, *Neoliberalism and Class Conflict in Latin America*. London: Macmillan Press/New York St. Martin's Press.

Veltmeyer, Henry, 1974, 'The Structuralist Interrogation of Marx's Thought: Levi-Strauss and Louis Althusser', *Science and Society*, Vol.38, No.4.

Veltmeyer, Henry, 1978, 'Marx's Two Methods of Social Analysis', *Sociological Inquiry*, Vol.48, No.3.

Vila, Pablo, 1985, *El movimiento de rock nacional: crónicas de la resistencia juvenil*, Buenos Aires: CEDES.

Vives, Cristian, 1985, *El Pueblo Mapuche: elementos para comprenderlo como movimiento social*, Santiago de Chile: ILET (Mimeo).

Vuskovic,, Pedro, 1993, *Pobreza y Disegualdad en America Latina*. Mexico, DF: Centro de Investigaciones Interdisciplinarias en Humanidades, UNAM.

Waylen, G, 1993, 'Women's Movements and Democratisation in Latin America', *Third World Quarterly*, Vol.14, No.3.

Williamson, J. (ed.), 1990, *Latin American Adjustment. How Much Has Happened?* Washington, DC: Institute for International Economics.

Woodward, David, 1992, *Debt, Adjustmkent and Poverty in Developing Countries*, Vol.1, London: Pinter Publishers.

Zambrano, Angel, 1987, 'Asociaciones de vecinos y procesos de democratización', in Luis Gomez Calcagno (ed.), *Los movimientos sociales: democracia emergente en el sistema político venezolano*, Caracas: CENDES.

THE METAMORPHOSIS OF LATIN AMERICAN PROTESTANT GROUPS:
A Sociohistorical Perspective*

Jean-Pierre Bastian
Universidad Autónoma Metropolitana, Iztapalpa

Study of religious phenomena in Latin America and the Caribbean covered by the generic term *Protestantism* has opened up a fertile field of research for sociologists, anthropologists, and historians in the last thirty years. The exponential growth in new non–Roman Catholic religious movements since the 1950s and the breadth of their organized networks have stimulated research based more often on sensationalism than on a scientific perspective. The complex and pluralistic manifestations of this heterodox religious phenomenon have generally been reduced to a notion of Protestantism rarely found in scholarly usage. The multiplicity of non–Roman Catholic religious movements cannot be reduced to some catchall category of "Protestantism." Moreover, one must also analyze the connection between usage of the term *Protestant* and a culture marked by the Spanish Inquisition, which shaped the Ibero-American collective unconscious for more than three centuries, in order to understand why a fair number of Latin American researchers look at religious dissidence rather superficially, reducing it immediately to "Protestantism."

Another frequent conflation has been to associate Protestantism with all new religious movements and with the generic concept of sect, a term that has been employed superficially and rarely from a sociological point of view. This confusion has resulted from the Latin American cultural perspective, a product of the Inquisition that pursued followers of "sects of Luther, Moses, and Muhammed" on the American continent in the sixteenth century. As it turned out, Islam never took hold in Latin America until recently, and Judaism has not survived except by the indirect means of "*marrano*" assimilation (covert Judaism in response to forced conversion). The only religious force (beyond indigenous "idolatries") that has gradually been recognized as a representation of heterodoxy has been the Lutheran heresy and its latter-day variations. To paraphrase Serge Gruzinski, it is possible to assert that Protestants thus join "the series

*This article was translated from French by Margaret Caffey-Moquin with funding from the Tinker Foundation.

33

of deviants, phantasms, and obsessions that haunt the imagination of the Iberian societies alongside the Jews, sodomites, and sorcerers" (Gruzinski and Bernand 1988, 163).

Amalgamation of the terms *Protestantism* and *sect* was reinforced in the nineteenth century during the apogée of Roman Catholic ultramontanism (advocacy of papal primacy) and the struggle against the liberalizing forces of modernity, when the "Protestant sects" were denounced by conservatives and intransigent Catholics in terms exceeding the normal political discourse of the nineteenth century. Thus it is not surprising that the tendency to label all sects as Protestant has reappeared since the early 1960s, along with the ideological polarization and violent politics that characterized the cold war (1950–1990). This same aggregation of *Protestantism* and *sect* was by this time also common in intellectual circles on the right and the left, notably among the younger generation of Latin American researchers for whom Marxist dogma supplanted Inquisitorial dogma. In this intellectual climate, numerous attempts were made to forge a "conspiracy theory" (see Stoll 1984). Such a theory thus represents a repetition of the clichés of the Inquisitorial culture surviving in the collective unconscious: denunciation of Protestant groups by suspecting them of representing the vanguard of U.S. imperialism, preparing to annex Latin America to the United States, destroying national identities and the unity of the Latin American peoples, being the chief agent of acculturation, presaging an invasion by U.S. capital, and so on.[1]

The durability of these clichés is all the more surprising because since the late 1960s, several solid sociological studies (Lalive d'Epinay 1968, 1975; Willems 1967) have proposed a typology and an interpretation of the Protestant movements that are still applicable in the 1990s. As a result, one can only ascribe the proliferation of uncritical and unscientific essays on this theme to the limited scientific background of researchers who have not assimilated the theoretical underpinnings of the sociology of religion and have instead substituted the rhetoric of Marxist "jargon" or inquisitorial Catholic culture for the rigor of a scientific approach.

Despite this severe handicap, some progress has been made in analyzing "Protestant" religious phenomena in Latin America and the Caribbean since the basic studies were undertaken by Christian Lalive d'Epinay and Emile Willems. Subsequent research has taken two directions: historical approaches have permitted an understanding of Latin American Protestant groups over the long term, while a number of anthropological monographs

---

1. Numerous examples of essays produced by former Catholic clergy can be cited, among them José Vaderrey, "Les Sectes en Amérique Centrale," *Pro Mundi Vita*, no. 100, no. 1 (1985): 1–39; and Gilberto Giménez, *Sectas religiosas en el sureste: aspectos sociográficos y estadísticos* (Mexico City: CIESAS, 1988); and Assman (1987). An example of a Marxist argument is the pamphlet by Erwin Rodríguez, *Un evangelio según la clase dominante* (Mexico City: Universidad Nacional Autónoma de México, 1982). On the conspiracy theory, see Stoll (1984).

34

have managed to capture the syncretic nature and the sociopolitical implications of religious dissension in indigenous settings.

Finally, three comprehensive studies of Protestant movements in Latin America appeared in 1990 (Bastian 1990; Martin 1990; Stoll 1990). All three attempt to explain the Protestant religious explosion in Latin America over the last thirty years. My study considers Protestantism over the long term from the perspective of its connections with political regimes and Latin American culture and concludes that these connections changed beginning in the 1960s. David Martin, in contrast, links Protestantism to the earlier Protestant outgrowths in England (Methodism) and the United States (Pentecostalism), perceiving Latin American Protestantism as an extension of Pentecostalism. David Stoll meanwhile views Protestantism in Latin America not as an invasion but as an evangelical awakening that offers new forms of organization to working-class sectors. All three studies affirm that the phenomenon in question is definitely Protestantism. None of them, however, have examined the topic itself.

The objective of this article is to explore the subject by using the following hypothesis as a point of departure: the flourishing of heterodox religion being witnessed in Latin America is a redeployment of "popular religion," of rural forms of Catholicism without priests. Thus rather than talking about Protestantism, it is necessary to ask whether the Latin American Protestant movements that have existed for over a century have undergone a metamorphosis. Such a change characterizes the now-fragmented religious world, one liberated by the economic and social transformations imposed on Latin American societies since the 1960s.

In this sense, recent research suggests a double question: can one still speak of "Protestant groups" in referring to the heterodox Christian religious phenomena found at the center of the Latin American religious world? And are these manifestations still part of a "Protestant logic," or are they forms of millenarianism and messianism similar to other minority heterodox religious expressions that proliferate when traditional societies crumble?

In analyzing the metamorphosis, this article will first address the relationship of Latin American Protestant movements to their history. Next, it will consider the statistical data that allow measurement of the growth of heterodox religious societies. Finally, I will explore the structure of the object of study by discussing four points that respond to recently published anthropological and sociological research.

THE RELATIONSHIP TO HISTORY

Recent Latin Americanist historiography, by emphasizing the long duration and the permanence of the mentalities and mental constructs of social control, affords a view of the constants within Latin American polit-

35

ical and social practices. In particular, the corporatism that permeates all social practices is usually perceived as the fruit of a pre-Hispanic and colonial double heritage. The Aristotelian-Thomist view of the social order as a natural order that is hierarchical, vertical, and integrated reinforced the pre-Hispanic values and practices that produced the authoritarian colonial culture of the old regime (see Pietschmann 1980; Mansilla 1989; Lafaye 1974).

The "natural social order" became above all a colonial order in which the top-down hierarchy legitimated the dominion of Spaniards over Indians, blacks, and the *castas* (mestizos or those of mixed race). The racial preeminence of whites over Indians and people of mixed race continued virtually unchanged by the political independence movements of the early nineteenth century, when the elite creoles (who were white) supplanted Iberian power. Ever since then, their dilemma has been how to modernize Latin American societies while maintaining their own privileges and control of the indigenous and black masses known to them as *las chusmas* (the rabble).

In resisting centrifugal social forces, Catholicism proved to be the essential cohesive factor for these fragile nationalities. Thus the basic problem for the first generation of liberal moderates was how to reconcile Catholicism, which increasingly favored papal power over national or diocesan authority, with liberal modernity without destroying that keystone of corporatist mentality and practices, the Catholic Church. Some radicalized liberal minorities attempted to resolve the problem of Catholic "intransigentism" by imposing by force of arms liberal constitutions and a forced secularization on the traditional mentality of the masses. In Latin America, liberal modernity could find no basis for a religious reform that would have allowed eventual transformation of the corporatist mentality. Partly for this reason, attempts at democratic reform of all types—whether authoritarian and oligarchic liberalism, neocorporatist populism, or caudillismo—succeeded to about the same degree (see Bastian 1990; Halperin Donghi 1985; Touraine 1988).

The power struggle between the deeply rooted mental constructs of Latin American societies and liberal democratic modernity caused the "Protestant question" to arise with particular force during the nineteenth century. This problem emerged for the creole elite as early as the beginning of the nineteenth century over the issues of free trade and the promotion of settlement in the colonies.[2] The question of religious tolerance and its radical corollary of liberty constituted the heart of the political

---

2. By the term *creole*, I mean Spanish and Portuguese descendants of second generation and later who were born in Latin America to white parents. In the Caribbean, the term *creole* is applied to those of mixed race.

36

debates of the liberal elites during the first half of the nineteenth century (see for example Rodríguez 1980).

But only in one context, when armed forces imposed grand liberal principles like the separation of church and state and the freedom of worship, can one speak of Latin American Protestantism. This form of Protestantism arose not from outside (as one Protestant hagiography would have it or as the superficial perception of numerous works would lead one to believe) but from within the liberal radical minorities, as demonstrated by the works of David Gueiros Vieira (1980), Marcos Antonio Ramos (1986), and my own studies (1989, 1990). All these works have shown that in Brazil, Cuba, and Mexico as far back as 1850, non–Roman Catholic schisms were proliferating along with Catholic evangelical associations modeled on the lodges or "evangelical" religious societies organized by radical-liberal Latin Americans long before U.S. missionaries arrived.

Thus these dissident religious networks already existed and were actually rebaptized for the most part (as Methodist, Presbyterian, Baptist, and so on) following negotiations between missionaries and dissident religious liberals. This process evolved by reinforcing the preexisting networks and their expansion (previously limited to a radical-liberal dimension) and by redirecting the missionaries' economic contribution toward developing radical-liberal religious presses, schools, and democratic models of religious administration. This process grew out of the liberal political culture of Latin American Protestant agents of change and adapted to the struggle against the larger traditional society, which was corporatist and Catholic. For this reason, the symbols of this liberal Protestantism—Martin Luther, John Calvin, and John Wesley—were replaced by Benito Juárez, Domingo Faustino Sarmiento, and José Martí, thus developing a liberal civic religion that was in effect a Protestant syncretism adapted to reflect Latin American liberal values.

Recognition of the fundamentally endogenous character of the Latin American liberal Protestant movements of the nineteenth century (excepting the transplanted Protestant denominations of Europeans who immigrated to the southern part of Latin America) leads to the perception that they shared the associative logic of other "societies of thought" that were their contemporaries.[3] In effect, these Protestant movements shared the

3. On the concept of "society of thought," see Furet (1978). For its application to Protestantism, see Bastian (1989, 1990b). According to Furet, a society of thought is "a form of socialization whose principle focuses on what its members should do, in order to conserve their roles, to divest themselves of all specificity and their real social existence—the opposite of what was called 'organizations' under the old regime, defined by a community of actual professional or social interests as such. The society of thought is characterized by the fact that for each of its members there is only one relationship to ideas. In this sense, these societies anticipated the functioning of democracy, because the latter equalizes individuals according to an abstraction sufficient to constitute them as such: the citizenship that contains and defines that part of sovereignty corresponding to each person" (Furet 1978, 220).

37

nineteenth-century passion for organization within civil society, as witnessed by the emergence of other similarly local associations that adopted the trappings of foreign associative systems in the form of lodges, spiritist circles, and mutual-aid societies.

These new forms of association were attractive to social sectors in transition (such as workers, small landowners, employees, and schoolteachers) and mestizo in origin, whose precarious economic status had alienated them from the traditional social order of the hacienda and the creole oligarchies who were imposing an authoritarian economic development. For the social sectors in transition, the Protestant associations and the other "societies of thought" served as a means for individuating oneself and inculcating democratic practices and values. This process occurred within a holistic larger society that remained corporative and dominated by collective social and political actors. With their synods, assemblies, general conferences, and conventions, the Protestant associations developed social countermodels and became veritable laboratories for administering modernity not only through egalitarian social relationships but also by applying democratic practices of religious administration that anticipated similar demands to be made of the larger social order.

Another trend was the ongoing participation of Protestant actors in the great democratic liberal and bourgeois struggles, the anti-oligarchic and anti-authoritarian campaigns that by the late 1850s had been going on for a century. Members of Latin American Protestant congregations could be found siding with the democratic forces at the heart of the republican and antislavery struggles in Brazil (1870–1889), during the Cuban independence movements (1868–1898), and in the Mexican Revolution (1910–1920). Latin American Protestants were also active in the movements opposing the dictatorship of Porfirio Díaz in Mexico (1876–1910), among the *tenientes* (lieutenants) in Brazil of the 1920s and 1930s, in the Peruvian *civiliste* movement (1920–1940), on the side of the Jacobo Arbenz regime and the agrarian revolution in Guatemala (1950–1954), and in the early days of the Cuban Revolution (1953–1961). The political and social vision characteristic of Latin American liberal Protestant movements appeared in the work of John Mackay (a disciple of Miguel Unamuno and a friend of Raúl Haya de la Torre), in the writings of Mexican Alberto Rembao, and in the review *La Nueva Democracia* (published from 1920 to 1961 in New York City). In these ways, the identity of the Protestant movements was forged as an agent of a reform that was religious as well as intellectual and moral, a precondition for democratic modernity.[4]

What is striking to historians today is the cohesive identity of the Protestant political position by the late 1950s, especially in comparison

4. For a general interpretation of the historical evolution of Latin American Protestant movements, see Bastian (1990) and Prien (1978).

38

with current Protestant movements, which are polarized into antagonistic camps on the left and the right, "progressives" versus "conservatives." It appears that toward the end of the 1950s, the Latin American Protestantism that had arisen from the political culture of radical liberalism and reinforced that culture was playing the role of a "society of thought," hoping to disseminate to the larger society the experiments carried out in temples and schools, where a new, ultra-minoritarian group of citizens (representative social actors in the classic sense of liberal democracy) was being created.

The relationship of Latin American Protestantism to radical liberalism allows researchers to investigate more confidently the heterodox religious phenomena that have been called Protestant, as well as contemporary Protestant groups that reflect more the extensive transformation of the current religious sphere than a preexisting Protestant heritage. There is even reason to ask whether the contemporary Protestant movements are not the opposites of the earlier "societies of thought." Although the traditional forms of Protestantism arose from the political culture of radical-liberal minorities and questioned the corporatist order and mentality, the contemporary "Protestant" religious schisms originated instead within the Catholic and shamanistic popular religious culture and no longer offer any countermodel to corporatism. On the contrary, they reinforce the order that accounts for their exponential growth and success.

THE EXPONENTIAL GROWTH OF RECENT PROTESTANT MOVEMENTS

One of the noteworthy phenomena in the evolution of Latin American and Caribbean societies over the last thirty years has been the metamorphosis of the religious sphere. Although the Catholic Church has remained dominant at the national level in many regions, it now represents less than half of the total religious forces that are present in these countries.

Since the early 1960s, a veritable atomization has occurred. For example, in 1985 there were 72 Protestant religious societies in Nicaragua and 106 in Guatemala, but in the early 1990s they can be counted by the dozens in both countries. Consequently, the available statistical data for 1960 and 1985 clearly reflect this exponential growth. Unfortunately, however, only a few countries (like Mexico) have implemented a ten-year census that includes questions on religion. The available statistical data on Latin America as a whole come from the religious organizations themselves. Although less reliable, these data also indicate the exponential growth of Protestant religious societies. Comparing the figures published in the U.S. journal *Christianity Today* in 1963 for the year 1960 with those of J. P. Johnstone for 1985 (published in 1986), one finds a broad trend in which some parts of Central America have fallen victim to social disin-

39

tegration, and a slower but similar tendency has characterized secularized countries like Venezuela and Uruguay.

A precise religious demography for each country (nonexistent as yet) could capture the distribution and regional impact of these societies. One such study has been completed on Central America based on statistical data gathered by the Proyecto Centroamericano de Estudios Socio-religiosos (PROCADES) in Costa Rica (see Bastian 1986). My analysis revealed exponential growth (see table 1) and distribution characterized by two strong poles of concentration for each country in the region. Protestant groups in Central America are clustered in two areas: in marginalized rural zones far from the traditional centers of political and religious power and on the periphery of the capitals and regional urban centers. Evidently, marginalization and migration are two of the key factors responsible for the expansion of Protestant societies in Central America. The statistical data from the Mexican census for 1980 confirm this duality in the strong concentration of non-Catholics in the southern states (Chiapas and Quintana Roo having 9 percent each, Tabasco 12.5 percent, and Campeche 10.5 percent) and also in the capitals of the central provinces and the North, where rural migrants abound.[5] In contrast, the west central provinces of the Bajío, a traditional region with strong Catholic influence since the colonial era, registered Protestant rates of less than 1 percent.

It should be noted nevertheless that because the statistical reports available are usually published by the Protestant organizations, such data tend to validate the Protestant religious phenomenon at the expense of other heterodox religious manifestations. This kind of research focuses on a single religious manifestation and thus tends to reinforce the inflexibility of the categories being considered (see Fonseca 1991). It should also be emphasized that since the 1960s, the fragmentation of Protestant denominations has been accompanied by a corresponding differentiation in the religious sphere with the result being that Protestant groups today in no way represent all the unofficial religious movements.

Pentecostal groups represent another important segment of heterodox religious movements, but numerous non-Protestant societies (such as Mormons, Jehovah's Witnesses, Christian Science, and Dianetics) are also proliferating, along with other movements that are syncretic (Luz del Mundo), miracle-oriented (El Niño Fidencio in Mexico, El Niño Jesús de Barlovento in Venezuela), and millennarianist Catholic (La Nueva Jerusalem). To this ever expanding religious universe should be added the new movements of Eastern origin that recruit their adherents among urban and university populations (such as the Moonies, Tibetan movements, Baha'i, and the Hare Krishna), the ancient esoteric sects (like the spiritism

5. See the Mexican census for 1980: *X Censo de Población: resultados preliminares* (Mexico City: Secretaría de Programación y Presupuesto, 1981), p. 75, t. 14.

40

TABLE 1 Percentage of Protestants in National Latin American Populations in 1960 and 1985

Country	1960 Protestants (%)	1985 Protestants (%)	Fringe Groups (%)
Argentina	2.1	5.5	1.1
Bahamas	–	56.4	1.1
Barbados	–	59.3	2.5
Belize	–	25.8	2.0
Bolivia	1.0	7.6	0.7
Brazil	7.8	17.4	0.5
Chile	10.8	22.5	2.0
Colombia	0.7	3.1	1.1
Costa Rica	4.3	7.7	2.2
Cuba	3.2	2.4	–
Dominican Republic	1.5	6.4	0.6
Ecuador	0.3	3.4	0.9
El Salvador	2.2	14.0	1.2
French Guyana	1.2	6.5	1.7
Guatemala	3.0	20.4	0.7
Guyana	–	28.0	1.8
Haiti	10.4	17.4	0.6
Honduras	1.5	9.9	0.7
Jamaica	–	38.6	5.0
Mexico	1.9	4.0	1.0
Nicaragua	4.5	9.3	2.1
Panama	7.6	11.8	1.0
Paraguay	0.7	4.0	0.3
Peru	0.7	3.6	0.9
Puerto Rico	6.9	27.2	2.7
Surinam	9.7	19.9	1.0
Uruguay	1.6	3.1	2.2
Venezuela	0.7	2.6	0.7

Sources: The data for 1960 were compiled for publication in *Christianity Today* 8, no. 21, 19 July 1963, p. 8. Data for 1985 are from J. P. Johnstone, *Operation World*, 4th ed. (1986) 26: 498–99. "Protestant" includes the historical churches as well as the Pentecostal denominations; "Marginal Groups" designates non-Protestant societies such as the Mormons and Jehovah's Witnesses.

of Alan Kardec), and the new esotericisms (La Gran Fraternidad). One of the first methodological consequences of the evolution of the Latin American religious world is that it is no longer possible to study the so-called Protestant groups themselves. A second consequence is that one can no longer explain the evolution of the religious field only in terms of Protestantism (the unfortunate assumption made all too often). Only comparative studies can go beyond the impasses of reductionism by employing a

41

theory of the religious sphere, as do the pioneering studies of Brazilian Carlos Rodrigues Brandão (1986, 1987).

PROTESTANT MOVEMENTS AS OBJECTS OF STUDY AND INTERPRETATION

Contemporary Latin American Protestant movements cannot be analyzed without first consulting the seminal studies of Lalive d'Epinay and Willems, the first to observe the accelerated transformation since the Protestant phenomenon began in the 1960s. The limitations of Lalive d'Epinay's work evident today are found in the choice of a region (Chile and Argentina) that is atypical of the indigenous, black, and mestizo continent and his strictly Protestant theme. He nevertheless posed the essential questions. On the one hand, Lalive d'Epinay developed a typology that locates the variants of Protestantism along the continuum of cult-sect-church, still a useful means of classifying the wide spectrum of religious movements. On the other hand, he (not Willems) was the first to perceive the Protestant sects' gradual adoption of the practices and values of popular religion and culture.

Within the framework of a theory of economic and social crisis and the resulting social disorder, Lalive d'Epinay understood Protestant sects as countersocieties in which what he called the "hacienda model" has reconstructed itself. Similarly, he placed at the center of such a religious society the role of the pastor or patron whose style of religious administration is typically authoritarian and antidemocratic. Because Protestant sects made up the majority of Protestant groups by the late 1960s, Lalive d'Epinay strongly emphasized the Protestants' tendency toward corporatist acculturation, even though he did not precisely describe the break with previous Protestant models implied by this tendency. He perceived Protestant sects as continuous with and reelaborating popular religious culture, and he questioned whether or not these Protestant movements "should be interpreted as a reform of popular Catholicism as much as a renewal internal to Protestantism." In pursuing this line of analysis, Lalive d'Epinay situated these Protestant sects within "the panorama of popular religions alongside the animisms, the spiritisms, the Afro-American religions, the messianisms, the popular forms of Catholicism set up around the sanctuaries, etc." (Lalive d'Epinay 1975, 178–79).

Whereas Willems explained the growth of Protestant forms as resulting from urbanization and the increasing rationalization of everyday life, Lalive d'Epinay observed the establishment of rural as well as urban Protestant sects and placed them within the logic of an adaptation to popular attitudes. Beyond this point, Lalive d'Epinay described their relationship to politics as one of "conformist disengagement," which he termed a "passive modality of the function of witnessing" (Lalive d'Epinay 1975, 279).

42

Since the work of Lalive d'Epinay and Willems, case studies have proliferated, particularly by anthropologists working in indigenous societies (see among others Miller 1979; Garma Navarro 1987; Muratorio 1981a; and Fajardo 1987). But only recently has it been possible to develop integrated approaches based on these studies: one from a historical perspective (Bastian 1990), another from an anthropological point of view (Stoll 1990), and a third from a sociological perspective (Martin 1990). My own extensive review of the literature discerned a rupture starting in the 1960s, marked by Protestant movements adopting the attitudes and values of popular religion as a result of the Pentecostal revolution.

Current Protestant movements are therefore less an expression of the original Protestantism than a redeployment of popular Latin American religion. On the basis of his participatory observation in Guatemala, Nicaragua, and Ecuador, Stoll has posited an expansion of Protestantism that offers a "new form of social organization and a new way to express their hopes" while it is "at least producing new leaders for popular movements" (Stoll 1990, 331, 330). In his view, it is not Protestantism that has become Latin American, but Latin America that has opted for Protestantism. Along this same line, Martin (1990) reviews an ample literature of field studies and perceives what he calls "the explosion of Protestantism in Latin America" via the Pentecostal movements. For Martin, these Latin American Pentecostal forms express an ongoing Protestant ferment that extended from eighteenth-century English Methodism to early-twentieth-century U.S. Pentecostalism. In his view, the Protestant explosion in Latin America is tangible proof of the vitality of Protestant Anglo-Saxon religious culture and of the Latin American masses' progressive acculturation. For Martin, the evangelical awakening is a paradigm that has recurred in three successive sociopolitical contexts.

The Pentecostal wave that is inundating Latin America is the manifestation of a long-term religious and sociopolitical reform leading to the secularization and rationalization of popular behaviors and values. All things considered, the set of questions developed by Stoll and Martin amplify and refine but do not modify or transcend the analyses of Lalive d'Epinay, which had already identified Pentecostal movements as vehicles for reform in Latin American popular religion. Hence arises the necessity of considering the questions raised by Lalive d'Epinay and his findings on the subject. They will be discussed and critiqued in the context of other interpretations, focusing on four points in the hope of stimulating future discussion and advancing the debate.

Protestant Expansion as a Renewal of Popular Religion

The expansion of "Protestant" societies and new religious movements corresponds neither to a "reform of popular Catholicism" nor to a

43

"renewal internal to Protestantism" but rather to a patchwork kind of renewal of popular religion and by the historic Protestant groups' adopting the practices and values of popular Catholic culture.

Throughout the 1970s, when the topic of popular religion was in vogue, many researchers stressed the autonomy of popular religious practices in response to control by the Catholic hierarchy—a juxtaposition of practices that were connected but not integrated (Queiroz 1986; Parker Gumucio 1987; Kohut and Meyers 1988). It is probable that the centralizing and vertical development of Catholicism (which has been called "Romanization") as well as the destruction of traditional social relationships of production in rural settings and ensuing migrations have all combined to foster instances of symbolic redevelopment among minority sectors of Latin American societies. In considering this interpretive perspective, a hypothesis advanced by Pierre Chaunu in 1965 may prove fruitful. In his view, the popular Protestant movements are actually substitutes for forms of Catholicism and thus fill a void: "This radical Protestantism, without dogmatic demands, wholly amenable to inspiration, wholly devoted to the revelation of God—when all things are considered—is it not closer to a Catholicism without priests [typical of the tradition of] part of the masses?" (Chaunu 1965, 17).

David Stoll's latest analysis views Latin American Protestant movements similarly as a reorienting (or rechanneling) of "the popular religiosity of folk Catholicism" (Stoll 1990, 112–13; see also Westmeier 1986). Several monographs on Pentecostal movements in indigenous settings demonstrate the plausibility of this hypothesis. In studying the Toba of the Argentine Chaco, Elmer Miller (1979) as well as Pablo Wright (1983, 1984, 1988) and Daniel Santamaría (1990) have all noted the continuity between shamanistic and Pentecostal religious practices as a kind of religious patchwork or composite assemblage. For Wright, the creation of the United Toba Evangelical Church in 1961, directed by an indigenous religious hierarchy according to the traditional norms of symbolic and political power, "represented an attempt to legitimize certain aspects of their culture through a language and an entity acknowledged and accepted by the surrounding non-indigenous society that discriminates without regard to the autochthonous codes of communication" (Wright 1988, 74). According to Santamaría, this sect involves a strategy of adaptation that redefines ethnicity via a new Christian cult resembling the surrounding society "but which, through its own symbolic manifestations, exists within the ancestral religious atmosphere" (Santamaría 1990, 12).

In Central America, Samandu detected a similar continuity in emphasizing that "Pentecostal beliefs make possible free expression of the popular religious world [that is] inhabited by demons, spirits, revelations, and divine cures . . . in such a way that the believers recognize in Pentecostalism 'their' religion with profound roots in the popular culture,

44

long discredited as superstition by the cultivated and educated classes" (Samandu 1988, p. 8; 1989). The Pentecostal sects' acculturation is not unique, however, because most of the historic Protestant churches have "Pentecostalized" themselves during the last thirty years by adopting charismatic practices and thus assuring themselves of continuing growth and even a rural indigenous base. Such is the case with the Iglesia Presbiteriana Nacional de México, which is strongly entrenched among the Maya of the Yucatán and Chiapas. Andrés Fajardo (1987) found a similar trend in Presbyterianism among the Ixil Maya in neighboring Guatemala (Fajardo 1987; Stoll 1990, 85–86).

To understand this process of acculturation better, it is necessary to consider the diverse expressions of the current Protestant movements within the scope of religious observance. As in the Brazilian case of the village of Santa Rita, "no particular observance of religious worship has succeeded in imposing its hegemony, and where religious mobility and a plurality of beliefs" often characterized popular practices (Saint Martin 1984, 114).

It is also necessary to note the "dynamic of interaction among the diverse religions of the people," as was observed by Cláudia Fonseca (1991) in a working-class neighborhood in Porte Alegre, in the Brazilian state of Rio Grande do Sul. There the Pentecostals are former "Catholics," while others among the informants in the neighborhood are former Pentecostals.

In other words, contemporary popular Protestant groups are participating in a patchwork religious culture in which "passages from one church to another are frequent; the faithful of the Assembly of God often frequent the *terreiro* of the Umbanda, and more rarely the Catholic Church" (Saint Martin 1984, 114; see also Samandu 1991). The enduring characteristics of popular religious culture within Latin American Protestant movements was observed by Roger Bastide in 1973:

What strikes me most as an ethnologist is the process of acculturation of Protestantism via Catholic mass culture: the Protestant seminarians wear chains with crosses or even saints' medals; the men and women separate into two opposite groups in the temples; the festivals (under the pretext of fund-raising) play a more important role than Bible studies; Hispanic "*caudillismo*" continues despite all the conflicts among the various churches, reinterpreted only in the form of dogmas or liturgical differences; institutional indifference wins over the younger generation, so that many individuals today are at the same time Catholic and Protestant, or Protestant and spiritist, or have even become strangers to the life of the churches in which they were baptized. (Bastide 1973, 146)

The assimilation of Latin American Protestant groups into the religious and political culture of millennarian and messianic movements causes them to be viewed today as being more continuous than discontinuous with the religious and cultural universe of the societies in which they prosper. Thus one can ask whether grounds exist for describing them

45

as Protestant or whether they are instead new syncretic religious movements that have become part of the strategy of a symbolic force of resistance or an adaptation to modernity in a religious patchwork produced by the lower strata of Latin American societies.

Protestant Movements as Means of Resistance and Adaptation

In the past dozen years, researchers have noted the growth of Pentecostal movements in rural societies where political conflicts with the landed regime are violent. Several case studies demonstrate the growing cacique-style control by mestizo or indigenous elites who, via popular Catholicism and management of a symbolic religious system, have maintained absolute power and a monopoly over land, commerce, and the political structure of rural society (Bastian 1984; Garma Navarro 1987; Burnett 1989, 137–38). Given the monolithic nature of the vertical and authoritarian political structures, reinforced by a popular Catholicism that was deflected from its reciprocal and redistributive functions, the new "Protestant" religious movements have become one of the few options for breaking with the past. Carlos Garma Navarro's pioneering (1987) work examined Protestant groups in the northern Sierra in the Mexican state of Puebla. He demonstrated that since the 1960s, faced with the mestizo elites' control of coffee commercialization and political power via popular Catholicism, the indigenous peoples have opted for "Protestant" religious practices in order to develop a counterforce. In doing so, the "Protestant" leaders have come to represent a renewal of politico-religious leadership in the region by questioning the mestizo elite.

Similarly, in a study of northeastern Brazil (1985), Regina Reyes Novaes highlighted the active participation of the Pentecostals in the peasant leagues of Francisco Julião during the 1960s, a movement promoting land claims and agrarian reform. In the Ecuadorian province of Chimborazo, the agrarian reform of the 1980s has been viewed more recently by various anthropologists as accompanied by an explosion of Protestant movements (see Casagrande 1978; Muratorio 1981a, 1981b; Santana 1981, 1983). Such studies regard this trend as "an ethnic revitalization" as it relates to the large landowners and to a Catholic hierarchy that (paradoxically) was progressive in the Diocese of Riobamba. Since the 1984 elections, the Asociación Indígena Evangélica del Chimborazo (AIECH) has become a means of expressing the fundamental demands of the Quechuas vis-à-vis the monopolies of land and religion (Stoll 1990, 302). In the southern part of neighboring Colombia, among the indigenous Paez and Guambianos, Joanne Rappaport (1984) noted similarly that "Protestantism" had reinforced ethnic identity while allowing the cult's realization without a nonindigenous intermediary and "while integrating their new beliefs into traditional systems of thought, particularly the aspects that legitimized

46

and structured their political activity oriented toward self-determination" (Rappaport 1984, 116, 112).

Such case studies suggest a mechanism of active resistance via adopting "Protestant" religious practices linked to a "creative symbolism" that allows for a restructuring of the dominated group's identity in the sense of modifying the relationship of political force to the dominant sectors of society in the hope of regaining short- and long-term advantages. One can similarly ask whether these rural indigenous "protesting" forms of Protestantism eventually become part of the millennarian and messianic forms that Maria Isaura Pereira de Queiroz (1968) sought to categorize in distinguishing the restorative movements from the reformist and subversive ones. Donald Curry (1968, 1970) also drew a parallel between Pentecostal movements and messianism in the Brazilian *sertão*. But even so, Protestant sects are not merely vehicles for passive conformism, as Lalive d'Epinay proposed. Particularly in rural and indigenous settings, where social acceleration occurs via modernization, Protestant sects are the manifestations of active resistance. In a thorough consideration of this analytical framework, passive conformism would also be one element of resistance by these minority sectors of society. As Leannec Hurbon (1987) observed, this kind of "passive resistance" can operate in the new religious movements of the Caribbean "through the secret workings of the system of symbols and images with the aim of producing a Caribbean culture that would not be reducible to Western culture" (Queiroz 1968; Hurbon 1987, 58). Through a process of "legitimation or rejection of symbolic activities and traditional images, the convert engages in a process of distancing himself or herself from the dominant values" (Hurbon 1987, 60). It is also true that the main expression of passive resistance and passive conformism is found, as Lalive d'Epinay showed, in the protection that a religious sect offers the individual while enfolding him or her within a countersociety and a minority religious culture. But in my view, it should be possible to enlarge understanding of passive conformism by discussing its relationship to the dominant political and religious culture, transformed by an authoritarian and antidemocratic corporatist symbolism that is identical with that of "Protestant" religious societies.

The Authoritarian and Vertical Religious and Political Culture of Latin American Forms of Protestantism

Rarely have studies of Pentecostal religious societies explicitly reapplied Lalive d'Epinay's analysis of the religious model as being transposed from that of the hacienda and the role of the pastor-patron. Although he attempted to show the innovative character of the Protestant leadership, which (unlike the hacienda) multiplies the possibilities for assuming power, he did not emphasize the elements of continuity that result from

47

reproducing the practices and values intrinsic in traditional and corporatist political and religious culture. Today the majority of Pentecostal churches have leaders who are the chiefs, owners, caciques, and caudillos of a religious movement that they themselves have created and transmitted from father to son according to a patrimonial or nepotistic model. Thus the large Pentecostal church known as Brazil para Cristo, which is affiliated with the Ecumenical Council of Churches, functions under the absolute control of its founder. As Ari Pedro Oro (1990) has shown, this sect has also developed miracle-working practices typical of the Afro-Brazilian movements. Similarly, La Iglesia de la Luz del Mundo, founded in 1926 by a *bracero* in Guadalajara, Mexico, has seen its founder, under the adopted name of Aaron, become a powerful messiah and the uncontested chief of the movement. Upon Aaron's death in 1984, his son succeeded him under the name of Samuel. In Peru the chief of the Pentecostal society known as Los Israelitas has proclaimed himself a messiah by taking the titles of "Grand Biblical Compiler, Grand and Unique Missionary General, Spiritual Guide, Prophet of God, Master of Masters, and Holy Spirit and Christ of the West."[6] This messianism, typical of all the large Pentecostal societies, reappears at all levels of the Pentecostal religious hierarchy. It starts at the level of the local congregation, in which the pastor is not only the proprietor of the temple and the land on which he has consolidated his religious enterprise (often begun in the street) but also the absolute master of it all.

Jacques Gutwirth (1991) found among those of modest means in the Pentecostal sects in Porto Alegre a passive acceptance of authoritarian practices:

This group seems to search and to find in the temples certainties implied by an understanding of the world that is at once very stereotyped and very limited; it also yields with submission to the authoritarian mode of the pastors, who take charge of the conduct of life [and] the way of thinking of the faithful. Miracles and secondarily exorcism are major elements of a religious system with despotic tendencies, conducted by a "charismatic" leader . . . who himself answers to the local directors of the churches. (Gutwirth 1991, 105)

As Wright concluded from studying Toba Pentecostalists, "religious leaders are recognized by their influence over the other members, influence based on some powers of supernatural origin—the contact with divinity— and also on their social and economic prestige" (Wright 1988, p. 74). It thus becomes necessary to analyze with greater rigor, as does Kamsteeg (1990), the networks of reciprocity and redistribution emanating from the Pentecostal leaders in order to perceive the extent to which these networks operate within the logic of the traditional corporatist political and reli-

6. On La Iglesia de la Luz del Mundo, see Ibarra Bellon (1972). On the authoritarian role of the pastor, see also Stoll (1990, 110–11).

gious culture and to recognize their absolute difference from the political culture of Latin American Protestantism of the nineteenth century and the first half of the twentieth.

Acculturation also affects the historical forms of Protestantism, which are partially "Pentecostalized" but have also assimilated the corporatist political culture, unlike the earlier Protestant models arising from the po-' litical culture of radical liberalism. A recent dissertation by Pedro Enrique Carrasco (1988) vigorously demonstrated the process of "episcopalization of the ranks of the Latin American Baptist leadership." Carrasco concluded that the "evangelical Baptist churches are directed by an elite with oligarchic tendencies that capitalizes on a symbolic power and an authority of tradition that function as ongoing institutional visibility" (Carrasco 1988, 231–32). This acculturation of one of the most radical Protestant societies (according to its original congregationalist and democratic model) mirrors a reality that affects the majority of the historical Protestant societies, with the exception of the European Protestant groups transplanted to the southern part of Latin America. Yet the 1960s and 1970s witnessed the same authoritarian model centered around an individual founder and patron within most of the ecumenical study centers arising from the influence of the World Council of Churches in places all over Latin America.[7] In these specific cases of ecumenical corporate enterprise, the abundant contributions received allow authoritarian control to be predicated on mechanisms of redistribution and reciprocity that reinforce the absolute power of the ecumenical "patron." A sociology of this "ecumenical practice" remains to be written. It is enough for now to concur with Carrasco's observation that "the episcopalization of the evangelical churches places the leaders in a posture of social nobility." I would add that this process also develops according to the norms of the dominant corporatist political culture.

In this regard, I made a comparative analysis of popular Protestant movements in Nicaragua and Guatemala (between 1980 and 1984) and their political behaviors under regimes that appear antagonistic because of their political ideologies but are actually governed by the same corporatist logic. I tried to show that in both countries each urban Protestant movement entered into a relationship with the government as the priv-

7. The abundant funding received by the centers for ecumenical studies sustained by the Ecumenical Council of Churches provides a basis for corporatist authority and for establishing relationships of reciprocity and redistribution, in which financial control by the individual founder and cacique is a key element of the power structure. Many examples can be cited of centers founded during the 1960s and 1970s that remain under the control of the founding cacique, among them: the Centro de Coordinación de Proyectos Ecuménicos (CECOPE) and the Centro Nacional de Comunicación Social (CENCOS) in Mexico City; and the Centro Antonio Valdivieso (CAV) in Managua.

49

ileged client of a patron state just when the tensions between the Catholic Church and the state had become acute (see Bastian 1986).[8]

One can thus hypothesize that the passive conformism character- istic of religious countersocieties, far from being merely a turning back on itself, is in fact a key element of the corporatist dynamic of the contempo- rary Protestant groups. These minority religious movements enter into negotiations with the state about the extent to which they can expect rein- forcement of their position in the religious sphere vis-à-vis the Catholic Church, the traditional monopoly-holder on religion. These negotiations follow the same corporatist logic as that of the larger society. Thus during the last twenty years, the Pentecostal leadership has been able to establish itself in certain Latin American countries as a political clientele of the authoritarian regimes in the traditional sense of corporatist mediator.[9]

Two studies of Brazil have shown that Protestant leaders encour- aged their members to vote for the military dictatorship in 1974 in order to obtain privileges and jobs in the administration (see Alves 1985 on the Presbyterians and Hoffnagel 1979 on the Assembly of God). This finding was also supported by Francisco Rolim, who observed that "the Pente- costal believers offered themselves as candidates in a major government party in the hope that the government would make available greater means of conceding favors and responding to demands" (Rolim 1985). Another specialist on the Brazilian Pentecostal movement has noted the perva- siveness of corporatist attitudes within the Pentecostal groups in the São Paulo region: "for the evangelicals, to have a representative in the munici- pal legislature signifies 'opening the door' to their specific interests, close to the public administration—particularly for concessions of land, trans- portation, etc. . . ." (Rolim 1985, 146). One Pentecostal from the Rio de Janeiro region forcefully expressed the traditional political attitude found in contemporary Latin American Protestant movements: "To vote for the candidates of the government parties, and preferably for the evangelicals, is to make your vote count for us" (Rolim 1985, 246). Today one can ven- ture the general hypothesis that Latin American Protestant movements are no longer the vehicles for a democratic religious and political culture.

---

8. Stoll observed in field studies the Guatemalan situation in the Ixil triangle in 1985. He noted that the indigenous Protestants were inclined toward a military regime mainly for reasons of survival in the face of death threats. He concluded that the growth of the evan- gelical churches was due not to U.S. financing but was instead a consequence of the revolu- tionary strategy of the Ejército Guerrillero de los Pobres, which was hardly consistent in its civil activities in the area (see Stoll 1990, 202-3).

9. This process was evident during the Chilean dictatorship of General Augusto Pinochet from 1973 to 1990 and is not exclusive to Pentecostal societies. A similar process developed in Nicaragua and Guatemala (see Bastian 1986). The situation is also similar in Cuba, where the Consejo Ecuménico de las Iglesias de Cuba plays the role of corporatist mediator and main- tains ideological control of the Protestant bases through a close relationship with the Depar- tamento para los Asuntos Religiosos of the socialist state.

50

On the contrary, they have adopted the authoritarian religious and political culture and are developing themselves within the logic of corporatist negotiation.[10]

This trend largely explains the emergence of politicians who have learned to use the new religious movements in a clientelist fashion, such as Alberto Fujimori in 1990 in Peru and Jorge Serrano, the first democratically elected Protestant Latin American president, in Guatemala in January 1991. At the same time, the negotiating capacity of the Protestant leaders and their skill at transforming their religious clienteles into a political clientele propel them along the corridors of power. Examples are the second vice-president of Peru elected along with Fujimori and some thirty deputies and senators from the rolls of Cambio 90 (the political party created for Fujimori's campaign). Even if the political displacement in favor of these sectors can be explained by the economic crisis of the 1980s, the political experience that they are acquiring and the exponential growth of their followings are creating long-term political actors who will have to be taken into account in a corporatist political culture that is unlikely to be replaced by a democratic one (Hermet 1973).

Endogenous Interests Mediating the Link between Latin American and U.S. Protestant Movements

An important issue not yet elucidated is the connection between Latin American Protestant movements and the international Protestant denominations. This area of research remains unexplored beyond the numerous pamphlets produced by the so-called conspiracy theory. This relationship must be approached from a comparative perspective, starting with the observation that the entire Latin American religious field is connected to international religious interests. This general rule applies to the Catholic Church as well as to the Protestant and newer religious movements. It is nonetheless probable that popular Protestant movements, because of their syncretism and their dominated position within the religious sphere, are much less influenced than the Latin American Catholic Church by decisions made outside Latin America. Taking a different ap-

---

10. It is interesting to note that in Peru, the presidential elections of April and June 1990 contained strong racial overtones in pitting the white candidate of the right against the non-white candidate of the left-center. Alberto Fujimori, who is of Japanese origin, was described by the press as "el chinito." His running mate for the vice-presidency was Carlos García García, a Peruvian Baptist pastor. It seems that part of the electoral surprise created by Fujimori in the first round, in which contrary to all expectations he received almost as many votes as Mario Vargas Llosa, was due to the effectiveness of the networks of the so-called Protestant groups in rapidly creating a political following. Compare the account of James Brooke, "Se preve una lucha entre las iglesias católica y evangelista," *Excélsior* (Mexico City), 29 Apr. 1990, pp. 2, 22, with that of Roque Félix, "Preocupan a la Iglesia los brotes racistas previos a la divisiva segunda ronda en Perú," *Excélsior,* 12 May 1990, 2d part, sec. A, p. 1.

51

proach, recent anthropological works have underscored the syncretic nature of rural Protestant movements to suggest their limited connections with international Protestant groups. The link exists nevertheless and merits analysis in studying the urban bureaucracies of Protestant churches. Particular attention should be paid to the selective usage made of international Protestant financial aid and to how such relationships help reinforce the corporatist power structures of Latin American Protestant sects (except for the transplanted Protestant movements of the Southern Cone and certain rare Latin American organizations).

An equally fertile field of research has been opened by David Stoll in analyzing the institutions of the U.S. Protestant religious Right and their support for U.S. government policies in Latin America (1982, 1990). Stoll has rigorously demonstrated the direct support provided by the Summer Institute of Linguistics and U.S. televangelists of the U.S. Central Intelligence Agency in the anti-Communist thrust and military takeovers during the 1960s and 1970s. But it should also be pointed out that the U.S. Protestant right wing was matched by a left wing represented by the National Council of Churches of Christ, an organization that regrouped most of the large denominations of the Protestant establishment that sympathized with the socialist regimes and democratic openings.

Stoll's recent study (1990) convincingly reconstructs in detail the close link between the U.S. Protestant right wing and the policies of President Ronald Reagan in Central America as well as the effective limits of their impact on Latin American Protestant movements. In his three case studies (Guatemala, Nicaragua, and Ecuador), Stoll found genuine autonomy in Latin American Protestant strategies regarding missionaries (Stoll 1982; 1990, 86, 202–3, 328). Likewise, Ari Pedro Oro's (1990) study of the use of the media by the Brazilian Pentecostal churches concluded that far from reproducing models imported from U.S. televangelism, these Brazilian churches recreate via radio or television syncretisms and miracle-working that are then broadcast by the media.[11]

Jacques Gutwirth (1991) has confirmed this finding of "a national audiovisual religion that is growing but escaping the control and norms of the established Protestant persuasions." It arose "according to modalities that were certainly 'deviant' in their connection with the 'established' Pentecostalism of American origin" (1991, 10). For Gutwirth, these churches constitute a "popular religion" that accentuates exorcism and miracle-working according to endogenous modalities: "in Brazil, televangelism of American origin thus plays a secondary role in the offensive advocated by the Rockefeller and Santa Fe connections" (Gutwirth 1991, 112).

In other words, international Protestant organizations are being

---

11. Oro (1990) and Gutwirth (1991, 102, 110, 111) take a position opposite to the "conspiracy" interpretation of Assman (1987).

52

increasingly rejected by Latin American Protestant groups as a consequence of the differing logics of their respective religious origins. Although it seems probable that they can influence the Latin American Protestant movements to some extent and in certain circumstances, the influence of the international organizations shows up primarily in the selection process engaged in by the Latin American Protestant leaders to reinforce their own traditional and corporatist religious authority. The international organizations are the source of their influence, insofar as these organizations can reinforce authoritarianism, but also reveal many limitations, as evinced by their failure to slow the processes of change or to combat syncretism successfully. The international Protestant organizations probably find themselves having the same kind of relationship with the Latin American Protestant sects that the Catholic Church has with Latin American popular Catholic movements.

CONCLUSION

In considering the overall evolution of Latin American Protestant movements since the second half of the nineteenth century, the metamorphosis they have undergone over the last thirty years is striking. In general, the Protestant movements of the nineteenth century arose from the political culture of radical liberalism, which was democratic and promoted individual free will. The current popular Protestant movements, in contrast, derive from the religious culture of popular, corporatist, and authoritarian Catholicism. Whereas nineteenth-century Protestant movements represented a religion of the written word, of civil and rational education, the current popular Protestant movements constitute an oral religion that is unlettered and lively. While the former were vehicles for practices that inculcated democratic liberal values, the latter are vehicles for caudillo-style models of religious and social control. The outcome of the popular Protestant sects is that, like an expanding model, the historical Protestant groups themselves (which are in the minority today) have largely broken with their liberal heritage and adopted the corporatist values of authoritarian political projects (Alves 1985). In this sense, study of these sects derives from a sociology of religious metamorphoses (Bastide 1970).

On the whole, it may be said that Latin American Protestant movements, with the exception of the transplanted churches of certain organizations arising from the historic denominations, are preponderantly syncretic in nature. In this sense, they are similar to the other new religious movements and should be approached by broadly analyzing the role and functions of the new religious movements within contemporary Latin American societies. In contrast to official Catholicism, which is highly structured, these movements belong to a loose system ruled by a kind of

53

informal religious economy. One should also ask, as Reyes Novaes does, whether these popular Protestant movements characterized by an intrinsic messianism and millenarianism "represent in some way, in very different historical circumstances, a historic redefinition of the nineteenth- or early-twentieth-century messianic movements, which are no longer currently viable" (Reyes Novaes, cited in Saint Martin 1984, 113). In my opinion, they are a renewal of popular religion in the sense of being a patchwork of resistance and development of a new relationship to the modernity imposed on them by Latin American governing elites. In this sense, a sociology of the Pentecostal movements should be undertaken to open new avenues of inquiry and to go beyond thinking in terms of religious syncretism or the more far-out phenomena. Certainly, the "Pentecostalized" indigenous groups do not limit themselves to bringing together two cults, as a conventional "religious" analysis would lead one to believe. They interconnect and establish within their practices and their vision of reality several systems of expression of familial and village identity and of the relationship of the individual to the community, to the environment, to production, to one's ancestors, and to one's self-image—facets that all merit thorough study.

Some recent studies take steps in this direction. Elisabeth Brusco's dissertation (1986) on the links between the adoption of evangelical religion and the modification of machismo in Colombia opens a promising avenue. Cecilia Mariz's (1990) article on the incidence of conversion to Pentecostalism and the struggle against alcoholism in Brazilian working-class society opens another. It would be interesting to analyze whether Pentecostalism is in reality something more than syncretism. That is to say, within popular cultures, Pentecostalism may provide the impetus for a new relationship to the community and to the family by imposing a new way of looking at the subject, a revolution in communication techniques. It is certainly a novel angle of research (as Martin 1990 acknowledges) that could make way for a sociology approximating anthropology in taking new steps while continuing to baptize these innovations as "Protestant."

Furthermore, instead of depicting a typology of messianic and millenarian movements and appending the rural and urban Pentecostal forms, it would be useful to modify the perspective by leaving aside the study of the movements themselves in order to address some of the larger issues. These questions should include the flexibility of popular religious traditions, the specificity of religion within the non-Western world, the mechanisms of control and power within Latin American societies, and the modalities of syncretism and Westernization.

Martin has described the explosion of Protestantism in Latin America: "The Evangelical religion now spilling over from North to South America is primarily Pentecostal" (1990, 42). Stoll meanwhile asks via the provocative title of his latest book, *Is Latin America Turning Protestant?* Unlike

54

those who have believed or wanted to discover within the Catholic movements of the popular church and liberation theology a continent-wide religious reform movement, Stoll believes that the Latin American Protestant sects are actually the authentic reform in expansion.

First of all, it should be made clear that neither the popular Catholic Church nor liberation theology fits the definition of a reform movement. Jean Meyer's recent book (1989) places them firmly in the continuum of the intransigent Catholic movements, bearers of a messianic hope for a reign of God on earth, the opposite of the secularizing Protestant reform that heralded modernity. Like the Mexican Cristeros of yesteryear, the *guerrillero* priests of not long ago believed that both Catholicism and socialist revolution referred to a revolutionary Catholic society. Second, neither the new Latin American religious movements nor the Protestant sects have any connection with religious reform and even less with political and social reform. They represent instead strategies of adaptation and resistance, fashioned by the lower strata of Latin American societies, which reinforce the autonomy of the authoritarian and corporatist popular religious culture.

Moreover, before speaking of "Protestant reform" as readily as Stoll and Martin do, one must consider the essential ambiguity of contemporary Latin American societies. Enrique González Pedrero describes it thus:

Is this not precisely the curse that hangs over [Latin Americans] of our times . . . having to be Catholic in a situation that could be called secularized Protestantism, which is the situation in today's world? Here is the question of what has happened to Latin Americans, born to life and history starting with Spanish Catholicism—which came first and solidified in the Counter-Reformation—and who must nevertheless act socially, politically, and economically within a society, a politics, and an economy that have been provided by a secularized Protestantism, which is not the religion of [Latin Americans'] origin. Does this not explain the permanent damage, the double life, the hypocrisy, and the horror of making it appear or simulating that we agree with the logic of industrial society, with modern political values, and with the contemporary neoliberal economy while in reality, these do not correspond to the world in which we were born and the values that shaped us? (González Pedrero 1990, 23; see also Paz 1959)

In terms of this basic question of an ambiguous modernity in Latin America, it makes sense to raise the question of their relationship to democratic modernity in Latin America before considering popular Protestant groups as religious reform movements. As has been amply shown, the historic Protestant movements were vehicles for this democratic modernity and were therefore central to the great democratic and liberal sociopolitical struggles against the forces of traditional society (see Bastian 1989, 1990). The historic forms of Protestantism sought recognition as the religious culture of modernity but did not succeed in transcending the constraints of radical liberalism. In contrast, the current popular Protestant

55

movements, which are constantly expanding, seem to have assimilated the popular political and religious culture of repression (Alves 1985).[12]

It is in this relationship to premodern traditional religious and political culture that one must comprehend the complete metamorphosis of Latin American Protestant movements. From their original role as protesters, these Protestant groups became witnesses, existing somehow as the religious expression of the rending of the Latin American individual faced with a modernity that was imposed but not assumed. Along this line, one can even ask whether it is still possible to speak, as does Martin (1990), of Protestant movements, that is to say, of movements of religious, intellectual, or moral reform. Is there instead a new modality of Latin American popular religious culture in the sense of an adaptation and a reinforcement of the traditional mechanisms of social control? To the extent that the "Protestant principle" becomes replaced by these "popular Protestant movements," the latter are less the expressions of a sui generis Protestantism than an ensemble of new non–Roman Catholic religious movements that are as eclectic and diversified as what continues to be the autonomous popular religion of a great part of the masses.[13]

In the end, one can ask whether the accelerated differentiation of the Latin American religious world and its fragmentation into hundreds of separate religious sects, each as authoritarian as the next, operate to reinforce the autonomy of civil society and to condition the formation of independent public opinion and democratic practices. As Alain Touraine has observed,

> Viable institutions can only exist if there first exist viable social actors. Democratization cannot be defined as a passage from chaos to liberty or from the masses to government. It presupposes the preliminary organization of social demands and the freedom of action of associations, of syndicates or other interest groups. It also presupposes that a debate will take shape before the one that takes shape in the political institutions—a debate in which the arena is public opinion. If this is dominated by confrontation of the [political] parties, the democracy lacks a base. (Touraine 1988, 447)

The Latin American Protestant movements of the nineteenth century, insofar as they were "societies of thought," were actually the ultra-minoritarian instrument for shaping public opinion via debate and the demands of free will. In contrast, the current popular Protestant movements, top-down and authoritarian, are a relay point for the vertical social control of a society blocked in its evolution toward a liberal and democratic modernity by the built-in tension between the actual country and

---

12. For development of this idea, see Bastian (1990, 261–73).
13. In the same sense, the nascent Chilean Pentecostal movement was viewed by the liberal press as "a ceremony of Indians" (compare Bastian 1990, 153–54). Le Bot observed that "Guatemalan Pentecostalism first arose at the very heart of indigenous society" (Le Bot 1987).

56

the legal country. Today the democratic transformation of Latin American societies seems to have been retarded, as Touraine notes. During the 1960s and 1970s, the military regimes triumphed, then the 1980s and 1990s seemed to herald a return to neocorporatist forms of populism that, according to the Mexican example, do not hesitate to lean on the Catholic Church to maintain their hegemony. In such contexts, the popular and millenarianist Protestant movements seem to be the tools for a project of restoration rather than of religious and social reform. As Touraine has emphasized, Latin American societies "continue to be stubbornly dualistic. On the one hand is the world of the word, that is to say of participation by not only the rich but the middle class and extending to a large part of the working class. On the other hand is the world of blood, that of poverty and repression." In such a dual world, the popular Protestant movements would arise out of the world of blood and would represent no more than an enormous effort to pass in the world of the word. The limitation of such a project is that it must be accomplished according to the logic of the world of the word, that is to say according to corporatist models of social control.

BIBLIOGRAPHY

ALVES, RUBEM
    1985   *Protestantism and Repression: A Brazilian Case Study.* Maryknoll, N.Y.: Orbis (1st ed. in Portuguese, 1979).
ASSMAN, HUGO
    1987   *La iglesia electrónica y su impacto en América Latina.* San José, Costa Rica: Departamento Ecuménico de Investigaciones.
BASTIAN, JEAN-PIERRE
    1985a   "Para una aproximación teórica del fenómeno protestante en América Central." *Cristianismo y Sociedad,* no. 85:61-68 (published in Mexico City).
    1985b   "Dissidence religieuse dans le milieu rural mexicain." *Social Compass* 32, nos. 2-3:245-60 (published in Louvain-la-Neuve, Belgium).
    1986   "Protestantismo popular y política en Guatemala y Nicaragua." *Revista Mexicana de Sociología* 48, no. 3:181-99.
    1988   "El paradigma de 1789: sociedades de ideas y revolución mexicana." *Historia Mexicana* 38, series 1, no. 149:79-110.
    1989   *Los disidentes, sociedades protestantes y revolución en Mexico, 1872-1911.* Mexico City: Fondo de Cultura Económica and El Colegio de México.
    1990   *Historia del protestantismo en América Latina.* Mexico City: Casa Unida de Publicaciones.
BASTIAN, JEAN-PIERRE, ED.
    1990   *Protestantes, liberales y francmasones: sociedades de ideas y modernidad en América Latina, Siglo XIX,* Mexico City: Fondo de Cultura Económica and the Comisión de Estudios de la Historia de la Iglesia en América Latina (CEHILA).
BASTIDE, ROGER
    1970   "Sociologie des mutations religieuses." In *Sociologie des mutations,* edited by Georges Balandier, 157-68. Paris: Anthropos.
    1973   "Contributions à une sociologie des religions en Amérique Latine." *Archives des Sciences Sociales des Religions,* no. 85:139-50.
BECKFORD, JAMES A., ED.
    1986   *New Religious Movements and Rapid Social Change.* Beverly Hills, Calif.: Sage.

57

BRUSCO, ELISABETH
1986   "The Household Basis of Evangelical Religion and the Reformation of Machismo in Colombia." Ph.D. diss., City University of New York.

BURNETT, VIRGINIA GARRARD
1989   "Protestantism in Rural Guatemala, 1872–1954." *LARR* 24, no. 2:127–42.

CARRASCO, PEDRO ENRIQUE
1988   "Les Cadres dirigeants babtistes latino-américains entre le croire et la pouvoir: Etude sociologique d'un processus d'épiscopalisation dans une société religieuse congrégationaliste en Amérique Latine." Ph.D. diss., Centre de Sociologie du Protestantisme, Université de Strasbourg.

CASAGRANDE, JOSEPH B.
1978   "Religious Conversion and Social Change in an Indian Community of Highland Ecuador." In *Amerikanische Studien*, edited by Roswith Hartmann and Udo Oberem, 105–11. Saint Augustine, Germany: Anthropos Institut.

CHAUNU, PIERRE
1965   "Pour une sociologie du protestantisme latino-américain." *Cahiers de Sociologie Economique*, no. 12 (May):5–18 (published in Le Havre).

CHRISTIANITY TODAY
1963   "Catholics and Protestants in Latin America." *Christianity Today* 7, no. 21 (19 July):5–8.

CURRY, DONALD EDWARD
1968   "Lusiada: An Anthropological Study of the Growth of Protestantism in Brazil." Ph.D. diss., Columbia University.
1970   "Messianism and Protestantism in Brazil's Sertão." *Journal of Inter-American Studies and World Affairs* 13, no. 3:416–38.

FAJARDO, ANDRES
1987   "From the Volcano: Protestant Conversion among the Ixil Maya of Highland Guatemala." B.A. honors thesis, Harvard College.

FOERSTER, ROLF G.
1988   "Milenarismo, profetismo y mesianismo en la sociedad mapuche contemporánea." *América Indígena* 48, no. 4:773–89.

FONSECA, CLAUDIA
1991   "La Religion dans la vie quotidienne d'un groupe populaire brésilien." *Archives des Sciences Sociales des Religions* 36, no. 73: (Jan.–Mar.):125–39.

FURET, FRANÇOIS
1978   *Penser la Révolution Française.* Paris: Gallimard.

GARMA NAVARRO, CARLOS
1987   *El protestantismo en una comunidad totonaca de Puebla.* Mexico City: Instituto Nacional Indigenista.
1988   "Liderazgo, mensaje religioso y contexto social." *Cristianismo y Sociedad* 26, no. 95: 89–100.

GONZALEZ PEDRERO, ENRIQUE
1990   "Reflexiones barrocas." *Vuelta* 14, no. 162 (May):22–27 (published in Mexico City).

GRANADOS, MANUEL JESUS
1988   "Los Israelitas." *Socialismo y Participación*, no. 41 (March):95–105 (published in Lima).

GRUZINSKI, SERGE, AND CARMEN BERNAND
1988   *De l'idolâtrie: une archéologie des sciences religieuses.* Paris: Seuil.

GUEIROS VIEIRA, DAVID
1980   *O Protestantismo, a Maçonaria e a Questão Religiosa no Brasil.* Brasília: Editora Universidade de Brasília.

GUTWIRTH, JACQUES
1991   "Pentecôtisme national et audiovisuel à Porto Alegre, Brésil." *Archives des Sciences Sociales des Religions* 37, no. 73 (Jan.–Mar):99–114 (published in Paris).

HALPERIN DONGHI, TULIO
1985   *Reforma y disolución de los imperios ibéricos, 1750–1850.* Madrid: Alianza.

HERMET, GUY
1973   "Les Fonctions politiques des organisations religieuses dans les régimes politiques à pluralisme limité." *Revue Française de Science Politique* 23 (June):439–72.

58

HOFFNAGEL, JUDITH CHAMBLISS
1979   "The Believers: Pentecostalism in a Brazilian City." Ph.D. diss., University of California, Berkeley.

HURBON, LAENNEC
1987   "Nuevos movimientos religiosos en el Caribe." *Cristianismo y Sociedad* 25, pt. 3, no. 93:37-64. English version in beckford 1986.

IBARRA BELON, ARACELI
1972   "La Hermosa Provincia: nacimiento y vida de una secta cristiana en Guadalajara, México." M.A. thesis, Universidad de Guadalajara.

JOHNSTONE, J. P.
1986   *Operation World.* 4th ed. Kent, Engl.: STL Books and WEC International.

KAMSTEEG, FRANS
1990   "Líderes y laicos entre los grupos pentecostales de Arequipa, Peru." *Cristianismo y Sociedad* 28, pt. 4, no. 106:59-76.

KOHUT, KARL, AND ALBERT MEYERS, EDS.
1988   *Religiosidad popular en América Latina.* Frankfurt: Verlag Klaus Dieter Vervuert.

LAFAYE, JACQUES
1974   *Quetzacoatl et Guadalupe: La Formation de la conscience nationale au Mexique.* Paris: Gallimard.

LALIVE D'EPINAY, CHRISTIAN
1968   *El refugio de las masas.* Santiago: Editorial del Pacífico. Published in English in London by Lutterworth in 1969.

1975   *Religion, dynamique sociale et dépendance: Les Mouvements protestants en Argentine et au Chili.* Paris: Mouton.

LE BOT, YVON
1987   "Cent Ans de Protestantisme au Guatemala: Notes et études documentaires." *La Documentation Française,* no. 4850:109-19 (published in Paris).

1991   "Présence religieuse et marché: le destin de l'Amérique Latine." *Le Monde,* 20 Aug., p. 13.

MANSILLA, H. C. F.
1989   "La herencia ibérica y la persistencia del autoritarismo en América Latina." *Cristianismo y Sociedad* 27, pt. 2, no. 100:81-94.

MARIZ, CECILIA L.
1990   "Pentecostalismo y alcoholismo entre los pobres del Brasil." *Cristianismo y Sociedad* 28, pt. 3:34-44.

MARTIN, DAVID
1990   *Tongues of Fire: The Explosion of Protestantism in Latin America.* Cambridge: Basil Blackwell.

MARTINEZ, ABELINO
1989   *Las sectas en Nicaragua: oferta y demanda de salvación.* San José, Costa Rica: Departamento Ecuménico de Investigaciones.

MEYER, JEAN
1989   *Historia de los cristianos en América Latina, Siglos XIX y XX.* Mexico City: Vuelta.

MILLER, ELMER S.
1979   *Los tobas argentinos: armonía y disonancia en una sociedad.* Mexico City: Siglo Veintiuno.

MURATORIO, BLANCA
1981a   "Protestantism and Capitalism Revisited in the Rural Highlands of Ecuador." *Journal of Peasant Studies,* no. 8:37-61.

1981b   "Protestantism, Ethnicity, and Class in Chimborazo." In *Cultural Transformations and Ethnicity in Modern Ecuador,* edited by Norman E. Whitten, 506-34. Urbana: University of Illinois Press.

ORO, ARI PEDRO
1990   "Religiones pentecostales y medios masivos de comunicación en Brasil." *Cristianismo y Sociedad* 18, no. 3:45-56.

PADILLA, RENE, ED.
1991   *De la marginación al compromiso: los evangélicos y la política en América Latina.* Buenos Aires: Fraternidad Teológica Latinoamericana.

59

PARKER GUMUCIO, CHRISTIAN
1986   *Religion y clases subalternas urbanas en una sociedad dependiente.* Louvain: Université Catholique de Louvain.
PAZ, OCTAVIO
1959   *El laberinto de la soledad.* Mexico City: Fondo de Cultura Económica
PIETSCHMANN, HORST
1980   *Staat und Staatliche Evolution am Beginn der Spanischen Kolonisation Amerikas.* Münster: Aschendorff. Spanish translation published by the Fondo de Cultura Económica in Mexico City in 1989.
PRIEN, HANS-JÜRGEN
1978   *Die Geschichte des Christentums in Lateinamerika.* Göttingen, Germany: Vandenhoeck und Ruprecht.
QUEIROZ, MARIA ISAURA PEREIRA DE
1968   *Historia y etnología de los movimientos mesiánicos.* Mexico City: Siglo Veintiuno.
1986   "Evolução Religiosa e Criação: Os Cultos Sincréticos Brasileiros." *Cristianismo y Sociedad* 25, no. 88:7-26.
RAMOS, MARCOS ANTONIO
1987   *Panorama del protestantismo en Cuba.* Miami, Fla.: Editorial Caribe.
RAPPAPORT, JOANNE
1984   "Las misiones protestantes y la resistencia indígena en el sur de Colombia." *América Indígena* 44, no. 1:111-27 (published in Mexico City).
REYES NOVAES, REGINA
1985   *Os Escolhidos de Deus: Pentecostais, Trabalhadores e Cidadania.* Cadernos do ISER no. 19. Rio de Janeiro: Instituto Superior dos Estudos da Religião (ISER).
RODRIGUES BRANDÃO, CARLOS
1986   *Os Deuses do Povo: Un Estudo sobre a Religião Popular.* São Paulo: Brasiliense.
1987   "Creencia e Identidad: Campo Religioso y Cambio Cultural." *Cristianismo y Sociedad* 25, pt. 3, no. 93:65-106.
RODRIGUEZ, JAIME E.
1980   *El nacimiento de Hispanoamérica: Vicente Rocafuerte y el hispanoamericanismo, 1808-1832.* Mexico City: Fondo de Cultura Económica.
ROLIM, FRANCISCO C.
1985   *Pentecostais no Brazil: Uma Interpretação Socio-Religiosa.* Petrópolis: Vozes.
ROUQUIE, ALAIN
1987   *Amérique Latine: Introduction à l'Extrême-Occident.* Paris: Seuil.
SAINT MARTIN, MONIQUE DE
1984   "Quelques Questions a propos du pentecôtisme au Brésil." *Actes de la Recherche en Sciences Sociales,* nos. 52-53 (June):111-14 (published in Paris).
SAMANDU, LUIS E.
1988   "El pentecostalismo en Nicaragua y sus raíces religiosas populares." *Pasos,* no. 17 (May-June):1-10 (published in San José, Costa Rica).
1989   "Los pentecostalismos en América Central." *Aportes* (June):34-35 (published in San José, Costa Rica).
1991   "Religión e identidades en América Central." *Cristianismo y Sociedad* 29, pt. 3, no. 109:67-86.
SANTAMARIA, DANIEL J.
1990   "Pentecostalismo e identidad étnica." *Cristianismo y Sociedad,* 28, pt. 3, no. 105: 7-13.
SANTANA, ROBERTO
1981   "El caso de Ecuarunari." *Nariz del Diablo,* no. 2:30-38 (published in Quito by CIESE).
1983   *Campesinado indígena y el desafío de la modernidad.* Quito: Centro Andino de Acción Popular.
STOLL, DAVID
1982   *Fishers of Men or Founders of Empire? The Wycliffe Bible Translators in Latin America.* London: Zed.
1984   "¿Con que derecho adoctrinan a nuestros indígenas? La polémica en torno al Instituto Lingüístico de Verano." *América Indígena* 44, no. 1:9-24 (published in Mexico City).

60

1990   *Is Latin America Turning Protestant? The Politics of Evangelical Growth,* Berkeley and Los Angeles: University of California Press.

TOURAINE, ALAIN
1988   *La Parole et le sang: Politique et société en Amérique Latine.* Paris: Odile Jacob.

VARGAS LLOSA, MARIO
1989   "Entre la libertad y el miedo." *Vuelta,* no. 147 (Feb.):15 (published in Mexico City).

WESTMEIER, KARL-WILHELM
1986   "The Enthusiastic Protestants of Bogotá, Colombia." *International Review of Mission* 75, no. 297 (Jan.):13–24 (published in Geneva).

WILLEMS, EMILE
1967   *Followers of the New Faith: Future, Change, and the Rise of Protestantism in Brazil and Chile.* Nashville, Tenn.: Vanderbilt University Press.

WRIGHT, PABLO G.
1983   "Presencia protestante entre los aborígenes del Chaco argentino." *Scripta Antropologica* 8:73–84 (published in Buenos Aires).

1984   "Quelques Formes du chamanisme Toba." *Bulletin de la Société Suisse des Américanistes,* no. 48:29–35 (published in Geneva).

1988   "Tradición y aculturación en una organización socio-religiosa toba contemporánea." *Cristianismo y Sociedad* 26, pt. 1, no. 95:71–88.

61

Three Moments in Brazilian Millenarianism: The Interrelationship Between Politics and Religion

Patricia R. Pessar

Brazilian millenarianism is a weave of religion and politics. Yet some, like the researcher, Rui Facó,[1] would have us believe that the religious thread is no more than gossamer, since the purportedly true motives of millenarianists are political ones hidden under the cloak of religious symbols. In stark contrast, for the followers of a millenarian movement I studied in Northeast Brazil, millenarianism belongs solely in the religious domain and is sullied when one mixes politics into religion, *fazendo politica na religião*. As I argue in this paper, what gives meaning and motion to Brazilian millenarianism is a dynamic tension between the warp of religion and the woof of politics.[2] In analyzing this dynamic relationship I will consider three "moments" in Brazilian millenarianism. The first "moment" is the pairing of an historical context with apocalyptic fears and millennial dreams. The second "moment" is the social construction of a messiah by the would-be leader and his followers. The third "moment" is the routinization and regeneration of millenarian movements.

The movements examined in this article are the following: Canudos (1893-1899), located in the state of Bahia and led by Antônio Conselheiro; Contestado (1910-1916), situated in Santa Catarina and headed by several monks *(monges)* named João and José Maria; Joaseiro (1899-present) located in Ceará and led by Padre Cícero; Caldeirão (1926-1935), found in Ceará and directed by *beato* José Lourenço; and Santa Brígida (1944-present), located in Bahia and led by Pedro Batista. Two unsuccessful movements attempted by João Gostava (late 1950s-1967) in Santa Brígida, Bahia and by *O Velho* (1970-1976) in Pernambuco will also be considered.[3]

THE FIRST MOMENT: THE EMERGENCE OF APOCALYPTIC FEARS AND MILLENARIAN DREAMS

In this section I will argue that rural Brazilians were attracted to messianic figures and participated in movements in the late 1800s and early 1900s because these expressed and provided a vehicle for people's resentment against members of the traditional elite who were unable or unwilling to fulfill traditional duties for their dependents. Folk Catholicism, I propose, provided the meanings, orientations, and roles with which rural Brazilians interpreted their radically changing political-economy and generated millenarian-inspired guides for action.[4]

Luso-Brazilian Review XXVIII, 1 0024-7413/91/000 $1.50
© 1991 by the Board of Regents of the University of Wisconsin System

My discussion challenges those students of millenarianism who either interpret a religious world view as a deterrent to political mobilization,[5] or, in contrast, who view religious symbols as a mask or expedient tool for pursuing political goals.[6] Both positions totally disregard the fact that in most societies in which millenarian movements develop and are oriented toward political goals, religious and political meanings and motives are intertwined and reinforcing. Political legitimacy and cause for rebellion are often predicated upon the elite group's fulfilling duties that have been sacralized through religious meaning and institutions.[7] Let us turn then to a consideration of some of the key principles of Brazilian folk Catholicism and the ways in which these helped to buttress a patrimonial political economy.

Supernatural Causes of Misfortune and Suffering

Although a modicum of suffering is anticipated simply because "we are not placed on earth solely for enjoyment,"[8] rural Brazilians often attribute disease, crop failure, and other misfortune to divine punishment.[9] While the transgressions cited as causes for this punishment are varied, the social consequences of the phenomonology of misfortune are quite specific. Under ordinary circumstances, these beliefs legitimate and reproduce relations and institutions of hierarchy and exploitation.

Misfortune to individuals and to the community at large is often publicly attributed to someone having criticized God or the saints for failing to act in the individual's self-interest. For example, during a month of unusual rainfall in which many agriculturalists lost their entire harvest of beans, I was told by most farmers that the rains were caused by "a man down the road" who had earlier cursed God for neglecting to send rain. In this case and many like it, rural Brazilians were affirming the norm of accepting the circumstances with which one is confronted (*conformar-se*) rather than chafing under it and receiving even greater hardship.[10] This prescription applies to what I would term natural as well as social phenomena. That is, many rural Brazilians maintain that "God loves the poor" and it is sinful to desire more material security and wealth than God has deemed sufficient for the individual. As a Northeastern Brazilian observed, "The poor do not have the right to protest; people can neither be all rich or all poor, because that is not what God desires."[11] Again, I heard many accounts about people who suffered divine punishment, such as falling mute or being reduced to pauperism, for complaining about their poverty and coveting the wealth and success of others.

Many anthropologists have observed that where supernatural intervention is an agent for social control, there is less reliance upon alternative legal and political mechanisms.[12] Others have noted that power is more easily sustained when leaders do not have to expend their resources on punitive activities such as expelling people from their land.[13] Application of these two principles to the rural Brazilian case shows that subjugation is facilitated by the belief that misfortune follows upon rebellion against one's condition, and by the further confirmation of these beliefs in public attributions of general misfortune, such as excessive rain and drought, to acts of divine retribution allegedly directed against transgressors.

Misfortune is also associated with failure to fulfill the norms of reciprocity and co-operation. Punishment may result, for example, when an individual fails to fulfill duties (*obrigações*) to the saints or God after a petition for assistance (*promessa*) has been honored.[14] Several community studies contain accounts of individuals who were afflicted with divine punishment owing to their impropriety during a saint's day or because of their refusal to contribute to a saint's day ritual in which the saint is honored for his or her favors to the community. For example, Eduardo Galvão reports that in the Amazonian town of Itá the diseases and misfortunes of merchants were often publicly attributed to their money-lending practices during saint's day rituals.[15] The causal link between the abandonment of the norms of reciprocity and cooperation, on the one hand, and misfortune on the other, is also apparent in beliefs about "black magic." In interviews with Northeasterners who had sought the assistance of local curers, I learned that many believed they had fallen victim to a neighbor's wrath upon failing to fulfill a traditional obligation such as cooperating in a labor exchange or providing a small loan.

As in most peasant societies, economic relations in rural Brazil are cast in moral and supernatural terms. We must look to the exigencies of peasant life for the reasons why reciprocity and cooperation are so important that their breach is buttressed with expectations of direct supernatural retribution or indirect supernatural punishment (black magic) through the actions of aggrieved individuals. Multiple indeterminacies produced by natural disasters such as drought, crop failure, disease, fluctuations in the market for cash crops and consumer goods, and changing political demands such as taxation and conscription leave peasant families and peasant communities highly vulnerable. Under these circumstances peasants must rely on intraclass cooperation and reciprocity. Institutions such as labor exchange, barter, and charity are mechanisms for coping with a highly stratified political economy characterized by profound inequalities in the distribution of land, capital, and political power. The other source of security for the rural poor is asymmetrical exchange with a patron.

As documented in many community studies and cross-cultural analyses of peasant societies, both categories of exchange perpetuate the peasant's subordinate position.[16] The fact that slightly more economically solvent peasants are expected to make available to the poor the already limited factors of production not controlled by the ruling class means that peasants are accommodated to, and in fact are collaborators in, maintaining their inferior structural position. That is, acts of cooperation, ennobled in spiritual and ethical symbolism, make the status quo livable by demanding sacrifices from the victims. If the practice of "shared poverty"[17] were not prescribed, it could be argued that the nature of and reality of peasant exploitation would be highlighted and protest would follow. In the case of vertical exchange, although the patron's provision of limited resources such as land and credit fits the peasant's need to maximize security and minimize risk, the contradiction in the relationship should not be obscured. The dependent's exchange of produce, labor, military support, and loyalty protects and enriches the ruling class while reproducing the peasantry's subordination and dependency. As Shepard Forman writes for Brazilian peasants:

> These dyadic relationships, with their mutual expectations of proper behavior and vague understandings about some sort of equivalency in reciprocal exchanges, have long been superimposed upon basic contractual land/labor arrangements, not simply offsetting the asymmetry of the economic exchanges by creating ties of affect and loyalty . . . but also providing the ideology that reaffirms, legitimizes, and justifies the authority of the landed class as a group, despite the tenuousness of the individual economic dyads.[18]

For the purpose of this essay, it is important to note that hierarchy and asymmetrical exchange became central elements within the conceptual and moral systems of the rural cultivators. Thus in the daily round, it was the proper completion of the norm of reciprocity and paternalism on the part of the patron rather than the justification of inequality itself that became the crucial issue for the poor.[19] Within this "moral economy"[20] power is conceived to be legitimately centralized within the hands of a small supernatural and societal elite. That elite distributes part of this good among those who believe in and uphold these hierarchical and inegalitarian systems.

Given this homologous relationship between the sacred and society, it is not surprising that the same term is sometimes used to refer to both God and the saints and a patron. God is sometimes conceived of as an "Almighty Patron" and as the *"bom pai da gente"*—a reference to "our good Father" that has been employed in political contexts "and carries with it the expectation of patronage and all the affective weight of personalism."[21] Alba Zaluar Guimarães notes that the word *manda-chuva* (rainmaker), clearly associated with the supernatural power of saints to send rain when they are petitioned by devotees is a synonym for patron.[22] She implies, as do other social scientists, that the symbolic congruence between sacred powers and secular authority is a source of mystification since temporal power is purportedly viewed by the poor as a divinely wrought replica of the celestial order.

That political institutions have become alienated from their producers through the process of sacralization[23] is apparent when we consider both the structural congruence between God and the saints and secular leaders, as well as popular homilies such as "God in Heaven and the president on earth." As will be discussed shortly, this sacralizing process is, nonetheless, doubled-edged. If the ruler and patron are secular versions of God and the saints, it is encumbent upon them to uphold the patriarchal duties that they share with their sacred counterparts, that is, to provide material security, spiritual growth, and physical protection for the poor.

A MILLENARIAN VIEW OF HISTORY

Folk Catholicism contains a millenarian view of history. Thus, added to the cycle of sinning, divine punishment, repentance, devotion and petitions for supernatural assistance and for salvation after death is the knowledge that God and the saints are becoming increasingly alienated from humanity because of its sins. This alienation will presumably culminate in the arrival of the Antichrist, the Apocalypse, the Day of Judgment, and Heaven on Earth for the few who will be saved.

Judeo-Christian millennial thought entered Brazil with the missionaries who carried the Bible and other religious texts like the *Missão Abreviada*, a text that abounds in apocalyptic passages, such as "This is also a truth, that after the time that is rapidly drawing to an end, an eternity will arise that will never end. The eternity must be happy or sad; there will be nothing between."[24]

Two factors contributed to the appeal of millenarian thought in Brazil. These are millennial-like beliefs held by indigenous tribes and Portuguese beliefs about the return of a messianic king. Prior to the arrival of Europeans, native leaders led followers on long migrations in search of a land without evil. Several anthropologists have concluded that these journeys were religiously inspired.[25] Doubtless more influential in the acceptance and growth of millennial thought in Brazil, were messianic beliefs held by many Portuguese colonists. Foremost among these was the ardent belief in the return of King

Sebastião, a Portuguese monarch lost in the 1578 battle of Alcacer Kebir against the Moors. According to legend, Sebastião would punish the wicked and lead the faithful to a terrestrial paradise. An example of Sebastianist beliefs is found in the following text from the Canudos movement:

> In truth I say unto you, when nation falls out with nation, Brazil with Brazil, England with England, Prussia with Prussia, then shall Dom Sebastião with all his army arise from the waves of the sea. . . .
> For a thousand and many, for two thousand, thou shalt not come!
> And on that day when he and his army shall arise, then shall he with the edge of the sword free all from the yoke of this Republic. . . .[26]

Millennial thought, especially of the apocalyptic sort, has been incorporated into rural Brazilian hymns *(benditos)*, literature *(literatura de cordel)*, and everyday discourse. Of the one hundred traditional *benditos* I collected in various Northeastern communities during 1973–1974, fifteen contained references to the impeding apocalypse, and more than one-half mentioned salvation. There is *literatura de cordel* in which rural bards discuss millenarian subjects, such as the arrival of a false prophet and an ancient friar's warnings about the Last Days.[27] Every rural Brazilian I asked to describe the Apocalypse could do so in vivid detail, and there was substantial agreement in the content of these accounts. Phrases such as "The year 2,000 will not come" were spontaneously voiced when people discussed unusual occurrences among themselves.

If we are to appreciate why millenarian movements developed in the late 1800s and 1900s, it becomes necessary to add the principle of "resentment"[28] to the analysis of folk Catholicism. The religions of the disprivileged classes often encompass the promise of divine vengeance against members of the elite. In Catholicism, for example, the pious poor are to be rewarded after death and again on Judgment Day for their faith and resignation. On the other hand, eternal torment faces those who have abused their power and wealth. As a traditional Brazilian *bendito* proclaims:

> The mighty of this world
> In the next they will find
> Our Lady crying
> And the devil well contented

Although belief in ultimate retribution may foster resignation in the face of ordinary suffering, in times of unusual and unexpected hardship—as occurred during the late 1800s and early 1900s—hate and resentment may increase against the elite who are expected to protect the poor against chaos and dearth. This motive may encourage collective acts to express the immorality of the elite and to call for divine punishment.

Let us trace the social transformations and natural disasters that undermined the traditional oligarchy and in its sway left the peasantry without the security they had strived to maintain through exchanging labor, loyalty, obedience, and deference and by forging ritual alliances with members of the landed elite.

Social Transformations and Natural Disasters

The major social transformations affecting rural Brazil over the late 1800s and early 1900s were political centralization and capitalist development. As I will briefly describe below, as a consequence of these changes many members of the landed elite could not fulfill the traditional moral obligations of ensuring subsistence and protection for the peasants. And worse, many openly identified themselves with the emerging group of capitalists who substituted casual, contractual relations for the traditional multi-stranded ties.[29]

The introduction into the Northeast's *sertão* of a drought-resistant strain of cotton in the 1850s illustrates the transition from subsistence farming to export-oriented agriculture. Stimulated by the cotton shortage created by the American Civil War, the crop prospered and attracted large numbers of rural workers from the neighboring *agreste* zone. A mixed cattle and cotton economy was established.[30]

After 1871 the *sertão's* economy suffered due to declining cotton prices and the subsequent decrease in local profits and wages. The situation was greatly exacerbated by five major droughts that struck the Northeast between 1877 and 1919. Unable to feed themselves, massive numbers of rural inhabitants were forced to migrate. Land-owners were either unwilling or unable to provide the rural population with jobs and protection during this difficult period. Many were never able to recover after the droughts and rural laborers were deprived of traditional patronage, since the elite found it increasingly difficult to maintain and support a fixed following on the land. With the demise of the traditional patronage came the rise of a new kind of patron who spurned paternalism and replaced multiple ties with one, that between salaried worker and boss.[31]

From 1877 onward *sertanejos* fleeing the drought migrated to the humid *serra* ("mountainous") zone in the *sertão,* and to the Amazon and the South where there were booms in rubber and coffee respectively, and to the cities. The population of Ceará's capital Fortaleza, grew from its normal 40,000 in 1887 to 160,000 in 1879. The inhospitable conditions that awaited these migrants and their herding together into camps. which by 1915 were referred to as "concentration camps," caused 6,000 deaths from starvation and disease in Fortaleza alone.[32]

In the South where the Contestado movement would unfold, foreign investors displaced traditional patrons and created entirely new relations of production. Siegel notes that "For a century and a half whatever demands [peasants] could make and rights they might expect to be fulfilled occurred within a complex patronage network to which they suddenly no longer had access."[33] The major foreign investments were destined for railroad construction, directly through the Contestado region, and for the establishment of a lumber company. Construction of the railroad brought only limited employment to the region, since the majority of the workers were recruited in Rio de Janeiro and in the drought-stricken state of Pernambuco. "What the railroad did bring to the hinterland was another element of discord: an intrusive entrepreneurial activity, labor force and organization. A professional security corps was established to maintain order, which it did by answering any complaints with repression."[34] When the construction was completed, no provisions were made for the workers, adding thousands of frustrated individuals to the ranks of dislocated peasants. Many of this latter group were expelled from their land by the American lumber company and passed over as workers. European immigrants were hired and relocated because of their preferred work habits. The Contestado movement attracted large numbers of workers and peasants whose material well-being and security had been disrupted by these new, intrusive developments.

Political centralization and a severe reduction in the power and status of local political chiefs followed the founding of the Republic in 1889. Local leaders were increasingly dwarfed by and dependent upon a new national bourgeoisie. On this point Duglas Teixeira Monteiro writes, "When the state oligarchies became involved in large scale economic and administrative projects that went beyond municipal and sometimes even state limits (land concessions, negotiations with national or foreign investors . . .), the local chiefs degenerated into peons or at best lesser elites involved in intense competition within an increasingly circumscribed local area."[35] The high degree of political centralization also militated against regional hegemony, a supremacy originally based upon the paramilitary actions of the *coronéis'* private militias.[36] With the Republic came the involvement of the army in local and state-wide disputes, as well as a high local-level responsiveness to changes in state and national politics. De Souza observes that:

> Under the *coronelista* structure, a heavy commitment was . . . required of the Northeastern chieftains. A series of political mobilizations took place throughout the First Republic's forty years of existence. . . . These struggles finally undermined the power resources of the local chieftains: for one thing, the commitment of their followings to large-scale political operations deprived their economic enterprises of a substantial number of laborers . . . The chieftains' political struggles also rendered them less capable of providing their followings with protection and sponsorship of violent actions.[37]

Finally, with the State promoting national and foreign capitalist investment in rural areas, the patrons' abilities to provide for their dependents' material security was undermined. This is clearest in the case of the Contestado movement. In recounting their motives for joining the movement, the survivors of Contestado explained that *"Coronel* Arthur da Paula and other political chiefs had taken their land and were unable to relocate them to fallow state lands because these were ceded to other political chiefs."[38]

In what way were millenarian movements consequences of and reactions to the changes in social relations between the elite and the poor? The movements were, in my opinion, rebellions against "modern" members of the ruling class and rejections of the emerging capitalist relations in rural areas.

In line with the belief that general misfortune follows from the moral transgressions of individuals and groups, it is likely that the rural poor attributed the droughts, suffering, and chaos of the late 1800s and early 1900s to the failure of many of the elite to fulfill their obligations to their poor dependents.[39] They may have believed that material and spiritual well-being would be re-established only with the repentance of the disobedient and a return to the traditional patronage system, or more drastically by the divinely ordained destruction of the ruling class and their political and economic innovations.

The motive of resentment and the creation of rebellions must be linked, then, to the disjunction between the cultural code for action prescribed for patrons and the actual behavior of many members of the rural elite during the late 1800s and early 1900s. While the homology between God and the saints and the ruler and the patrons elevated the ruling class by placing them within a sacred cosmology, it implied as well that this group's legitimacy, and the obedience and loyalty of the poor, were contingent upon the elites' fulfilling certain duties. Deference and gratitude were expressed, and hate and anticipation of divine revenge ("resentment") submerged, while the powerful were adhering to the norms that authenticated their dominance. As a consequence of political and economic transformations rural patrons could not maintain the moral obligations dependents expected. And a new elite emerged whose relations with the masses were stripped of all paternalistic pretense. The abandonment of the cosmological and moral meanings and duties associated with patronage released and legitimated the resentment against members of the rural ruling class. Resentment was channeled into collective action, whose goal was the destruction of the immoral elite.

Consistent with the rural Brazilian worldview and its motive of resentment, the millenarianists anticipated divine retribution against members of the elite who, according to the followers of Antônio Conselheiro, had substituted "Satan's law" for "God's law." These "satanical laws" consisted of new rational-bureaucratic institutions that aggregated the peasants and were unresponsive to the indeterminacies in peasants' lives. They included taxation (when new tax regulations were promulgated Antônio Conselheiro denounced them as autos da fé and publicly burned the decrees);[40] land seizures and sales to entrepreneurs (the millenarianists of Contestado protested: "We don't have any rights to land, which is for the people of Oropa");[41] and government censuses (rural priests warned parishioners that census takers were recording their names as members of Satan's army).[42] Within their sacred cities millenarianists rejected the new values and institutions. There followers redistributed their wealth, land was often worked communally, and millenarianists lived as brothers and sisters under the authority of the messiah.

My interpretation of the millenarianists' motives not only accounts for their cooperation with certain traditional political chiefs but also clarifies the promonarchial ideology of the Canudos, Contestado, and Joaseiro movements. Who after all best epitomized the meaning and values that morally united the vulnerable peasant with the elite than the monarch? The millenarianists of Canudos awaited the return of the divine king Sebastião who would lead a devout army against the powerful antichrists and re-establish the sanctified monarch. After José Maria and many followers were killed in a battle in which they were minor actors in a litigation dispute between the states of Santa Catarina and Paraná, the surviving millenarianists insisted that the messiah and their fallen comrades would be resurrected in one year. Once again, it was believed that king Sebastião would lead the Enchanted Army that would defeat the Republic. Finally when the *romeiros* (pilgrims) of Padre Cícero took part in the revolt of 1914, this insurrection was termed a holy war by his devotees. Allegedly the messiah had been advised by the Virgin Mary that the enemy's bullets would not harm the *romeiros*. "The millenarianists believed that the final victory would coincide with the reestablishment of the Monarchy, that was the government of God."[43]

In this section we have seen how religious beliefs about moral authority, society, and cosmology were drawn upon by rural Brazilians to interpret the major political-economic changes characterizing the late 1800s and early 1900s. At this time Folk Catholicism temporarily lost its conventional role of inclining poor rural Brazilians to accomodate to asymmetrical forms of economic and political exchange. Rather, the usually supressed principle of "resentment" was unleashed when local patrons and State officials refused to uphold their traditional obligations as inscribed in the patrimonial "moral economy."

Having considered why millenarian movements emerged at the turn of the century, let us now turn to a topic that has received scant attention in the study of millenarianism, in general, and Brazilian millenarianism, in particular. I refer to the process by which a religious figure claims charismatic power and is authenticated as a messiah by his followers.[44]

THE SECOND MOMENT: THE SOCIAL CONSTRUCTION OF A MESSIAH

I was with my Padrinho Pedro Batista in 1940 when we met a very extraordinary man. This was the only person I've ever seen my *Padrinho* take a blessing from! This man, who was filled with *mistério*, advised my *Padrinho* that his mission was not to enter into the world of men. His mission was another. This man said that many would try to murder my *Padrinho*, but none could succeed. He warned that my *Padrinho* could only be undone if he entered into politics... So when my *Padrinho* entered more and more into politics, I reminded him of the sacred man's message. But it was too late. He had entered into the world of men and had sacrificed his mission.[45]

This account related by the successor of the deceased messianic leader, Pedro Batista, captures the strict dichotomy between religion, and more particularly charisma *(mistério)*, on the one hand, and politics on the other. In my investigation of the successful and failed careers of would-be messiahs during what may be called the "sacralizing moment," I have observed that those who do succeed must symbolically separate themselves from secular markers—especially those associated with politics. To do so, is to leave the social world of the "persons" who populate rural Brazil.[46]

In order to appreciate the process by which messiahs ceased to be "persons," we must recognize the interdependency between politics and kinship in the rural Brazilian social structure and cultural system. As several scholars have observed, kinship and political alliances identified an individual and informed his or her actions.[47] As Pereira de Queiroz writes:

To explain who a man was, it was essential to say whose son and kinsman he was. Only then was it clear what relations held between any two people: whether of cooperation or conflict... In the Northeast as in the Contestado, kinship determined the socio-political position of the different estate-owners, and the political affiliations... The idiom of the region itself still tends to express this intra-kinship solidarity and the importance of kin for the socio-political localization of the individual. To ask a *jagunço* of the south who he is, is to invite the answer "I belong to "colonel" so-and-so's folk," and in turn the "colonels" tend to use the expression "my people."[48]

If a surname and *parentela* (extended bilateral kindred) located a rural Brazilian within a socio-political space, having no such name and kinship ties removed an individual from this sphere. This denial of kinship, and by extension, a fixed location

within the political landscape, appears to have been one of the ways in which would-be
messiahs' *mistério* was authenticated. For example, a verse from a *literatura de cordel* about
Padre Cícero claims:

> Mãe Quinó gazed at her new born babe
> and the nurse went out to change her robes.
> An angel came down to close the sainted mother's eyes.
> She exchanged the babe for baby Cícero.
> Baby Cícero born not from woman, knowing no sin.
> Mãe Quinó, his sainted mother could never see again.[49]

As for Pedro Batista, it is written:

> Where he came from no one knows.
> No one can understand.
> The people would ask him
> But he would not respond.
> This was his duty.
> For the secrets of God
> Are for no one to know.[50]

As if to make Pedro Batista's kinship more elusive, his followers emphasized that in all
the years that they knew him not one person appeared claiming to be his relative. As
one *romeiro* related, "his adopted family was unknown and his real family was not of this
world."[51]

In 1974 I witnessed an attempt by many *romeiros* to replace Pedro Batista's successor,
Maria das Dores, with an elderly man, *O Velho,* who some claimed was the reincarnation of Pedro Batista. Kinship was one of the points that the detractors of *O Velho*
stressed when they sought to discredit his *mistério* as a messiah. They noted the existence of an extended family in the state of Alagoas known to many in the community
and the suspicion that *O Velho* had fathered an illegitimate daughter.

Folklore also plays a key role in the social construction of charisma and messianic
authority in Brazil. Within this folkloric tradition, religion and politics—or sacred and
secular authority—are pitted against each other. A central theme in many of the stories
told about messianic figures holds that the messiah both transcends and overcomes secular power relations and leadership.[52] The following story about Pedro Batista not only
contains this theme, but also underscores the *mistério* associated with a messiah's name.

> My uncle was an important political figure in Joaseiro. He invited
> me to a neighbor's farm where an old penitent was curing and preach-
> ing. My uncle was amused by this. He insisted that as I was a young
> penitent, I should accompany him. We were joined by the political
> chief.
>   The first time I saw my *Padrinho* my whole body went cold and tears
> brimmed in my eyes. I knew from the first moment that my mission
> and his would be one. But I remained quiet. I just stood and watched
> him cure the poor.

Suddenly two hired killers appeared. The woman who owned the house ordered the men away, saying that they were trespassing. I'd never seen a woman talk so forcefully to men! When they did not respond, she turned to the political chief and asked for his intervention. He said he could do nothing. But it became apparent that they had been sent by him. The woman began to berate the men again, and my *Padrinho*, gently but firmly, told her to "remain silent." The assassins approached him and shouted, "Are you Pedro Batista da Silva, *Curador?*" He said "I am called..." He said a name, but to this day, neither I nor anyone else who was there can replicate it! Such is the mystery of my *Padrinho*. Then they said, "Are you prepared to die?" "If God wills it," he replied. Then standing right before him, they began to shake violently, and in a moment, their guns and holsters had fallen to the ground! Shocked, they fell to their knees and begged for his pardon. My *Padrinho* responded, "You receive the pardon from Pedro Batista da Silva, here. But, the next time you ask for my pardon, you will call me by another name!"[53]

In the case of Padre Cícero, Candace Slater also emphasizes the role *romeiro's* stories have assumed in establishing his transcendent authority. She points in particular to the genre of stories which contrast the secular, modern, and fallible politician, Dr. Floro, with the spiritual, traditional, and omniscient leader, Padre Cícero. According to Slater these stories not only often place Dr. Floro in a compromised position for having disobeyed Padre Cícero's higher authority, but they also place the blame for unpopular, "civil" decisions on Dr. Floro rather than Padre Cícero.[54] This is a "conceit" which apparently suited the Northeastern conceptions of the separation between religion and charismatic authority, on one hand, and politics and secular authority, on the other. Through this literary device, Padre Cícero could continue to be perceived as the upholder of a higher form of moral authority which could not injure or exploit the poor. Any actions associated with him that proved disadvantageous to the poor were transformed through folktales into actions provoked by the disobedient and misguided Dr. Floro.[55]

In contrast to Pedro Batista and Padre Cícero, *O Velho* failed to assert his will over local authorities. The latter rebuked his attempts either to visit Santa Brígida or relocate there permanently. As I observed, many undecided *romeiros* anxiously watched these encounters for a sign of divine power, such as those contained in the stories about Pedro Batista and Padre Cícero. The same woman who related the story about Pedro Batista and the assassins stated,

Everytime *O Velho* met up with the authorities, I secretly prayed for a sign, because I so wanted him to be my *Padrinho*. But he has never triumphed. Some predicted that after *O Velho* was banished by Antônio, Antônio would fall deathly ill as did those politicians who tried to interfere with the mission of my *Padrinho* Cícero and my *Padrinho* Pedro. But as you can see Antônio and all his family are well and prospering. I can only conclude that *O Velho* is as weak and mortal as any poor sinner.[56]

It is quite likely that if *O Velho* had either triumphed over his political adversaries or had been jailed—and thus been transformed into a martyr, the corpus of folktales dealing with moral authority and transcendence would also have been applied to him. It is noteworthy that local politicians rejected the option of jailing *O Velho* precisely because they did not want, in their words, to "flame the fires of fanaticism by giving the people a martyr"[57] to celebrate in myth and acts of devotion.

In this section we have considered that moment in the development of messianic movements when the charisma or, *mistério*, of a would-be messiah is socially constructed by the leader and his followers. I have argued that this is a symbolic process whereby the charismatic figure must be separated through actions and myth from secular markers of identity and secular figures of authority.

Just as the tension between secular and sacred authority animates the initial phase of establishing the authenticity of a messianic leader, so does this tension persist, if not intensify, as successful movements gain several thousands of adherents as well as the attention of local and national political figures. In the next section we will consider this phase of routinization and how it has sometimes led to the regeneration of new offshoot movements.

THE THIRD MOMENT: THE ROUTINIZATION AND REGENERATION OF MOVEMENTS

In an earlier piece I described the process by which messiahs like Antônio Conselheiro, João Maria, Padre Cícero and Pedro Batista became involved with local and regional *chefes políticos.*[58] I traced this involvement to an earlier phase in the social construction of charisma when these religious figures were recipients of gifts of charity *(esmolas)* from their devotees. Befitting an individual with *mistério* as opposed to a secular patron, these figures did not hoard these goods, but rather redistributed them among their poor followers. Such acts of beneficence served both to distinguish messianic leaders from other secular leaders and to attract hundreds if not thousands of needy devotees.

I have argued further that over time these messianic leaders were forced to cooperate with local and national political leaders in order to gain protection and material assistance for a growing body of followers who could not be self-supporting without at least initial assistance from these formal channels. In some cases, such as Canudos, the messianic leader chose the wrong political allies and paid dearly—Antônio Conselheiro being witness to the destruction of his movement by military force. In other cases, such as the Padre Cícero and Pedro Batista movements, the leaders' cooperation with representatives of the State and the capitalist economy jeopardized many of the communal, egalitarian, and folk religious values that had characterized the movement. These actions led to a backlash among members of that strata of the movement who were excluded from the political and economic benefits that this cooperation brought to an "elite" within the body of followers. It was the former group who were receptive to new "messiahs" who appeared to be truer to the initial, spiritual and social goals of the millenarian movement. To illustrate this process whereby routinization and hierarchy lead to off-shoot millenarian activity, I will consider the cases of João Gostava, *O Velho,* and *beato* José Lourenço. Each of these cases emerged in a context when the messianic leader and or his closest advisors had entered into political and economic agreements that tied the millenarian community firmly to the State and capitalist economy. Let us begin with the Pedro Batista movement.

Beginning in 1945 Pedro Batista settled his approximately 4,000 followers in the remote rural community of Santa Brígida, Bahia and purchased several large *fazendas* to be worked cooperatively by his *romeiros.* In exchange for votes, the *romaria* was allowed to settle and given political protection by the local *chefe político* of Geremoabo, Colonel Sá. As a reward for the *romaria's* political loyalty to Colonel Sá and his party, Santa Brígida was elevated in the early 1950s to the status of *sede de distrito* (district seat) with its own justice of the peace and system of records. Finally in 1963 it was accorded the status of municipality.

According to informants, by the mid-1950s with his health faltering, Pedro Batista began to worry about the future material well-being of his *romaria.* Apparently he was persuaded by a politician from the state capital in Bahia to cede 5,117 hectares of his land to the federal government in 1959 for the construction of a government run "cooperative." While this act was supposed to bring modern management and technology to the 160 *romeiro* families settled in the *núcleo colonial,* it brought instead corrupt government officials who expropriated and sold the seeds and material destined for Santa Brígida. An infirm and politically naive Pedro Batista proved unable either to stem this graft, nor stop many of the affected families from migrating temporarily to cities in order to recoup their financial losses.

The *núcleo colonial* failure brought other unintended outcomes. The older children of the families who had temporarily migrated from Santa Brígida returned to the *romaria* with a vision of individual upward mobility and an appreciation of modern national political and economic institutions. This vision contradicted the collective, egalitarian values espoused by Pedro Batista as well as the insularity and suspicion of modern national institutions held by older *romeiros.* Nonetheless, as attested to by the elevation of Santa Brígida to a municipality, throughout the 1950s and 1960s, the community continued to cement its ties with the larger political-economy; and it was members of this younger generation of *romeiros* who came to assume administrative and political leadership positions and to establish themselves as commercial middlemen between Santa Brígida and regional markets. On the one hand, these political and commercial contacts with Brazilian national institutions brought the upward mobility these youthful *romeiros* sought. On the other hand, their actions promoted socio-economic stratification within the *romaria.* Moreover, the poorer *romeiros* feared that with these changes the *romaria* was veering away from its sacred mission to live an other-worldly, sacrificial, and penitenial life in order to usher in the millennium. This belief was intensified by the *romeiros'* realization that their once all-powerful messiah could no longer protect them from the misdeeds of corrupt government officials.[59]

It was in this context of a messianic leader impotent before secular authority and a once egalitarian *romaria* divided socio-economically that enthusiasm grew among the poor and powerless *romeiros* for a *romeiro* named João Gostava. In the words of one *romeiro:*

> At first everyone paid attention to João Gostava, because some of his words were good. He criticized the *romeiros* for caring more for money and comfort than penitence. . . He said that Santa Brígida had become infiltrated by demons and that my *Padrinho* could no longer protect his *romeiros* from the evil forces. He said that if we did not accept him as

leader, God would soon build a guillotine, and heads would begin to roll in the streets. The streets would run with blood, that is what he preached.[60]

João Gostava insisted that the *romeiros* abandon modern values and institutions by returning to *a antiga lei* (the old ways). Among the traditional institutions he reestablished among his followers were collective work teams *(mutirões);* these had gradually been replaced in Santa Brígida with contractual labor. That this collective form of organizing labor had to be resurrected, provides further evidence of the socio-economic stratification which had emerged within the *romaria*.

An uneasy *modus vivendi* existed between the authorities of Santa Brígida and the approximately one-hundred followers of João Gostava. This accommodation disppeared two months after Pedro Batista's death in November 1965. At that time João Gostava, who had renamed himself, *O Rei* (the King), declared his intention to move into the deceased messiah's home and "to claim his throne." This declaration caused concern within the *romaria*, especially among the more progressive elements. In the hopes of countering a confrontation between the followers of João Gostava and those *romeiros* who labeled him a "fanatic," a meeting was set up between Gostava and Santa Brígida's sheriff, policeman, and police department secretary. When the three approached Gostava's door a cry of "pia-ba-pau" went up, and they were dragged into the house. In the words of the secretary:

> All I could see around me were clubs. But I was lucky. Someone was hitting Oscar (the policeman) over the head with the large cross! We were totally surrounded and I was sure that my time to die had arrived. But then Mário (the sheriff) in some way managed to extricate his gun. He fired three shots and João Gostava and his second in command were mortally wounded. João Gostava's son had been hit in the shoulder. In the sudden excitement we managed to escape. . . We gathered up some reinforcements and led the men to the jail. It was a night of torment. The women wept over the bodies of the slain, and begged the King to come back to life! The children cried for their mothers to feed them. Santa Brígida had been turned into Hell![61]

The following morning the sheriff reported the deaths to the police commissioner in the closest city, Paulo Afonso; word was also sent to the deputy of police in the state capital. According to informants, police and military officials in Paulo Afonso interpreted these deaths as signs of rampant fanaticism in Santa Brígida. There was some sentiment in these circles that Santa Brígida represented a potential Canudos, and for this reason should be disbanded. It was only through the intercession of supportive, influential leaders from Geremoabo, Paulo Afonso, and Joaseiro that Santa Brígida was not placed under military rule nor the *romaria* dispersed. Nonetheless, police and government officials had clearly communicated their disdain for "fanaticism," and their desire for the *romaria* to be placed under the tutelage of its more progressive members.

This message was not lost on these *romeiros* when some six years later, millenarian enthusiasm once again gripped the poorer ranks of the *romaria*. It was now *O Velho* who appealed to their millennial dreams and to their resentment against the progressives. As I personally learned from these *romeiros*, they believed that his teachings about religion, communalism, and "the old ways" represented a way in which the values and concerns of traditional *romeiros* might return to the forefront of the *romaria*. As one pro-*Velho* supporter stated:

> It is the merchants, warehouse owners, and truckers who make all the money off us poor farmers. They set the prices and we have no recourse. At the time of my *Padrinho*, he looked after the poor, but all that has changed now. We need a new *Padrinho* to look after us and set the others on the right path again. We need *O Velho*.[62]

While the pro-*Velho* faction had more members, they confronted a more politically and economically powerful group of progressive *romeiros*. In claiming to represent and speak for the best interests of the *romaria*, the leaders of the progressives drew their authority from their appointed and elected positions in local government. As the following quote shows, these officials threatened *O Velho* and his supporters with legal intervention and prosecution should the would-be messiah attempt to relocate to Santa Brígida.

> How can I expect to get assistance for modern schools and equipment when the legislators in Salvador hear from rival politicians in neighboring municipalities that the citizens of Santa Brígida are a bunch of ignorant fanatics!...I and the more educated among us must take responsibility for the weak-minded within the *romaria*. One way we will do this is by continuing to threaten *O Velho* and his supporters with imprisonment in Paulo Afonso should they attempt to visit Santa Brígida again.[63]

As I described above, such threats, in combination with *O Velho's* inability to overcome these challenges, were factors which slowly undercut his support among the poorer *romeiros*. By 1976 when I returned again to Santa Brígida, support for *O Velho* had diminished to only a handful of devotees who visited him occasionally at his home in Pernambuco.

My contention that routinized millenarian movements can generate their own brand of "resentment" and off-shoot movements among those who have been excluded from the social and material benefits of routinization, can be well documented in the case of the Pedro Batista movement. My own ethnographic research in Santa Brígida has greatly assisted me in tracing the role assumed by local and external representatives of the State and capitalist economy in promoting both routinization and "resentment." Now I will turn to the case of *beato* José Lourenço, a devotee of Padre Cícero. Here my remarks regarding the regenerative nature of another millenarian movement must be more inferential. They are based both on my own first hand observations of the development of the Pedro Batista movement, and my bringing these observations to the interpretation of secondary source materials on Joaseiro and the *beato's* settlement in Caldeirão.

At the time of Padre Cícero, Joaseiro attracted many thousands of devotees. The votes, labor power, and markets these newcomers represented proved attractive to those politicians and merchants who favored the fuller integration of developing rural communities, like Joaseiro, into regional and national institutions. Within this process of centralization, Padre Cícero emerged as a key figure in regional politics. The rewards this status brought to Joaseiro and the *romaria* included the establishment of Joaseiro as an autonomous juridical district *(comarca)*. This meant that Joaseiro had its own justice of the peace as well as a public notary, "perhaps the most important legal institution in Brazil during the 'Old Republic.' "[64] As for Padre Cícero, Ralph Della Cava writes:

> As Vice-President of Ceará... as a distributor of political patronage and of cheap manpower throughout the backlands, the Patriarch was showered with deference by Cariry *coronéis*. Only with his advice did they appoint local officials, support state and federal candidates; and only with his endorsement did they solicit government subsidies for public works and economic development... The Patriarch... used his influence for the advancement of Joaseiro and the Cariry Valley.[65]

As we have seen already in the case of Santa Brígida, the greater integration of Joasciro into the regional and national political economy carried implications for the millenarian activity of Padre Cícero's *romaria*. Acts of "religious fanaticism" were suppressed under the direction of Dr. Floro. As Della Cava writes of Floro,

> Understandably, as a *bacharel* and urban oriented professional man it was unpleasant for him to be scoffed at in the Federal Congress as the *"deputado dos fanáticos."* During the minor drought of 1919 he violently suppressed the recrudescence of a society of penitential flagellants, a religious institution which had existed in the Cariry even before Padre Cícero's arrival in 1872. Under Floro's orders, the *penitentes* were disbanded. So too, was a small millenarian sect known as "the celestial hosts," whose members took the names of saints and resided, in sexual deviance, in the Hôrto. The religious garb and ceremonial accoutrements of both the flagellants and the "celestial hosts" were ordered burned in public by Floro, while the unrepentant were forcibly put to work in repairing the streets and sidewalks of Joaseiro.[66]

In Floro's attempts to modernize and "sanitize" a routinized Joaseiro of its "fanatical" elements, we again see signs of the tension between religion and politics. In taking these civic actions Floro attacked cultural features that were central to Brazilian millenarian values and goals. For example, based on my participant observation of the Pedro Batista movement and my reading about earlier movements, I feel confident in claiming that the outlawed ritual acts of penitence must have been viewed by the practicing *romeiros* as key sacred acts—acts that were required to usher in the millennium and to better ensure the salvation of the practitioners and other sinners.

As for the policies which integrated Joaseiro into the larger polity and economy, these created opportunities for a political and economic elite among the followers of Padre Cícero. This development contradicted what have been central values in most Brazilian millenarian movements—egalitarianism and collective work relations.

It is my opinion that the millenarian community of Caldeirão founded by José Lourenço in 1926 was a reaction to the hierarchical trends and anti-folk Catholic orientation that had developed in Joaseiro. In this regard, it is revealing that José Lourenço relocated his flock of some 5,000 followers away from the periphery of Joaseiro after Dr.

Floro directed two repressive acts against the *beato* and his people. First, Floro ordered the butchering of an ox which Padre Cícero had given to José Lourenço. This act followed José Lourenço's declaration that the beast was sacred and had curative powers. Second, the *beato* was a member of the celestial hosts which had been banned by Floro.[67] Indeed José Lourenço was jailed for a short time by Floro for his activities in the millennial sect. It is telling that Padre Cícero actually ceded the Caldeirão property to José Lourenço.[68] Perhaps this indicates that the priest himself was resigned to secularizing trends within the confines of Joaseiro, but nonetheless valued the millennial values and activities of his more zealous followers.[69]

As was the case with João Gostava, José Lourenço also instituted social and economic "reforms" which promoted egalitarianism and collectivism among his followers.

> Upon entering the community all the devotees had to hand over "all their valuables, the cattle, goats, chickens, even the smallest personal objects, for 'nothing was for anyone' and 'all was for everyone.' " Money did not circulate within the colony, and any that was brought by the new followers "was immediately invested in goods destined for the common good." José Lourenço also distributed the items of consumption and other commodities according to need, a policy he followed, as well, when assigning people to daily tasks. The work was collective based on the *mutirão*. José Lourenço never contemplated accumulating the surplus from his property, but rather distributed it among his *romeiros*, friends, and neighbors.[70]

As occurred later in the case of the millennial enthusiasm that crystalized around João Gostava and *O Velho*, José Lourenço soon drew the attention and contempt of local politicians and capitalists. The latter railed against the numerous workers who relocated to Caldeirão and were therefore pulled away from service on sugar mills and farms. In 1935 a contingent of local policemen were dispatched to Caldeirão with the message to disperse since "the State could not permit such a dangerous settlement"[71] When the *romeiros* refused to leave Caldeirão peacefully, they were attacked by soldiers, their homes destroyed, and José Lourenço forced to flee with a handful of followers to a community in Pernambuco, far from Joaseiro. Two later attempts to reestablish a *romaria* on the "sacred site of Caldeirão" attempted by two other *beatos* allied to José Lourenço ended tragically with police and military intervention and the deaths of many of the *romeiros*.[72]

CONCLUSION

There has been a tendency in studies of Brazilian millenarian movements to dismiss the religious meanings and motives so evident in the ideologies and actions of the messianic leaders and their followers. Rather, movements have been simplified when attributed merely to factors such as social change, modernization, or class struggle. In this article I have attempted to give just due to both the ideological and political-economic underpinnings of millenian activity in rural Brazil. In doing this, I have argued that Folk Catholicism provided the meanings and motives—such as a "moral economy" encompassing patrons and clients, and "resentment"—which assisted rural Brazilians to interpret political-economic changes which threatened their precarious way of life. Folk Catholicism also provided guides for remedial action. I have rejected both native and conventional social scientific explanations of millenarian activity which privilege either religion or politics. Rather, I have argued that in three distinct "moments" of Brazilian millenarianism, the organizing principle has been the dynamic relationship "between" religion and politics.

Let me close with some final observations about these three moments. In Brazilian millenarianism, as with so many social phenomena, the social forces that initially promoted millenarian movements in the late 1800s and early 1900s were not the sole elements that facilitated the perpetuation of movements into the latter half of the 20th century. While the later movements do share the search for a perfect traditional patron, they also are responsive to what may be called a symbolic paradigm of unfulfilled millennial dreams. This paradigm is most visible in popular beliefs about Padre Cícero and Pedro Batista—beliefs that have fanned the fires of millennial enthusiasm. For example, when Padre Cícero died (or in his *romeiros'* terminology *se mudou*), the belief emerged that Padre Cícero would return.[73] When Pedro Batista appeared, his followers believed he was the "reincarnation" of Padre Cícero. Finally when Pedro Batista *se mudou* his *romeiros* incorporated the Trinity theme into their belief system. Consequently, they claimed that Padre Cícero was God the Father, Pedro Batista, God the Son, and *O Velho*, God the Holy Ghost. This paradigm with its themes of return, reincarnation, and the final culmination of the millennial drama, is available to those rural Brazilians who feel that the prevailing political-economic system has left them marginalized and vulnerable.

Several theorists have suggested that millenarian movements will disappear as individuals learn to express their needs and demands in political rather than religious terms.[74] There are two assumptions underlying this proposition. The first holds that millenarianism is, at root, a political phenomenon. The second maintains that religious expressions are examples of false consciousness and as such will be replaced by more appropriate and realistic political ones.

While I agree with this conclusion, I do so based on very different grounds. Rather than millenarianism being doomed by a "maturing consciousness," what I believe has been more injurious to millenarian activity worldwide is a "maturing State." As we have seen in the case of Brazil, many of the movements clustered during that period of political transition when power and legitimacy were uncertain. At that time certain politicians tolerated popular movements in a bid to obtain the followers' arms, votes, and labor power. It is noteworthy that in the cases of the Padre Cícero and Pedro Batista movements once an accommodation was forged between the messianic leader and local politicians, the space for "unsettling" millennial enthusiasm within the confines of the millenarian community was narrowed if not completely closed. Consequently, even though these millennial movements did continue to spawn millenarian expectations among the disposed in their midst, these outbursts were quelled by the movements' "secularized" elite who emerged as local representatives of and guardians for the State.

If it is the maturing State that has progressively narrowed the social space for millenarian activity in Brazil, it is also representatives of the State who have assumed a key role in defining and mystifying this activity. Euclides da Cunha first drew on the confidence of a modernizing State with its emerging bourgeoisie to label Antônio Conselheiro and his followers as, "backward, fanatics."[75] Many years later Santa Brígida's later-day upholders of the modern State also used the delegitimating tag of "fanaticism" to characterize the struggle of the poor and excluded in their midst. It is indeed because representatives of the State have so often claimed exclusive rights to define the meaning and motives of social movements that we, as social scientists, must search for and reclaim the words and deeds of *o povo* (the common people). It is only in this way that we can write balanced histories of millenarian movements and produce measured social analyses.[76]

NOTES

[1]Rui Facó, *Cangaçeiros e fanáticos,* (Rio de Janeiro: Civilição Brasileira, 1972).

[2]For a review of competing explanations of Brazilian millenarian movements, see Patricia R. Pessar, "Millenarian Movements in Rural Brazil: Prophecy and Protest," *Religion* 12 (1982): 187–213.

[3]The material presented on the Pedro Batista movement and on the failed movements of João Gostava and *O Velho* were collected by me over the periods September 1973–December 1974 and June–August 1976. Materials for the other movements come from secondary sources which are cited later in this article.

[4]Many of the ideas presented in this section are found in two of my previous publications, see Pessar, "Millenarian Movements in Rural Brazil," op. cit.; and Pessar, "Unmasking the Politics of Religion: The Case of Brazilian Millenarianism," *Journal of Latin American Lore* 7:2 (1981): 255–278.

[5]See Mair, "The Pursuit of the Millennium in Melanesia," *British Journal of Sociology* (1958) 9: 175–182.

[6]See Peter Worsley, *The Trumpet Shall Sound* (London: MacGibbon and Kee, 1957); Facó, *Cangaçeiros e fanáticos,* op. cit.

[7]See Norman Cohn, *The Pursuit of the Millennium* (New York: Oxford University Press, 1961); James Scott, *The Moral Economy of the Peasant* (New Haven: Yale University Press, 1976).

[8]Emílio Willems, *Uma vila brasileira* (São Paulo: Difusão Européia do Livro, 1961), p. 149.

[9]See Eduardo Hornaert, *Verdadeira e falsa religião no Nordeste* (Salvador: Editôra Benedina Ltda., 1972).

[10]Ibid.

[11]Ibid. p. 61.

[12]See I.M. Lewis, *Ecstatic Religion* (Middlesex: Penguin Books, Ltd., 1971).

[13]See Marc Swartz, Victor Turner and Arthur Tuden, *Political Anthropology* (Chicago: Aldine Press, 1966).

[14]See Shepard Forman, *The Brazilian Peasantry* (New York: Columbia University Press, 1975); and Donald Pierson, *Cruz de Almas* (Washington D.C.: Smithsonian Institute, 1948).

[15]Eduardo Galvão, *Santos e visagens* (Rio de Janeiro: Editôra Nacional Rio de Janeiro, 1957); also see Emílio Willems, op. cit., p. 149 for an account of ritual sponsors who allegedly died because of their failure to give all the money they collected to the saint, The Holy Ghost.

[16]See Allen Johnson, *Sharecroppers of the Sertão* (Stanford: Stanford University Press, 1971); Shepard Forman, op. cit.; Joel Migdal, *Peasants, Politics, and Revolution* (Princeton: Princeton University Press, 1974).

[17]See Clifford Geertz, *Agricultural Involution* (Berkeley: University of California Press, 1974).

[18]Shepard Forman, op, cit., p. 206.

[19]See Duglas Teixeira Monteiro, *Os errantes do novo século* (São Paulo: Livraria Duas Cidades, 1974).

[20]For a discussion of the concept of "moral economy" within peasant society, see James Scott, op. cit.; also see Allen Johnson, op. cit., pp. 123–131, for a discussion of the reciprocal rights and duties which bind contemporary Brazilian landlords and their workers.

[21]Shepard Forman, op. cit., p. 217.

[22]Alba Zaluar Guimarães, "Sobre a lógica do catolicismo popular," *Dados* (173): 173–194; see also Pierson, op. cit.

[23]See Peter Berger, *The Sacred Canopy*, (New York: Doubleday, 1967).

[24]Padre Manoel José Gonçalves Couto, *Missão abreviada* (Pôrto, Portugal, 1873) p. 199.

[25]See René Ribeiro, "Brazilian Messianic Movements," in S. Thrupp, ed., *Millennial Dreams in Action* (The Hague: Mouton, 1962).

[26]Euclides da Cunha, *Rebellion in the Backlands*, (Chicago: University of Chicago Press, 1944), p. 136.

[27]See *literatura de cordel* by Francisquinho Pereira da Costa, "A carta misteriosa de Frei Vidal da Penha sobre o fim dos tempos," and by Augusto de Souza Lima, *Este é o falso profeta*.

[28]See Friedrich Nietzsche, *The Philosophy of Nietzsche* (New York: The Modern Library, 1954), p. 647; and Max Weber, *The Sociology of Religion* (Boston: Beacon Press, 1963), p. 110.

[29]See Todd Diacon, "Capitalists and Fanatics: Brazil's Contestado Rebellion, 1912–1916," Unpublished dissertation, University of Wisconsin, Madison, 1987.

[30]Anthony Hall, *Drought and Irrigation in Northeast Brazil* (New York: Cambridge University Press, 1978), p. 4.

[31]Ibid.

[32]Ibid.

[33]Bernard Siegel, "The Contestado Rebellion, 1912–1916: A Case Study in Brazilian Messianism and Regional Dynamics," in R. Fogelson and R. Adams, eds., *The Anthropology of Power* (New York: Academic Press, 1977) p. 329; see also Diacon, *op cit*.

[34]Ibid., p. 328.

[35]Duglas Teixeira Montero, op. cit. p. 25.

[36]See Billy Jaynes Chandler, *The Feitosas and the Sertão of Inhamuns* (Gainesville: University of Florida Press, 1972).

[37]Amaury de Souza, "The Congaçeiro and the Politics of Violence in Northeast Brazil," in R. Chilcote, ed., *Protest and Resistance in Angola and Brazil* (Berkeley: University of California Press, 1972) pp. 122–123.

[38]Teixeira Monteiro, op. cit., p. 46.

[39]For an analysis of how apocalyptic visions contained in religious texts and *benditos* may have promoted the belief that the drought and suffering of this period were supernatural harbingers of the end of the world and the dawning of the millennium, see my "Millenarian Movements in Rural Brazil," op. cit.

[40]Euclides da Cunha, op. cit., p. 141.

[41]Maurício Vinhas de Queiroz, *Messianismo e conflicto social* (Rio de Janeiro: Editôra Civilização, 1966), p. 202.

[42]Abelardo Montenegro, *Antônio Conselheiro* (Forteleza, 1954), p. 33.

[43]Maria Isaura Pereira de Queiroz, *O messianismo no Brasil e no mundo* (São Paulo: Universidade de São Paulo, 1965), p. 245.

[44]For a discussion of the way in which *mistério* is constructed in miracle narratives about Padre Cícero, see Candace Slater, *Trail of Miracles* (Berkeley: University of California Press, 1986), pp. 112–116.

[45]Story told by Maria das Dores in Santa Brígida, 1974.

[46]The term "persons" is a term used by anthropologists to connote the status of social actors in hierarchical, face-to-face societies, such as rural Brazil, where the "individual" is subordinated to and defined in relation to higher order institutions, such as the family and the community. See, Louis Dumont, *Homo Hierarchicus* (Chicago: University of Chicago Press, 1970). Robert da Matta argues that it is the marginal, liminal individual, like the bandit and messiah who escapes the status of "person" in Brazilian society to emerge as an autonomous "individual." See Roberto da Matta, *Carnavais, malandros e heróis: para uma sociologia do dilema brasileira* (Rio de Janeiro: Zahar, 1979).

[47]See Gilberto Freyre, *The Masters and the Slaves: A Study of the Development of Brazilian Civilization* (New York: Alfred A. Knopf, 1946); Djacir Menezes, *O outro nordeste* (Rio de Janeiro: Livraria José Olympio Editôra, 1937); and Rui Facó, op. cit..

[48]Maria Isaura Pereira de Queiroz, "Messiahs in Brazil," *Past and Present* 31, pp. 68–69.

[49]*Literatura de cordel* recounting the miracles surrounding Padre Cícero's life. When I transcribed this verse in Joaseiro in 1974, I inadvertently neglected to record the title and author of the *cordel* story.

[50]*Literatura de cordel* composed by João Alves Oliveira, "Vida e morte de meu Padrinho Pedro Batista."

[51]As is the accepted convention in ethnographic research, most of the informants' quotes are presented without individual attribution; *romeiro*, Batok, Bahia, 1974.

[52]See also Candace Slater, op. cit., chapter 6.

[53]Story told by Maria das Dores, Santa Brígida, 1974. It should be noted that similar stories about assassins shaking and losing guns and knives are told about Padre Cícero. When I queried the narrators about the similarity of these stories, they usually smiled and explained that this was because both men shared the same *mistério.* It would appear that there is a shared corpus of miracle tales that believers attach to social actors to whom they believe to have *mistério.* This process in turn heightens the charisma of the protagonist in these miracle tales, since they not only separate him or her from worldly beings, but also establish a homologous relationship between the new charismatic figure and previous sacred figures.

[54]Candace Slater, op. cit., p. 177.

[55]Consistent with the argument developed in the first section concerning followers' of messianic movements being motivated by desires to reinstate the traditional form of patronage, Slater writes of Padre Cícero and Dr. Floro:

"The priest is not only a symbol of spiritual power but also the idealization of a landowning system in which the patron is supposed to embody the ethical force known in Portuguese as *moral.* Floro, in this context, stands for a secular, modernizing state in which interpersonal obligation is perceived to yield to physical force... Moreover his lack of respect for the rules casts unwelcome doubt on their validity, adding to the insecurity of the dispossessed... The priest is not simply an incarnation of some vague celestial authority but is a recognizably Northeast Brazilian patron. Floro, for his part, exemplifies a new order that storytellers find alien because it negates the long-established view of power as a personal relationship binding two individuals of unequal social status. (pp. 183, 184).

[56]Comment of Maria das Dores, Santa Brígida, 1974.

[57]Comment by *romeiro*, Santa Brígida, 1974.

[58]See Patricia R. Pessar, "Unmasking the Politics of Religion," op. cit.

[59]In a interview one *romeiro* stated:

One day Dr. Portela arrived and said each family was to receive 200 *cruzeiros.* But the next day he held another meeting and said, 'Do you know, if I give you the money you will all just waste it on gambling and alcohol.' So of course he kept the money, like always. My *Padrinho* knew about this, but he told us to be calm and patient. What could he do; he had placed the *romaria* in the hands of the *doutores.*

[60]Interview with *romeiro*, Santa Brígida, 1974.

[61]Interview with ex-police department secretary, Santa Brígida, 1974.

[62]Comment of *romeiro*, Batok, 1974.

[63]Interview with *romeiro* local government official, Santa Brígida, 1974.

[64]Ralph della Cava, *Miracle at Joaseiro* (New York: Columbia University Press, 1970), p. 162.

[65]Ibid.

[66]Ibid., p. 170.

[67]Maria Isaura Pereira de Queiroz, *O messianismo*, p. 261.

[68]Ibid.

[69]In this regard it is revealing that Candace Slater states that all three of the people she knew who had lived in Caldeirão indicated that the community was "more religious" than Joaseiro, p. 52.

[70]*O Messianismo*, p. 263.

[71]Ibid., p. 266.

[72]See Ibid, and Raymundo Duarte ("Notas preliminares do estudo do movimento messiânico de Pau de Colher," unpublished manuscript, n.d.).

[73]A popular *bendito* states:

> In the year, '34
> He told us
> My children, I am going on a journey;
> My Father in the sky has called me.
>
> I am going, but I will return.
> Follow my commandments
> With faith recite your rosaries
> So you will be able to see me.

[74]See Peter Worsley, *The Trumpet Shall Sound* (London: MacGibbon and Kee, 1957); and Ian Jarvie, *The Revolution in Anthropology* (New York: Humanities Press, 1964).

[75]Euclides da Cunha, op. cit..

[76]For discussion of the conditions for and constraints upon the production of authoritative statements ("truths") and labels in historical and ethnographic documents and analyses, see Michel Foucault, *The Archeology of Knowledge*, pp. 215–237 (New York: Harper and Row, 1976); and James Clifford and George Marcus, eds., *Writing Culture* (Berkeley: University of California Press, 1984).

For a recent treatment of the problem of labeling in the study of bandits and peasant resistance, see Gilbert Joseph, "On the Trail of Latin American Bandits: A Reexamination of Peasant Resistance," *Latin American Review* 25:3 (1990), 7–53.

Feminism, Antifeminism, and Electoral Politics in Postwar Nicaragua and El Salvador

KAREN KAMPWIRTH

National elections marking a transition from civil war to relative normality occurred in 1990 in Nicaragua and in 1994 in El Salvador. While the long process of political transformation in Central America should not be reduced to elections, these electoral moments do capture many of the dilemmas inherent in transforming guerrilla organizations into leftist parties, and in transforming gender relations from the exceptional conditions of wartime to the relatively normal, but reformulated, conditions of peacetime.

Seen from a feminist perspective, the first post-civil war election in Nicaragua was close to disastrous. Violeta Barrios de Chamorro, the presidential candidate of the fourteen party UNO (Unión Nacional Opositora) coalition, ran an explicitly antifeminist campaign in 1990 and won. The gendered images drawn upon by Daniel Ortega, the incumbent from the Sandinista party (Frente Sandinista de Liberación Nacional or FSLN) were not explicitly antifeminist, but they could hardly be labeled feminist either.

Antifeminist tactics rhetorically respond to and attack feminist organizing. This concept builds upon the work of Sonia Alvarez, who argues that gender may be politicized in two basic ways. Feminine organizing "grows out of and accepts prevailing female roles and asserts rights on the basis of those roles, [while feminist organizing] seeks to transform the roles society assigns to women, challenges existing gender power arrangements, and claims women's rights to personal autonomy and equality."[1]

[1] Sonia Alvarez, *Engendering Democracy in Brazil: Women's Movements in Transition Politics* (Princeton: Princeton University Press, 1990), 24; a similar argument is made by Maxine Molyneux, "Mobilization Without Emancipation?" in Richard Fagen et al., eds., *Transition and Development: Problems of Third World Socialism* (New York: Monthly Review Press), 280–302.

KAREN KAMPWIRTH is assistant professor of political science and chair of the Latin American studies program at Knox College. Her forthcoming book, *Feminism and Guerrilla Politics in Latin America*, considers the cases of Nicaragua, El Salvador, and Chiapas, Mexico.

243

Recently, the feminine/feminist distinction has been criticized. Some of those criticisms begin with what I think is a misreading of the theory. For example, one critic claimed that the theory "tends to assume exclusionary interests, that one cannot move from one category into another."[2] Another claimed that the feminine/feminist distinction marginalizes feminine organizing by defining it as private, in contrast with public feminist organizing."[3] A third argued that the distinction is a way of promoting middle-class (feminist) groups over working-class (feminine) groups.[4]

All three critics observed that many women's groups utilize both feminine and feminist strategies. That is clearly true, though not incompatible with my reading of Alvarez. The argument is not that there are two kinds of activists (feminine and feminist) but that there are two kinds of strategies. They are both public strategies that in practice are both used by middle-class and working-class women. The main difference between the two strategies is their impact on power inequality based on gender: either directly challenging it or at best indirectly challenging it. I am still convinced that what kind of strategy is used matters. Apparently, many Latin American activists agree, as they continue to make these distinctions.[5]

So while I think the feminine/feminist distinction remains useful, I think Alvarez's two concepts are even more effective when complemented by a third concept: antifeminism. Antifeminism is not the same as feminine organizing, though both accept power differences between men and women as natural. The difference is that while feminine organizing simply reinforces the status quo, antifeminist strategies are employed in response to a threat to the status quo. In this case, the threat was the decade of the Sandinista revolution.

In Nicaragua, as antifeminist claims were made by presidential candidate Violeta Chamorro, the women's movement basically sat on the sidelines and made little effort to influence the campaign except to echo the campaign rhetoric of the Sandinistas. In contrast, in El Salvador, feminists seized the opportunity of their first post-civil war election to try to extract promises from all the political parties. The rhetoric that the parties employed in 1994 was largely gender neutral, but the two top vote-getters did endorse the feminist demands of

---

[2] Jennifer Schirmer, "The Seeking of Truth and the Gendering of Consciousness" in Sarah Radcliffe and Sallie Westwood, eds., *Viva: Women and Popular Protest in Latin America* (New York: Routledge), 60–61.

[3] Lynn Stephen, *Women and Social Movements in Latin America* (Austin: University of Texas Press, 1997), 11–12.

[4] Amy Lind, "Power, Gender and Development" in Arturo Escobar and Sonia Alvarez, eds., *The Making of Social Movements in Latin America* (Boulder, CO: Westview Press), 137.

[5] Mariana Fernández and Graciela Freyermuth, "Migration, Organization, and Identity: The Case of a Women's Group from San Cristóbal de las Casas," *Signs* 20 (Summer 1995): 972; Comité Centroamericano, *Memorias del VI Encuentro Feminista* (Managua: Editorial UCA, 1993), 39, 43, 44, 53, 59, 117; Mercedes Olivera, "Practica Feminista en el Movimiento Zapatista de Liberación Nacional" in Rosa Rojas, ed., *Chiapas y las mujeres, que? Tomo II* (Mexico City: Editorial La Correa Feminista, 1995), 177.

the Women '94 platform. That agreement was surprising given the divergence between the ideologies of the rightwing ARENA party (Alianza Republicana Nacionalista), which had been linked to death squads during the civil war,[6] and the leftwing Coalition, whose largest member (Frente Farabundo Martí de Liberación Nacional or FMLN) was a guerrilla force that fought the ARENA party as late as two years before the electoral campaign.

The election that signaled the end of the civil war in Nicaragua was highly gendered in terms of the strategies employed by the major candidates, but organized feminists had no role to play in that election and were quite dismayed by its outcome. In contrast, the election that marked the end of the Salvadoran civil war was characterized by campaign strategies with very little gendered content, but by a significant role for organized feminists. The differences in the campaigns, in countries that are otherwise very similar in cultural and historical terms, are striking.

Historically, both Nicaragua and El Salvador were characterized by economic dependency on a few agricultural products, accompanied by well entrenched political authoritarianism.[7] Elections did occur but, given the sort of power held by big landowners and politicians (who were often the same people), those elections were not terribly meaningful. This article, with its focus on electoral politics, would have made little sense as recently as a generation ago.

Several major transformations had to occur before there would be any point to analyzing electoral politics in Central America. These changes included the growth of export-oriented agriculture and the creation of the Central American Common Market in the 1950s and 1960s, which had a negative impact on the standard of living of the average Central American. Among the effects of rising land concentration and unemployment was a drop in per capita food consumption.[8]

At approximately the same time as the economies of these countries were changing, so was the Catholic Church. While parts of the traditional church continued to side with Central American elites, "[s]ome factions in the church began to weld the poor and dispossessed into a new social force, organizing base communities, and call[ing] for 'a preferential option for the poor.'"[9] These socioeconomic changes helped create the conditions for several decades of civil strife. Informed by the transformed Catholic Church and the example of the

---

[6] See Clifford Krauss, "U.S., Aware of Killings, Kept Ties to Salvadoran Rightists, Papers Suggest," *New York Times*, 9 November 1993.

[7] Hector Pérez-Brignoli, *A Brief History of Central America* (Berkeley: University of California Press, 1989); Ralph Lee Woodward, *Central America: A Nation Divided* (New York: Oxford University Press, 1985).

[8] T. David Mason, "Women's Participation in Central American Revolutions: A Theoretical Perspective," *Comparative Political Studies* 25 (April 1992): 68–70.

[9] Morris J. Blachman and Kenneth E. Sharpe, "The Transitions to 'Electoral' and Democratic Politics in Central America" in Louis W. Goodman, William LeoGrande, and Johanna Mendelson Forman, eds., *Political Parties and Democracy in Central America* (Boulder, CO: Westview Press, 1992), 37.

Cuban revolution, one response to increasing impoverishment and governmental violence was the emergence of guerrilla movements in the three Central American countries with the most dictatorial regimes—Nicaragua, El Salvador, and Guatemala—from the 1960s through the beginning of the 1990s.

The postwar election campaigns in Nicaragua and El Salvador in the early 1990s suggest a number of questions about the relationship between electoral and social movement politics, especially in a postwar context. How does the legacy of war shape electoral politics? Under what circumstances is antifeminism or feminism an effective campaign strategy for a candidate? And from the perspective of social movement activists, how are the opportunities and dangers presented by elections best approached to make gains, or at least not to lose disastrously?

Many have argued that social movements play critical roles in democratizing politics.[10] Recently, however, Judith Adler Hellman advised caution about asserting this connection, arguing that in the case of Mexico there is little evidence that social movements are serving to democratize national politics.[11]

One of the reasons that this assertion about the connection between social movements and democratization is frequently made (even in cases where evidence is scant) is that, with some notable exceptions,[12] writers on Latin American social movements do not devote much space to the formal mechanisms of democracy. The democratization that most concerns writers on social movements is the democratization of civil society, or economic democratization, or

---

[10] Alvarez, *Engendering Democracy in Brazil*; Susan Eckstein, *Power and Popular Protest: Latin American Social Movements* (Berkeley: University of California Press, 1989); Arturo Escobar and Sonia Alvarez, *The Making of Social Movements in Latin America: Identity, Strategy, and Democracy* (Boulder, CO: Westview Press, 1992); Joe Foweraker and Ann Craig, *Popular Movements and Political Change in Mexico* (Boulder, CO: Lynne Rienner Publishers, 1990); Jane Jaquette, *The Women's Movement in Latin America: Participation and Democracy,* (Boulder, CO: Westview Press, 1994); Elizabeth Jelin, *Women and Social Change in Latin America,* (London: Zed Brooks, 1990); Temma Kaplan, "Community and Resistance in Women's Political Cultures," *Dialectical Anthropology* 15 (1990); Ernesto Laclau and Chantal Mouffe, *Hegemony and Socialist Strategy: Toward a Radical Democratic Politics* (New York: Verso, 1990); Daniel Levine, *Religion and Political Conflict in Latin America* (Chapel Hill: University of North Carolina Press, 1986); Sarah Radcliffe and Sallie Westwood, *Viva: Women and Popular Protest in Latin America* (New York: Routledge, 1993); William Rowe and Vivian Schelling, *Memory and Modernity: Popular Culture in Latin America* (New York: Verso, 1991); Helen Safa, "Women's Social Movements in Latin America," *Gender and Society* 4 (September 1990); David Slater, "Power and Social Movements in the Other Occident: Latin America in an International Context," *Latin American Perspectives* 21 (Spring 1994).

[11] Judith Adler Hellman, "Mexican Popular Movements: Clientalism and the Process of Democratization," *Latin American Perspectives* 21 (Spring 1994).

[12] Alvarez, *Engendering Democracy in Brazil*; Eckstein, *Power and Popular Protest*; Escobar and Alvarez, *The Making of Social Movements in Latin America*; Foweraker and Craig, *Popular Movements and Political Change in Mexico*; Jaquette, *The Women's Movement in Latin America*; Safa, "Women's Social Movements in Latin America"; Alfred Stepan, ed., *Democratizing Brazil: Problems of Transition and Consolidation,* (New York: Oxford University Press, 1989).

the rise of more democratic identities. In this view, "[t]he process of democratization of society . . . goes beyond the boundaries of political democracy."[13]

While political analysis may be sharpened by thinking beyond the boundaries of political democracy, analysis also has to happen within those boundaries. Unfortunately, the social movement literature tends to downplay or ignore the formal mechanisms of democracy, including elections, that are the focus of the literature on transitions to democracy in Latin America.[14] Too often, the literatures on social movements and formal democratization address similar issues but talk past each other, making it difficult to evaluate the assertion that the actions of social movements play a significant role in shaping formal politics. Jane Jaquette expressed this dilemma well, noting that "few who study Latin American politics have thought about the growing impact of women's participation, and few who study women's movements have cared about political parties or the state. Democracy, and women, deserve better."[15]

This article is an attempt to meet Jaquette's challenge. The first two sections of the article analyze the election campaigns of 1990 in Nicaragua and 1994 in El Salvador, focusing on the role gender images and organized feminists played. The final section shows why the electoral campaigns took the shape that they did. I argue that the differences in the way women were integrated into national politics during the 1970s and 1980s explain how they were integrated into the electoral processes of the 1990s.

Analyzing the electoral role of feminism as an organized movement (rather than feminists as individual voters) means that the questions I will ask and the data I will use to answer them differ from many other studies of electoral politics. The polling data that informs most electoral studies is well suited to explain electoral outcomes or voting behavior, but often poorly suited to analyze the participation of social movements or the shape of campaigns. Since my main questions concern process (the unfolding of the electoral campaigns) rather than outcome (which candidate won or what sort of people voted), my answers are based on qualitative data (interviews, media analysis, participant-observation) rather than quantitative data.[16]

---

[13] Slater, "Power and Social Movements," 24.

[14] See Guiseppe Di Palma and Lawrence Whitehead, eds., *The Central American Impasse* (New York: St. Martin's Press, 1986); L. Diamond et al., eds., *Democracy in Developing Countries: Latin America* (Boulder, CO: Lynne Rienner, 1989); Terry Lynn Karl, "Dilemmas of Democratization in Latin America," *Comparative Politics* 23 (October 1990); Juan Linz and Arturo Valenzuela, eds., *The Failure of Presidential Democracy* (Baltimore: Johns Hopkins Press, 1994); George López and Michael Stohl, eds., *Liberalization and Redemocratization in Latin America* (New York: Greenwood Press, 1987); Scott Mainwaring et al., eds., *Issues in Democratic Consolidation: The New South American Democracies in Comparative Perspective* (Notre Dame, IN: University of Notre Dame Press, 1992); Guillermo O'Donnell and Philippe Schmitter, *Transitions from Authoritarian Rule: Tentative Conclusions about Uncertain Democracies* (Baltimore: Johns Hopkins University Press, 1986); Robert Pastor, ed., *Democracy in the Americas: Stopping the Pendulum* (New York: Holmes and Meier Publishers, 1989).

[15] Jaquette, *The Women's Movement in Latin America*, 235.

[16] I collected this data in Nicaragua from October 1990 to July 1991 and in El Salvador in March 1994 and in July to August 1994.

1990 IN NICARAGUA: ANTIFEMINISM WINS

Having presented herself as a traditional, long-suffering mother who would re-unite the Nicaraguan family, Violeta Chamorro was elected president. The an-tifeminist image of womanhood that she presented in her campaign illustrates a view of gender that apparently still resonates with large sectors of the Nicara-guan population, despite a decade of revolutionary transformation. It is worth asking why those antifeminist images were not directly challenged, either by her main rival for the presidency, Sandinista candidate Daniel Ortega, or by Nicaraguan feminists.

The image of womanhood that doña Violeta[17] projected was a multifaceted one. Principally, those facets were doña Violeta as loyal wife and widow, recon-ciling mother, and Virgin Mary. Throughout the campaign, doña Violeta re-minded voters that she was the widow of Pedro Joaquín Chamorro, a well known hero of the struggle against the Somoza dictatorship, who was assassi-nated in 1978. Not only was her widowhood emphasized, but the type of wife she had been was important as well. As she told a reporter: "'I am not a feminist nor do I wish to be one. I am a women dedicated to my home, like Pedro taught me.' Later she would claim 'to be marked with the branding iron of the Cha-morros.'"[18]

Not only did doña Violeta present herself as an exemplary wife and widow but also as an exemplary mother who managed to keep her children united against the odds.[19] The message was that she could also reunite the whole Nica-raguan family, which had been divided by more than a decade of civil war. In a "New Year's Message from doña Violeta" she promised that: "[In 1990] the Nicaraguan family will return to reunite with joy. In 1990 the people are going to choose our moral option and there will not be any more war nor misery nor hate because we will all be brothers."[20]

Consistent with the first two facets of the doña Violeta symbol, those of loyal wife/widow and reconciling mother, was a third facet—that of the Virgin Mary. Throughout doña Violeta's presidential campaign, she was photo-graphed in white, a symbol of purity, in this case of her lack of taint with the filth of politics. This symbolism is powerful in a predominantly Catholic country like Nicaragua. And doña Violeta played on the Virgin Mary symbol in a num-

---

[17] I will call her doña Violeta, for that is what she is most commonly called, and it is what she calls herself. Doña is an honorific that is used before the first name of an older woman.

[18] Scarlet Cuadra, "Electorado Feminino por la Revolución," *Barricada*, Managua, 13 January 1990.

[19] Those odds are considerable. Her four children are politically divided: two are Sandinista activists and two are committed anti-Sandinistas like Violeta herself. On the Chamorro family, see Shirley Christian, *Nicaragua: Revolution in the Family* (New York: Vintage Books, 1986); Patricia Taylor Ed-misten, *Nicaragua Divided: La Prensa and the Chamorro Legacy* (Pensacola: University of West Flor-ida Press, 1990); Denis Lynn Daly Heyck, *Life Stories of the Nicaraguan Revolution* (New York: Routledge, 1990); Brook Larmer, "Struggle to Rule Nicaragua Begins: Hints of Dynasty," *Christian Science Monitor,* 1 March 1990.

[20] *La Prensa,* Managua, 5 January 1990.

ber of ways. Like the Virgin, who suffered the murder of her son, doña Violeta suffered the murder of her husband. While the Virgin was the mother of a martyred savior, doña Violeta is the widow of such a savior. The Virgin Mary image provided an alternative to the most radical Sandinista image of womanhood, that of the woman guerrilla. Doña Violeta made it clear that she was not a guerrilla or even knowledgeable about politics; and precisely because of that distance from politics, she would be able to end the contra war. Through these images of traditional womanhood, what normally would be a liability for a politician—lack of political experience—was presented as an asset.[21]

Doña Violeta's main rival in the race for the presidency in 1990, Sandinista Daniel Ortega, also faced a number of challenges that he, less successfully, tried to overcome through a variety of gendered images. During the campaign, posters of Daniel embracing his baby daughter Camila were plastered across the country. Juxtaposed with the image of Daniel, the good father, was Daniel as a cowboy and Daniel dancing at political rallies with young women to the beat of the Beatles' "All You Need is Love."

These images did not mesh well with the policy promises of the FSLN. Symbolically, Daniel Ortega took various forms—a loving father, a sex symbol surrounded by young women, a cowboy leading a charging herd of men on horses. Practically, the Sandinistas could not promise an end to the war; that decision was in the hands of the UNO's ally, the U.S. Government. So what they promised was dignity, solidarity, and further anti-imperialist struggle, loosely tied together with the slogan, "Everything Will Be Better."

While these highly gendered images were projected, the social movement that might be expected to be most engaged with such a campaign—the women's movement—largely watched from the sidelines. To the extent that the women's movement was an actor in the campaign, it was largely as a cheerleader for the Sandinistas. For instance, a mural painted by the Asociación de Mujeres Nicaragüenses Luisa Amanda Espinoza (AMNLAE) read "Women and Daniel in One Love." It was illustrated with a big red heart pierced by an arrow.

During the campaign, the broad-based women's movement (and self-identified feminists within that movement) did nothing to directly counter the gendered images of the major candidates. This left doña Violeta free to promise to reunite and reimpose the traditional Nicaraguan family, and left Daniel to project a mishmash of masculine images. Doña Violeta's maternal reconciliation message would carry the election, as she was elected president with nearly 55 percent of the vote.

[21] For more on the campaign and its policy implications, see Karen Kampwirth, "The Mother of the Nicaraguans: Doña Violeta and the UNO's Gender Agenda," *Latin American Perspectives* 23 (Winter 1996).

1994 IN EL SALVADOR: "WOMEN DECIDE FOR OURSELVES"

The relationship between electoral politics and feminist mobilization was reversed in the Salvadoran election, where a campaign with little overt gender content was met with a loud and persistent response from feminists. The lack of gender politics in campaign discourse was consistent with the near absence of political debate of any sort in campaign advertising. While the nine parties were far from indistinguishable, all the major parties chose the strategy of bland, feel-good television advertisements.[22]

But as the major parties seemingly tried to sweep the political battles of the previous decade under the electoral rug, organized feminists tried to shake that rug. In January 1993, over a year before the election, a number of women's organizations joined forces to gain a voice in national politics. The result was a coalition known as "Women '94."[23]

While there are disagreements about what really happened in the development of the Women '94 coalition, there is remarkable agreement over its origins. Every activist who discussed those origins with me noted that it was the most autonomous and most radically feminist current with the movement (*Concertacion de Mujeres por la Paz, la Dignidad, y la Igualdad* or Women's Coalition for Peace, Dignity, and Equality) that was responsible for initiating the effort. I would suggest that this was due to the greater autonomy of that current in relationship to the political parties, particularly the FMLN. The feminist organizations that belonged to this current had already waged sometimes nasty battles for autonomy and so enjoyed the necessary space to try to influence the political parties.[24]

The coalition spent the first eight months of its existence (January 1993 to August 1993) developing a platform through working groups on women and violence, health, education, environment, work, legislation, development, land, and political parties. About fifty women were involved in each group, and they were women who felt the direct impact of policies in these areas. For instance,

---

[22] Advertisements mainly consisted of flying flags, and brief endorsements from smiling men and women. The exception was a series of advertisements, sponsored by the rightwing Freedom and Democracy Institute (ILYD) or by unidentified sources, in which the Left coalition was blamed for the civil war of the 1980s. See Jack Spence et al., *El Salvador: Elections of the Century, Results, Recommendations, Analysis* (Cambridge, MA: Hemisphere Initiatives, July 1994), 18–27. The Left might have responded with "anonymous" advertisements of its own, pointing out the well-documented links between ARENA and the death squads. Perhaps fearing further polarization, it did not run such advertisements.

[23] The exact number of members of the coalition is disputed. Twenty-eight organizations and numerous individuals officially formed the coalition. See Mujeres 94, "Plataforma de las Mujeres Salvadoreñas: Edición Popular," unpublished document, August 1993. But in separate interviews, Mirna Rodríguez and Lorena Peña told me that forty groups participated. The disagreement may be due to the difficulty of defining membership.

[24] Mujeres por la Dignidad y la Vida, *Hacer Política Desde Las Mujeres: Una propuesta feminista para la participacíon política de las mujeres salvadoreñas* (San Salvador: Doble G Impresores, 1993), 115–132.

the majority of the members of the working group on land and credit were peasants.

In August 1993 the platform was officially presented to the political parties in a ceremony that began with a march of 5,000 or 6,000 women and ended in a fancy hotel in San Salvador. But only two major candidates attended, both from the leftist coalition: presidential candidate Rubén Zamora and Shafik Handal, the candidate for mayor of San Salvador. Individual women from ARENA and secondary representatives from the Christian Democrats (PDC) also attended the presentation of the platform.

There were fourteen demands in the main version of the platform.[25] Of those, nine could be considered feminist, as they represented a direct challenge to power dynamics between men and women. Those points included demands for "comprehensive sex education without prejudice," "free and voluntary motherhood" (a euphemism for contraception and abortion rights), and "fifty percent of leadership positions for women." Another three of the fourteen demands could be called feminine, for they addressed women's interests within the gender division of labor in El Salvador, but without directly challenging male power. These included a call for "stabilization of food prices" and "more and better public hospitals." The final two demands could be either feminist or feminine, depending on the interpretation.

The parties were left to consider these demands until the beginning of the new year, when they were called to a public debate. Partisan response to that debate, like the response to the initial presentation, was lukewarm. Once again, the Left coalition and the PDC were the only parties to send official representatives.

Finally, the parties were asked to commit to the platform in a signing ceremony held on 8 March 1994, International Women's Day. This time, the PDC did not send an official representative, but ARENA did. So the final version of the platform was signed by Rubén Zamora, of the left-wing coalition and Gloria Salguero Gross, of the right-wing ARENA party.

While it is undeniable that the partisan response to the platform was less than ecstatic, the two parties that endorsed the platform were the two top vote getters. The Coalition and ARENA won 73.9 percent of the votes cast in the election of March 1994. They were the two participants in the run-off election

[25] Not surprisingly, the platform is very long. One version of the platform lists seventy-eight demands, another lists sixty-three demands. An illustrated popular education booklet lists thirty-three demands. Posters were distributed with a list of fourteen demands. Finally, an even more reduced list of ten demands was presented to the parties. Mujeres 94, "Plataforma de las Mujeres Salvadoreñas: Edición Popular"; Mujeres 94, "Plataforma de las Mujeres Salvadoreñas," unpublished document, (31 August 1993); Mujeres 94, "Compromisos De Los Candidatos(as) Con El Movimiento De Mujeres De El Salvador," unpublished document, 8 March 1994; Julio Soro et al., *Como Los Partidos Políticos Incluyen A Las Mujeres En Sus Plataformas Políticas* (San Salvador: Red por la Unidad y el Desarollo de las Mujeres Salvadoreñas, 1994); U.S.–El Salvador Institute for Democratic Development, "Platform of the Women of El Salvador," unpublished document, 1994.

held in April of that year, which ARENA won easily.[26] Arguably, Women '94 achieved its partisan goals by gaining the endorsement of the two biggest parties in the country.

But that begs the question: what did endorsement mean? In the case of ARENA, the answer seems to be not much, at least in the short term. One week after Gloria Salguero Gross signed the platform in the name of ARENA and four days before the election, ARENA celebrated the "grand closing" of the "women's crusade." At this "very important event," the wives of the presidential and vice-presidential candidates presented a document that contained "the principal necessities and aspirations of the Salvadoran woman."[27]

ARENA's document on women was presented by women whose status within the party was that of wife, rather than by any of ARENA's female candidates. The symbolism of this choice is fairly straightforward and was reinforced by ARENA's platform, which mentions women only three times. Women were promised subsidies to "mother-infant programs," implementation of a new family code to "protect women, children and old people," and nutritious rations for "pregnant mothers and children."[28] The authors of a study of the platforms conclude that the "analysis that we have done of ARENA's platform, both in its general proposals for society, and its specific proposals for women, demonstrates a profound opposition to all that is demanded in the Women '94 platform."[29]

The impact of the Women '94 platform on ARENA's platform was quite limited at best. Still, it would have been too much to expect a far-right party like ARENA to give a strong endorsement to a feminist platform. In fact, personal animosities between most members of the women's movement and ARENA that had built up over the course of the war could have led ARENA to conduct an anti-feminist campaign like Violeta Chamorro did. That ARENA conducted a fairly gender-neutral campaign and that it signed the Women '94 platform represents a small step forward in feminist influence within right-wing party politics in El Salvador.

But what of feminists' relationships with the left-wing coalition, and especially the largest coalition member, the FMLN? To what extent did feminists have an impact on the coalition's campaign? The official platforms of the parties that made up the coalition were almost all more feminist-friendly than ARENA's platform. Those platforms referred to women more frequently than did ARENA's and, most importantly, the platforms of the three members of the leftist coalition and that of the Christian Democrats explicitly addressed the problem of discrimination against women, which ARENA's platform did not.[30]

[26] Spence et al., *El Salvador*, 37.
[27] Advertisement, *El Diario de Hoy*, 15 March 1994.
[28] Julio Soro et al., *Como Los Partidos Políticos Incluyen A Las Mujeres*, 31–32.
[29] Ibid., 80.
[30] Ibid., 42.

Given that these platforms were not widely read, a better measure of feminist success may be what occurred at public events during the campaign. Women '94 was a very visible presence at some of the coalition's rallies through booths in which information was provided and Women '94 T-shirts were sold. Furthermore, the leaflets distributed by the FMLN at these rallies promised to fulfill many of the feminist's demands. In one pamphlet, entitled "Now's the Time for Real Solutions," ten promises were made that included combating delinquency, increasing employment, stabilizing prices, improving health and education, and promoting "the rights and participation of women." Another pamphlet was focused directly at women. Entitled "First our Demands: Woman, Vote for Yourself, Vote FMLN," the pamphlet outlined seven ways in which the FMLN would improve women's lives, all of which may have been taken directly from the Women '94 platform.

Most importantly, given the high levels of illiteracy in El Salvador, both pamphlets were illustrated with progressive images of gender relations including a little boy standing on a box to cook, two women working as carpenters, women and men receiving land, and a female member of the new National Civilian Police stopping a knife-wielding delinquent. Through words and images, the leftist coalition (and especially the FMLN) identified themselves with organized feminism.

EXPLAINING THE ELECTORAL DIFFERENCES

The national elections that marked the end of the civil wars in Nicaragua and El Salvador were both highly gendered, but in ways that could not have been more different. In Nicaragua, an electoral campaign with a strong gender content was greeted with feminist silence, while in El Salvador, a campaign with little overt gender content was met with a loud and persistent response from feminists.

Why were such different choices made during these transitional electoral campaigns? One possible explanation might be that the Nicaraguan women's movement did not wish to play a greater role, because it is inherently less feminist and more partisan than the Salvadoran women's movement. But that theory was disproved by events following the 1990 elections, when independent, nonpartisan feminism fairly exploded in Nicaragua.[31] I will argue that the differences were not because of inherent differences in the political culture of the two

---

[31] On the women's movement after 1990, see Norma Stoltz Chinchilla, "Feminism, Revolution, and Democratic Transitions in Nicaragua" in Jaquette, ed., *The Women's Movement in Latin America*; Ana Criquillon, "The Nicaraguan Women's Movement: Feminist Reflections from Within" in Minor Sinclair, ed., *The New Politics of Survival: Grassroots Movements in Central America* (New York: Monthly Review Press, 1995); Margaret Randall, *Sandino's Daughters Revisited: Feminism in Nicaragua* (New Brunswick, NJ: Rutgers University Press, 1994); Margaret Randall, *Gathering Rage: The Failure of 20th Century Revolutions to Develop a Feminist Agenda* (New York: Monthly Review Press, 1992).

countries or their movements. Rather, they were a legacy of Central American politics in the 1970s and 1980s.

The two countries have much in common. Both the FSLN and the FMLN began their political lives as guerrilla movements that mobilized large numbers of women (and men) as armed combatants and in support work.[32] But there was one crucial difference. The FSLN of Nicaragua overthrew the Somoza dictatorship in 1979 and then governed the country for over a decade until it lost the election of 1990. While the FMLN represented a significant threat to the military-dominated government of El Salvador (holding up to a third of the national territory for a period of years[33]), it never managed to overthrow the national government.

First, the central factor that explains the differences in the role of organized feminists in the first post-civil war elections is the history of the revolutionary organizations in the previous decades, only one of which benefited from the economic and political power that is inherent in controlling the state.

My second argument is that because the FSLN controlled the state for over a decade, it had considerable control over would-be feminist dissidents within the revolutionary coalition. Feminism existed as an undercurrent in social movement politics within Nicaragua throughout the revolutionary decade. But it could not break the surface (feminists could not seek autonomy), because the Sandinista party had enough political and economic power to keep possibly threatening feminist currents submerged. In contrast, the FMLN never had control of the state and its concomitant economic and political power. Therefore, the FMLN was forced to reach out to its feminist base during the first post-civil war election campaign through ideological appeals. The FSLN felt the need to make no such appeal.

[32] Compared with previous guerrilla movements in Latin America, women participated in the guerrilla struggles in Nicaragua (1961–1979) and El Salvador (1970–1992) in unusually large numbers. Within the FSLN of Nicaragua, an estimated 30 percent of the combatants and many guerrilla leaders were women. See Helen Collinson, ed., *Women and Revolution in Nicaragua* (Atlantic Highlands, NJ: Zed Books, 1990), 154; Patricia Flynn, "Women Challenge the Myth" in Stanford Central American Network, ed., *Revolution in Central America*, (Boulder, CO: Westview Press, 1983), 416; Linda Lobao Reif, "Women in Latin American Guerrilla Movements," *Comparative Politics* 18 (January 1986): 158. In contrast, Carlos Vilas disputes the widespread belief that women comprised 30 percent of the FSLN's combatants, suggesting that the figure was closer to 6.6 percent. Carlos Vilas, *The Sandinista Revolution: National Liberation and Social Transformation in Central America* (New York: Monthly Review Press, 1986), 108–109. Approximately 40 percent of the FMLN membership, 30 percent of the combatants, and 20 percent of the military leadership were women. See Mason, "Women's Participation in Central American Revolutions," 65; Tommie Sue Montgomery, *Revolution in El Salvador: From Civil Strife to Civil Peace*, (Boulder, CO: Westview Press, 1995), 123. In the case of the FMLN, these estimates were confirmed during the process of demobilization, which was supervised by the United Nations Observor Group in El Salvador (ONUSAL). 29.2 percent of the 8,506 combatants and 35.5 percent of the 4,093 FMLN *políticos* (political personnel) that were registered by ONUSAL were women. See Ilja Luciak, "Women in the Transition: The Case of the Female FMLN Combatants in El Salvador" (paper presented at the conference of the Latin American Studies Association in Washington DC, 28–30 September 1995), 3.

[33] Eric Selbin, *Modern Latin American Revolutions* (Boulder, CO: Westview Press, 1993), 145.

Finally, the third factor that helps explain the role played by feminism and antifeminism in the first post-civil war elections also flows out of the political history of the previous two decades. The personal histories of the candidates, especially the role they had played during the civil wars, limited their abilities to launch certain kinds of campaigns, and made it possible for them to launch other kinds.

The Importance of Controlling the State

While women were active participants in the struggle to overthrow the Somoza dictatorship, the guerrilla struggle was not a feminist one. Initially, women tended to justify their active involvement in the guerrilla movement in terms of feminine interests. Armed struggle was a new way of fulfilling an old female role: the protection of children. As Gloria Carrión explained: "The widespread repression, and particularly the way this repression centered on our youth, outraged women of all classes. The repression was so bad that it was a crime just to be young. . . . We had outright political assassinations of children eight, nine, ten years old."[34] Out of such early defenses of feminine interests, feminist thinking would sometimes develop. For instance, Ana Criquillon, a long-time feminist activist, talked about her work with women in the eastern neighborhoods of Managua: "I was not a feminist when I arrived in Nicaragua [in 1972]; I worked with Christian women. . . . They were housewives, almost none of them had graduated from high school. . . . Afterwards I realized that the majority had safe houses. It was the first case of consciousness raising without our realizing what we were doing."[35]

With the Sandinista's triumphant march into Managua on 19 July 1979, the transformation of Nicaraguan society expanded. In recognition of their role in the guerrilla struggle, women were a central part of that transformation, especially in the early 1980s. One important channel for women's participation was through the women's movement, which underwent some changes after the Sandinistas took power. AMPRONAC,[36] the women's organization affiliated with the Sandinistas during the guerrilla struggle, changed its name to AMNLAE,[37] and went public. State-movement relations represented a break with the past. Instead of the antagonism between AMPRONAC and the Somocista state, there was cooperation between AMNLAE and the Sandinista state.

Starting in July 1979, the state was transformed in multiple ways, many of which directly affected women. This transformation included legal reform, the expansion of adult education and formal education, the opening of state-funded day care centers, the beginning of a campaign against domestic vio-

---

[34] Quoted in Randall, *Sandino's Daughters*, 13.
[35] Ana Criquillon, interview with author, 6 June 1991.
[36] AMPRONAC stood for the Asociación de Mujeres Ante La Problemática Nacional.
[37] AMNLAE stood for the Asociación de Mujeres Nicaragüenses Luisa Amanda Espinoza.

lence, and the nationalization of health care.[38] While most of the reforms that transformed women's conditions could be called feminine (that is, they improved women's lives without challenging power dynamics between men and women), some Sandinista reforms, especially in the first few years of the revolution, were genuinely feminist and therefore very controversial.[39]

Close ties to the FSLN meant that AMNLAE rightfully shared some of the credit for Sandinista reforms. Early in the Sandinista period, the organization's main goal was to provide support for the government's programs. AMNLAE provided support for the male-dominated FSLN, without directly challenging sexual inequality. In 1980, AMNLAE hoped that its 25,000 members would "defend the revolution by joining the popular militias; participate in organizations that directed state policy in areas like education, health, supplies, employment and salaries; fight for legal equality and the creation of childcare centers; join the literacy campaign; create health brigades, control contraband and hoarding and encourage productive collectives of women."[40]

One of the ways that AMNLAE sought to put many government policies into practice was through Women's Houses that were built in all the regions of Nicaragua, fifty-two by the early 1990s. These houses served as intermediaries between the state and individuals by providing services in the areas of health, psychological counseling, and legal counseling, as well as workshops in areas such as sexuality, contraception, and job training.[41] AMNLAE played a crucial role as a link between the state and the population in all of these endeavors.

But in this link a contradiction arose, which became more acute over time. AMNLAE ended up devoting tremendous resources to preserving the power and legitimacy of the Sandinista-controlled state. What might have been a reasonable assumption that the further emancipation of women was dependent on the well-being of their emancipator, the FSLN, was to eventually undermine the movement. The contra war that dominated the mid-1980s exposed the contradictions inherent in the assumption.[42]

[38] Collinson, *Women and Revolution in Nicaragua*; Maxine Molyneux, "The Politics of Abortion in Nicaragua: Revolutionary Pragmatism—or Feminism in the Realm of Necessity?" *Feminist Review* 29 (May 1988); Maxine Molyneux, "Mobilization without Emancipation? Women's Interests, the State, and Revolution" in Richard Fagen et al., eds., *Transition and Development: Problems of Third World Socialism* (New York: Monthly Review Press, 1986); Martha Luz Padilla et al., "Impact of the Sandinista Agrarian Reform on Rural Women's Subordination" in Carmen Diana Deere and Magdalena León, eds., *Rural Women and State Policy* (Boulder, CO: Westview Press, 1987); Lois Wessel, "Reproductive Rights in Nicaragua: From the Sandinistas to the Government of Violeta Chamorro," *Feminist Studies* 17 (Fall 1991).

[39] Karen Kampwirth, "Legislating Personal Politics in Sandinista Nicaragua, 1979–1992," *Women's Studies International Forum* 21 (Winter 1998).

[40] Clara Murguialday, *Nicaragua, revolución y feminismo (1977–89)* (Madrid: Editorial Revolución, 1990), 104.

[41] María Dolores Alvarez (director of AMNLAE's Documentation Center), interview with author, November 1990; Irene Rojas (director of AMNLAE's Erlinda López house), interview with author, 26 March 1991.

[42] Peter Rosset and John Vandermeer, eds., *Nicaragua: Unfinished Revolution* (New York: Grove Press, 1986); Edgar Chamorro, *Packaging the Contras: A Case of CIA Disinformation* (New York:

Some activists who continued to work within AMNLAE in the early 1990s admitted that they made mistakes in their relationship with the party. Too often, they said, AMNLAE played the role of the "submissive wife of the FSLN." This submission may have been the legacy of the movement's origin as a semiclandestine FSLN affiliate. It was certainly enhanced by the dual crises of war and economic embargo.

Klemen Altamirano, a sociologist from the Masaya Women's Center, suggested that the mobilization of older mothers to the exclusion of others, the caution which characterized their mobilization and, more generally, AMNLAE's relationship with the state were all products of the contra war. "Because of the war it was necessary to use up many resources, resources that were not just material but also ideological. That was part of the fall of the FSLN."[43]

One of the ideological resources that might have been lost in the war was the political courage to mobilize older women to challenge their vulnerability rather than to glorify it. They might have mobilized them in a way that questioned rather than reinforced women's traditional submission. In other words, had the party felt less vulnerable, it might have been willing to take some feminist risks. Those risks could have had the ultimate benefit, from the party's perspective, of building the commitment of older mothers for a revolutionary agenda. Instead, by reinforcing the traditional role of mothers, the FSLN unwittingly supported the logic used effectively by the UNO in the 1990 election. According to the UNO's position, good mothers should protect their children from war and that meant voting against the FSLN. Ironically, measures that were taken to ensure the longevity of the FSLN ultimately may have contributed to its electoral loss.

AMNLAE and, indirectly, the FSLN helped to create the feminist movement by opening a space for it to develop that had been closed before 1979. But the FSLN was unwilling to grant feminists the autonomy they would have needed to lead a campaign like Women '94 in El Salvador. The Sandinista party made the common assumption that feminists had nowhere to go and so would never desert them in 1990. The party assumed that its ability to control and coopt feminists meant that it was free to lead an electoral campaign that was not meant to appeal to feminists but rather to the elusive middle-of-the-road voter.

The FSLN had been publicly committed to ending gender inequality from as early as 1969. It then presided over more than a decade of revolutionary rule in which women were actively mobilized and some feminist reforms were enacted. That led many Nicaraguans to associate feminism with Sandinismo and antifeminism with anti-Sandinismo. Ironically, limited but real feminist successes over the course of the previous decades left the Nicaraguan public open

Institute for Media Analysis, 1987); Roger N. Lancaster, *Life Is Hard: Machismo, Danger, and the Intimacy of Power in Nicaragua* (Berkeley: University of California Press, 1992).
[43] Klemen Altamirano, interview with author, 3 February 1991.

to an antifeminist campaign, which forced feminists into silent support for the Sandinistas, just at the time when many of them wanted to break away from the FSLN.

In contrast, the FMLN did not enter its first post-civil war election at the end of over a decade of political rule. Instead, it entered that electoral campaign at the end of over a decade of guerrilla war, which had resulted in stalemate. The FMLN did not have the ability to coopt and control feminists that its Nicaraguan counterpart had. So it was in its interest to try a different electoral strategy. Rather than try to mobilize middle-of-the-road voters over gender issues, it tried to mobilize its base (including feminists and other women's movement activists) with ideological promises.

But having a party that is receptive to social movement appeals is not enough. Social movements needs to be capable of making those appeals. In El Salvador, they were. Salvadoran feminists did have the autonomy they needed to participate in electoral politics

Organizational Legacies of the Civil Wars

The relationship between the political parties and women's organizations, some of which later became feminist organizations, first took shape during the guerrilla struggle. Since many of the political parties and most of the social movements that are active today first emerged out of the civil wars, they have particular characteristics that differ from parties and movements in many other countries. One is that social movements have had a hard time influencing these parties from within. This difficulty is rooted in hierarchical decision-making traditions developed over years of guerrilla struggle, which may have been appropriate in wartime, but which are quite inappropriate once the war is over.

The simple declaration of political party status does not always equip former guerrilla organizations to face the challenges of competitive politics. After the transformation of these guerrilla movements into political parties in 1979 in Nicaragua and in 1992 in El Salvador, tensions which had been submerged during the guerrilla wars reemerged, as the wildly differing agendas within the revolutionary coalitions became apparent. One of the tensions that had been submerged by these wars was the debate over feminist reform.

A further factor that shaped the relationship between feminist movements and the leftwing parties was the priority given to work against inequalities rooted in class, rather than inequalities rooted in gender. Most obviously, this tendency derived from the influence of Marxism both as theory and as experienced in socialist countries. This preferential option for the poor (and not for women, or for gays, or for indigenous people) also emerged out of radical Catholicism. Whatever the origins of the tendency, it made it harder for feminist movements to gain a voice within these parties than for other kinds of social movements, such as unions. The FSLN's and FMLN's self-image was of parties that sided with the most vulnerable, generally understood in class terms. This created difficulties for those social movements, such as the feminist movements, which often incorporated class concerns into their work but were not fundamentally class-based movements.

To gain a voice within their parties, many social movements found it necessary to seek autonomy from the parties. In Nicaragua, the quest for autonomy came years after the transformation of the FSLN into a party; in El Salvador it came nearly at the same time as the FMLN became a party. In 1990, Nicaraguan feminist activists faced the dilemma that universally faces radicals within coalitional political parties—those on the left end of left-center coalitions like the FSLN, or those on the right end of right-center coalitions.[44] In the absence of another politically viable option, leaving the party is not a very plausible threat.[45] On the other hand, staying within the coalition but vocally criticizing it is also a risky strategy. It might mainly benefit the coalition's opponents. Given the tone of the UNO's campaign, feminists may well have thought the risk of a UNO victory was simply too high; better to support the FSLN, despite its imperfections.

This explanation however, implies that Salvadoran feminists should have been equally cautious during their first postwar election in 1994. They, too, represented the left wing (measured in terms of gender politics) within a left-center coalition. Yet they chose to vocally criticize and pressure the political parties. For even though Salvadoran feminists faced the same electoral dilemma faced by Nicaraguan feminists, they faced it with a considerably greater degree of movement autonomy.

While a few independent feminists groups broke off from the Sandinista-affiliated women's movement in the late 1980s, the vast majority of Nicaraguan feminists remained in organizations that were closely tied to the Sandinista party.[46] In Nicaragua, the height of the autonomy struggle took place in 1991 and 1992. The autonomy struggle was important, for it reshaped social movement/party relations, but it was too late to influence the 1990 election and possibly too early to influence the 1996 election.

[44] See Anthony Downs, *An Economic Theory of Democracy* (New York: Harper and Row, 1957); Duane Oldfield, *The Right and the Righteous: The Christian Right Confronts the Republican Party*, (Lanham, MD: Rowman and Littlefield, 1996); Ronald Walters, *Black Presidential Politics in America: A Strategic Approach* (Albany: State University of New York Press, 1988).

[45] Arguably, this thesis that radicals will tend to stay in large parties only applies in a simple-majority single ballot system. Proportional representation favors multiple parties, since small radical parties may plausibly win some offices. Maurice Duverger, *Political Parties: Their Organization in the Modern State* (New York: John Wiley, 1963), 239. In Nicaragua and El Salvador, these arguments are far less clear-cut, since the electoral systems are amalgams of simple-majority and proportional representation, with different rules for presidential, congressional, and municipal offices, all of which may be determined in a single election.

[46] Randall, *Sandino's Daughters Revisited*; Midge Quandt, *Unbinding The Ties: The Popular Organizations And The FSLN In Nicaragua*, (Washington, DC: Nicaragua Network Education Fund, 1993).

In El Salvador the height of the autonomy struggle took place between 1990 and 1992. But while the two autonomy struggles took place at about the same time if measured in real time, they did not occur simultaneously if measured in electoral time. In contrast to the Nicaraguan case, the Salvadoran feminist autonomy struggle occurred at a very propitious time to influence the first postwar election in El Salvador.

The Salvadoran autonomy battle was early enough but not too early in relation to the 1994 election, so that a number of organizations had enough autonomy to speak to the political parties from without. But the energy generated in the autonomy battle might have been dissipated had that battle occurred years before the election. The lost resources that are the price of autonomy catch up with organizers in the conditions of extreme poverty that characterize Central America.

The role of social movement autonomy in electoral politics (and, by implication, in democratization) is contradictory. In El Salvador, the increased autonomy of feminist organizations had some democratizing effects upon national politics. Feminist demands for improvements in the quality of life of the majority of the population were inserted into party discourse, if sometimes unenthusiastically. If any of those demands are met, then women will have increased opportunities for participation in national politics and for gaining influence over the future development of those politics. The promise of democratic participation will have been realized to a greater extent than if feminists had remained silent.

But autonomy is not an unmitigated good. Despite the inherent disadvantages, there are many advantages to affiliation with a political party. Parties can provide a space for gaining organizing experience, and they can provide critical material resources. The same guerrillas-converted-into-parties that eventually constrained these Central American feminists were also to a large degree initially responsible for the emergence of feminism within what remained profoundly sexist societies. Cutting the ties that constrained feminists also meant cutting some of the resources that sustained them. At the height of the autonomy struggle, the advantage of autonomy probably outweighed the costs of lost resources; after the initial autonomy struggle, the costs of those lost resources become more apparent.

A number of Nicaraguan feminists observers suggested to me in 1994 and 1995 that the energy of the autonomy battle might have worn off, as groups were torn apart by infighting over limited resources. The campaign leading up to the October 1996 election in Nicaragua reenergized the feminist movement to a limited extent. But political divisions within Nicaragua, within the parties as well as the social movements, also created an opportunity for another anti-politics candidate similar to doña Violeta, far-right populist, Arnoldo Alemán, now president of Nicaragua. The case of Nicaragua suggests that there is a thin line between political autonomy and political fragmentation.

Personal Histories of the Candidates

The history of guerrilla war and revolutionary government that shaped the ideological reputation of the parties and the relationship of the social movements with those parties also shaped the sorts of people that candidates were. That legacy created strategic opportunities for some candidates and limited the options of others.

Violeta Chamorro was in a better position than any of the other major presidential candidates to run an antifeminist, antiwar campaign. All the other presidential candidates, with the exception of one minor candidate in El Salvador, were men. While in theory, male candidates could run on an antifeminist platform, they could easily be accused of being antiwoman, something no candidate wants, since women are allowed to vote. But making an antiwoman accusation stick on Violeta Chamorro would have been difficult. Another reason why only Violeta Chamorro could have run this sort of campaign against the civil war (and the implied link between war and feminism) was that she was the only major candidate in either country who had not been directly involved in the civil war.

Finally, doña Violeta's near total lack of political experience meant that her best option was to run on her record as a mother. Daniel Ortega's strategy, while also gendered, was not an attempt to express a gendered message but was instead an effort to run away from the economic disaster and civil war of the 1980s. It could be argued that a more confrontational campaign emphasizing the many positive aspects of the Sandinista record, including the feminist elements of that record, might have been more effective. But it would have been very hard for Daniel to attack doña Violeta (an older women who spent most of her campaign in a wheelchair with her leg in a cast) without coming across as a bully, a typical *machista* man.

In the Salvadoran case, both the leftwing coalition and the rightwing ARENA party had many members who had been directly involved in the civil war. The main member of the coalition, the FMLN, had been a guerrilla group only two years earlier, while the ARENA party and its presidential candidate Armando Calderón Sol were closely linked to the death squads responsible for most of the violence of the war. So neither party could convincingly run on a pacifist antiwar platform. Instead, both tried to downplay the legacy of the civil war.

But either party might have utilized a gendered campaign instead of the bland politically empty campaigns that both chose. They did not, because an antifeminist campaign would have seemed vulgar to many and because neither of the major parties was particularly feminist. Furthermore, ARENA members assumed, correctly I believe, that few if any feminists would consider voting for ARENA, and coalition members assumed that they could count on feminist votes in exchange for very little.

CONCLUSIONS

I have argued that the gendered differences in these elections were principally due to three factors. The main difference between the two cases is that the FSLN of Nicaragua succeeded in overthrowing the Somoza dictatorship and governing for over a decade. In contrast, the FMLN never succeeded in overthrowing the militarized government of El Salvador. The other two factors flow out of this central difference. Because of the long period of Sandinista rule, organized feminists in Nicaragua were much less autonomous and much less able to organize independently than their counterparts in El Salvador at the time of the first post-civil war elections. Finally, the electoral strategies that candidates chose were shaped by their personal histories. Because she had not participated actively in the war, Violeta Chamorro had the option of running on the image of a long-suffering mother who preferred familial reconciliation to war. In El Salvador, members of both major parties were actively involved in the civil war and so could not take pacifist, antiwar positions, but instead had to downplay the war's legacy.

The legacy of the civil war years in both cases severely constrained the electoral strategies of certain actors and opened up opportunities for others. Social movements helped set the stage for the elections, both as organizations with relations to the guerrillas and the political parties, and as carriers of ideas that then became associated with certain parties. Yet, once the election campaigns began in each country, the formerly fluid rules of politics began to solidify. The gendered outcomes in both cases were as much a function of relations between the women's movements, the guerrillas, and the political parties in the period leading up to the elections as they were due to the role of women's movements in the election campaigns themselves.

Election campaigns are dynamic events in which social movements may play significant roles. However, as this comparison showed, there is no guarantee that social movements will choose to or be able to participate in these events. If they do not do so, the extent to which they will be a democratizing force is necessarily limited. So those who assert the democratizing potential of social movements need to pay more attention to the mechanisms of formal politics. It is often through these mechanisms that a potential becomes a reality.

These cases also suggest room for improvement in the way elections are studied by political scientists. Mainstream election studies, with their emphasis on numerical results and polling data, do a good job of analyzing formal shifts of power as parties are voted in and out of office. But they often do a poor job of analyzing more informal shifts of power. Here attention to social movements could enhance our understanding of electoral politics. The informal shifts in societal power that often result from campaigns have as much to do with the role of social movements throughout the campaign and the images and rhetoric utilized by candidates as they do with the final vote.

This distinction between formal shifts and informal shifts was illustrated in comparing the first post-civil war elections in Nicaragua and El Salvador. In both of those elections, the right-wing parties won. And yet the power dynamics that resulted from the campaigns were quite different, if seen from the perspective of organized feminists. A better nuanced view of power dynamics will be gained by students of both social movements and elections if the interactions between movements and parties are located at the center of more of our studies.*

*I am grateful to Cynthia Enloe, Duane Oldfield, Eric Selbin, and Jack Spence for their insightful comments on earlier drafts of this article.

From Clientelism to Cooperation:
Local Government, Participatory Policy,
and Civic Organizing in Porto Alegre, Brazil

REBECCA ABERS

A growing number of scholars and policy makers agree that improving the quality of life in impoverished urban areas—both in the "First" and "Third" Worlds—depends on the capacity of local residents to form social networks and civic organizations. Much recent work argues that such capacity will only develop with the retreat of the state, which has historically worked against the capacity of communities to help themselves by paternalistically providing services and welfare directly to individuals and, in some cases (especially in the Third World), by repressing civic groups outright. Some recent studies, however, have shown that state actors can actually promote the empowerment rather than the weakening of civic organizations. This article looks at one particularly impressive example of such *state-fostered civic organizing*.

Since 1989, the local government of Porto Alegre, a city of 1.3 million people in southern Brazil, has implemented what it calls the "participatory budget." One of the central goals of this policy is to hand over decisions about the distribution of municipal funds for basic capital improvements—paved streets, drainage and sewer investments, school construction, and so on—to neighborhood-based forums. The policy has fostered a dramatic increase in neighborhood activism in the poorest neighborhoods of the city, with over 14,000 people participating each year in budget assemblies. Innumerable new neighborhood organizations have appeared in response to the policy, often in areas that were previously dominated by closed, ineffective associations that served as little more than tools of clientelist party politics. The Porto Alegre policy has combined a substantial amount of

POLITICS & SOCIETY, Vol. 26 No. 4, December 1998 511-537
© 1998 Sage Publications, Inc.

government investment in social programs with a successful state-sponsored effort at capacitating civic groups to control that investment and, in doing so, to dramatically improve their quality of life.

This article will examine how this process of civic empowerment occurred.[1] The next section will consider the role that state actors can play in helping those with little previous experience to begin to organize collectively. I then go on to briefly examine the history of neighborhood associationalism in Porto Alegre and to describe the budget policy. The main body of the article looks at one district of the city that, prior to 1989, had virtually no experience with broad-based, participatory civic organizing, showing how the budget policy mobilized neighborhood groups, discouraged clientelist forms of neighborhood action, and promoted the emergence of participatory groups that not only struggled collectively to bring benefits to their neighborhoods but also learned to work in collaboration with other neighborhood groups in the pursuit of broader goals.

Clientelism, Associationalism, and the State

It has often been suggested that strong democratic institutions will only emerge once strong civic groups have formed that can, essentially, force the state to represent them. That is, the organization of civil society is a prior condition for democratization. In an influential 1993 study, for example, Putnam[2] argues that the primary explanation for the rise of democratic institutions in northern Italy is that region's long history of civic organizing, a legacy that goes back nearly a thousand years. The result is a rather deterministic view of democratization: only those regions that have an ingrained culture of associationalism are likely to develop a responsive, accountable, participatory state. Others have suggested, however, that a culture of civic organization can be created in places where communities do not benefit from such legacies. In their recent work on "associational democracy," for example, Cohen and Rogers[3] argue that associative environments are "artifactual." Networks of civic organizations can be created and transformed as political circumstances, institutional environments, and balances of power change. With this possibility as a starting point, this article will explore how, under certain circumstances, state actors can be the transformative force that helps promote the growth of associationalism.

Lacking the long civic history of northern Italy, Brazil much more closely resembles the Italian south, where Putnam argues that clientelist traditions have almost inexorably suppressed the emergence of organized civil society. In political systems dominated by clientelism, those in power use their access to state resources to provide personal favors to a broad-based clientele who, in turn, mobilize votes for their patrons. In Brazil, clientelist traditions have led to the development of vast political machines that link local bosses to state-level and federal politicians through such *troca de favores*, or favor exchange. In the cities, neighborhood associations play a critical role in these linkages. *Cabos eleitorais*, or ward bosses, head up a large percentage if not most neighborhood associations and use them to mobilize votes for their party candidates by conveying promises of favors to local residents.[4]

Associations that are linked to clientelist schemes are typically characterized by their closed, nonparticipatory character. Unlike protest-based, collective organizations that use the power of numbers to pressure politicians, they procure community benefits through an exclusive relationship between association leaders and their political higher-ups. Within clientelist systems, clients are discouraged from building up social ties with one another. Instead, relationships "are *based on individual ties to a leader* rather than on shared characteristics or horizontal ties among followers."[5] In the context of clientelism, more participatory forms of civic organizing are rare for two reasons: on one hand, there are few incentives to collective organizing since the privileged mode of obtaining benefits is not through protest and pressure but through personal favor exchanges articulated by a single neighborhood leader. On the other hand, because there is little reason to organize collectively, people have little previous experience with cooperative action. As Putnam notes, in a context where "two clients of the same patron, lacking direct ties . . . have no occasion to develop a norm of generalized reciprocity and no history of mutual collaboration to draw on,"[6] people have little information about how others are likely to act that might lead them to believe that cooperation might be fruitful. For Putnam, this lack of incentives and experience creates a vicious circle of nonorganization that is exceedingly difficult to break. Where cooperation is unusual, people lack the basis of mutual trust (at least outside of family ties). The result is high degrees of discord and individual isolation that make organizing difficult.[7]

Yet a number of recent authors have shown that certain types of state institutions, usually implanted "from above" by reformers, can build up civic activism among groups that have little previous experience with community-based cooperation. In a recent issue of *World Development*, Peter Evans brings together a series of studies that demonstrate how such state-fostered civic empowerment can occur.[8] Ostrom describes a participatory sewer construction policy in Recife, Brazil, where participation was directly facilitated by government officials.[9] Lam argues that the success of a decentralized irrigation policy in Taiwan grew out of the close and flexible relations between government workers and farmer participants.[10] Fox argues that even in the context of authoritarianism, reformers within the Mexican government were able to promote policies that gave power to and strengthened peasant organizations.[11] In related work, Tendler writes of how government practice in the Brazilian state of Ceará rapidly moved "from bad to good" with the implementation of policies that included efforts by the state government to assist directly in the organization of civil associations in the municipalities.[12] In all of these cases, both the close ties that developed between government officials and citizens and the fact that the state policies explicitly encouraged civic

organizing led not only to strengthening civic groups but also to a growing political capacity of those organizations to pressure for government accountability and
effective policy. The importance of what Evans calls "state-society synergy" suggests that the relationship between civil society and strong democratic institutions
is far from a simple, one-way, bottom-up process.

To understand how state actors can promote associationalism, it is useful to
look at how the literature on social movements has explored what causes people to
mobilize. Many authors have noted that purely economic explanations are not sat-
isfactory: associationalism does not seem to be related to certain levels of misery
or well-being. Instead, political factors seem to best explain why civic organizing
booms at certain times and places and not others. General changes in political
conditions provide "windows of opportunity" in which *enabling environments*
emerge that make people believe that collective action is likely to be fruitful.[13]
'Social movements form when ordinary citizens, sometimes encouraged by leaders, respond to changes in opportunities that lower the costs of collective action,
reveal potential allies and show where elites and authorities are vulnerable."[14]

At the same time, studies have shown that poor people's movements often only
mobilize with the direct help of outsiders. *External agents* can help people acquire
financial resources and political skills for taking advantage of windows of opportunity. Those who have more resources—disaffected elites who sympathize with
a cause or organized groups seeking to build up potential allies—can provide the
funding and the technical skills that make it possible for those with few resources
or previous experience to mobilize.[15] In Latin America, the Catholic church, student activists, left-wing militants, nongovernmental organizations, and liberal
professionals have historically played a critical role in helping popular organizations get off the ground.[16]

For the most part, the social movement literature envisions the state's impact
on civic organizing as an indirect one. The state is seen as highly unlikely actually
to encourage autonomous civic groups to form, and any attempt on the part of the
state to act as an "external agent," directly intervening in local communities to
help associations gain organizing capacity, is often assumed to be no more than an
attempt to co-opt them. Porto Alegre provides us with an unusual example in
which state reformers took on a more proactive role, not only providing an *enabling environment*, in which the formation of civic groups was explicitly promoted, but also working directly and closely with local communities to help them
organize.[17] Examining how this occurred can help us rethink the potential relationship between state and civil society.

NEIGHBORHOOD ORGANIZATIONS AND THE
PARTICIPATORY BUDGET POLICY IN PORTO ALEGRE

In the twenty-year democratic period prior to the 1964 military coup, Socie-
dades de Amigos de Bairro, or Neighborhood Friends Societies (SABs), began to

appear throughout Brazilian cities. These early neighborhood associations, formed largely by poor residents seeking the extension of social services into their neighborhoods, rarely mobilized large numbers. Preferring instead to negotiate with local politicians, association leaders would rally neighborhood votes in exchange for promises of investments once their candidates were elected. As they gained political importance over the 1950s and early 1960s, SABs expanded dramatically in Brazil's booming cities.[18] In Porto Alegre, most were connected to the Partido Trabalhista Brasileiro (PTB), a center-left populist party with a discourse of working-class rights and a practice of using strong-hand tactics to co-opt civic organizations and labor unions. In 1959, a statewide umbrella organization of SABs, the Federação Riograndense de Associações Comunitárias e de Amigos de Bairro, or FRACAB, was created largely to coordinate clientelist relations between the associations and PTB political leaders.[19]

In 1964, the military took power in Brazil and the PTB was outlawed. FRACAB was taken over by ARENA, the military-aligned party. Those SABs that continued to be active did so by supporting the regime and by generally avoiding making demands. As the regime began to weaken after 1974, however, renewed possibilities for clientelist politics began to emerge as ARENA sought to generate backing for the regime by distributing patronage to supporters.[20] But in the late 1970s, dissatisfaction with the military spread throughout Brazil, and protest movements of all kinds began to gain strength. During the military period, a massive migration from the countryside had occurred, and Brazil's cities were swelling with impoverished settlements totally lacking in basic infrastructure. For the vast majority of neighborhoods, fragile promises and petty exchanges with local bosses were nowhere near capable of satisfying the need for public transportation, paved streets, running water, sewers, basic health care, and other services. At the same time, the weakening regime was becoming more responsive to popular demands. Within this window of opportunity, a new kind of neighborhood organization emerged in Brazilian cities that refused to play according to clientelist rules.

As elsewhere, in Porto Alegre, during this period a number of neighborhood groups began to challenge the clientelist leaders dominating local associations, creating more open and participatory organizations that sought to obtain benefits for their neighborhoods through pressure and protest rather than through personal, closed-door negotiations. With the help of "external agents"—such as progressive church activists and local nongovernmental organizations—groups of neighborhoods formed coalitions in the three districts of the city where such "combative" groups were strongest: the hillside squatter settlement areas of Cruzeiro and Glória and the working-class area in the northern (Norte) part of the city where most industries were located. In the early 1980s, massive demonstrations took place in these three districts as residents fought against relocation and demanded basic infrastructure. By the mid-1980s, these coalitions had become trong protest organizations that played an important role in local politics. Unlike lientelist associations, they were broad based and participatory, shunning per-ɔnal exchanges and backroom deal making. They were dominated by an ideol-gy of egalitarianism, equal rights, and grassroots participation, mobilizing large umbers of neighborhood residents.[21]

Nevertheless, such "combative" neighborhood groups never represented more ian about one-third of the city's neighborhood associations.[22] Although by the nd of the 1980s, several other districts of the city had formed similar neighbor-ood coalitions, most city neighborhoods were still dominated by clientelist asso-iations that had also been expanding, especially under the aegis of the Partido 'emocrático Trabalhista (PDT), the successor to the pre-coup PTB. The PDT had eveloped a powerful network of neighborhood leaders that helped elect it to the iayor's office in 1985. Vast impoverished districts of the periphery continued ιrgely unmobilized, with their only associations controlled by ward bosses work-ιg for political parties, who discouraged more participatory forms of organizing.

In 1988, in a surprise victory, Olivio Dutra, the "dark horse" candidate of the artido dos Trabalhadores, or PT, won the election for mayor of Porto Alegre. A ːmocratic-socialist party, the PT was founded in 1980, at the height of the protest ιovement against the military regime, out of a coalition of grassroots move-ιents, radical labor unions, and formerly revolutionary leftist militants and intel-ːctuals. Although it included many traditional left-wing activists among its)unding members, since the beginning the PT took care to distance itself from the ːntralism of earlier Brazilian socialist parties. The party was organized into ιuclei"—small groups in neighborhoods, schools, and workplaces that met, ιade decisions, and elected delegates to zonal, municipal, and regional party con-ːrences. The idea behind this "pyramidal" system was to ensure bottom-up deci-on making in which a large party base rooted in popular movements ideally ould have contact with the top leadership. Over the course of the 1980s, a ιguely defined conception formed within the party of a democratic system of ɔverning that would parallel the pyramidal party structure. The proposal was to ːvelop a system of "popular councils" in neighborhoods and workplaces that ould take over much of the work of local government decision making. By the ιd of the decade, the party platform centered on two themes: "the redirecting of ɔvernment priorities towards the poor" and "popular participation."[23]

In 1989, the PT came to office in Porto Alegre, proclaiming that participatory ɔuncils would be created in all areas of government decision making. But once in ower, the administration faced a number of difficulties in implementing these leas. The government structure was in disarray, left bankrupt by the previous ɟministration. The new administration, headed up by a group of activists with lit-e experience in governing, immediately discovered that simply providing basic ːrvices to the population would be an extremely difficult task. At the same time, lthough strong civic organizations existed in some parts of the city, most neighborhoods had no organizations that could effectively represent them in participatory forums. In this context, it took several years for participatory initiatives to get off the ground and even more time before neighborhoods in historically unmobilized districts of the city would begin to participate effectively.

The participatory budget policy was created in 1989 and, over the course of several years, became the central participatory effort of the administration. The city was divided into sixteen "budget districts" following the contours of the neighborhood coalitions and, where those did not exist, more general geographic features. Each year, two rounds of general assemblies were held in each of these districts, where government officials would present the public with general information about the city budget and where participants would elect their representatives to year-round forums. After the first assembly, meetings were held in each neighborhood, where residents would draw up lists of priorities for investment in seven categories ranging from street paving to storm drainage to school construction. Then, in the second assembly, delegates of each of the sixteen District Budget Forums would be elected. One out of every ten assembly participants could be elected to the forums, which would thus represent each neighborhood in the district in the proportion that they sent residents to the assemblies. At the second round of assemblies, each district also elected two members and two alternates to the citywide Municipal Budget Council. In the months following the big district assemblies, the delegates in District Budget Forums would negotiate among themselves to come up with districtwide "priority lists" of infrastructure projects in each investment category. The Municipal Budget Council would determine how to distribute funds for each category among districts. Then, each district's quota would be applied following the district priority lists so that those neighborhoods that had been given higher priority by the District Budget Forums would be the first to have their projects included in the following year's budget. Both the District Budget Forums and the Municipal Budget Council had broader tasks as well. The forums would monitor investments year-round and would engage in regular discussion with government personnel on issues related to service provision more generally. The council was responsible for overseeing the formulation of the entire city budget, approving the expenditure plans of each city agency. In 1994, five "thematic forums" were added into the process. Mirroring the district process, five large thematic assemblies elected delegate forums to debate broader policy areas such as economic development and health policy. The assemblies also sent members to an expanded Municipal Budget Council. But even with this addition, most participants continued to focus on discussing how neighborhood-level capital improvements should be distributed.

Elsewhere, I have explored at length how the participatory budget policy evolved over time and why it became a central policy of the PT administration while other participatory programs fell by the wayside.[24] Briefly, as the PT reorganized the administration, generated revenues by passing new tax laws and streamlining spending, and worked to build broader political support, it found that the budget policy was more viable than the other participatory efforts. On one hand, it clearly corresponded to the two PT party mottoes by promoting both popular participation and investment of public resources in poor neighborhoods. In doing so, it attended the demands that the "combative" neighborhood coalitions had long been making: the systematic allocation of basic infrastructure in poor neighborhoods and the control over infrastructure decisions by neighborhood residents themselves.

On the other hand, the policy was politically popular. Once revenues were available, small-scale infrastructure investments were highly visible projects that immediately affected the lives of large numbers of people. Although some elite groups—especially large property owners—were now paying higher taxes to pay for the policy, others—such as the construction agencies contracted to carry out the construction—benefited from the surge in public spending in basic infrastructure. A growing progressive middle class also supported the policy, which was seen as a much-needed challenge to traditions of closed-door decision making, corruption, and favoritism that had historically led to the misuse of government resources.

Perhaps most important, the budget policy proved to have a tremendous capacity to mobilize. As people realized that, through mobilization, they could bring tangible benefits to their areas, participation in neighborhood associations boomed. Although the majority of participants in the budget policy were not PT militants, as the government showed its commitment toward attending their demands, they naturally grew to sympathize with the party. This legion of neighborhood activists was essential for maintaining the budget policy: on numerous occasions, budget participants flooded the city assembly chambers to demand that the deputies approve the budget they had designed and vote for tax increases that financed investments. They also helped mobilize support for the PT at election time, although not in the traditional clientelist fashion. Rather than providing political support in exchange for favors, the budget participants promoted the re-election of a government that had effectively attended their needs in an open, transparent way. In part because of the support generated around the budget policy, the PT has been reelected two times and continues with high levels of approval to this day.

FROM CLIENTELISM TO COOPERATION: THE EXTREMO SUL DISTRICT

The remainder of this article will examine how the budget policy succeeded in mobilizing neighborhoods that had been previously dominated by clientelism and how this led to a more general strengthening of civil society in Porto Alegre. The discussion will focus on one district of the city where I conducted extensive interviews and participant observation over the course of a two-year period: the Extremo Sul district. In earlier times, the "Extreme South" of Porto Alegre, a

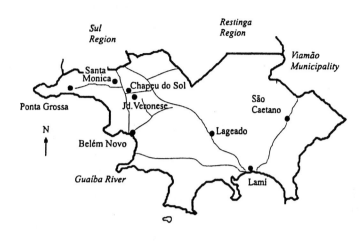

Figure 1.   Map of the Extremo Sul District.

beautiful area of green hills bordering the Guaíba River, was known best for the riverside settlement of Belém Novo, the city's most accessible waterside resort until the mid-twentieth century. When paved highways made travel easy to the ocean beaches of Rio Grande do Sul State, the area lost its importance as a vacation spot. Eventually bathing became altogether impossible there, as Porto Alegre's rapid growth during the 1960s and 1970s led to the contamination of the river as far as the next municipality. The district was largely ignored by city officials for many years as development efforts were directed toward the northern "industrial zone." But by the early eighties, the largely rural southern periphery had become a district of expansion, not of economic investment, but of people seeking affordable housing. In the Extremo Sul, lower middle-class people who could not afford to purchase land elsewhere could buy a nice-sized lot, albeit in a subdivision totally lacking in basic infrastructure. Along the district's dirt roads, dozens of impoverished settlements and tiny roadside land invasions also appeared, where people collected who were too poor to make it even in the in-town squatter settlements. By the 1990s, about 24,000 people lived in the district. Figure 1 is a map of the district identifying some of the larger settlements.

As in many other districts of the city, wide-scale community organizing in the Extremo Sul district was virtually nonexistent prior to the PT administration. Official neighborhood associations were largely dominated by a few of the better-off residents with clientelist ties to political parties, especially the PDT. Most of the neighborhoods and settlements in the district either had no association at all, or associations were closed to the participation of residents in general. Except for older parts of Belém Novo, none of the district's settlements had basic

273

sanitation, storm drainage, or pavement infrastructure, and transportation to the city on the unpaved roads was extremely slow and expensive. Occasional candidates would travel through the district promising to bring the much-needed infrastructure if elected, but the promises were rarely fulfilled. In the years after the PT came to office in Porto Alegre, however, a dramatic transformation of this picture occurred, as a result of the budget policy.

Mobilizing Neighborhood Residents

In an effort to bring better service provision to the south of the city, in its first year in office, the PT administration created a Centro Administrativo Regional (District Administrative Center; CAR) in Restinga, a more densely populated district adjacent to the Extremo Sul. The CAR staff was faced with the difficult task of making contact with neighborhood leaders in the Extremo Sul and of promoting the participatory budget policy. The task was daunting in such a large, sparsely populated district, and the administration's initial financial difficulties made things more complicated. Without even an automobile in the first year to travel through the district, initially the only way to call people to the budget assemblies was a mailing list of formally established neighborhood associations. The vast majority of associations on that list were of the traditional, nonparticipatory clientelist type. Association leaders were invited to the first participatory budget assembly in Belém Novo in 1990. Elections for the Extremo Sul representative in the Municipal Budget Council held at the very poorly attended meeting gave the job to two wealthy men, one who owned most of the land around Lami and dominated the neighborhood association there and another who was an aspiring politician who a few years later would be elected to the City Assembly by the PDT. Making little effort to meet with the Extremo Sul residents, these councillors formulated a very long and unordered list of demands, most of which would be left unattended in a year that the PT administration still had few funds for capital improvements.

The following year, the annual districtwide assembly drew eighty people, still largely from the Belém Novo area. The new budget councillors elected were a PT militant active in the progressive Catholic church and a small-time politician who worked for a conservative state congressman. To collect information on the district's needs, they traveled through the district talking to residents. Still only one general assembly to discuss district priorities took place. The first major investment of the new administration in the Extremo Sul district—the pavement of Chapeu do Sol Road—resulted out of this process. "If there had been any real participation," one neighborhood leader I interviewed remarked, "that road would never have been voted on, because very few people live there" (Pedrosa).[25]

Yet the Chapeu do Sol project had an important *demonstration effect.* As the CAR director noted, "even though it wasn't an important project from a technical perspective, it was still very important because it showed that through the participatory budget, things actually happen." Many Extremo Sul residents found out about the participatory budget policy after contacting the CAR (or some other municipal agency) to find out why the city was paving Chapeu do Sol Road and to request similar investment in their neighborhoods. The response would invariably be an explanation of the participatory budget process: "If you want such investment in your neighborhood, you need to organize and take part in next year's budget assemblies."

In addition to thus advising those who came to them with questions about district investments, the CAR staff also went out into the district—especially after 1991, when they obtained a car—and sought out potential neighborhood organizers. One major "discovery" in 1992 was Senhor Azevedo, an extremely energetic retired rail worker living in Ponta Grossa who had been a militant of the underground Communist Party during the dictatorship. Identifying him as a "potential leader," the CAR director encouraged him to found a neighborhood association. Another neighborhood, Lageado—which was suffering from lack of potable water—also began to mobilize after CAR officials encouraged residents to join the budget assemblies. In response to these efforts, in 1992, mobilizing for the big district budget assemblies in the Extremo Sul intensified: 569 people attended the second-round assembly, mostly from Lageado and Ponta Grossa neighborhoods. Sr. Azevedo and a Lageado resident were elected to the Municipal Budget Council, and regular assemblies of delegates were scheduled for the first time. Not surprisingly, the district's official priorities for that year were the paving of Ponta Grossa Road and the provision of potable water for Lageado. Large numbers had begun to participate for the first time, but still mostly from these two neighborhoods.

In the following years, however, as the first investments started to be implemented, other neighborhoods began to mobilize. In my interviews with participants from Belém Novo, Lami, São Caetano, Jardim Veronese, and Chapeu do Sol, I heard story after story of how they saw the administration investing elsewhere and how the demonstration effect of those capital improvements first implemented brought them into contact with administration officials who then encouraged them to take part in the budget assemblies. Mobilization and revitalized neighborhood organizations meant that by 1993, the dispute for investments in the Extremo Sul was no longer limited to Ponta Grossa and Lageado. The larger neighborhoods of Belém Novo, Lami, São Caetano, Santa Monica, Chapeu do Sol, and many other tiny settlements began to participate effectively. Over the years, different groups were able to mobilize a majority and to obtain major investments in their parts of the district: a health post in Lami; pavement in Ponta Grossa, Chapeu do Sol, São Caetano, Belém Novo, and Lageado; a major resettlement project for squatters on the river's edge in Belém Novo; storm drainage and sewer projects dispersed throughout the district; and new and more frequent bus lines all the way to Lami and São Caetano. For the first time ever, major city investments were being made in this distant periphery of the city. Each one of those investments corresponded to a neighborhood organizing effort.

It is clear that such mobilization only occurred because the administration was able to convince skeptical residents that participation would actually bring them fruits.

I know people who today are budget delegates who used to say, "[Participating] is not worth the trouble. Where have you ever seen the people decide anything?" And today they are participating and believing. (Solange)

The constant attention of high-level administration staff who regularly appeared at meetings and who saw to it that smaller demands outside of the participatory budget (such as road maintenance) were attended gave further credibility to the participatory process. The fact that upper-echelon administration personnel would go all the way to the Extremo Sul district and meet with residents carried a lot of weight. In my interviews, statements like the following were common.

Before, we never had so much proximity. If you wanted to talk to a secretary, there was a huge bureaucratic procedure. Today it is easy. The administration even comes to the community! (Solange)

People who didn't believe in the process would see that we got things by participating. Then they also started to participate. They would notice that with the participatory budget, they had a lot of power. . . . Before, you would have to go to a city deputy, who might be able to arrange a meeting for you with the mayor. Now, I can go directly to the mayor and speak to him. More than that, it is no longer me that needs to speak to him, but he who needs me! (Claudia)

Opening Closed Neighborhood Associations

The organizing that occurred throughout the Extremo Sul district was only possible because emerging neighborhood leaders were able to break with traditional associations that prohibited the broader based participation of residents and that made little effort to bring government services to the neighborhoods, especially when that government was in the hands of an opposition party. This usually took some time, since even after they knew of the opportunities presented by budget policy, residents often expected the "official leadership" of their associations to organize discussions about capital improvement priorities. In many cases, however, some residents eventually tired of waiting and began to work together on their own. The first neighborhood to thus topple a clientelist neighborhood association was Lageado, which for years had a "lifelong" president who, according to residents, never did anything except knock on doors at election time. By 1992, with the scarcity of clean running water in the neighborhood reaching intolerable proportions, residents were able to force an election in the association and to begin holding regular meetings in which many residents participated. It was this new organization that had the capacity to mobilize the neighborhood in sufficient numbers to put "water for Lageado" at the top of the district's priority list for that year.

A similar process occurred in a number of other neighborhoods as the years went by. One particularly impressive tale of a rejuvenated neighborhood associa-. tion took place in Lami, where a very wealthy landowner, Lira, had been president for thirteen years, never holding open meetings. In the first years of the participatory budget, Lira participated in the district budget assemblies and presented demands for Lami without holding any discussions in his neighborhood or informing residents about the policy. Lami residents only began to meet after administration officials, concerned that few were participating there, called an open assembly in the neighborhood to explain the budget process. At the first such meeting, only six residents showed up, and it was canceled for lack of quorum. But a month later, those six brought with them another forty, and from that time on participation grew in the neighborhood. As one of the original six noted,

We now knew that the only way to get anything for Lami was through the participatory budget. The way it was, Sr. Lira and Getúlio, when they would make demands, would only ask for things that served them. They did not even want to discuss it with us. They had cars and thought the public transportation system was great. What they really wanted was to keep the neighborhood the way it had always been. (Solange)

The result of this parallel mobilization was the appearance of new leaders in the neighborhood who began to push Lira to hold elections for the association executive committee.

We pressured and pressured. He didn't want to hold the election. But finally he accepted. He went out with a loud speaker car saying, "Vote for Lira, twelve years your president and all going well." I thought at the time: that's the wrong thing for him to say. People are going to realize that it's wrong that he has been there twelve years. . . . It's time to change presidents. And you know, there were people there whom he brought with him to vote and who voted against him. We won by two hundred votes! (Oswaldo)

The revitalized neighborhood association went on to become one of the most effective associations in the Extremo Sul district, holding large and regular meetings, bringing in many participants from the impoverished settlements near Lami village, and promoting a number of activities that went beyond the budget discussion.

At the same time, in another part of the district, a very different process occurred: one neighborhood leader managed to combine the mobilization required by the budget policy with what might be called "quasi-clientelist" techniques. Nelson, a small-time politician affiliated with the PDT, mobilized residents in one of the poorest squatter settlements in the Ponta Grossa area to attend the big district assemblies with promises that if they voted him into the Municipal Budget Council, he would get basic improvements for the settlement. According to residents, he even promised investments that they later discovered were not within the purview of the participatory budget, such as electricity, which was a

277

state government service. Providing buses for transportation and, according to some rumors, other fringe benefits (ranging from sandwiches to children's shoes, depending on the source of the rumors), he brought dozens of residents to the big district assemblies and was elected by them to the Municipal Budget Council. Having mobilized so many people, he also claimed the right to appoint his friends and neighbors to a large number of seats in the District Budget Forum. But rather than using the influence he thus gained in the District Budget Forum to propose improvements to the settlement he had originally mobilized, he rallied to pass a project that would pave the road passing in front of his house in a different part of Ponta Grossa.

This process, which strikingly resembled the vote-getting techniques of client-elist neighborhood leaders, is what Porto Alegrenses call *inchaço*, or the one-time "swelling" of assemblies by people who do not participate regularly, who do not have reliable information about the process, and who simply vote according to the dictates of their leader. It was a relatively common problem in a participatory process that privileged those neighborhoods that could bring large numbers to the assemblies. But, as I will discuss further below, such practices became increasingly difficult to carry out in the Extremo Sul as the rest of the district organized. In any case, whatever the method of mobilizing—through collective discussion and participation, or through quasi-clientelist techniques—many more people were joining neighborhood associations and attending public assemblies in the district than ever before.

Building Cooperative Alliances

While the budget policy stimulated neighborhood mobilization in the competitive effort to win investments, the policy also tended to promote *cooperation* among neighborhoods. This is because the dynamics of decision making in the forums not only encouraged neighborhood associations to mobilize residents but also to make alliances with other neighborhoods. The District Budget Forums incorporated representatives from too many neighborhoods to allow a single one to fully dominate decision-making sessions. In 1994, for example, the Extremo Sul elected representatives from about ten settlements. Other, more densely occupied districts included up to thirty neighborhoods and settlements. This meant that even well-mobilized neighborhood groups usually sought alliances with others to ensure that their demands were included in the district's top priorities for a particular year.

In the Extremo Sul, Nelson's above-described attempt to monopolize district priority-setting assemblies had the unexpected effect of encouraging neighborhoods in the rest of the district to unify. Since it had the majority at the big district assembly in 1994, Ponta Grossa was in the unusual position of being able to name over half of the district's delegates for the 1995 budget year. Most of these delegates did not regularly participate in the District Budget Forum. But on the day that the forum discussed how the district's "pavement" quota would be divided up among subdistricts—a meeting that took place only after several months of discussion within the forum—Nelson successfully mobilized the full body of delegates from his area. The result was that he pushed through an agreement in which Ponta Grossa would receive twice as much investment in street pavement as any other neighborhood. This lopsided distribution infuriated residents from the rest of the district. At the next forum meeting, they argued that the inchaço of Ponta Grossa delegates the month before had been unfair and demanded a new vote. Ponta Grossa still had a majority of delegates at this meeting, but the other neighborhoods had also ensured that all non–Ponta Grossa delegates were present at the assembly. In addition, they lured a number of Ponta Grossa delegates to their side, taking advantage of a dispute occurring between Nelson and others within the neighborhood who feared that the pavement would only go to his part of the neighborhood. This new majority voted in a much more equal distribution of pavement. It also voted to hold a recall assembly to revoke Nelson's election to the Municipal Budget Council. A few weeks later, he was removed from office. In the end, his attempt at inchaço did little more than bring about his own demise because it led participants from other neighborhoods to unite against him.

In the following years, the group that led the organization against inchaço made a special effort to help the residents of the settlement Nelson had used to get elected to organize on their own. This group became a regular presence within the District Budget Forum. What is more, this first attempt at cooperating among districts led to the development of a long-term alliance of emerging neighborhood leaders in the Extremo Sul. In the following year, those who organized the resistance against Nelson's inchaço attempt made speeches throughout the district on the importance of unity, of defending "the needs of the district" rather than the "needs of specific neighborhoods," and of ensuring that all the neighborhoods that participated had at least some of their demands attended each year. This discourse proved highly popular. At the end of that year's budget cycle, the "cooperative group" put together a coalition for the Municipal Budget Council elections, selecting representatives from four different neighborhoods and waging a campaign that emphasized the importance of districtwide unity. This coalition won the elections several years in a row and thus came to be the major force within the District Budget Forum.

Under the leadership of this group, investments in the district were from then on distributed much more fairly, a result of annual accords in which each participating neighborhood would be benefited. The group also proceeded to promote a series of larger districtwide projects that depended on the allied support of a number of neighborhoods. One such effort was a project to resettle and rehouse a group of squatter settlements to a well-localized area supplied with infrastructure. Throughout the Extremo Sul, there were dozens of tiny settlements on public lands, most in areas unfit for habitation because they were subject to flooding and erosion, because the soil was too porous for pipelines and sewers, because they were ecological preservation areas, or because they occupied the shoulders of roads. In 1994, the new leadership in the District Budget Forum went to all the neighborhood assemblies in the Extremo Sul to convince budget participants that the district's first priority should be resettling residents of such areas. They succeeded in passing a project to purchase a new area along the district's main road to be used for resettlement. The following year, they mobilized even more intensely to give districtwide priority to the construction of houses for the settlers on the new subdivision. The growing concern for the district's general development was also reflected in the intense participation of Extremo Sul budget participants in a series of public meetings in 1995 and 1996, organized by leaders from the budget forums of the southern part of the city and by local small farmers living in the rural area within the municipality. This discussion led to the formulation of a "sustainable development plan" for the district that was presented to the municipal government.

Transforming Participants' Perspectives

All this shows that within a few years after the budget policy was initiated, people who had initially joined up to obtain localized benefits for their neighborhoods were now thinking more broadly about the potential of the district as a whole and about how neighborhood groups could work together to realize that potential. This reflected changes not only in the way people voted, but in the way they *perceived* the process of deliberation. There were several aspects to these changes.

In the first place, participants with little or no previous experience in collective action had to learn the elementary rules of holding a meeting. Few of the participants in the Extremo Sul forum had previously been activists—for the most part, they were just ordinary people hoping to improve their neighborhoods. But in order to do so, they had to learn some basic democratic practices—simple ones, such as how to hold a meeting. In the period that I attended assemblies in the Extremo Sul—which coincided with the period of consolidation of the District Budget Council there—a slow but clear transition occurred. Initially, the meetings were chaotic, everyone interrupted everyone, people yelled and cursed, and offended participants walked out before decisions were made. Numerous "scenes" occurred, in which residents angry with decisions made or with perceived betrayals of loyalty disrupted meetings. Such conflicts alienated many participants. As one remarked, "We don't want to be insulted with obscenities. People should use their good sense. Many delegates stopped participating because of all that mess" (Francisco). Many of my informants interpreted the chaos of the meetings in the initial phase as a result of self-centered attitudes:

All these aggressions in the assemblies have happened because people still haven't put it into their heads that this here is a whole, a collective. . . . They are always trying to get their cut. If everyone saw that what we do is for the whole, this would all work much better. . . . This is [a question of] culture. The culture of the leadership. (Elza)

Over time, the leaders in the forum, many of whom initially engaged in such personal disputes, name calling, and temper tantrums, began to see that those tactics were not working. As they were criticized by their peers for inappropriate behavior and as assembly attendance notably declined after such scenes took place, the more fiery leaders began to temper their ways. At the same time, calmer neighborhood residents noticeably rose in favor among participants. The cooperative group mentioned above, which came to coordinate the meetings, slowly learned to control interruptions, to keep discussion on the agenda, to hold careful and well-counted votes, and so on.

This transformation was much more complex than simply getting people to hold their tongues. People also had to learn to create rules guiding speech that would ensure all voices being heard. By the end of my observation period, it had become commonplace to hold lengthy discussions prior to substantive debates about whether all who wanted to speak should be able to, whether each neighborhood should have one representative present its case, or whether all individuals should have their say, how much time would be given to a certain issue, and how much time each participant could speak. Participants also learned the necessity of carefully defining voting rules. The budget prioritizing process often involved very complex voting procedures as the group placed seven budget categories in order of priority and then placed numerous specific demands in order within each category. The simple yes or no vote did not work for these intricate orderings. But it required some experience before meeting coordinators learned how to explain the purpose of the vote and how to make the rules clear. Developing skills in "rule setting" was the first step in working together collectively.

As they learned to work together, participants' reasons for participating also tended to change. Most people joined the assemblies with very specific, narrow goals in mind: I want the street paved in front of my house, I want to stop the seasonal flooding in my neighborhood. The confrontation between these localized concerns and the similar concerns of others often forced them to change perspectives. Participants from better-off areas began to recognize that some neighborhoods had far greater needs and began to give preference to them.

The districtwide support for relocating squatter settlements, mentioned above, was an example of such emerging solidarity. That process began with the pleas of one riverside squatter settlement resident, Dona Carolina. She was the only delegate of her weakly organized settlement and was therefore unable to pass the demand for resettlement to a better area without the support of others. But with the help of the cooperative leadership, she was able to convince the vast majority of delegates in the district that the needs of her area were so great that they should give it preference. The project, which eventually expanded to include other squatter settlements, was voted "top district priority" largely because delegates came to believe that in addition to dramatically improving the quality of life of squatter residents, it would also increase the general economic potential of the erstwhile tourist region by beautifying the riverside areas and reducing the pollution of swimming areas caused by untreated sewage. Although this rationale suggests that delegates voted for the project at least in part because they themselves would indirectly benefit, this decision still involved putting put their original, neighborhood-based demands in second place. The fact that this occurred showed that, through participation, people not only began to feel solidarity for others but also began to see their own interests more broadly. Many of the people who began to participate for the sake of their street were, a year or two later, champions of "districtwide" issues, defending projects that would promote the economic revitalization of the southern part of the city or protect ecological reserves in the rural area of the municipality.

What is perhaps most impressive about the learning process that occurred through the budget debates is that participants slowly began to develop the capacity to systematize their changing attitudes into general rules for how resources ought to be distributed. As they gained experience, they began to discuss the criteria that should determine which neighborhoods should receive their demands before actually discussing the demands themselves, thereby abstracting from specific interests to think more generally. At least up to the end of my research period, this process of developing rules was only incipient in the Extremo Sul district, seeming to result from a sort of exhaustion as after much fighting budget delegates sought a more peaceful way to resolve their differences. At the suggestion of the city-employed organizer, delegates agreed to use a system in which each neighborhood would list general priorities (sanitation, health care, pavement, etc.). First priority for the district in each category would be given to the neighborhoods that gave first priority to that category. When more than one neighborhood put the same category first, "technical" considerations would be taken into account: how many people would benefit, did the road go by a school or allow for an extension of bus lines, and so on. In this way, final distributions would not simply reflect which neighborhoods could mobilize more votes. Those projects that were located in more needy areas or that would benefit larger numbers would prevail.

Ultimately, in the Extremo Sul, the rule system ended up being combined with a certain amount of direct negotiation in which those neighborhoods that had elected more delegates pressured to get their projects even if they could not be justified "technically." Even so, with the growing awareness that decisions should correspond to such rules made it more difficult to argue that the group with more delegates on the day of the vote should simply have its way. In other districts of the city that I studied, the use of distributional rules had developed even further by the period of my research, becoming the central focus of debate as participants designed complex "point" systems to decide which neighborhoods should have priority. This sort of discussion represented a whole new level of deliberation:

people began to think about what they thought "distributional justice" should practically mean.

These social learning processes were complex, slow, and often frustrating. One week participants might agree on a set of general rules that should guide decision making, and the next week those same rules might be utterly ignored. But it is certain that over a period of months and years, the rules slowly began to stick as participants became conscious of their broader interests, beginning to consider how their personal concerns could be made compatible with the interests of others and, ultimately, even campaigning for others' causes. This process of developing what Benhabib[26] calls "enlarged thinking" started, however, only because people were drawn to the participatory process in the pursuit of more narrow, individualistic concerns and, through that process, were forced to confront their own concerns with those of others. That is, the fact that the participatory budget provided the *incentives to participate* discussed earlier ultimately created the conditions in which people gained *experience with participation* that not only gave them a chance to build ties of trust and reciprocity with others but also to build new, enlarged worldviews.

CONCLUSIONS: LOCAL POLICY AND CIVIC ORGANIZING

In 1989, when the participatory budget was initiated, the capacity for neighborhood mobilization was distributed very unevenly throughout Porto Alegre. But the result was not that those more organized neighborhoods and districts dominated the process over time as some might have expected.[27] Instead, certain characteristics of the budget policy and of the way it was implemented led to mobilization in poor neighborhoods where previously residents had little or no experience with collective action. Although I have focused here on the Extremo Sul, that district was not particularly unusual. In other districts of the city where neighborhood organizations had been similarly weak before the PT came to office, the budget policy also created an enabling environment in which associations gained membership and force and districtwide alliances consolidated. In those districts where civic organizing had been strong before the budget policy, important transformations also occurred, with new neighborhoods gaining strength and older leadership losing influence.[28] These processes did not occur without conflict. In the Extremo Sul and elsewhere, it took four or five years after the policy was initiated before strong civic groups emerged. But within six or seven years after the PT came to office, civic organizing was no longer the purview of a few "historically combative" districts of the city: there had appeared innumerable new neighborhood and districtwide organizations that mobilized large numbers, met regularly with administration staff to discuss government policy, worked together to articulate demands, and engaged in broader and more general discussions on how to improve their communities.

Quantitative data on the budget policy confirm these observations. In the first place, assembly attendance changed dramatically over the years that the policy was in place. In 1989, 60% of budget participants at the district assemblies lived in the six districts of the city that had some history of protest-based neighborhood activism, while only 40% came from the ten districts that had little activist history. By 1995, this picture had reversed dramatically: 62% of participants came from the latter ten districts.

In the second place, questions on participation in neighborhood associations asked during a 1995 survey of participants in the district assemblies[29] showed that associationalism had increased as a result of the budget policy. Of those interviewed, 67% were members of some kind of civic association. Of those, 83% participated in associations located in their neighborhoods, including not only official neighborhood associations but also "community centers," "mothers clubs," and informal "street commissions." When asked how their participation in civic groups changed since the policy began, 33% of those who were members responded that prior to the budget policy, they did not participate in civic groups at all. Another 25% said that they had previously participated in civic groups, but since the budget policy, that participation had increased. This means that nearly 60% of those who were active in associations had become more active in the context of the budget policy.

Finally, confirming my qualitative evidence that the residents of poor neighborhoods have been the prime mobilizers in the budget policy, a comparison of our assembly survey data with the 1991 population census shows that the budget participants had significantly lower income levels than the municipal population as a whole. While 29% of the Porto Alegre's households earned three times the minimum salary or less, 45% of participants in the district assemblies declared a household income in this range.[30] Likewise, while 53% of Porto Alegre's households had incomes of more than five times the minimum salary, only 34% of those participating in district assemblies had household incomes at this level. This corroborates the conclusion that the processes of civic organizing described here have been particularly intense for social groups that have been historically disempowered in Brazil: poor and working-class people living in an urban periphery grossly lacking in basic services and infrastructure.

As noted earlier, theorists of social movements have pointed out that people mobilize when there are windows of opportunities that lead them to believe that action will more likely bring results. Often, such *enabling environments* have to do with changes in the state power structure, such as the weakening of a powerful elite or the strengthening of reformist policy makers. Obviously, the creation of a responsive, participatory policy represents a particularly radical change in the "opportunity structure" for collective action. Some people are born activists, struggling for improvements even when government is not responsive to them. Others may be interested in their communities and in improving their conditions but are unwilling to go through the long, tortuous, and usually frustrating process of organization and protest. Many of those who began participating in the participatory budget policy fit into this second category. For them, the participatory budget policy provided an environment in which, for the first time, it was easy and rewarding to participate in public life. As one participant I interviewed noted,

I was always a sociable person. I knew everyone in the neighborhood. But I never even thought of participating in anything like this, of trying to improve my community. There just never was the opportunity. When the participatory budget came along, I discovered that my familiarity with the neighborhood and with the neighbors could become something more. (Joana)

The first step in a state-sponsored process of promoting civic organizing is that the state must be genuinely open to participation and genuinely responsive to participant demands. But that is not enough: potential participants also have to *become aware* of that responsiveness. In Porto Alegre, this did not occur immediately. Indeed, after such a long history of having the promises of government officials go unfulfilled, it took some time before a large numbers began to participate in earnest. The administration had to prove its credibility by consistently providing publicly perceivable responses to the demands that participants prioritized in a fairly short period of time. A *demonstration effect* helped provide previously unmobilized groups with the *incentives* to organize their neighborhoods.

At the same time, participants also responded to the policy because the issues it targeted were easily comprehensible and clearly relevant to their lives. The policy focused on basic needs that all residents of poor neighborhoods would agree were important to resolve. Where people do not fully understand the purpose of a policy issue, it is much less likely that they will mobilize. One example of such difficulties was the attempt by the same Porto Alegre administration to carry out a participatory debate on reformulating the city's Master Plan within the District Budget Forums. Although Master Plan regulations—determining the minimum width and maximum incline of roads, the size of lots, and so on—have a dramatic effect on the neighborhood infrastructure issues with which budget participants were preoccupied, the municipal agency responsible for the process was never able to clearly communicate to the residents how the Master Plan affected their lives. The use of planning jargon dominated, and educational efforts to translate that jargon into "popular" terms were never carried out on a large scale. In consequence, initial interest by neighborhood delegates soon petered out, and the participatory process was dominated by more educated representatives of sectoral organizations, nongovernment organizations, and business groups.[31]

While both its "demonstration effect" and the fact that the budget policy targeted issues that were meaningful to poor neighborhood residents helped people recognize that participation could bring *benefits*, other factors helped reduce the *costs* of participation. In the first place, the fact that the budget forums were open to new participants and to providing benefits to them reduced the costs for newcomers to join up. The institutional structure created by the administration was critical for ensuring this openness: all adult residents could participate in the assemblies, and proportional representation rules ensured that minority groups would hold seats in the District Budget Forums and the Municipal Council. Another effort at reducing the costs of participation was to send government officials to far-away neighborhoods rather than obliging participants to travel to the city center. High-level agency officials were required to spend a significant amount of their time traveling throughout the city to meet with residents to discuss capital improvements and other city services. The creation of a number of District Administrative Centers also brought city services and officials closer to the residents of the impoverished city periphery. The result was that, as suggested by some of the comments cited earlier, participants were often surprised by the regular appearance of high-echelon city officials, including the mayor himself, at neighborhood and district assemblies. This proximity made the participation of poor residents less costly, since they no longer had to travel long distances to engage in negotiations with city officials about capital improvements.

But perhaps the most important effort by the administration to reduce the costs of participation and to increase awareness of potential benefits was the work of community organizers who acted as *external agents*, visiting unmobilized neighborhoods, seeking out new leaders, helping people organize, and disseminating information about what could be gained through collective action. In the Extremo Sul district, direct contact with government organizers was absolutely essential for drawing new neighborhoods into the process. One government-employed community organizer referred to this integration as "politicizing the pothole." The administration had a coherent policy of encouraging all people who came to government offices with small demands to begin to think about the larger needs they may have and to organize their communities in the pursuit of those demands. Often, this required innumerable trips to unorganized neighborhoods to help residents call assemblies and to present information to neighborhood groups on what they needed to do in order to participate effectively in the budget process. Indeed, such "popular education efforts" on the part of administration officials could have been used even more intensely in other areas of decision making. For example, had more effective information seminars been held around the Master Plan discussion, that policy might have been better able to mobilize residents.[32]

While all these aspects of the policy helped provide *incentives* for collective action by increasing the expectation of benefits and reducing the costs of participation, the policy also provided an environment in which people could gain experience with *cooperative action* and, in that context, could become aware of broader needs going beyond their own neighborhoods. The specific institutional structure of the policy helped encourage associations to become more inclusive and cooperative. On one hand, neighborhoods had to mobilize in order to obtain benefits. In all the neighborhoods I examined, associations membership increased and open discussions of priorities occurred, although in some cases, quasi-clientelist techniques were used to attract people to the assemblies. On the other hand, the dynamics of decision making within the District Budget Forums, through which neighborhood groups had to negotiate with one another to come up with lists of priorities, encouraged the formation of alliances among neighborhood groups. The experience of building alliances from year to year contributed to the creation of strong formal and informal districtwide networks of neighborhoods throughout the city. Individuals within the networks changed the way they understood their own interests, beginning to see themselves as members of larger groups and beginning to take the interests of others into account. In these ways, the budget process discouraged long-standing traditions of clientelism and promoted what some authors would call "social capital," or networks of reciprocity and trust.

The role of the government as an *external agent* was also important in promoting those networks. Government officials sought to mobilize residents in areas where clientelist associations predominated, calling open meetings in neighborhoods, such as Lami, where the association president refused to disseminate information to residents about the budget policy. In the case of Ponta Grossa, where a neighborhood leader engaged in inchaço, the government-employed community organizers worked closely with other budget participants to bring better information to residents and to help them organize on their own. The organizers working with the District Budget Forums also helped reduce discord and to promote agreements among delegates. In the Extremo Sul, although budget delegates coordinated the meetings, an administration organizer provided a constant source of information, advising the leadership on how they could better coordinate discussion and promoting "cooperative values" and the use of "distributive rules." This work much resembled the guidance that church activists, student groups, liberal professionals, and other groups always have provided in helping neighborhood groups organize.

The picture presented here of state-sponsored civic organizing sharply contrasts prevailing perceptions that government spending and proactive policy making are only likely to discourage collective action. Much to the contrary, the mobilization and organization I have described in the Porto Alegre case was the direct result of a policy that involved a great deal of government investment in two fundamental ways. First, countering international policy trends toward promoting self-financing and "cost recovery" in infrastructure investments, the Porto Alegre government gave top priority to raising revenues through taxation and administrative streamlining in order to pay for capital improvement expenditures.[33] It spent between 12% and 20% of city revenues on that rubric each year—amounting in 1995 to about sixty million dollars—most of which went to neighborhood-level projects. In the context of the participatory budget policy, this intensive government spending set off, rather than discouraged, a boom in civic action throughout the city.

Second, the policy also prioritized a different type of investment: an investment in building a new relationship between government personnel and local citizens. The efforts of community organizers hired by the administration, and of many other government workers who regularly attended neighborhood meetings, reflected a new type of governing that privileged accessibility, flexibility, and negotiation. It was successful largely because of the willingness and passion of several hundred politically appointed employees who worked outside conventional hours going to meetings at night and on weekends. It was also successful because of extensive efforts within the administration to promote an "esprit de corps" of respecting ordinary citizens and avoiding bureaucratic rigidity. The result was that through a "case-by-case" process of organizing, popular education, and negotiation, the Porto Alegre administration helped neighborhood groups organize, providing inexperienced neighborhood leaders with practical assistance in mobilizing their communities, helping them learn the basic skills of organizing, and promoting values of cooperation and reciprocity.

None of this occurred, of course, outside the realm of politics. As always with state-sponsored participatory processes, the actions of the government were influenced by the need to generate political support for the PT. But since the administration sought to do so in part by gaining allies in poor neighborhoods and in part, as mentioned earlier, by building a more general reputation for "democratic" governing, the administration's interests largely coincided with those of neighborhood organizations: both sought a transparent process through which neighborhoods could obtain access to government infrastructure and services.[34] This coincidence of interests was perhaps the key that led to the cycle of civic organizing I have described, since while, on one hand, the government found that by providing infrastructure and services to those neighborhoods that effectively participated, it could build credibility and support, on the other hand, neighborhood residents tended to mobilize only when they believed that their participation would bring fruits. The end result went well beyond mere electoral strategy, leading to a fundamental transformation of political life in Porto Alegre as neighborhoods residents that had earlier served as powerless cogs in clientelist machines were now active participants in public life, organized into representative civic associations and engaging in an open, transparent debate about government policy.

NOTES

1. See Rebecca Abers, "Inventing Local Democracy: Neighborhood Organizing and Participatory Policy-Making in Porto Alegre, Brazil" (Ph.D. diss., University of California, Los Angeles, 1997) for a more detailed examination of these issues, as well as a more general discussion of the politics of implementing the budget policy in Porto Alegre. Both the dissertation and this article are based on over a year and a half of field research in Porto

Alegre between 1993 and 1997, funded by the Inter-American Foundation, the Fulbright U.S. Student Program, and the UCLA Latin American Center. The research involved extensive interviews with more than 50 local government officials and more than 40 budget participants. I also collaborated in the application of a sample survey of 622 participants throughout the city (see note 9) and conducted participant observation at over 100 public assemblies and neighborhood meetings. Participant observation and interviews focused on two regions of the city—one with a long history of civic organizing and another where neighborhood organizations were historically weak. This article focuses on the latter region.

2. Robert D. Putnam, *Making Democracy Work: Civic Traditions in Modern Italy* (Princeton, NJ: Princeton University Press, 1993).

3. Joshua Cohen and Joel Rogers, "Secondary Associations and Democratic Governance," *Politics and Society* 20, no. 4 (1992): 393-472.

4. On clientelism in Brazil, see Frances Hagopian, *Traditional Politics and Regime Change in Brazil* (Cambridge: Cambridge University Press, 1996) and Eli Diniz, *Voto e maquina política: patronagem e clientelismo no Rio de Janeiro* (Rio de Janeiro: Paz e Terra, 1982). On the specific role of neighborhood associations in clientelist machines, see also Geert A. Banck, "Poverty, Politics and the Shaping of Urban Space: a Brazilian Example," *International Journal of Urban and Regional Research* 10 (1986): 522-540, and Robert Gay, "Community Organization and Clientelist Politics in Contemporary Brazil: A Case Study from Suburban Rio de Janeiro," *International Journal of Urban and Regional Research* 14, no. 4 (1990): 648-666.

5. James C. Scott, "Patron-Client Politics and Political Change in Southeast Asia," *American Political Science Review* 66 (1972): 91-113, cited in Luigi Graziano, "A Conceptual Framework for the Study of Clientelistic Behavior," *European Journal of Political Research* 4 (1976): 149-174.

6. Putnam, *Making Democracy Work*, 175.

7. Ibid., 177.

8. Peter Evans, "Introduction: Development Strategies across the Public-Private Divide," *World Development* 24, no. 6 (1996): 1033-1037.

9. Elinor Ostrom, "Crossing the Great Divide: Coproduction, Synergy and Development," *World Development* 24, no. 6 (1996): 1073-1087. See also Gabrielle Watson, *Good Sewers Cheap? Agency-Customer Interactions in Low-Cost Urban Sanitation in Brazil* (Washington, DC: The World Bank, Water and Sanitation Division, 1995).

10. Wai Fung Lam, "Institutional Design of Public Agencies and Coproduction: A Study of Irrigation Associations in Taiwan," *World Development* 24, no. 66 (1996): 1039-1054.

11. Jonathan Fox, "How Does Civil Society Thicken? The Political Construction of Social Capital in Rural Mexico," *World Development* 24, no. 6 (1996): 1089-1103. See also Jonathan Fox, "Popular Participation and Access to Food: Mexico's Community Food Councils," in Scott Whiteford and Anne E. Ferguson, eds., *Harvest of Want: Hunger and Food Security in Central America and Mexico* (Boulder, CO: Westview, 1991), 209-242.

12. Judith Tendler, *Good Government in the Tropics* (Baltimore, MD: Johns Hopkins University Press, 1996).

13. Charles Tilly, *From Mobilization to Revolution* (Reading, MA: Addison-Wesley, 1978) and Sidney Tarrow, *Power in Movement: Social Movements, Collective Action and Politics* (Cambridge: Cambridge University Press, 1994).

14. Tarrow, *Power in Movement*, 18.

15. J. Craig Jenkins, "Resource Mobilization Theory and the Study of Social Movements," *Annual Review of Sociology* 9 (1983): 527-553; John D. McCarthy and Mayer N.

Zald, "Resource Mobilization and Social Movements: A Partial Theory," *American Journal of Sociology* 82, no. 6 (1977): 1212-1241; and Tilly, *From Mobilization to Revolution*, 52-97.

16. For the Brazilian case, Jacobi argues that while the window of opportunity represented by the weakening of the dictatorship promoted the rise of popular movements in the early eighties, the work of a variety of external agents helps explain why those movements were stronger in some neighborhoods, cities, and regions than others. Pedro Jacobi, *Movimentos sociais e políticas públicas* (São Paulo: Cortez, 1989).

17. Although unusual, the Porto Alegre case is not unprecedented. For an interesting study of a similar policy in a U.S. city, see Haeberle's study of the Citizen Participation Program in Birmingham, Alabama. As in Porto Alegre, Haeberle finds that local government investment in directly promoting citizen participation dramatically strengthened the associational environment of that city. Steven H. Haeberle, *Planting the Grassroots: Structuring Citizen Participation* (New York: Praeger, 1989).

18. Sonia Alvarez, " 'Deepening' Democracy: Popular Movement Networks, Constitutional Reform, and Radical Urban Regimes in Contemporary Brazil," in Robert Fisher and Joseph Kling, eds., *Mobilizing the Community: Local Politics in the Era of the Global City* (London: Sage, 1993), 195; Lúcio Kowarick and Nabil Bonduki, "Espaço urbano e espaço político: do populismo à redemocratizaçao," in Lúcio Kowarick, ed., *As Lutas Sociais e a Cidade: São Paulo Passado e Presente* (Rio de Janeiro: Paz e Terra, 1988), 133-167; and Paul Singer, "Movimentos de Bairro" in Paul Singer and V. C. Brant, eds., *São Paulo: O Povo em Movimento* (São Paulo: Cebrap, 1980).

19. Sérgio Gregório Baierle, "Um Novo Princípio Etico-Político: Prática Social e Sujeito nos Movimentos Populares em Porto Alegre nos Anos Oitenta" (master's thesis, Universade Estadual de Campinas, 1992), 97-98.

20. Hagopian, *Traditional Politics and Regime Change in Brazil*.

21. Baierle, "Um Novo Princípio Etico-Político."

22. Here I loosely define the "combative" camp of neighborhood organizations as including those organizations officially affiliated with the citywide organization created by the "combative" leadership, UAMPA (Uniao das Associaçoes de Moradores de Porto Alegre). The figure is reported in Baierle, "Um Novo Princípio Etico-Político."

23. On PT history and ideology, see Moacir Gadotti and Otaviano Pereira, *Pra Que PT: Origem, Projeto e Consolidaçao do Partido dos Trabalhadores* (São Paulo: Cortez, 1989); Margaret E. Keck, *The Workers' Party and Democratization in Brazil* (New Haven, CT: Yale University Press, 1992); and Rachel Meneguello, *PT: A Formaçao de um Partido, 1979-1982* (São Paulo: Paz e Terra, 1989). On the experiences of other PT administrations, see Rebecca Abers, "From Ideas to Practice: The Partido dos Trabalhadores and Participatory Governance in Brazil," *Latin American Perspectives* 91, no. 23 (1996): 35-53; Alvarez, " 'Deepening' Democracy"; William Nylen, "Popular Participation in Brazil's Workers' Party: 'Democratizing Democracy' in Municipal Politics," *The Political Chronicle* Fall (1996): 1-8; and William Nylen, "Reconstructing the Workers' Party (PT): Lessons from North-Eastern Brazil," in Douglas A. Chalmers et al., eds., *The New Politics of Inequality in Latin America: Rethinking Participation and Representation* (Oxford: Oxford University Press, 1997), 421-446.

24. Abers, "Inventing Local Democracy."

25. All the names of budget participants and other community activists interviewed have been changed.

26. Seyla Benhabib, *Situating the Self: Gender, Community and Postmodernism in Contemporary Ethics* (New York: Routledge Kegan Paul, 1992).

27. For a discussion of theories of participation that assume that those who are best organized early on will continue to dominate over time, see Rebecca Abers, "Learning Democratic Practice: Distributing Government Resources through Popular Participation in Porto Alegre, Brazil," in Michael Douglass and John Friedmann, eds., *Cities for Citizens: Planning and the Rise of Civil Society in a Global Age* (Chichester, UK: Wiley, 1998), 39-65.

28. See Abers, "Inventing Local Democracy," for an examination of how the budget policy affected organizing patterns in one historically active region.

29. I conducted this survey in collaboration with two local nongovernmental organizations (CIDADE and FASE-RS) and the community relations department of the Porto Alegre municipal government. Questionnaires were applied at the second round of big annual assemblies, held during the month of June 1995. About 10% of the participants in each of sixteen regional and five thematic assemblies were interviewed, reaching a total of 622 questionnaires. The survey addressed socioeconomic statistics, participatory experiences, participation in civil associations, and opinions about the budget process. For a report on the results, see Luciano Fedozzi, Maria Regina Pozzobon, and Rebecca Abers, "Orçamento Participativo: Pesquisa Sobre a Populaçao Que Participou da Segunda Rodada de Assembléias do Orçamento Participativo da Prefeitura Municipal de Porto Alegre" (unpublished manuscript, CIDADE/FASE, Porto Alegre, 1995).

30. In 1995, when the assembly survey was carried out, the monthly minimum salary was about US$100.

31. In her study of participation in land use decisions in the Brazilian city of Petrópolis, Gondim notes, "It does not seem realistic to expect residents of the metropolitan periphery to go to the work of mobilizing themselves around legislation based on abstract land use planning concepts. People do not experience 'current land use patterns.' They experience concrete everyday effects of the disordered occupation of urban space. In other words, what matters is not the lot size in itself, but the lack of space for children to play or for the family to increase its living space. People are not worried about 'minimum adequate densities,' but about traffic jams, lines and insufficient water supply. Nor do they worry about 'incompatible uses,' but simply want to avoid the effects of pollution." Linda M. Gondim, "Dilemas da participaçao comunitária," *Revista de administraçao municipal* 35, no. 187 (1988): 12. In the Porto Alegre Master Plan discussion, planners had great difficulty bringing planning jargon to the level of ordinary citizens. In consequence, it is not surprising that most of the assemblies were dominated by professionals and academics.

32. The work of an extension group from the local university's Urban Planning Program showed how it was possible to translate the Master Plan issues into terms more comprehensible to ordinary participants. They held a seminar with members of the budget forum in the Glória region to help them respond to the Master Plan process. With some guidance about how physical planning and legal issues affected their region, a vigorous debate took place as participants mapped the region and located areas that represented particular problems or that were sites of potential improvements.

33. City revenues nearly doubled over the first four years that the PT was in office in Porto Alegre, largely as a result of increases in the municipal taxes on property and services. For a detailed description of revenue changes, see Guillerme Cassel and Joao Verle, "A política tributária e de saneamento financeiro da Administraçao Popular," in Carlos Henrique Horn, ed., *Porto Alegre: o Desafio da Mudança* (Porto Alegre: Ortiz, 1994), 29-47.

34. See Rebecca Abers, "Practicing Radical Democracy: Lessons from Brazil," *Plurimondi* (forthcoming), for more on how the PT's political strategy made participatory policy possible.

FROM POPULISM TO NEOLIBERALISM
Labor Unions and Market Reforms in Latin America

By M. VICTORIA MURILLO*

A TALE OF THREE CARLOSES

CARLOS Salinas, Carlos Andrés Pérez, and Carlos Menem were inaugurated between December 1988 and July 1989 as presidents of Mexico, Venezuela, and Argentina, respectively. They not only shared the timing of their administrations[1] but also the task of turning populist labor parties toward neoliberalism. All three had been the candidates of populist labor-based parties that had advanced protectionism and state intervention in the postwar period. Once in office and facing tremendous fiscal crises and capital flight, all three presidents reduced state intervention and opened the economies of their countries. This shift in development strategy not only was the most important policy turnaround of the postwar era in all three Latin American countries, but it also moved their labor-based parties away from the policies upon

*Earlier versions of this paper were presented at the twenty-first meeting of the Latin American Studies Association, Chicago, September 24–26, 1998, and at the conference "Space, Place, and Nation: Reconstructing Neoliberalism in the Americas," University of Massachusetts, Amherst, November 20–21, 1998. I would like to thank Arun Agrawal, Ernesto Cabrera, Ernesto Calvo, Javier Corrales, Miguel Glatzer, Miriam Golden, Pauline Jones-Luong, Robert Kaufman, Steven Levitsky, James McGuire, Nicoli Nattrass, Phillip Oxhorn, Héctor Schamis, Jeremy Sikkins, and four anonymous reviewers for helpful comments to previous versions of this paper, and Antonieta Mercado for her research assistance in Mexico. I would also like to thank Alberto Alesina, Robert Bates, David Cameron, John Coatsworth, Jorge Domínguez, Geoffrey Garrett, Peter Hall, Ian Shapiro, Juan Carlos Torre, and Deborah Yashar, who provided useful comments to clarify the ideas presented in this paper. I gratefully acknowledge the financial support of the Mellon Foundation, the Harvard Academy for International and Area Studies, and the David Rockefeller Center for Latin American Studies at Harvard University, as well as the Institute for the Study of World Politics. I also want to acknowledge the institutional support of the Department of Political Science at Yale University; the Instituto Torcuato Di Tella in Argentina; the IESA in Venezuela; the Colegio de México, Flacso, and ITAM, and Intelmex in Mexico.

[1] Salinas was president of Mexico from the end of 1988 to the end of 1994, and Carlos Andrés Pérez was president of Venezuela from the beginning of 1989 to mid-1993. To hold the international conditions constant in the comparison with Mexico and Venezuela, I analyze the first administration of Carlos Menem in Argentina, which ran from mid-1989 to mid-1995.

which their historic relationships with long-term union allies had been built.

Despite the parallel convergence of labor-based populism turning into neoliberalism and the common challenge faced by unions in Argentina, Mexico, and Venezuela, union responses to neoliberal reforms were diverse. Union-government interactions varied across these countries and across sectors within the same country. For instance, the Mexican Workers' Confederation subordinated to Salinas's policies, endorsing them in corporatist pacts and even campaigning actively for the North American Free Trade Agreement (NAFTA). To the contrary, the Venezuelan Workers' Confederation opposed Perez's reforms by organizing the first economic general strikes in the history of Venezuela. Argentine teachers unsuccessfully resisted the decentralization of schools; their militancy accounted for more than a third of the total strikes in the two years before the government, with no union input, finally implemented the reform. In Mexico, however, teachers successfully opposed key pieces of the decentralization process and limited its scope. Meanwhile, Mexican telephone workers negotiated with their government to support the privatization of their company in return for job stability, handsome social benefits, and easy financing for the purchase of almost 5 percent of the shares in the company.

Such variation in union-government interactions in response to market-oriented reforms has considerable political importance. First, unions can organize support for or opposition to the reforms, thus changing the costs of reform for policymakers. Their actions can affect the feasibility, design, and implementation of reforms, as shown by the delays in the reform of labor market regulations in all three countries. Unions should therefore be included in the analysis of the politics of economic reforms.

Second, unions can have a direct impact on the governance of administrations led by labor-based political parties. Unions not only have organized the core constituency of labor-based parties and provided them with political machines for electoral campaigns, but they also have shared a long-term partisan identity with governing politicians. As a result, the interaction between unions and labor-based parties implementing market-oriented reforms can influence the future of the electoral coalition that brought these parties to power. Argentina, Mexico, and Venezuela are key cases in that regard because the alliance between unions and labor-based parties had shaped the national party system fifty years earlier.[2]

[2] Ruth Berins Collier and David Collier, *Shaping the Political Arena* (Princeton: Princeton University Press, 1991).

Thus, a theory that accounts for the cross-sectoral and cross-national variations in union-government interactions in these countries can help solve the puzzle of the transition from closed to open economies in Latin America.[3] Moreover, an explanation of such variation has broad comparative implications for our understanding of similar stories in other regions of the world where the pressure of globalization turned labor-parties toward policies that challenged their long-standing agreements with labor allies.

Theories of union politics suggest that union behavior varies according to either differences in national-level institutions or interests of economic sectors with regard to market policies and international integration. Yet, in Argentina, Mexico, and Venezuela, the interactions between unions and labor-based governments over market-oriented reforms cut across national borders and sectoral cleavages. Explanations based on either economic interest or national institutions are thus insufficient to understand such patterns of interaction. I argue instead that the incentives created by partisan loyalties, partisan competition, and union competition explain these interactions. Partisan loyalty results from the long-term affiliation of a union with a political party. Partisan competition is the struggle for control of the unions among union leaders affiliated with different political parties. Union competition is the rivalry among labor organizations for the representation of the same workers, which can take place in diverse national and sectoral contexts. Loyalty derived from a long-term affiliation with the incumbent party facilitates collaboration between labor unions and the government. Yet, if loyal union leaders are afraid of being replaced by activists affiliated with the opposition parties because of partisan competition, their incentives for militancy increase to show their responsiveness to the rank and file hurt by market reforms. Union competition for the representation of the same workers makes coordination more difficult thereby weakening unions and making them less likely to obtain concessions from the government despite their partisan loyalty. I use the empirical evidence from eighteen cases, including national confederations and individual unions in five economic sectors in Argentina, Mexico, and Venezuela to test this theory.

The article is divided into six sections. The first section introduces the policy shift of labor-based parties from populism to neoliberalism

---

[3] The politics of Argentina, Mexico, and Venezuela have a strong effect in Latin America and the Caribbean. By 1995 they made up 32 percent of the regional population, 43 percent of the regional gross domestic product, and 48 percent of regional exports. Inter-American Development Bank, *Economic and Social Progress in Latin America* (Baltimore: Johns Hopkins University Press, 1996), 357–61.

in Argentina, Mexico, and Venezuela. The second examines the relevant literature upon which I build my analysis. The third describes the patterns of union-government interaction in the context of market-oriented reforms. The fourth presents my hypothesis for explaining those patterns. The fifth section reports the test of my hypothesis on the case studies, and the last offers some conclusions.

FROM POPULISM TO NEOLIBERALISM

On October 17, 1945, a multitude of workers organized by their unions marched into downtown Buenos Aires to demand the release of imprisoned Colonel Juan Perón and to defend the social legislation he had implemented as secretary of labor. In the elections of February 1946, the Labor Party—organized by the leaders of those same unions—led the political coalition that elected Perón to the presidency. Most workers voted for Perón and taught their children to be Peronist, creating one of the strongest partisan loyalties in Latin America. After all, Perón and the Peronist unions had changed their lives by providing better wages and labor benefits, social security, and even paid vacations at union resorts. Since labor benefits compensated them for previous frustration in dealing with indifferent employers and hostile governments, the unions identified with Peronism and served as Peronist political machines. Peronism, which became the symbol of workers' rights, promoted import substitution industrialization and state intervention as development strategies.[4] It also turned unions into key players in the Argentine political system.

In 1989 a Peronist candidate, Carlos Menem, won the presidential elections. During his populist electoral campaign, Menem promised wage hikes and social justice, and he threatened not to pay the external debt. After his inauguration, however, he delivered austerity, followed by trade liberalization, privatization, and adjustment of the public sector. As state intervention had done forty years earlier, the retreat of the state and market-oriented reforms reshaped state-society relations. The national labor confederation, the Peronist-dominated General Confederation of Labor (CGT), although surprised by the policy turnaround, accepted market-oriented reforms and reduced the number of general

---

[4] Import substitution industrialization (ISI) was a development strategy adopted by most Latin American countries after the Great Depression. They originally raised tariffs to compensate for the shortage of foreign exchange produced by the crisis, but this policy gradually evolved into active protectionism that included subsidized exchange rates for importing inputs with closed markets. ISI created few incentives for developing internationally competitive industries and, thus, exporting.

strikes from thirteen against the previous administration of the Civic Radical Union (UCR) (1983–89) to only one under the first Menem administration (1989–95). Peronist unions, though, were able to negotiate concessions on the reforms of social security, labor legislation, and privatization.

In Mexico during the same period, the story of the policy turnaround of labor parties in government was similar to that in Argentina. Unions entered the political arena during the Mexican Revolution. They first formed six "Red Battalions" that fought with the army of President Venustiano Carranza in 1915. In 1919 they organized a Labor Party, which supported the elections of Presidents Alvaro Obregón and Plutarco E. Calles. In return, unions obtained political appointments and favorable labor legislation to compensate for their weakness in collective bargaining with private employers. In 1936 President Lázaro Cárdenas promoted the organization of the Mexican Workers Confederation (CTM). In 1938 he founded the Party of the Mexican Revolution (PRM) and integrated labor into its functional structure. Unions became political machines for the PRM, which would become the Institutional Revolutionary Party (PRI), and were included in the party structure. Unions also gave Cárdenas a suitable excuse—in the form of a labor conflict—for the nationalization of oil in 1938. In return, workers received social benefits, and union leaders gained political influence they could use in the industrial arena. The PRI also implemented policies of import substitution industrialization while using the state as the main instrument for economic development.

Half a century later, however, PRI labor leaders witnessed a PRI president, Carlos Salinas, become the champion of economic liberalization, state shrinkage, and market-oriented reforms. The main national confederation, the PRI-dominated CTM, explicitly supported Salinas's stabilization plan and structural reforms both in the annual corporatist pacts signed with government and business representatives and in an agreement to increase labor productivity signed in 1992. Moreover, it campaigned for Salinas's proposal to integrate Mexico into NAFTA. In spite of the CTM's acquiescence, the administration ignored most of its demands even while paying lip service to the alliance between the PRI and the labor movement.

During the same period, a similar story of policy turnaround was being written in Venezuela, where Democratic Action (AD) had traditionally been a champion of democracy and nationalism as well as of union organization. During its first administration (1946–48), AD promoted an upsurge in union organization and social mobilization.

Democratic Action union leaders promoted the founding of the Venezuelan Workers Confederation (CTV), and its labor bureau integrated union leaders into the party structure. Unions provided AD with political machines while channeling workers' loyalty and supporting AD development policies based on state intervention and import substitution industrialization. In return, AD administrations provided workers with social and labor benefits, and union leaders with political influence.

In 1988 AD union leaders endorsed the populist Carlos Andrés Pérez in the primaries of AD and in his campaign for the presidency. Pérez extended state intervention, established a minimum wage, and made dismissals more difficult during his first administration in the 1970s. After his inauguration in February 1989, however, he surprised foes and followers with his announcement of the "Great Turnaround." The Great Turnaround included trade liberalization, macroeconomic adjustment, and structural reforms of the state. The response of Perez's union allies to his reforms differed from that encountered by his Argentinean and Mexican counterparts. The AD-controlled CTV responded to his policy shift by organizing the first economic general strike in Venezuelan history, followed by a series of demonstrations and other strikes that boycotted most of Pérez's reforms in the labor and social sectors. Opposition by the CTV resulted in diverse concessions related to labor-market and social-security reforms until the government reformist intentions receded under the pressure of social protests and two failed military coups.

THE POLICY TURNAROUND AND THE CHALLENGE FOR
LABOR UNIONS

These convergent policy turnarounds in Argentina, Mexico, and Venezuela resulted from the failure of strategies based on state intervention and import substitution industrialization. The 1982 debt crisis highlighted their strategic limitations while it worsened fiscal deficits and balance-of-payment difficulties. Macroeconomic instability and recession followed during the 1980s, the "lost" decade. By the end of the eighties, incumbent populist labor-based parties in Argentina, Mexico, and Venezuela had shifted toward market-oriented reforms.[5] Accord-

[5] Market-oriented reform included short-term stabilization measures, fiscal restraint, tax reform, financial liberalization, competitive exchange and interest rates, trade liberalization, privatization, and deregulation of most markets, including the labor market. See John Williamson, *Latin American Adjustment: How Much Has Happened?* (Washington, D.C.: Institute for International Economics, 1990).

ing to Cukierman and Tommasi, labor-based parties have a comparative advantage in implementing market-oriented policies that bring uncertainty to their constituencies because they enjoy their trust.[6] That is, they are more credible when they claim that it was the exogenous shock rather than ideology that had induced them to implement market-oriented reforms. Yet, to bring capital back into their economies, labor-based parties in government have to overcome business's distrust of their previous populist character. Their policies, therefore, should be more drastic to show their new commitment to the market.

Drastic market reforms, though, had costs for labor unions and workers whose influence had developed based on state expansion, protectionism, rigid labor markets, and political clout. Trade liberalization increased differences among workers across and within sectors, making it harder to organize labor unions based on horizontal solidarity. International competition and privatization also provoked labor restructuring and layoffs in sectors that had been among the most highly unionized in the past, thus reducing the relative influence of unions. Higher unemployment hurt union bargaining power and increased job instability for union constituencies.[7] Stabilization policies that relied on wage restraint and international competition further reduced their wage bargaining power.[8] Moreover, the reform of social and labor regulations challenged institutions that had provided unions with legal and political clout—from appointments on social security boards to monopolies of representation—which they would not have been able to achieve based solely on their industrial power. More importantly, mar-

---

[6] Alex Cukierman and Mariano Tommasi, "Credibility of Policymakers and of Economic Reform," in Federico Sturzenegger and Tommasi, eds., *The Political Economy of Reform* (Cambridge: MIT Press, 1998).

[7] In Argentina, according to the permanent household surveys of the National Institute of Statistics and Censuses (INDEC), unemployment increased from 6.5 percent in 1988 to 18.6 percent in 1995. In Venezuela unemployment rose from 6.9 percent in 1988 to 9.6 percent in 1989 and 10.4 percent in 1990, although it fell to 6.5 percent in 1993. See Keila Betancourt, Samuel Freije, and Gustavo Márquez, *Mercado labora: Instituciones y regulaciones* (Labor markets: Institutions and regulations) (Caracas: IESA, 1995), 5. In Mexico, according to the International Labour Organisation, (ILO), unemployment measurements are highly contentious, but open unemployment peaked in 1983 and 1984. See ILO, *Yearbook of Labour Statistics* (Geneva; ILO, various years). In addition, the combined official rate of open unemployment and underemployment grew from 6.8 percent in 1989 to 8 percent in 1994. See Carlos Salinas de Gortari, *VI Informe de Gobierno* (VI State of the union) (Mexico City: Presidencia de la Nación, 1994).

[8] In Argentina, hyperinflation cut manufacture real wages by 36.3 percent between January 1989 and March 1991. Even after the success of stabilization, manufacture real wages fell by 12 percent between April 1989 and June 1995. Consejo Ténico de Inversiones, *La economía argentina:. Anuario 1997* (The Argentine economy: Yearbook 1997) (Buenos Aires: CTI, 1997), 65. In Venezuela the real industrial wage fell 35 percent in the 1989–93 period. Unido Industrial Statistics Database, 3-digit (1998). In Mexico real wages in manufacturing had dropped by almost 40 percent between 1982 and 1988, and despite improvements during the Salinas administration, they did not recover their 1982 level. ILO (fn 7).

ket reforms introduced a high degree of uncertainty about the future positions of union constituencies in the labor market, which often induced them to reject the changes. All these effects were more acute in the sectors that had previously enjoyed high levels of protection from competition (such as the public and the manufacture sectors).

In spite of the effect of market-oriented reforms on unionized labor, incumbent labor-based parties and their allied unions in Venezuela, Mexico, and Argentina had strong incentives to bargain with each other. Both sides preferred to avoid costly militancy and to be governed by labor-based parties rather than by other parties implementing the reforms. Yet, while some of the unions discussed in this study collaborated with their allied parties in government, others engaged in costly militant activities, and some of them undermined the governance of labor-based administrations. What conditions explain labor loyalty to or betrayal of long-term party allies? Furthermore, the success of labor unions in obtaining their objectives was varied, whether they chose restraint or militancy. Why did government officials grant concessions in some cases and not in others?

INTEREST, INSTITUTIONS, AND COMPARATIVE ANALYSIS

Various bodies of literature provide important insights into these questions. Interest-based theories have focused on classes, factors, and sectors as the unit of analysis. These demand-driven theories derive the policy preferences of different actors from their economic interests, explaining policies as a result of these demands.[9] Some of them focus on the effect of globalization and market-oriented reforms on the economic interest of diverse sectors, such as exposed and protected or public and private.[10] According to these theories, the policy preferences of

[9] Jeffry Frieden, "Invested Interests: The Politics of National Economic Policies in a World of Global Finance," *International Organization* 45 (Autumn 1991); Peter Gourevitch, *Politics in Hard Times: Comparative Responses to International Economic Crises* (Ithaca, N. Y.: Cornell University Press, 1986); and Ronald Rogowski, *Commerce and Coalitions* (Princeton: Princeton University Press, 1989).

[10] For example, Frieden presents a general argument about sector-driven policy preferences and applies it to unions and exchange rate policies. Frieden (Ibid.); and idem, "Labor and Politics of Exchange Rates: The Case of the European System," in Sanford Jacoby, ed., *The Workers of Nations: Industrial Relations in a Global Economy* (New York and London: Oxford University Press, 1995). Peter Swenson focuses on cross-class coalitions based on sector-level preferences with regard to collective bargaining decentralization and state adjustment. Swenson, "Bringing Capital Back In, Or Social Democracy Reconsidered," *World Politics* 43 (July 1991). The Latin American literature uses a similar logic to explain populist coalitions between urban workers and industrialists producing for the domestic market based on the transfer of resources from exporting to protected sectors for import substitution industrialization. Fernando Henrique Cardoso and Enzo Faletto, *Dependencia y desarrollo en América Latina* (Dependency and development in Latin America) (Buenos Aires: Siglo XXI, 1969); and Guillermo O'Donnell, *Modernization and Bureaucratic-Authoritarianism* (Berkeley: University of California, Institute of International Studies, 1973).

employees (and employers) in the internationally exposed (or protected) sectors are based on their economic interests in international markets or their dependence on state subsidies. These theories provide a robust account of the origin of union preferences, based on union interests vis-à-vis economic liberalization. These theories, however, present some empirical limitations for explaining the patterns of interaction in my case studies because I found variation within sectors that share a common economic interest. For instance, although both Mexico and Venezuela are oil exporters and oil production in both is monopolized by the state, their oil workers' unions reacted to management attempts to increase labor productivity very differently.

Interest-based theories overlook the effect of institutions on shaping social demands. Institutional variables influence the bargaining power of unions and their relationship with governments. In particular, explanations based on the economic interest of unions alone cannot account for the influence of populist legacies or of organizations on members who are uncertain about the effect of market-oriented reforms on their future interests. Institutional analyses focus either on "formal-public institutions" that influence the responses of governments to social demands or on "socioeconomic institutions" that shape the distributional pressures from social organizations.[11] Regarding formal-public institutions, the recent literature on the politics of economic liberalization centers on policymakers and looks at the capacity of governments to control social demands that may derail market-oriented reforms.[12] Regarding socioeconomic institutions, the literature on corporatism emphasizes the effect of macrolevel organizational variables, including union internal dynamics and long-term partisan alliances, on union

[11] Geoffrey Garrett and Peter Lange, "Internationalization, Institutions, and Political Change," in Robert Keohane and Helen Milner, eds., *Internationalization and Domestic Politics* (Cambridge: Cambridge University Press, 1996).

[12] Volumes by Joan Nelson, Steven Haggard and Robert Kaufman, and Dani Rodrik assume that liberalization has concentrated costs and diffused benefits, making it difficult to organize collective action in support of reform. Nelson, ed., *Economic Crisis and Policy Choice: The Politics of Adjustment in the Third World* (Princeton: Princeton University Press, 1990); idem, *Fragile Coalitions: The Politics of Economic Adjustment* (New Brunswick, N.J.: Transaction Books, 1989); Haggard and Kaufman, eds., *The Politics of Economic Adjustment* (Princeton: Princeton University Press, 1992); idem, *The Political Economy of Democratic Transitions* (Princeton: Princeton University Press, 1995); and Rodrik "Understanding Economic Reform," *Journal of Economic Literature* 36 (March 1996). Therefore, the management of reform implies the thwarting of societal resistance and the insulation of reformist policymakers. Catherine Conaghan and James Malloy and Carlos Acuña and William Smith also point out the combination of repression, co-optation, and insulation by skillful policymakers for the implementation of market reforms for Latin America. Conaghan and Malloy, *Unsettling Statecraft: Democracy and Neoliberalism in the Central Andes* (Pittsburgh: University of Pittsburgh Press, 1994); Acuña and Smith, "The Political Economy of Structural Adjustment: The Logic of Support and Opposition to Neoliberal Reform," in Smith, Acuña, and Eduardo Gamarra, eds., *Latin American Political Economy in the Age of Neoliberal Reform* (New Brunswick, N.J.: Transaction Publishers, 1994).

preferences and strategies vis-à-vis governments.[13] The West European version of corporatism assumes open economies and societal corporatism. The Latin American version assumes closed economies and puts greater emphasis on the use of state institutions to control labor organization.[14]

While interest-based theories disregard institutions, macrolevel institutional analysis does not sufficiently explain variation in union behavior within the same country.[15] My case studies, though, show diversity in the union-government interaction within each country. Hence, following a path set by Pizzorno and Crouch[16] and reexamined by the recent comparative literature on union politics and the effects of globalization or market reforms on different sectors and across different countries,[17] I shift the focus of analysis to unions as organizations and to their interactions with governments in a variety of contexts. I pro-

[13] A number of scholars have analyzed the effect of union density and concentration, centralization of wage bargaining, and partisan affiliation on union behavior. See, for example, Phillipe Schmitter, "Still the Century of Corporatism," *Review of Politics* 36 (January 1974); David Cameron, "Social Democracy, Labor Quiescence, and the Representation of Economic Interest in Advanced Capitalist Society," and Peter Lange, "Unions, Workers, and Wage Regulation: The Rational Bases of Consent," in John H. Goldthorpe, ed., *Order and Conflict in Contemporary Capitalism* (Oxford: Clarendon Press, 1984); Lars Calmfors and John Driffill, "Centralization and Wage Bargaining," *Economic Policy* 3 (April 1988); R. Michael Alvarez, Geoffrey Garrett, and Peter Lange, "Government Partisanship, Labor Organization, and Macroeconomic Performance," *American Political Science Review* 85 (June 1991); and Peter Lange and George Tsebelis, "Strikes around the World: A Game Theoretic Approach," in Jacoby (fn. 10).

[14] In Schmitter's original definition, organized interests in "societal" corporatism emerged more autonomously from the state than in "state" corporatism. In the comparative Latin American literature, Ruth Berins Collier and David Collier emphasize state "incorporation" of labor, and Francisco Zapata stresses the deeply political character of union activity resulting from the high degree of state intervention. Country studies confirm this view. In particular, these three countries are classified by both Zapata and Collier and Collier as having historically high levels of state intervention and legal benefits for formal workers. Collier and Collier (fn. 3); idem, "Inducement versus Constraints: Disaggregating 'Corporatism,'" *American Political Science Review* 73 (December 1979); Zapata, *El conflicto sindical en América Latina* (Labor conflict in Latin America) (Mexico City: El Colegio de Mexico, 1986); and idem, *Autonomía y subordinación en el sindicalismo latinoamericano* (Autonomy and subordination of Latin American unionism) (Mexico City: Fondo de Cultura Económica, 1993).

[15] Katrina Burgess's dissertation, an institutionalist work on the reshaping of the alliance between organized labor and labor parties, focuses on the external costs created by political parties on the decision making of unions at the national level. Instead, I propose to analyze the internal dynamics of unions and the effect of competition for leadership or for members on their relations with political parties. Burgess, "Alliances under Stress: Economic Reform and Party-Union Relations in Mexico, Spain, and Venezuela" (Ph.D. diss., Princeton University, 1998).

[16] Allesandro Pizzorno, "Political Exchange and Collective Identity," in Colin Crouch and Pizzorno eds., *The Resurgence of Class Conflict in Western Europe since 1968*, vol. 2 (New York: Holmes and Meier Publishers, Inc., 1978); and Crouch, *Trade Unions: The Logic of Collective Action* (Cambridge: Fontana Paperback, 1982).

[17] Volumes edited by Miriam Golden and Jonas Pontusson and by Christopher Candland and Rudra Sil provide a nice sample of new work in this direction for the developed and the developing world respectively. Golden and Pontusson, eds., *Bargaining for Change: Union Politics in North America and Europe* (Ithaca, N. Y.: Cornell University Press, 1992); and Candland and Sil, eds., *Industrial Relations in the Age of Globalization* (Oxford: Oxford University Press, forthcoming).

pose a partisan theory of union-government interactions that can be applied both to national confederations across countries and to individual unions in different sectors within the same country by focusing on the interaction of variables that can be singled out in different contexts. The comparison across countries and sectors allows me to isolate the effect of interest at the sector level and of institutions at the national level.

PATTERNS OF UNION-GOVERNMENT INTERACTION

The interaction between unions and governments involves either union militancy or restraint and the capacity to obtain concessions from the government through these means. Militancy here means union-organized protest that affects labor relations; it is the most usual measurement of union behavior. Militancy can disrupt production and undermine governance, especially of labor-based parties who are in power because part of their electoral appeal is based on their control of labor. Militancy is usually measured by counting the number of strikes, their duration, and their scope. Repertoires of protest vary, however, depending on institutional and cultural legacies.[18] Other means of protest include demonstrations, boycotts, sabotage, hunger strikes, sit-ins, and the like.

The interaction does not end with union militancy or restraint because the government can respond by granting or refusing concessions. Since militancy is costly for unions, union leaders prefer to threaten industrial action rather than actually to exercise it. If the union is strong, this threat should suffice to obtain concessions from the government because conflict also involves costs for the government. Yet, some strong unions choose militancy to achieve their demands despite the cost. Indeed, even weak unions that have more to lose and less to win from labor conflict sometimes opt for "heroic defeats," to borrow Golden's metaphor.[19]

To understand this apparent irrationality in the behavior of unions as well as its effect (if any) on the government granting them concessions, I combined the reactions of both actors into four possible inter-

---

[18] Due to the effect of institutional and cultural constraints, militancy was measured using diverse forms. For instance, the meaning of a general strike in Argentina, where they have occurred often in the past—even under Peronist administrations—is different from that of a general strike in Venezuela, where there were no antecedents of such means of protest for economic demands. See James W. McGuire, *Peronism without Peron: Unions, Parties, and Democracy in Argentina* (Stanford, Calif.: Stanford University Press, 1997); and Steve Ellner, *Organized Labor in Venezuela, 1958–1991* (Wilmington, Del.: Scholarly Resources, 1993).

[19] Miriam Golden, *Heroic Defeats: The Politics of Job Loss* (Cambridge: Cambrige University Press, 1997).

WORLD POLITICS

TABLE 1
CLASSIFICATION OF POSSIBLE UNION-GOVERNMENT INTERACTIONS

	No Militancy	Militancy
Concessions	Successful restraint or "cooperation"	Successful militancy or "opposition"
No concessions	Unsuccessful restraint or "subordination"	Unsuccessful militancy or "resistance"

actions. Four categories resulted from the combination: successful militancy or "opposition," unsuccessful militancy or "resistance," successful restraint or "cooperation," and unsuccessful restraint or "subordination." The classification is presented in Table 1.

I applied this classification to the main national labor confederations in Argentina, Mexico, and Venezuela, as well as to unions in five economic sectors deeply affected by market reforms: automobile, education, electricity, oil, and telecommunications.[20] The national labor confederations were the Argentine CGT, the Mexican CTM, and the Venezuelan CTV.[21] The individual unions organized sectors that were under state management, with the exception of the automobile sector, which enjoyed preferential protection in all three countries.[22] These sectors were chosen because their previous conditions strengthened their bargaining power during the period of protectionism but made them more vulnerable to economic liberalization and state retrenchment. This research design facilitates comparisons across countries, sectors, and even different levels of union organization and facilitates the isolation of the common effect of the independent variables on the dependent variables in these diverse contexts. Since about half of the unions experienced a change in strategy during the period under dis-

[20] National confederations are multisectoral economy-wide organizations to which industry-specific unions adhere.

[21] In all three countries, I compare the responses of the main national confederations to a set of policies: stabilization, privatization, trade liberalization, social security, changes in the regulations for labor organization, and labor market flexibility.

[22] The unions involved in the study in Argentina were the Union of Automobile Workers (SMATA), the Federation of Light and Power Workers (FATLyF), the Federation of Telephone Workers (FOETRA), the Union of State-Owned Oil Workers (SUPE), and the Argentine Federation of Teachers (CTERA) with its rival unions. In Mexico, the unions in the study were the Mexican Union of Telephone Workers (STRM), the Mexican Union of Oil Workers (STPRM), the Mexican Union of Electricity Workers (SME), the National Union of Education Workers (SNTE), and the local union of Ford Motors Workers at Cuatitlán. In Venezuela, the unions studied were the Federation of Telephone Workers (FETRATEL), the Federation of Electricity Workers (FETRAELEC), the Federation of Oil Workers (FEDEPETROL), the Ford Motors' Section of the Federation of Automobile Workers (FETRAUTOMOTRIZ), and the multiple unions in the education sector. In all these cases, I analyzed the process of industrial restructuring and reform that involved bargaining with the specific union studied.

TABLE 2
UNION-GOVERNMENT INTERACTIONS BY COUNTRY AND SECTOR

Sectors	Countries Venezuela	Mexico	Argentina	Sectoral Variation	Total Cases
Oil	C[a] → O	S[b] → S	C → C	C=3, O[c]=1, S=2	6
Automobile	C → C	R[d] → S	O → C	C=3, O=1, S=1, R=1	6
Telecom.	C → O	C → C	O → C	C=4, O=2	6
Electricity	C → O	C → O	O → C	C=3, O=3	6
Education	R → R	O → O	R → R	R=4, O=2	6
Nat'l. conf.	O → O	S → S	S → C	C=1, O=2, S=3	6
Nat'l Variation	C=5, O=5, R=2	C=3, O=3, S=5, R=1	C=6, O=3, S=1, R=2		
Total cases	12	12	12		36

[a] C= cooperation (successful restraint)
[b] S= subordination (unsuccessful restraint)
[c] O= opposition (successful militancy)
[d] R= resistance (unsuccessful militancy)

cussion, two observations are reported for each union, thus doubling their number (N=18x2=36) to show the continuity or change in union strategies.[23] Table 2 summarizes all studied interactions by country and sector. The arrows show the passing of time between the first and the second observation. The indicators for militancy and concessions are provided in the Appendix.

Table 2 shows that the case studies provide an array of observations of different union-government interactions with no apparent national or sector-level pattern. It illustrates the need to go beyond country and sector-level variables. The bottom row of the table shows that each of the countries presented at least three different types of interactions despite common national contexts (defined in terms of political institutions and macroeconomic conditions). In turn, the data in the right-hand columns of the table also show diversity in the interactions within each of the economic sectors despite the similarity of interests. In the next section I propose a hypothesis to account for this variation.

A PARTISAN THEORY OF UNION-GOVERNMENT INTERACTION

Union members have different preferences for wages, work conditions, and job stability derived from their diverse labor-market alternatives.

[23] Changes in the independent variable from one category to another were used as cut-off points when possible. When there were no changes in the independent variable, the cut-off was based on two diverse reform initiatives (for example, privatization and restructuring) when possible.

Union leaders thus aggregate a particular combination of such preferences into specific union demands. Union leaders also organize collective action (either strikes or restraint) and make possible the control of workers' behavior for the intertemporal exchange of current restraint for future benefits.[24] Hence, union leaders, as workers' representatives, are the agents of any exchange with government officials.

Unions, however, are not perfect agents, and the preferences of union leaders need not be the same as those of workers.[25] Union leaders also have their own objectives in the exchange besides those of their constituencies. For example, union leaders may seek ideological or material rewards while acting as workers' representatives, or they may prefer to maximize the long-term rather than short-term goals of workers. It is possible, however, to assume that they want to maximize leadership survival. That is, whatever the objectives of union leaders, their primary constraint is to "remain in power because otherwise they would not be able to pursue their objectives."[26] Hence, while their objectives can be perceived as a cost for their agency role in the exchange, union leaders are constrained by their constituencies' preferences to the extent that they want to avoid being replaced as workers' agents.[27] Union leaders want to avoid replacement by internal or external rivals. They can be replaced by new leaders who propose a different set of union demands (partisan or leadership competition), or their members can leave the union for other unions whose banners have become more attractive for them (union competition).[28]

Previous attempts at leadership survival have led union leaders to build long-term alliances with political parties to complement industrial muscle with political influence. Political parties channeled labor demands through the state and helped mobilize support from other sectors.[29] Partisan alliances built on historical exchanges created loyalty

---

[24] Pizzorno (fn. 16), 278.

[25] Crouch (fn. 16), 161. The imperfection of the union agency may be a desirable goal for workers that select union leaders not just to carry their demands but also to articulate them and to calculate the benefits of intertemporal exchanges.

[26] Henry Farber, "The Analysis of Union Behavior," in O. Ashenfelter and R. Layard, eds., *Handbook of Labor Economics* (Amsterdam: North-Holland, 1986), 1080.

[27] Farber argues that the democratic constraints on the leadership range from cases where the limits are so loose that the leadership can maximize their objective function without regard to the constraints of the political process (dictatorship) to cases where the leadership is severely hampered by the political process and the need to answer the rank and file. Yet, he shows that the possibility of insurgency constrains leaders even in imperfect democracies. Ibid.

[28] In a Hirschmanian sense, replacement by alternative leaders can be assimilated to "voice" within the same organization while the abandonment of the union by members is similar to his concept of "exit." Albert Hirschman, *Exit, Voice, and Loyalty* (Cambridge: Harvard University Press, 1970).

[29] J. Samuel Valenzuela, "Labour Movements and Political Systems: Some Variations," in Marino Regini, ed., *The Future of Labour Movements* (Newbury Park, Calif.: Sage Publications, 1992).

bonds between parties and unions, thus influencing both their ability to bargain and the attitudes of union leaders toward incumbent politicians. Thus, partisan loyalty implies that, all things being equal, union leaders should be more willing to restrain their militancy when their allied parties are in the government and to increase it when those parties are in the opposition.[30] It follows that if allied union leaders are replaced by others associated with opposition political parties, the change will affect not only the union leaders but also the terms of union-government interactions.

Strategic politicians consider the effect of partisan loyalty on union attitudes. Loyal unions can facilitate the implementation of government policies and provide electoral support. Incumbent politicians should prefer to reward their loyalty rather than support unions that have no attachment to the governing party[31]—in particular, nonallied union leaders, who have no ideological and electoral attachments to the government and who, therefore, have fewer incentives for restraint. The identity of the party in government thus affects the organizational dynamics of labor unions. Partisan loyalty may facilitate fulfilling constituencies' demands at the time of the original alliance. If, however, market reforms implemented by labor-based parties increase the uncertainty of workers about their future, partisan loyalties can become contradictory with constituencies' demands, thereby affecting leadership survival and the incentives of labor leaders in their interaction with governments.

PARTISAN OR LEADERSHIP COMPETITION

Diversity in labor partisan affiliations implies that various parties appeal to organized labor. In Europe these parties tend to be the Communist, the Socialist, and the Christian Democratic Parties. In Latin America strong populist labor parties have historically competed with leftist parties for union influence. The higher costs of leadership competition in a less democratic context also increased the value of subsidies provided by political parties in Latin America. Leadership competition between rivals associated with different political parties could take place within a single union in the form of partisan competition or across diverse unions combining partisan and union competi-

---

[30] Walter Korpi explains this pattern as the result of a trade-off between industrial and political resources. Korpi, *The Working Class in Welfare Capitalism* (London: Routledge and Kegan Paul, 1978). In the Latin American context, Zapata explains the empirical regularity of political strikes by the influence of the state on industrial relations. Zapata (fn. 14, 1986).

[31] The cost of bargaining with nonallied union leaders is higher due to the lack of mutual trust while part of the agency costs may indirectly feed the coffers of opposition parties.

tion for membership. A partisan monopoly exists when the union leadership affiliated with the labor party faces no competition, such as in the Mexican telephone union. Partisan competition occurs when activists of diverse parties compete or even share leadership positions through proportional representation in the same organization, such as in the Venezuelan CTV.

In some cases, diverse factions of the same party compete for union leadership. Such competition still implies the risk of the allied union leaders being replaced as representatives. For the incumbent labor-based parties, partisan competition implies the threat of allied union leaders being replaced by hostile activists associated with the electoral opposition. Leadership competition among factions will only imply such a threat if the winning faction is likely to defect from the party and join the opposition.

If allied union leaders perceive that leadership competition grows (for example, by losing local union elections), they will try to recover the following of their constituencies to avoid replacement. If they believe that rival leaders are taking advantage of their restraint vis-à-vis market reforms, their incentives for militancy will increase to avoid replacement. Calls for militancy aim to show their constituencies that they have not "sold-out." Leadership survival increases incentives for militancy—even if it is not the best bargaining strategy considering their available information—because if labor leaders are replaced, they will not be able to continue bargaining.

UNION COMPETITION

Union competition, or organizational fragmentation, is the rivalry among unions for the representation of workers in the same sector. Where a union monopoly exists, a single union represents all the workers in the sector. In Mexico, for example, the teachers' union was the only union in the education sector, and teachers had no option but to join. Where there is union competition, however, several organizations vie for the membership of the same workers. In Venezuela, for instance, thirteen federations competed for the representation of teachers by 1991.

Union competition introduces the need to coordinate the action of different unions to organize collective action, whether militancy or restraint. The larger the number of unions competing for the same members, the harder it is to coordinate them for collective action.[32] Union competition makes coordination and its enforcement more difficult by

---

[32] Mancur Olson, *The Logic of Collective Action* (Cambridge: Harvard University Press, 1971), 48.

creating incentives to attract members from rival organizations, thereby increasing coordination costs for unions engaging in collective action.[33] Unions trying to attract members from rival organizations are more likely to differentiate themselves by breaking coordination to become the most appealing to potential members. This situation is heightened if unions have diverse partisan identities that generate not only different attitudes toward the government but also different bargaining costs among competing unions.

In addition to coordination costs, each union is also weaker than a single monopolistic union because each leader controls the militancy or restraint of only a share of the involved workers. As a result, government officials put less value on the exchange with individual unions because they have to enter multiple interactions in their negotiations with the sector, thereby increasing bargaining costs. Thus, although government officials prefer to reward loyal unions, they should be less likely to make concessions to competing unions. Government response to loyal unions, therefore, is more related to the strength of the union than to its militancy.

THE PARTISAN THEORY AND UNION-GOVERNMENT INTERACTIONS

The effect of union competition and leadership competition on the interaction between union leaders and government officials varies according to the party in power. When labor-based parties implement market-oriented reforms, allied union leaders are willing to collaborate despite the uncertainty and distress of their constituencies due to their loyalty to long-term allies. Loyal union leaders are predisposed to collaborate and can expect some concessions in return. Moreover, they have better information about the commitments and constraints of their partisan allies and the need to implement these policies.

Yet, when labor-based parties shift their policy, they leave void the populist space of those who disagree with market-oriented policies. Opposition political parties from the left or disgruntled politicians splitting from the governing party (on ideological grounds) can take advantage of the policy shift to occupy that space. This movement may facilitate the growth of militant union activists allied with political parties or partisan factions opposed to market-oriented reforms and may

---

[33] Miriam Golden shows that coordination in wage bargaining is most likely when union monopoly is high because the competition for members "provides a strong incentive for unions to try to maximize their wage gains in order to retain members or to attract them away from competitors." Golden, "The Dynamics of Trade Unionism and National Economic Performance," *American Political Science Review* 87 (June 1993), 441.

enhance leadership and partisan competition. Indeed, in Mexico, Venezuela, and Argentina, new political parties occupying this populist space emerged.[34] Furthermore, this movement more likely turns factional competition into partisan competition. Partisan competition, in turn, increases the likelihood of militancy. These effects are more likely in sectors where the high uncertainty of workers about the sudden shift from public to private or from protection to exposure is likely to prompt them into militancy. Additionally, market-oriented reforms can sharpen union competition by provoking splits over how to respond or by aggravating the distributive struggle for shrinking resources among rival unions. In their attempts to attract members from rival organizations to increase their representation in these disputes, unions have more incentives to boycott coordination efforts as a strategy of differentiation, thereby weakening all the unions within the sector.

These explanatory conditions are not fixed. The party in power may change with elections. Union competition and partisan competition within the union movement can also change. Governments, though, cannot usually manipulate these variables in the short-term, although their policies can influence their changes. Market reforms in particular can affect all these variables by improving or damaging the electoral opportunities of incumbents, thus affecting the likelihood of challenges to labor leaders and making it harder for unions to coordinate their strategies. If these changes in the explanatory conditions occur, changes in the dependent variable should follow, thereby explaining variations in the union-government interaction during the period under discussion. Table 3 summarizes the expected union-government interactions when a labor-based party implements market-oriented reforms.

"Cooperation," or successful restraint for concessions, is more likely in the absence of union and partisan competition—when only one union organizes all workers and is affiliated with the governing party. Partisan loyalty reduces the incentives for militancy and facilitates bargaining while union monopoly boosts the bargaining power of the union because government officials want the collaboration of a strong and loyal union.

"Opposition," or successful militancy, can more likely be expected in the presence of growing partisan competition and union monopoly—

---

[34] Market reforms created a new critical juncture in the electoral politics of these countries (together with a simultaneous process of democratization or decentralization) that resulted in the emergence of new parties or divisions in the incumbent labor-based parties. Argentina experienced the emergence of FREPASO or Front for a Country with Solidarity (originating in a splintering of Peronism). Mexico saw the organization of the PRD or Party of the Democratic Revolution (also emerging from a division within the PRI). In Venezuela, Causa R grew to become a national political party and was followed by an array of new political options that reshaped the traditional two-party system.

TABLE 3
PREDICTED BACKGROUND CONDITIONS FOR LOYAL UNIONS AND
LABOR GOVERNMENTS

		Partisan Competition for Leadership	
		Monopoly (one party)	Competition (many parties)
Union Competition for Members	Monopoly (one union)	Cooperation (successful restraint)	Opposition (successful militancy)
	Competition (many unions)	Subordination (unsuccessful restraint)	Resistance (unsuccessful militancy)

when leaders affiliated with different parties compete for the control of a single union. Growing partisan competition based on protesting the consequences of the policy shift increases the incentives for "irrational" militancy[35] because allied union leaders are afraid of being replaced and the sections controlled by contenders have already turned militant. Since the union is strong, government officials are more likely to grant concessions so that allied union leaders can show a better record than their contenders.

"Subordination," or unsuccessful restraint, more likely results from competition among different unions affiliated with the governing party. While partisan loyalty facilitates restraint, union competition weakens all unions despite their loyalty. Government officials may also choose to reward only the most compliant unions. This selection should also prompt competing unions to comply to avoid losing resources and becoming less attractive for members than other competing unions.

"Resistance," or unsuccessful militancy, more likely happens when partisan competition and union competition overlap—competing unions affiliated with different parties. Union competition weakens all unions and, together with partisan competition, makes coordination more difficult. Unions associated with opposition parties protest to differentiate themselves from cooperative loyal unions. If they succeed in attracting members due to their bellicose stance, loyal unions will turn more militant to avoid losing members although union competition makes them weak and unlikely to be successful.

---

[35] Since union monopoly makes the union strong and the government can observe this strength, it seems unnecessary to enter a conflict to show it in terms of the external interaction, but partisan competition prompts union leaders to protest for reasons linked to their internal power.

APPLYING THE PARTISAN THEORY IN
ARGENTINA, MEXICO, AND VENEZUELA

According to the partisan theory, union-government interactions in Argentina, Mexico, and Venezuela should have felt the effects of partisan ties because the incumbent parties were labor-based. In this context, leadership competition should have increased the likelihood of labor militancy, and union competition should have decreased the likelihood of concessions for unions. This section provides a brief description of the dynamics of the case studies, relating them to the predicted background conditions for each interaction, which are summarized in the Appendix.

In Venezuela, although AD historically controlled the CTV, other parties competed for leadership and displaced AD briefly in the 1960s. Also the system of proportional representation reinforced the pluralism of the CTV in its leadership, resulting in the inclusion of minority parties in the executive committee.[36] In 1989, after Pérez announced the reforms, urban riots signaled the general discontent of the population. Union leaders of AD, afraid of losing control of the CTV to opposition parties protesting the reforms, called the first economic general strike in Venezuelan history for May 1989. The tension between partisan loyalty and leadership survival divided the AD union leadership between those with positions in the CTV who were more favorable to the strike and those with party appointments who were more reluctant about it.[37] Pérez's concessions included emergency wage hikes, suspension of layoffs, and retaining price controls for basic staples. In 1990 and 1991, however, Causa R, a new political party, grew rapidly in the union movement by rejecting reforms, especially among public sector workers, further increasing partisan competition. As a result, the CTV called additional protests despite Perez's move to halt the reform of the severance payment system and social security and his acceptance of union demands for the resignation of the labor minister. Hence, union monopoly and increasing partisan competition explain the CTV opposition.

In spite of the national tendencies in union behavior, Venezuela experienced variation in union-government interactions. In the case of the privatization of the state-owned monopoly of telecommunications,

---

[36] Ellner (fn. 18).

[37] Author's interviews with AD union leaders of different factions confirmed the account of Steve Ellner. See Ellner, "Organized Labor's Political Influence and Party Ties in Venezuela: *Acción Democrática* and Its Labor Leadership," *Journal of Interamerican Studies and World Affairs* 31 (Winter 1989).

the combination of union monopoly and partisan monopoly exercised by the AD union leadership resulted in cooperation. Labor restraint was exchanged for concessions that included employee-owned stock, job stability, and labor directors. Subsequent worker discontent with the privatization, however, resulted in Causa R winning the union elections in the main local union (Caracas) while growing in other regions by protesting market reforms and privatization. As a result, a new AD leadership took control of the union and increased the militancy of the national union against labor restructuring to show their responsiveness to the discontented rank and file. In spite of attempts at broad restructuring, the company could not change work conditions from the privatization agreements. In this case, the increase in partisan competition combined with union monopoly to move the union into opposition.[38]

Very similar dynamics explain the shift from cooperation to opposition in the cases of the electricity workers' union of the state-owned electric company (CADAFE) and of the state-owned oil company (PDVSA). Union monopoly and an unchallenged AD leadership facilitated cooperation when the Pérez administration decentralized CADAFE. Concessions to the union included handsome monetary incentives for transfers, job stability, and wage increases for workers in the interior. Yet, the subsequent discontent of workers also gave the election of the Caracas's union to Causa R, who had led the local union into a wildcat strike. Subsequently, the AD leadership increased the militancy of the union and successfully boycotted industrial restructuring. Again, the increase in partisan competition combined with union monopoly resulted in opposition. In PDVSA, the combination of union monopoly and no partisan competition for the AD leadership favored cooperation in 1991. In return, the union retained hiring prerogatives. Afterward, workers' discontent resulted in increasing partisan competition, not only from Causa R but also from other left-wing parties—the Movement to Socialism (MAS) and the Electoral Movement of the People (MEP). As a result, the AD leadership took a more combative stance against management proposals in 1993 and tried to gain legitimacy by decreasing its discretionary use of hiring prerogatives and obtaining a halt to the reform of commissaries.[39] Thus, partisan competition, along with union monopoly, explains the shift of the union to opposition.

Contrary to the unions in public enterprises, the two remaining cases show a different pattern. The union of Ford Motors, a local union

---

[38] Union leaders, government officials, and company managers, interviewed by the author, Caracas, June–July 1994, May–July 1996.
[39] Ibid.

based in Carabobo, opted for cooperation. The union restrained and accepted layoffs and new working rules in return for participation in the selection of those laid off, reincorporated, and trained. In this case, cooperation resulted from the combination of union monopoly and partisan monopoly. In a personal interview, the labor relations' manager said that cooperation for restructuring and training was possible because the AD uniqn leadership did not face competition from left-wing parties.[40] In education, the overlap of union competition and partisan competition in thirteen federations affiliated with diverse political parties and groups resulted in militant but unsuccessful resistance to the administrative reform initiated by Minister Gustavo Roosen. While coordination was difficult, the militancy of the rank and file rewarded the free riding of bellicose organizations. This situation brought the vice minister of education, Francisco Castillo to complain, "I think that there is a competition among unions, where the one that strikes the most is the one that is the most supported by the rank and file."[41] In spite of the differences between these two cases, both sectors contrast with telecommunication, electricity, and oil in that the levels of union competition and partisan competition did not change during the period studied, and neither did the studied interactions.

In Argentina,[42] Peronism's policy shift divided the CGT. All three competing factions, though, remained within the ranks of Peronism. The Menem administration was unwilling to make concessions, in particular to the most "populist" faction, although it provided selective incentives (such as guaranteed monopolies of representation and execu-

---

[40] Author's interview with Ford's labor relations manager and AD union leader was confirmed by Consuelo Iranzo, Luisa Bethencourt, Hector Lucena, and Fausto Sandoval Bauza. See Iranzo, Bethencourt, Lucena, and Bauza, "Competitividad, Calificación y Trabajo: Sector Automotriz Venezolano" (Competition, qualifications, and work: Automobile sector in Venezuela) (Manuscript, Cendes, 1996).

[41] Cite from El Nacional, January 9, 1991. Former Minister Gustavo Roosen and union leaders of FetraMagisterio and Fenatev confirmed this account derived from a press chronology, in interviews with the author, Caracas, June 1996.

[42] The information on the Argentine cases is derived from a press chronology, union annual reports and other documents, interviews with union leaders of all factions, three ministers of labor and other government officials, as well as labor relations managers in the involved companies. The Argentine press chronology was elaborated in the archives of the newspaper Clarin and includes newspapers such as Clarin, La Nacion, La Rozon, Cronica, ElCronista Comercial, Pagina 12, and Ambito Financiero. Union sources included the internal constitution, annual minutes, and balances for the 1988 to 1994 period for SMATA, FATLyF, CTERA, FOETRA, and SUPE. Documents included collective bargaining contracts signed by the unions and approved by the Ministry of Labor, bill proposals, parliamentary information on introduced, modified, and passed bills. Interviews included SUPE and CGT union leader Antonio Cassia (Buenos Aires, 1993, 1995), FATLyF union leader Carlos Alderete (Buenos Aires, 1993), CTA union leader Victor De Gennaro (Buenos Aires, 1995), CTERA union leader Marta Marffei (Buenos Aires, 1995), ministers of labor Armando Caro Figueroa (Buenos Aires, 1994), Rodolfo Diaz (Buenos Aires, 1992, 1995), and Enrique Rodriguez (Buenos Aires, 1992, 1995), managers of labor relations, such as YPF's Roberto Teglia (Buenos Aires, 1995), and Telecom's Juan Giar (Buenos Aires, 1995).

tive appointments) to the most compliant. Peronist labor unions were unable to halt a new law that introduced temporary hiring and decrees that established wage restraint and deprived them of collecting and administering union health-fund fees. As a result, many important unions moved out of the populist faction, and in 1992 all three factions decided to unify under a leadership dominated by the most cooperative union leaders. Thus, from 1989 to 1992 the combination of partisan monopoly and union competition subordinated Peronist unions to the administration. After its unification, the CGT recovered its union monopoly and maintained its Peronist loyalty, moving from subordination to cooperation. As a result, it was rewarded with concessions that included changes in the reforms of pensions, social security, subsidies for health funds, and the maintenance of legislation on collective bargaining and labor organization.

Argentina also shows diversity in union-government interactions although national institutions and conditions remain the same. Menem also privatized the state-owned monopoly of telecommunications, ENTEL. Unlike its Venezuelan counterpart, the union opposed privatization by increasing its militancy. A combination of union monopoly and leadership competition explains this outcome. Leadership competition in the telephone workers' union increased when a populist faction that opposed market reforms and privatization won control of the union in Buenos Aires (the largest in the federation) and increased union militancy.[43] A monopolistic union, nonetheless, was able to obtain concessions, including the administration and representation of employee-owned stock, handsome retirement packages, and subsidies for the union health fund. After privatization, the loyal Peronist leadership won control of the rebellious locals and curtailed leadership competition. Hence, with the absence of union and partisan competition, the union cooperated with the new private management in discussions of labor restructuring. Concessions at this stage included union participation in training, contracts for union-organized companies, and voluntary retirement packages. The privatization of state-owned electric companies also resulted in initial opposition due to a combination of union monopoly and leadership competition. The local unions, which the populist militant faction controlled and which competed with the

---

[43] The policy-shift of Peronism encouraged the formation of a splinter group, which together with some left-wing parties, formed, in turn, a new opposition political party in 1992 that would became the FREPASO in 1994. Among its core organizers was a group of union leaders that had broken ties with the Peronist union movement and organized a new small confederation, the CTA (Congress of Argentine Workers) in 1992.

loyal leadership, joined the CTA in 1992. Since the national federation was a member of the CGT, the dissident unions were expelled. As a result, leadership competition receded. Lacking union competition and partisan competition, the union began to cooperate. In the first period, union concessions included employee-owned stock, subsidies for the union health fund, and contracts for union-organized cooperatives of former employees. In the second period, they included subsidies for union participation in the privatization of companies—public utilities, an energy transmission company, and the concession of a coal mine—as well as voluntary retirement packages.

The cases of the restructuring and privatization of the state-owned oil company (YPF) and of the decentralization of education differed from the previous two examples. In the case of the YPF, the Peronist union leadership faced no competition and had a very close relationship with Menem that facilitated bargaining for concessions, which included subsidies for the union to buy the oil fleet, contracts for union companies employing laid-off workers, and voluntary retirement packages. Thus, leadership monopoly and union monopoly resulted in cooperation. Unlike the oil company, the education sector, as in Venezuela, was fragmented into various unions. Many of them gathered into a national confederation, CTERA, whose leader, Mary Sánchez, was one of the Peronist union leaders who had left the party and the CGT to found the FREPASO and the CTA in protest of the policy shift. Yet, many others unions did not belong to the national confederation and competed with CTERA unions in every province. Many of the non-CTERA unions were Peronist. In this case, the overlapping of union competition and partisan competition coincided with resistance or unsuccessful militancy against the decentralization of education to the provincial level enacted by Congress in 1992. In spite of the restraint of oil workers and of the militancy of teachers that accounted for more than a third of total strikes in 1991 and 1992, in both cases the levels of union competition, partisan competition, and union-government interactions remained the same during the period under discussion.

Lastly, the national union of automobile workers moved from opposition to cooperation in 1991. In this case, union monopoly with no partisan competition made the union's initial opposition unexpected, although the subsequent cooperation coincides with the theory. The increasing militancy of the union until 1991 is related to the rejection of trade liberalization in a heavily protected sector. The consequence of this militancy together with lobbying by business was to persuade the government to grant an industrial regime of protection and gradual opening for the sector after 1991. The industry was thus exceptionally successful in shielding itself from the conditions created by a sudden trade opening. After the regime was granted, the government became again an important partner, and partisan loyalties moved the union toward cooperation.

The Mexican cases highlight the importance of contextualizing the explanatory variables within the constraints created by the political regime on the means of expressing militancy and the costs of partisan competition.[44] Yet at the same time, even in the most constrained environment, where the regime is not totally democratic, the interaction between unions and the government varies. This variation cannot be explained by traditional theories based only on the features of the Mexican regime. The Mexican CTM subordinated to Salinas's policies. The only important concession that it was able to obtain was the prevention of labor-code reform. The same variables—partisan monopoly combined with union competition—explain the confederation's subordination and its exception to cooperation in relation to the labor code.[45] The CTM competed with other national labor confederations also associated with the monopolistic PRI. While partisan loyalty reduced their incentives for militancy, government officials manipulated union competition for scarce resources among the various PRI-related national confederations and rewarded the most compliant of them with selective incentives (such as public recognition and favorable treatment in arbitration boards) to weaken CTM claims. The only exception was when the CTM unified with all other PRI-confederations and reduced union competition to boycott the reform of the labor code successfully. The same institutional mechanism that provided a common forum for all of them to unify, an umbrella organization called the Congress of Labor, had previously facilitated union competition because decision making was based on consensus or unanimity.[46]

[44] State imposed limits on strike activity discard the usefulness of using strikes as a measure of militancy but do not imply that militancy does not take place. Mexican workers have held illegal strikes, used strike petitions as a threat to show their militancy, and resorted very often to sit-ins, demonstrations, and even extreme measures such as going naked or on hunger strikes. On repertoires of protest, see the account of Maria Lorena Cook, *Organizing Dissent* (University Park: Pennsylvania State University Press, 1996). For a historial analysis of the evolution of union strategies, see Alberto Aziz Nassif, *El estado mexicano y la CTM* (The Mexican state and the CTM) (Mexico City: Ed. La Casa Chata, 1989); Ilán Bizberg, *Estado y sindicalismo en México* (State and unionism in Mexico) (Mexico City: El Colegio de México, 1990); and Kevin Middlebrook, *The Paradox of Revolution* (Baltimore: John Hopkins University Press, 1995).

[45] Graciela Bensusán confirms interviews with union leaders and government officials. Bensusán, "Los determinantes institucionales de la flexibilización laboral" (Institutional influences on labor flexibility), *Revista Mexicana de Sociología* 1 (1994).

[46] For instance, the Revolutionary Confederation of Workers and Peasants (CROC) and the Revolutionary Confederation of Mexican Workers (CROM) explicitly boycotted CTM protest against wage ceil-

As in Venezuela and Argentina, the state-owned monopoly of telecommunications, Telmex, was privatized in Mexico. In this case, cooperation in relation to both privatization and restructuring corresponds to the overlap of union monopoly and leadership monopoly, which remained unchanged during the entire period studied. The latter, held since 1974 by a charismatic PRI union leader, Francisco Hernández Juarez, who had co-opted the opposition, successfully provided benefits for his constituencies and developed a close relationship with the president, who often used this union as an example of modern unionism. Moreover, since this union was not affiliated with the CTM, it had more room to maneuver and even organized the Federation of Goods and Services Workers (FESEBES), a new labor confederation competing with the CTM.[47] The union obtained employee-owned shares and a labor director in the private company, wage increases, job stability, and the maintenance of work conditions during privatization. Afterward, concessions included participation in joint committees with management for training and restructuring and increases in wage and nonwage benefits.

The union of electricity workers of the Company of Light and Power, which was not a CTM-affiliate either, also joined the FESEBES. Its charismatic union leader, Jorge Sanchez, also had a close relationship with the president. In this case, the absence of union and leadership competition led to cooperation between the union and management. Cooperation led the government to bail out the company, establish guarantees for union survival, and develop joint union-management committees to discuss productivity and financial issues. Unlike Hernández Juarez, though, the loyal leader lost the union elections in 1993 and was replaced by an independent leadership, breaking the loyalty strings. As expected, this situation increased union incentives for

ings in the Congress of Labor and were publicly rewarded by the government. Subsequent exit of unions from the CTM into preferred organizations, most notably the CROC, increased the pressure on its leadership. See my press chronology, which derives from the archives of Entorno Laboral and which includes newspapers such as *La Jornada, Excelsior, El Sol de Mexico, Uno mas Uno,* and *Reforma.*

[47] Ruth Berins Collier and James Samstad analyze the development of the FESEBES and the "new unionism" in "Mexican Labor and Structural Reform: New Unionism or Old Stalemate?" in Riordan Roett, ed., *The Challenge of Institutional Reform in Mexico* (Boulder, Colo.: Lynne Rienner, 1995). Interviews with union leaders, government officials, and company managers confirmed the numerous accounts on the strategy of this union. For telecommunications, see Enrique De La Garza, "Sindicato y restructuración productiva en México" (Union and labor restructuring in Mexico), *Revista Mexicana de Sociologia* 1 (1994); and De La Garza and Javier Melgoza, "Reestructuración y cambio en las relaciones laborales en la telefonía mexicana" (Restructuring and change in labor relations in the Mexican telephone industry), in Jorge Walter and Cecilia Senen González, eds., *La privatización de las telecomunicaciones en América Latina (Privatization of telecommunications in Latin America)* (Buenos Aires: Eudeba, 1998). For electricity, see Javier Melgoza, "El SME y la productividad: Los saldos de la negociación" (SME and productivity: Outcomes of bargaining), *Polis* 93 (1994).

militancy (although less than if the leadership was associated with an opposition party). It also, however, reduced the partisan incentives of the government to grant concessions to the union, which nonetheless included a reduction of productivity targets and the maintenance of job stability. In this case, the tension between partisan loyalty and leadership survival was broken by the replacement of the loyal leader and his succession by an independent and more militant union leadership.

In Mexico, the education sector was not as fragmented as in Argentina and Venezuela. The National Union of Education Workers (SNTE) which also was not a CTM-affiliate, had a union monopoly and was controlled by PRI union leaders. A discontented rank and file, organized by dissidents in the National Coordinating Committee of Education Workers (CNTE), had toppled the previous PRI leadership. The new PRI leader, Elba Ester Gordillo, therefore, had to win legitimacy to avoid replacement. As a result, the SNTE became more bellicose after the change in leadership while including the dissidents within the executive committee through proportional representation and increasing internal debate.[48] In 1991 when the decentralization law was discussed, a leak from the secretary of education mentioned the division of the centralized union. The SNTE not only became more militant but also joined forces with the dissident CNTE. The government responded by granting centralized national work conditions and earmarked budgets for the states as well as salary hikes and nonwage benefits for the union. Hence, the combination of union monopoly and partisan competition resulted in opposition.

The unions of oil workers and Ford automobile workers in Mexico, both CTM-affiliates, provide interesting cases to illuminate the limits of my explanatory framework. In such cases, partisan competition may be punished by a nondemocratic government that can resort to coercion. Both unions faced sharp restructuring due to the opening of their sectors to private capital and international competition. Both attempted to resist the changes and were forced into subordination by the repression of the CTM and the state. The workers of the Ford Motors plant at Cuatitlán rejected restructuring and chose an independent leadership (linked with left-wing parties), which broke the tension between partisan loyalty and leadership survival and brought the local union to resist industrial restructuring—albeit unsuccessfully—in 1988 and 1992. The

---

[48] Although my account derives from a press chronology and interviews with union leaders, government officials, and experts, the process of modernization and democratization of the union has been widely studied. See, for instance, Cook (fn. 44); and Joe Foewaker, *Popular Mobilization in Mexico, the Teachers' Movement 1977–87* (Cambridge: Cambridge University Press, 1993).

local union not only increased its militancy but also attempted to withdraw from the CTM-affiliated national union. The CTM, upheld by the government and the company, responded to the militant leadership and their supporters with violent repression, forcing the local and the national union into subordination.[49] In the case of the oil workers' union, the PRI union leader had supported the opposition presidential candidate, Cuahutemoc Cárdenas,[50] by delivering votes in the oil regions, although PRI local candidates carried the elections. As a result of the partisan threat, the state gave a fatal blow to the union by putting the union leader in prison under fabricated murder charges and by bringing the union into subordination, thereby shifting the issue of leadership survival from workers to state officials.[51] In both cases, the restrictions on political pluralism of the regime limited partisan competition in the unions and tipped the balance in favor of partisan loyalty by dramatically raising the costs of noncompliance with government officials.[52] The Mexican political regime restricted partisan competition in the union movement, thus limiting the explanatory power of this variable for certain unions. Yet, other non-CTM unions, such as the teachers', telephone workers', and electricity workers' unions—and even the CTM itself—retained their relative autonomy, thus permitting the use of the explanatory variables based on union dynamics to illustrate their interaction with the government.

Table 4 shows the high correspondence between the patterns of union-government interaction presented in Table 2 (and summarized in the Appendix) and the explanatory conditions defined by my partisan theory and presented in Table 3.

This high correspondence between the observed outcomes and the explanatory conditions provides a better account than either macrolevel or sector-level theories for the interactions studied. In a context of al-

---

[49] Interviews and press releases are confirmed by Marisa Von Bulow, "Reestructuración productiva y estrategias sindicales. El caso de la Ford en Cuahutitlán 1987–1993" (Production restructuring and union strategy: The case of Ford in Cuahutitlán 1987–1993) (M.A. thesis, Facultad Latinoamericana de Ciencias Sociales-Sede México, 1994); and Jorge Carrillo, "La Ford en México: Restructuración industrial y cambio en las relaciones sociales" (Ph.D. dissertation, El Colegio de México, Centro de Estudios Sociológicos, 1993).

[50] Cárdenas split from the PRI because he rejected the policy shift and failed to be selected as its presidential nominee. He launched a new coalition, later to be renamed as the PRD, and he delivered the strongest electoral blow to the PRI by dramatically reducing its share of votes (and even claiming victory stolen by fraud) in 1988.

[51] Fabio Barbosa gives a graphic account of the process that confirms interviews and press releases. Barbosa, "La reestructuración de Pemex" (The restructuring of Pemex), *El Cotidiano* 46 (March–April 1992).

[52] These two cases related to Burgess's argument about the PRI imposing external costs on union leaders' decisions. Burgess (fn. 15).

TABLE 4
EXPLANATORY CONDITIONS AND UNION-GOVERNMENT INTERACTION IN
ARGENTINA, MEXICO, AND VENEZUELA

	Explanatory Conditions Assuming Partisan Loyalty		Frequency of Each	Interactions Corresponding with
Possible Interactions	Partisan Competition	Union Competition	Interaction in the Study	Explanatory Conditions
Cooperation (successful restraint)	No	No	13	13
Subordination (unsuccessful restraint)	No	Yes	6	3
Opposition (successful militancy)	Yes	No	12	11
Resistance (unsuccessful militancy)	Yes	Yes	5	5
Totals			36	32

lied labor parties implementing market reforms, partisan competition and union competition influenced the interaction between loyal union leaders and government officials in different sectoral and national contexts. Additionally the explanatory conditions in the studied interactions varied as expected over the short-term, further reinforcing the implications of this explanatory logic.

Other patterns of interaction also deserve attention. In Argentina a pattern of cooperation between unions and government tended to arise mainly from opposition but also from subordination at the national level. In Venezuela a pattern of opposition between the two arose mainly from cooperation, although arriving early in this interaction at the national level. Finally, although Mexico shows a less clear trend, it is where most cases of subordination concentrate. These trends in the interactions studied are related to national institutions that can facilitate the emergence of union competition and partisan competition, thus explaining these patterns.

In Argentina national regulation established monopolies of representation for collective bargaining except in the public administration. As a result, union competition is limited except at the peak level and in the public administration, where the cases of union competition leading to subordination or resistance emerged. The strong partisan identity of labor unions combined with their ability to obtain concessions from the government helped Peronist labor leaders retain control of their unions. In Venezuela collective bargaining rules also facilitated effective union monopolies.[53] The education sector was an exception, excluded from collective bargaining and faced with union competition, as in Argentina. The growth of leadership competition that increased labor incentives for militancy in many AD unions is related to the political changes brought about by the combination of market reforms and political decentralization. These changes made room for new political options not only in the union movement but also in the electoral arena.[54] In Mexico the characteristics of the regime allowed the government to overcome the effect of the explanatory conditions in the cases of oil workers and the Ford Motors' workers of Cuatitlán. These cases do not contradict the explanatory logic but highlight its limitation. In the oil workers' union, partisan monopoly and union monopoly had previously led to labor restraint in return for sizable concessions including nonwage benefits for workers, hiring prerogatives, contracts for union companies, and fees over suppliers' contracts for the union. After its leader challenged the election of Salinas, however, the union was forced into subordination. In the case of Ford Motors, when alternative leaders won local elections, breaking loyalty ties and increasing labor militancy, the government and the CTM also forced the union into subordination. Thus, in Mexico the opportunities for leadership or partisan competition were limited in most cases by a regime that had also curtailed political pluralism in the electoral arena.

National patterns also had important policy consequences. The prevalence of opposition in Venezuela weakened the pace of market reforms until they finally were suspended. The predominance of cooperation in Argentina facilitated the rapid implementation of market reforms and the adoption of union strategies more akin to a market economy. In Mexico, although subordination eased the implementation of reforms, it also slowed the adaptation of union strategies to the new environment. In spite of national trends, though, some cases in each country entered into different interactions explained by other combinations of union competition and partisan competition.

At the sector level there were less clear patterns. The cases in the oil and automobile sectors exhibited a large variation in interactions. Telecommunications and electricity do not have a single predominant interaction, but unions in both sectors successfully obtained concessions through cooperation or opposition (and enjoyed union monop-

[53] International Labour Organization, *Relaciones de Trabajo en Venezuela* (Labor relations in Venezuela) (ILO report, 1991).

[54] Not only did Causa R grow in the unions and in the 1994 elections, but also many political outsiders, including current President Chávez, challenged the traditional political parties after that election.

oly). In the education sector, both resistance and opposition interactions are associated with higher militancy. This finding is consistent with predictions of higher militancy in public-sector workers[55] and with the politicization of the education sector[56] that facilitates the emergence of partisan competition. While partisan competition in Argentina and Venezuela had been an enduring feature of teachers' organizations, in Mexico it took an internal rebellion to allow for increasing partisan pluralism within the union.[57] Thus, although some sector-level patterns emerged, they are insufficient to account for the studied interaction.

CONCLUSIONS

This article attempts to complement the focus on policymakers that has predominated the literature on the political economy of market reforms in developing countries by providing some perspective on labor organizations, which have been neglected. The findings underscore the effect of partisan identities on creating a tension for union leaders when their allies implement market-oriented reforms. In my case studies, union leaders, on the one hand, were pulled by their partisan loyalties—based on long-term goals or on their own personal gain. On the other, they had to respond to their constituencies—based on the short-term goal of political survival. Partisan loyalty to governing allies on the part of union leaders increases incentives for restraint, while leadership or partisan competition pushes them toward militancy if demanded by constituencies. At the same time, union competition affects the strength of the union and its ability to obtain concessions from the government. This theory explained most of the interactions in my study between union and labor-based governments implementing market-oriented reforms in Argentina, Mexico, and Venezuela. In these countries, partisan loyalties inherited from the original postwar alliance between the Peronism, PRI, and AD with labor unions had an important influence on the transition to open economies. The interaction of partisan loyalties with union competition and partisan competition, how-

---

[55] Geoffrey Garrett and Christopher Way, "The Rise of Public Sector Unions, Corporatism and Macroeconomic Performance, 1970–1990," in Barry Eichengreen and Jeffry Frieden, eds., *The Political Economy of European Integration* (New York: Springer-Verlag, 1995).

[56] Ivan Nuñez, "Sindicatos de maestros, Estado y Políticas Educacionales en América Latina" (Teachers unions, state and education policy in Latin America), in M. L. P. B. Franco and D. M. L. Zibas, eds., *Final do Seculo: Desafios da educacao na América Latina (End of the century: Challenges for education in Latin America)* (Sao Paulo: Cortes Editora, CLACSO REDUC, 1990).

[57] Cook (fn. 44).

ever, can also influence the attitudes of unions and governments toward each other for nonlabor parties in government. The absence of partisan loyalties can make restraint and negotiations more difficult for unions and governments affecting the influence of leadership competition for militant labor leaders and of union competition in noncooperative unions. Further testing in other cases will show the extensions and limitations of this partisan theory.

If my argument is correct and political actors were aware of the effect of union competition and leadership competition, unions should have tried to affect these variables. In the previous section, I analyze the effect of legal institutions and electoral dynamics in shaping national patterns of union competition and leadership competition and thus union-government interactions. According to Collier and Collier the incorporation of labor shaped both legal institutions and the political system.[58] When the alliance between labor unions and political parties was established, the corporatist labor legislation that emerged shaped the opportunities for union competition and leadership competition because unions sought to strengthen their bargaining power and politicians wanted to reinforce labor loyalties. In Argentina, Mexico, and Venezuela, the labor legislation included restrictions to exit (ranging from permission to close shops to monopolies of representation) and facilitated the controls over leadership selection by incumbents.[59] At the same time, the partisan loyalties derived from the alliance were reinforced by the delivery of wage and social benefits when labor-based parties were in government.[60] National patterns thus resulted from the diverse emphasis on these variables that emerged from the original alliance. Union competition, however, was "stickier" than partisan competition because it was harder to modify on an individual basis without a legislative reform. This stickiness explains why leadership competition varied more frequently than union competition in the cases studied, making changes in militancy levels more likely than changes in the ability of unions to obtain concessions in the short term.

Although market reforms affect both conditions as analyzed above, changes are not easy to manipulate in the short term. Politicians cannot easily control electoral dynamics unless they resort to repression. Indeed, they are usually subject to the electoral dynamics unleashed by their shift toward the market and by the new alliances that this critical

[58] Collier and Collier (fn. 2).
[59] Collier and Collier (fn. 14, 1979).
[60] Zapata (fn. 14, 1986).

juncture allowed in the union movement.[61] They could reform the rules for labor organization, but these regulations have remained unchanged in all three countries during the period studied. Reforms to the regulations on labor organization affecting union competition would have also risked changing the partisan ties between labor unions and governing politicians on which incumbents counted to implement their policies and remain in power.[62]

The conclusions of this study resonate with Michels's claim that although organization is the weapon of the weak in their struggle with the strong, "it is the organization which gives birth to the dominion of the elected over the electors, of the mandataries over the mandators, of the delegates over the delegators."[63] He considers, however, that leadership competition should limit the iron rule of oligarchy in organizations because the "ascent of the new leaders always involves the danger, for those who are already in possession of power, that they will be forced to surrender their places to the newcomers. The old leader must therefore keep himself in permanent touch with the opinions and feelings of the masses to which he owes his position."[64] Coincidentally with Michels and Hirshman, this study shows that although union competition provides exit options for workers, it weakens unions. Instead, leadership or partisan competition provides voice options to increase representation but without weakening their bargaining power to the same extent.[65]

Finally, this study suggests that future research should address the interaction between different levels of analysis. Such research would not only look to recover forgotten actors (such as individual unions) from oblivion but also to move beyond the national-level bias to include units of analysis defined at the level of sectors, subnational units, and even organizations. The multilevel research design of this study combined cross-country and within-country comparisons to facilitate

[61] The new political parties emerging during the policy shift—FREPASO in Argentina, PRD in Mexico, and Causa R in Venezuela—built alliances with labor unions. Labor leaders, however, were more aware of the costs of corporatism once the state started its retrenchment, and the terms of new associations tended to be more fluid than in the past, thus affecting the extent of future "loyalties."

[62] Maria Victoria Murillo, "The Corporatist Paradox: Labor Parties and Labor Reform in Latin America" (Paper presented at the conference "Institutional Reforms, Growth, and Human Development in Latin America," Yale Center for International and Area Studies, April 16–17, 1999).

[63] Roberto Michels, *Political Parties: A Sociological Study of Oligarchical Tendencies in Modern Democracy*, trans. Eden and Cedar Paul (New York: The Free Press, 1962), 365.

[64] Ibid., 172.

[65] These implications are consistent with Hirschman's claim on the superiority of voice over exit as a mechanism for improvement in certain contexts when exit is not easily available or could provoke the demise of the organization.

the testing of alternative explanations within a relative small N. In turn, a small N made possible the collection of the data necessary to test causal mechanisms based on organizational dynamics. Theoretically this research design demonstrates the possibility of holding national institutions and macroeconomic conditions constant in comparisons within countries as well as sector-level variables constant in comparisons within sectors. Empirically it provides a better picture of the complex reality of the countries studied and the organizational dynamics of each case while advancing comparative analysis.

APPENDIX:
CLASSIFICATION OF CASES

Venezuela			
Case	*Militancy*	*Concessions*	*Category*
CTV-1 1989–92 (after 1992 coup attempt market reforms are suspended)	First general strike in history in 1989; followed by other two general strikes, public demonstrations, and protests	Emergency wage hike, unemployment insurance, suspension of layoffs for six months, price controls for basic staples; more rigid labor law; no reform of severance payment system or social security institution; inclusion of workers' shares in privatization schemes	Opposition
Telecom. 1991 (privatization)	From five yearly strike petitions in 1989 and 1990 to only three in 1991	Employee-owned stock, labor directors, job stability, stability of collective bargaining contract	Cooperation
Telecom. 1991–93 (restructuring after growth of internal opposition)	In 1992 forty-two weeks were lost on wildcat and legal strikes in five unions of the national federation, and nine unions presented strike petitions; in 1993 twelve unions presented strike petitions	Restructuring only within the limits set by privatization agreement	Opposition

	Venezuela		
Case	*Militancy*	*Concessions*	*Category*
Electricity 1989–91 (decentralization of the company)	No strikes in 1989, one in 1990, and none in 1991	Wage increases to the workers in the interior of the country, stability of work conditions across the company, handsome monetary incentives for transfers to the interior; job stability	Cooperation
Electricity 1992–93 (restructuring)	Four legal strikes and a wildcat strike in 1992; drastic increase in strike petitions, boycotts, and work unrest in 1993	Halt to restructuring attempts	Opposition
Oil 1991 (restructuring)	One strike in 1989, none in 1990, and one in 1991	Union allowed to retain hiring prerogatives in exchange for accepting the introduction of merit incentives on wages	Cooperation
Oil 1993 (restructuring)	Five strikes (one wildcat) in 1992 and six wildcat strikes in 1993	Union halts the dismantling of commissaries, but AD union leaders accept a reduction in hiring prerogatives demanded by management and internal competitors	Opposition
Auto 1989–92	No strikes or protests	Union accepts layoffs and introduction of new working methods in exchange for participation in selection of those laid off and trained in new technologies; after recovery, the union continues to participate in selection for training and reincorporation of laid-off workers	Cooperation

Venezuela			
Case	*Militancy*	*Concessions*	*Category*
Education	Strike petitions in the Ministry of Labor increased from nine in 1989 to thirty-one in 1990 and twenty-four in 1991 and dropped to four in 1992 and 1993; strikes also grew from three in 1989 to seven in 1990, eight in 1991, nine in 1992, and seven in 1993; occupation of buildings and street protests as well	No concessions administrative reform	Resistance

Mexico			
Case	*Militancy*	*Concessions*	*Category*
CTM-1	Fall in the number of strike petitions from a yearly average of 9,818 under the previous administration to a yearly average of 7,007	No concessions except halting the labor code reform	Subordination (except on the labor code where the unification of all PRI affiliates resulted in negotiation)
Electricity-1 1988–93 (attempt at privatization or liquidation of company)	From a 1987 strike (the first since 1936) under a previous opposition leadership to a public campaign, including a meeting of twenty thousand electrical workers, and lobbying to congress and to the president; public support for concertation pacts and NAFTA	Bail out of the company and creation of a new public company; monopoly of representation to the union; job stability; new fringe benefits and retirement plan; stability of work conditions and union participation in two union-management committees in charge of productivity and financial analysis; union right to information	Cooperation

	Mexico		
Case	*Militancy*	*Concessions*	*Category*
Electricity-2 1993–94 (restructuring)	Rejection of 1993 agreement signed by previous leader, first union to reject signing of the concertation pact in 1994; end of support for Salinas's policies; workers' mobilizations during bargaining in 1994; threats of strike	Reduction of the 1993 productivity targets in 1994, maintenance of job stability	Opposition (loyalty break)
Telecom.-1 1990–91 (privatization)	None	Employee-owned shares; labor director; increase in wages and permanent personnel; job stability; stability of work conditions	Cooperation
Telecom.-2 1992–94 (restructuring)	None	Committees for union participation in training and restructuring of work conditions, wage and benefits hikes	Cooperation
Oil (restructuring)	No strikes	No concessions and loss of job stability, work conditions, and union prerogatives	Subordination
Auto 1989–94 (restructuring)	Tradition of militancy in the 1970s, strike and sit-ins in 1989, plant takeover in 1990, none in 1991; demonstrations, sit-ins, meetings, stoppages, and "going naked" in 1993	Company-imposed conditions despite workers' resistance and sheer repression in 1990 and 1993	Resistance 1988–90 and 1992–93; Subordination 1990–91 and 1993–94

Mexico			
Case	*Militancy*	*Concessions*	*Category*
Education-SNTE (decentralization 1992)	Militancy by dissidents (CNTE) before 1989, but SNTE as well since 1989; militancy by SNTE peaked in 1991 against the fragmentation of the union and together with CNTE, including eight local strikes (besides four by the CNTE), three parades (besides three by CNTE), and many sit-ins, meetings, and a national process of consultation with the rank and file and joint public demands with the CNTE in November 1991	Limits to decentralization with guarantees of national work conditions and salaries by earmarking the state budgets, salary and benefits' hikes	Opposition

Argentina			
Case	*Militancy*	*Concessions*	*Category*
CGT 1 1989–92	From thirteen general strikes (1984–89) to one (1989–92); from 38.5 monthly strikes between January 1984 and June 1989 to 19.9 monthly strikes between July 1989 and March 1992	Unions could not stop hiring flexibility, wage restraint, and the loss of the collection of fees for their health funds	Subordination
CGT-2 1992–95	One general strike and 16.8 monthly strikes between April 1992 and July 1995	Union participation in the privatization of pensions, no reform to labor code, limits of competition for social security provision to health funds controlled by unions, permission for wage bargaining, union and workers' participation in privatization with government subsidies, bailing out of union debts	Cooperation

330

	Argentina		
Case	*Militancy*	*Concessions*	*Category*
Electricity-1 1989–92 (privatization and restructuring)	Eleven yearly strikes in 1992 after a yearly average of less than three strikes in 1984–88	Employee-owned stock, labor directors, voluntary retirements, subsidies for union health fund; start-up contracts of privatized companies for union organized companies hiring laid-off workers	Opposition
Electricity-2 1992–95 (after expulsion of militant local unions)	No strikes by the national federation; (two yearly strikes in 1993–95 by expelled local union)	Subsidies for union participation in privatization of utilities and coal mines; union participation in company defining the spot price of electricity	Cooperation
Telecom.1 1989–90 (privatization and restructuring)	Nine yearly strikes in 1990 is the peak after an average of 4.5 yearly strikes during the previous administration	Employee-owned stock and labor director, voluntary retirements for layoffs, subsidy for the union health fund, executive appointments for the allied leaders	Opposition
Telecom.2 1991–94 (restructuring and outsourcing)	Drop in strikes to one yearly strike	Union participation in training, voluntary retirements for layoffs for the workers in the main companies	Cooperation
Oil-1 1990–91 (restructuring)	Drop in average yearly strikes from 4.6 in 1984–88 to 1.5 in 1990–91	Voluntary retirements for layoffs; subsidies to the union to organize its own health fund	Cooperation

331

	Argentina		
Case	*Militancy*	*Concessions*	*Category*
Oil-2 1992 (privatization)	Yearly strikes averaged 0.5 in 1992–93	Union obtained monopoly of representation despite the existance of private oil workers' union; subsidies to the union to buy parts of the firm sold out by private owners with start-up contracts for hiring laid-off workers	Cooperation
Auto-1 1990–91 (between trade liberalization and the automobile regime)	Militancy increased from an average of 14.2 yearly strikes in 1984–89 to 18.5 yearly strikes in 1990–91	In 1991 unions and producers obtained a regime that protected the industry from competition	Opposition
Auto-2 1992–94 (automobile regime)	Militancy drops to 4.3 yearly strikes in 1992–94	Union and producers obtained the renewal of the automobile regime	Cooperation
Education-1 (decentralization law 1992)	Teachers' militancy was high with forty-four yearly strikes in 1989–94; proportion over total strikes increases to 44.5 percent in 1991 and 35.4 percent in 1992	No concessions	Resistance

SOURCES: Militancy data on Venezuela comes from the annual reports of the Secretary of Labor, a press chronology, and information of the labor relations' departments of CANTV, CADAFE, Ford Motors, and PDVSA. Militancy data on Mexico comes from a press chronology based on the archives of Entorno Laboral and from the Secretary of Labor. Strike data in Argentina is from the annual reports (1984–95) of the Consejo Técnico de Inversiones. Sources for concessions are labor contracts, government and union documents, press chronologies, and personal interviews with actors.

Acknowledgments

Loveman, Mara. "High-Risk Collective Action: Defending Human Rights in Chile, Uruguay, and Argentina." *American Journal of Sociology* 104, no. 2 (1998): 477-525. Reprinted with the permission of the University of Chicago Press, publisher. Identical copyright notice.

Lambrou, Yianna. "The Changing Role of NGOs in Rural Chile After Democracy." *Bulletin of Latin American Research* 16, no. 1 (1997): 107-116. Reprinted with the permission of Plenum Press.

Keck, Margaret. "Social Equity and Environmental Politics in Brazil: Lessons from the Rubber Tappers of Acre." *Comparative Politics* 27, no. 4 (1995): 409-424. Reprinted with the permission of the editors of Comparative Politics.

Collier, Ruth Berins and James Mahoney. "Adding Collective Actors to Collective Outcomes: Labor and Recent Democratization in South America and Southern Europe" *Comparative Politics* 29, no. 3 (1997): 285-303. Reprinted with the permission of the editors of Comparative Politics.

Houtzager, Peter and Marcus Kurtz. "The Institutional Roots of Popular Mobilization: State Transformation and Rural Politics in Brazil and Chile, 1960-1990." *Comparative Studies in Society and History* 42, no. 2 (2000): 394-424. Reprinted with the permission of Cambridge University Press.

Davis, Charles, Edwin E. Aguilar, and John G. Speer. "Associations and Activism: Mobilization of Urban Informal Workers in Costa Rica and Nicaragua." *Journal of Interamerican Studies and World Affairs* 41, no. 3 (1999): 35-66. Reprinted with the permission of the University of Miami, Graduate School of International Studies.

Veltmeyer, Henry. "New Social Movements in Latin America: The Dynamics of Class and Identity." *Journal of Peasant Studies* 25, no. 1 (1997): 139-169. Reprinted with the permission of Frank Cass.

Bastian, Jean-Pierre. "The Metamorphosis of Latin American Protestant Groups: A Sociohistorical Perspective." *Latin American Research Review* 28, no. 2 (1993): 33-61. Reprinted with the permission of the Latin American Research Review.

Pessar, Patricia. "Three Moments in Brazilian Millenarianism: The Interrelationship between Politics and Religion." *Luso-Brazilian Review* 28, no. 1 (1991): 95-116. Reprinted with the permission of the University of Wisconsin Press.

Kampwirth, Karen. "Feminism, Antifeminism, and Electoral Politics in Postwar Nicaragua and El Salvador." *Political Science Quarterly* 113, no. 2 (1998): 259-279. Reprinted with the permission of the author and The Academy of Political Science.

Abers, Rebecca. "From Clientelism to Cooperation: Local Government,
    Participatory Policy, and Civic Organizing in Porto Alegre, Brazil." *Politics
    and Society* 26, no. 4 (1998): 511-537. Reprinted with the permission of
    Sage Publications.
Murillo, M. Victoria. "From Populism to Neoliberalism: Labor Unions and Market
    Reforms in Latin America." *World Politics* 52, no. 2 (2000): 135-174.
    Reprinted with the permission of the Johns Hopkins University Press.